W9-BRN-747
3 1011 00000 2372

THE BEST THINGS IN LIFE ARE FREE

THE ULTIMATE MONEY-SAVING TRAVEL GUIDE

ARTS & CULTURE

SPORTS & LEISURE

MUSIC & FILM

ARTS & CULTURE

© Deric Olschner | 500px, © Matt Munro, © Lottie Davies, © Gavin Quirke | Getty Images

CONTENTS

SPORTS & LEISURE

FESTIVALS & EVENTS

ARTS & CULTURE

FOOD & DRINK

CONTENTS

Mate

INTRODUCTION

Last year, while taking our children on their first foray into Africa we visited Marrakesh in Morocco. On our first evening we walked into the Djemaa el-Fna (page 16), the city's world famous open square. It was like walking into another world. The smoke and smells from food stalls, the sound of drummers and the clamour of people shouting, singing and hawking their wares. Everyone's eyes were out on stalks, senses in overdrive. I had been worried it would be too much, but the kids asked to go again the following night. One of the most memorable moments I've had travelling cost nothing beyond the gumption to walk into the square that night.

The monetary value implied in the term *free* can misrepresent what's on offer within these pages. The quality of an experience, after all, is not attached to a price tag. Many of the suggestions here involve unearthing the world's secret wonders, whether that's swimming around Sydney's ocean pools (page 267) or strolling the tombs and monuments of Delhi's Lodi Gardens (page 37). Walkers tackling the great tracks of New Zealand (page 260) will find themselves close to the soul of those beautiful islands.

For many of us, when we take our first steps travelling free things are not only appealing but essential if we're to make our backpacking days last as long as possible. And it's not just formative forays - many unforgettable blasts of freedom and discovery tend to be budget affairs. You quickly realise that cheap can mean much, much better. No Roman dinner will ever match the bread and cheese picnic in Villa Celimontana, a short walk from the Colosseum, on my first visit to the Eternal City. And if we're talking life lessons, there are few better insights into the human condition than sharing a dorm room with a dozen others from around the world.

Nations all around the world recognise the value of making the wonders under their stewardship accessible. 5000 years of Chinese history? Free (National Museum of China, page 28). 19 museums and galleries in Washington DC? Free (Smithsonian Institution, page 242). Britain's national parks? All free. Donations always welcome, of course. And if you want to experience all those popular places at their best then get up early and get their before the crowds arrive. The priceless calm of early mornings doesn't come with a price tag either, by the way.

It's an exaggeration to say that everything good is free, so you'll find plenty of excellent value cheap things to experience throughout this book. Dip into your spare change for classy street food like a *choripán* (chorizo sandwich) in Buenos Aires (page 277), the best views of Hong Kong's skyline from the Star Ferry (page 48) and a Boston brewery tour (page 179). Great memories, a happier you and a grateful wallet; one glance through these pages and you may never aspire to the indulgences of top-end travel again.

Tom Hall

AFRICA

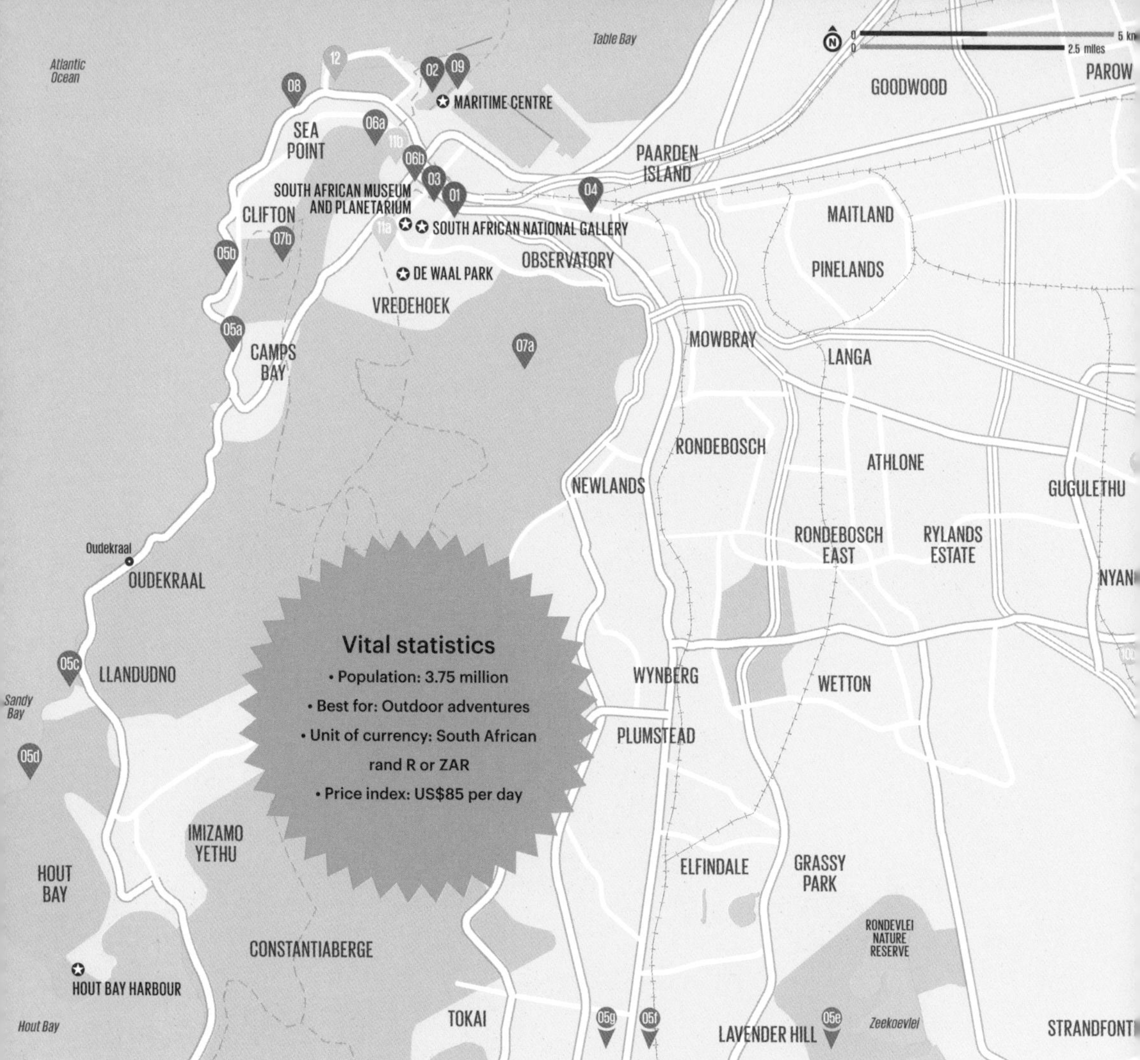

CAPE TOWN

South Africa's proudly multicultural Mother City sits between the Rainbow Nation's most iconic natural feature, Table Mountain, and the appropriately named Cape of Good Hope. Both mountain and ocean offer myriad opportunities for free recreation, and Cape Town comes to the party with countless cool activities and attractions.

01 District Six

Once a tight-knit community historically comprised of freed slaves, artisans, labourers and immigrants, District Six was torn apart under apartheid. By 1966 it was a white area; 60,000 occupants had been evicted and their homes bulldozed. You can independently explore the reclaimed streets, but don't miss the **District Six Museum** *(districtsix.co.za; 25a Buitenkant St; 9am-4pm Mon-Sat; R30)*, which also runs **Sunset Walking Tours** *(5.50pm spring-summer; R100)* led by ex-residents.

02 Free diamond tour

South Africa has been synonymous with diamonds since the 1840s, as the **Cape Town Diamond Museum** (*capetowndiamondmuseum.org; Clock Tower, Level 1, Waterfront; 9am-9pm; R50*) explains. Entry usually costs, but download a voucher from **Shimansky** (*shimansky.com*) to score a free tour. You even get a *gratis* glass of South African wine as you're walked through the cutting factory, manufacturing workshop, and diamond and tanzanite showroom. Exit through the gift shop...

03 St George's Cathedral

Even if a guided trip to the jail that once held Mandela and other political prisoners, **Robben Island** (*robben-island.org.za; R300*) is beyond your budget, don't miss the 'People's Cathedral', where Archbishop Desmond Tutu led a dignified decades-long struggle against apartheid. The cathedral choir gives occasional free performances. The main service takes place at 9.30am on Sundays, but visitors are always welcome. Tours of the Victorian-style church are also available. *sgcathedral.co.za; 5 Wale St; free.*

04 Whatiftheworld Gallery

Occupying an ubercool space in a decommissioned Woodstock synagogue, this forward-facing gallery has provided hanging space for contemporary Southern African artists since 2008. Many of the young artists originally championed have since shaped the country's artistic landscape, but there's always a new wave coming though. *Check the website for exhibitions. whatiftheworld.com; 1 Argyle St, Woodstock; 10am-5pm Tue-Fri, 10am-2pm Sat; free.*

05 Beach life

Cape Town's beautiful beaches are legendary. **Camps Bay** (5a) and **Clifton** (5b) are the trendy city options; Atlantic-facing **Llandudno** (5c) is for surfers; remote **Sandy Bay** (5d) for nudists;

05

THE LOCAL'S VIEW

"Cape Town's shops and premier art galleries stay open late on the first Thursday of the month, which is cool. Picnics on Signal Hill are sensational in summer, when you can also score free concerts in De Waal Park on Sunday afternoons. I'm from Hout Bay, though, and most sunny Sundays I hit the market by the harbour (after saying 'hi' to Bob, the resident seal), where there's great food, a bar and live music. Later, I might enjoy a bottle of wine on the beach or head to Noordhoek Farm Village (*noordhoekvillage.co.za*) to hear more live music." – Katie Owens, company director.

sheltered **False Bay**'s **Muizenberg** (5e) and **St James** (5f) are family friendly, with water warmed by Indian Ocean currents. All are free, except Simons Town's **Boulders Beach** (5g; *8am-6.30pm, longer in Dec-Jan; R60)* with its 3000 endangered African penguins.

06 Bo-Kaap

On the side of Signal Hill, Bo-Kaap, the former Malay Quarter, is famous for its streetscapes, mosques and cuisine-based tourism. Wander freely around the streets, visit the cheap **Bo-Kaap Museum** (6a; *bokaap.co.za/museum; 71 Wale St; 10am-5pm Mon-Sat; R20*) or do a **cooking course/tour** (*bokaapcookingtour.co.za; R700, including dinner*). Nearby is **Long St** (6b), home of the city's underground entertainment scene, alongside second-hand bookshops and boho boutiques.

07 Howl at the lion

Table Mountain National Park (7a) has hundreds of trails, wending around the Twelve Apostles, Devil's Peak, Signal Hill and Table Mountain. Most are free-access, but there are four pay points. Various routes scale the vertical kilometre to Devil's Peak, but if you're here during a full moon, join locals trekking with beers to **Lion's Head** (7b) to watch moonrise over the Hottentots Holland Mountains.

08 Sea Point promenade

Loved by everyone from runners and skaters to hand-holding couples and kids, this 11km-long, wave-splattered, careless and car-free coastal stretch is full of playgrounds and amazing outdoor artwork. You can swim for free in the wild Atlantic, or seek sanctuary in one of the world's finest public pools, the open-air **Sea Point Pavilion** (*www.capetown.gov.za; 7am-7pm summer, 9am-5pm winter;*

IZIKO MUSEUMS

The Iziko Museums of South Africa (*iziko.org.za*) is an 11-strong collection of Cape Town's top museums and attractions, including the Bo-Kaap Museum, the South African National Gallery (*Government Ave, Company's Garden; 10am-5pm*), South African Museum and Planetarium (*25 Queen Victoria St; 10am-5pm*), Maritime Centre (*Union-Castle House, Dock Rd, V&A Waterfront; 10am-5pm*) and Groot Constantia Manor House (*Groot Constantia Estate; 10am-5pm*), the oldest wine-producing estate in the country. These museums typically charge about R30, but for eight or nine days each year, typically public holidays, they all throw their doors open for free. Check the website for up-to-date details.

R21) with diving boards, splash puddles and two Olympic-size lap pools.

09 Victoria & Alfred Waterfront

A former wharf transformed into a swanky waterfront entertainment, eating and shopping arena, the V&A offers everything from free wi-fi to meetings with freedom fighters Nelson Mandela and Desmond Tutu – albeit in bronze form. Selfie-snappers shouldn't pose too long next to the seals, though – they're the real deal. Street performers provide entertainment, and free events take place year-round. *Robben Island tours depart here. waterfront.co.za; 9am-9pm; free.*

10 Going downtown

Visiting a Township is an essential Cape Town experience; combine it with a budget feed at **Mzoli's** (10a; *Gugulethu; 9am-6pm; meals R50–100*). Buy meat at this Gugs butcher and get it cooked on a traditional *braai* (barbecue), while supping beer and bouncing to Kwaito beats. Excellent tours (*laurastownshiptours.co.za; R400*) can be done, and shack accommodation is available at **Vicky's B&B** (10b; *Khayelitsha Township*), complete with Xhosa-style home cooking.

11 Wine tasting

South Africa produces some of the planet's best palate-pleasing plonk and it would be criminal not to try a few drops. Lucky then, that **Wine Concepts** (11a; *wineconcepts.co.za; 50 Kloof St*) offers complimentary wine tasting six days a week (*4-7pm Mon-Fri, noon-3pm Sat*). **Tjing Tjing Rooftop Bar** (11b; *tjingtjing.co.za; 165 Longmarket St*) also offers free wine tasting from 5pm to 7pm on Wednesdays.

12 Cape Town Carnival

Born on Long St amid the orgy of euphoria and energy that surrounded SA's hosting of the 2010 Football World Cup, this carnival has since grown into a massive annual gathering to celebrate South Africa's diversity. Some 50,000 people watch and participate in festivities that engulf Green Point, with floats, music, dancing and after-partying. *capetowncarnival.com; Fanwalk, Green Point; Mar; free.*

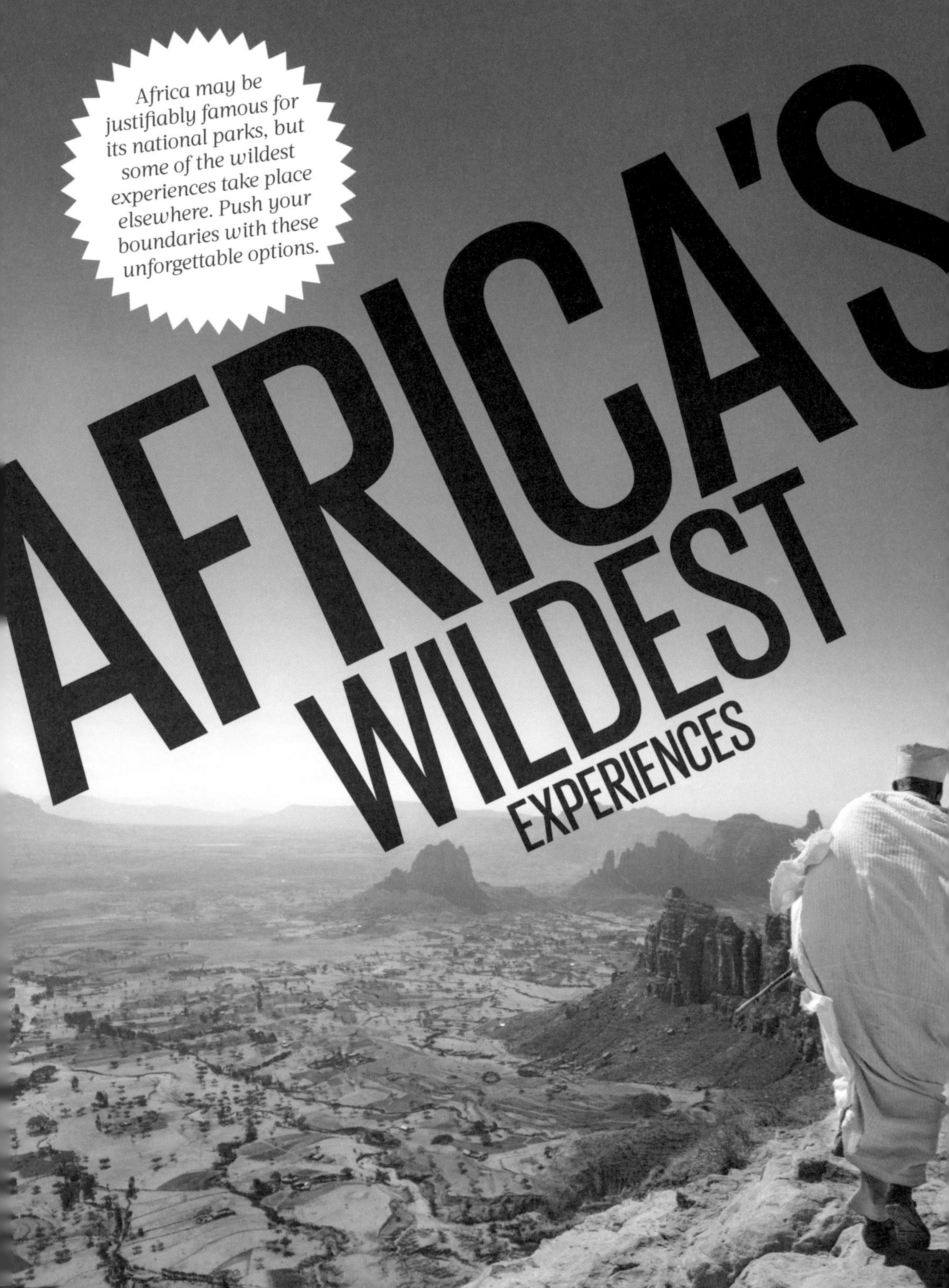

AFRICA'S WILDEST EXPERIENCES

Africa may be justifiably famous for its national parks, but some of the wildest experiences take place elsewhere. Push your boundaries with these unforgettable options.

SURF SWELL IN LIBERIA

Ride some of the best breaks on the continent with a growing cast of Liberian surfers. The golden beaches stretch to the horizon, and at night the crashing waves glow with phosphorescence. Pack your surfboard! *Robertsport, Liberia; free.*

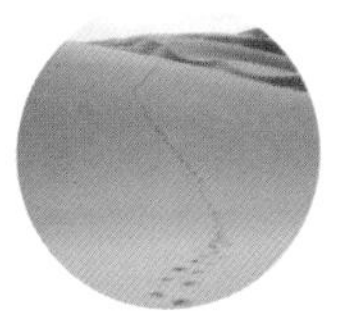

DUNE-WALK IN THE NAMIBIA

While huge swathes of the Namib's famous dunes sit within national parks, those just south of Swakopmund do not. Head out on the road to Walvis Bay and explore. Unique characteristics of the sand make some dunes hum as you walk along the crests. *Swakopmund, Namibia; free.*

SET EYES ON THE JADE SEA

The lake's eastern shore at the village of Loyangalani may be at the end of an incredibly long and uncomfortable transport-truck journey, but the volcanic landscapes, Jade Sea views and vibrant Turkana people are out of this world. *Lake Turkana, Kenya; free.*

HYENAS OF HARAR

The adventurous can take to the narrow alleys of Harar's old town at night to catch glimpses of the city's hyenas. Or shell out US$2.50 and you can watch them being fed outside the 16th-century walls each evening – double it and you can feed them yourself... *Harar, Ethiopia; evenings; free.*

VISIT THE WORLD'S MOST DANGEROUS CHURCH

Carved into a sheer cliff face many centuries ago, the church of Abuna Yemata Guh requires visitors to climb a 6m-high vertical wall with no ropes and negotiate a narrow ledge over a 200m drop. Tips for local guides expected. *Abuna Yemata Guh, Tigray, Ethiopia; US$7 plus tips.*

WILD FLOWERS OF NAMAKWA

The semi-desert of Namakwa erupts in a cornucopia of colour each spring when wildflowers carpet the landscape. Let's be clear, this is not a flower show or a larger-scale version of your granny's garden – it is one of Africa's most impressive sights. *Namakwa, South Africa; Aug-Sep; free.*

MARALAL INTERNATIONAL CAMEL DERBY

Join spectators to witness these epic cross-country camel races. Mingle with the crowds, attend the notorious parties and, if you're game, rent a camel and ride in the amateurs' race. *www.kenyasafari.com/maralal-camel-derby.html; Maralal, Kenya; free.*

TAKE A DIP IN DEVIL'S POOL

Drop into the Zambezi and swim in a natural pool on the edge of Victoria Falls while water slides past you and plummets over the 100m drop. Free it is not, but it's so wild it is worth the splurge (an incredible breakfast is included). *tongabezi.com; Livingstone Island, Victoria Falls, Zambia; May-Oct; US$95.*

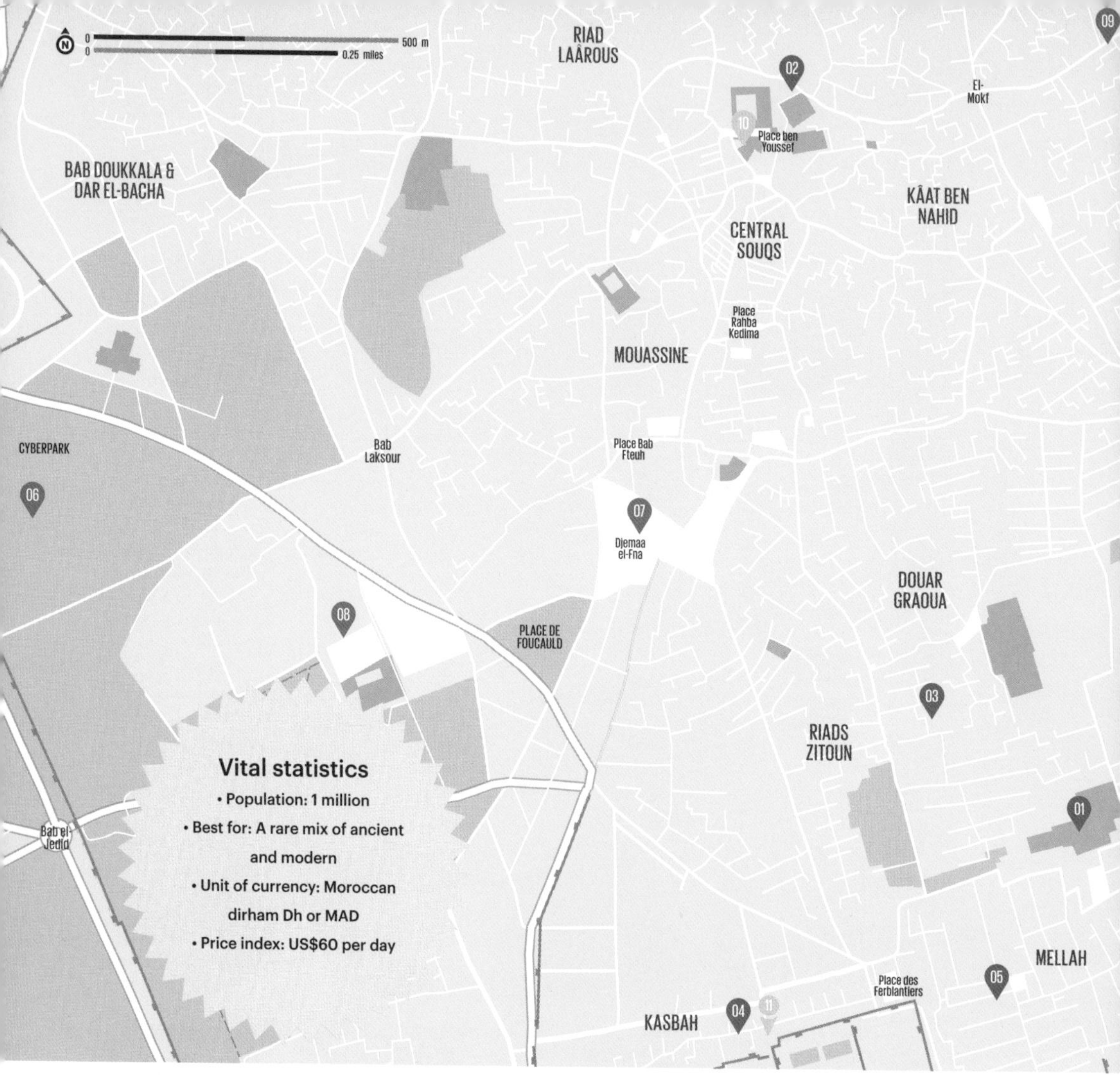

MARRAKESH

A trip to Marrakesh might conjure up images of the Rolling Stones buying up half the medina or A-listers partying in private suites at La Mamounia, but rest assured, this bustling, spicy, unforgettable city has plenty of attractions for mere mortals that don't demand you dish out all your dirhams.

01 **Bahia Palace**
This somewhat dilapidated late-19th-century palace is exceptional value. Built over 15 years by Vizier Ahmed Ibn Moussa as a retreat for his harem, La Bahia ('Palace of the Beautiful') is a 160-room complex of intricately patterned rooms, polished cedar ceilings, cool marble and secluded courtyards, surrounded by 8 hectares of landscaped gardens. *Rue Riad Zitoun el-Jedid; 8.30-11.45am & 2.30-5.45pm Sat-Thu, 8.30-11.30am & 3-5.45pm Fri; Dh10.*

02 **Dar Bellarj**
The non-profit Dar Bellarj Foundation showcases Moroccan arts and crafts in this former 'stork hospital' (literally, a hospice for injured birds). Now one of the city's leading venues for material arts, it hosts changing exhibitions of weaving, painting and other genres. There are also kids' workshops in traditional Moroccan music, and concerts during Ramadan and the Ashura festival. *9-7 Toualate Zaouiate Lahdar; 9.30am-12.30pm & 2-5.30pm Mon-Sat; free.*

03 **Dar Si Said**
It's hard to know what's more impressive: the 1000-year-old collection of Moroccan and Berber artefacts or the Hispano-Moorish palace that houses them. Bejewelled weapons, beaten-copper adornments, High Atlas carpets and lavish antique costumes are well worth the scant entrance fee, as is the domed wedding salon, faced with cedar intricately carved by *mâalems* (master artisans) from Fez. *Derb Si Said; 9am-4.45pm Wed-Mon; adult/child Dh10/3.*

04 **Museum for Photography and Visual Arts (MMVPA)**
The world's largest museum dedicated to photography and the visual arts is due to open opposite Menara Gardens in 2016; meanwhile, you can catch free exhibits in the temporary gallery in El Badi Palace. Giving a sense of what the finished museum will offer, the MMVPA focuses on images from Morocco and Northern Africa. *mmpva.org; Ksibat Nhass; 9am-5pm Wed-Mon; free.*

05 **The Mellah**
Marrakesh's 15th-century Jewish quarter is distinguished by its maze of *derbs* (alleys) and mud-brick buildings. No longer home to many Jews, their legacy survives in the **Lazama Synagogue** (*Derb Manchoura; tip expected*) and the *miaâra* or **Jewish cemetery** (*Ave Taoulat El Miara; tip expected*). Don't miss the **Mellah Market** (*Ave Houmane el-Fetouaki; 8am-1pm & 3-7pm; free*) and the artisans' showrooms around Pl des Ferblantiers.

01

ONE-DAY FREE PASS

If your time is as limited as your budget, this mini-itinerary will give you a good day's sightseeing. Start your morning catching the current exhibition at the Dar Bellarj, then wend your way south-east through the Medina's maze of souqs until you reach Djemaa el-Fna (p016), the perfect spot for a snack and some snake charming. From here it's a short ramble south to the Jewish architecture of the Mellah. Finally, get some culture with your colossal camel burger at Café Clock (p017).

06 Cyber Park

You'll find these tranquil gardens – full name: the Arsat Moulay Abdeslam Cyber Park – not far from Djemaa el-Fna. Originally laid out by Prince Moulay as a market garden in the 18th century, it became an ornamental park in 1920. The 2005 redevelopment, combining lemon, olive and pomegranate trees, water features, neat paths and free wi-fi, pays homage to both antecedents. *morocco.com; Ave Mohammed V; 9am-7pm; free.*

07 Djemaa el-Fna

Djemaa el-Fna ('Assembly of the Dead') is Morocco's largest, best-known public square. It's listed by UNESCO for its Intangible Cultural Heritage of Humanity. Created as a site for public executions in AD 1050, it is now filled by day with snake charmers, magicians and orange juice vendors. At night, add street-food hawkers, musicians, storytellers, healers, dancers and pedlars. People-watching doesn't get any better. *9am-1am; free.*

08 Koutoubia Mosque & Gardens

Koutoubia, built in the 12th century on the site of an earlier mosque imperfectly aligned with Mecca, is one of Marrakesh's great sights. The interior is off-limits to non-Muslims, but it can be appreciated externally. Its 70m-high minaret, topped with gleaming copper balls, is best viewed while strolling through the peaceful, palm-strewn gardens that surround it. *Cnr Rue el-Koutoubia & Ave Mohammed V; gardens open 8am-8pm; free.*

09 Tanneries

If you can stand the horrendous smell, then the outdoor tanneries are one of Marrakesh's classic free sights. The hides are treated in hundreds of concrete

MEDINA ETIQUETTE

Marrakesh has always been a mercantile metropolis: it pays to come prepared if you want to maximise your dirham. The hard sell is commonplace in the souqs, so be ready to stand your ground. Stallholders can be very forward, but are willing to haggle; just don't get involved in protracted negotiations if you don't plan to buy. You might also get the idea that guides are trying to edge you towards certain stalls: trust your instincts – of course they are! – and feel free to politely insist on looking further afield before committing to buying anything.

vats, following medieval techniques that involve quicklime, water, blood and even pigeon poo. Producing the many-hued leathers sold in the city's souqs is back-breaking, dirty work; sadly, now chemicals are also involved, it's unhealthy too. *Ave Bab el-Debbagh; dawn-dusk; free.*

10 Ben Youssef food stall qissaria

The food stalls in this *qissaria* (covered market) are often tiny operations where everything is done with skill and economy. They sell such unorthodox delights as snails, stewed sheep's head and grilled hearts, so be prepared. When you've sized up the offerings (including less challenging options like tagines, grilled meats and salads), grab a bench and eat al fresco. *Off Souq Shaaria, near Koubba Ba'adiyn; 11.30am-3.30pm; free.*

11 Café Clock

Moroccan tradition meets modern multimedia at this unique cafe. On Mondays, traditional storytellers practise their art (in English and Arabic), Wednesdays are jam sessions open to anyone with an instrument, Saturdays are for guest artists and Sundays feature sunset concerts of hypnotic Gnawa music. There's also a constantly changing array of art on display, and the kitchen serves up a mean camel burger. *cafeclock.com; 224 Derb Chtouka; 10am-10pm; mains Dh55-80.*

12 Festival of Popular Arts

This midsummer festival lights up the streets of Marrakesh every July. International performers join Berber minstrels, Gnawa musicians, sword-swallowers, acrobats, dancers, snake charmers and street performers from across Morocco. Performances can be seen at outdoor venues across the city over the festival's 10 days, focused in the courtyards and gardens of the El Badi Palace, near Place des Ferblantiers. The extravaganza culminates in an intoxicating parade through Djemaa el-Fna. *morocco.com/theater/marrakech-popular-arts-festival; July; free.*

$AFARI WITHOUT THE BIG BUCKS

African safaris can cost upwards of US$1000 per person per day, so here are some destinations where the wild rewards vastly outdo the price tag.

CYCLE SAFARI – KENYA

Beneath the basalt cliffs of this volcanic landscape are zebras, giraffes, impalas and other iconic species. Large carnivores are rare, however, so it's possible to spend a day walking or cycling; bikes can be rented nearby for an additional US$6. Camping is available. *kws.go.ke; Hell's Gate NP, Kenya; US$30.*

WEST AFRICAN SAFARI – GHANA

Known for its elephants, the savannah also hosts buffaloes, kob, baboons, warthogs and numerous bird species. Share the park's vehicle hire (US$20 per hour) with others to make it more of a bargain. Budget accommodation too. *molemotel-gh.com; Mole NP, Ghana; US$8, plus guide US$2.50/hr.*

NAMIBIAN SAFARI – NAMIBIA

The desert-like environment around the massive Etosha salt pan is captivating, but it is the wildlife that frequents the waterholes here that make it one of Africa's best parks. Great roads mean small rental cars are an option, and camping is possible. *etoshanationalpark.org; Etosha NP, Namibia; US$7.*

Illustration | Owen Gatley

BIG FIVE SAFARI – SOUTH AFRICA

Kruger is one of the world's greatest parks – the Big Five are all here, along with an extensive cast of other safari species. Independent access is a breeze, camping options are plentiful and there are 19,485 sq km of incredible landscapes. *sanparks.org; Kruger NP, South Africa; US$20.*

WALKING SAFARI – TANZANIA

Think of a thousand hippos sharing a mud bath and you're on the right track. The park comes to life in dry season (August to October). Camp in nearby Sitalike and share the armed guide fee (US$20 per group). *tanzaniaparks.com; Katavi NP, Tanzania; US$80 (including walking permit).*

OKAVANGO DELTA MOKORO SAFARI – BOTSWANA

Being poled through the Okavango Delta in a dugout canoe is one of Africa's greatest, and most expensive, experiences. However, Old Bridge Backpackers offer self-catered camping options ranging from US$70 (one day) to US$140 (four days). *maun-backpackers.com; Old Bridge Backpackers, Maun, Botswana; from US$70.*

WEST AFRICAN SAFARI

The coastal town of St Lucia is on the doorstep of two great parks: iSimangaliso (isimangaliso.com) and Hluhluwe-iMfolozi (hluhluwegamereserve.com). The latter is a classic Big Five destination, while the former hosts both land animals and aquatic ones. Budget safaris and accommodation available. *St Lucia, KwaZulu-Natal, South Africa; from US$40.*

TRACKING GORILLAS – UGANDA

The value of sharing a glance with a gorilla in the wild is something that can't be quantified. Visit Bwindi during low season (April, May and November) and permits are US$350 instead of US$600. Permits in Rwanda are US$750. *ugandawildlife.org; Bwindi Impenetrable NP, Uganda; from US$350.*

ASIA

鴨賞

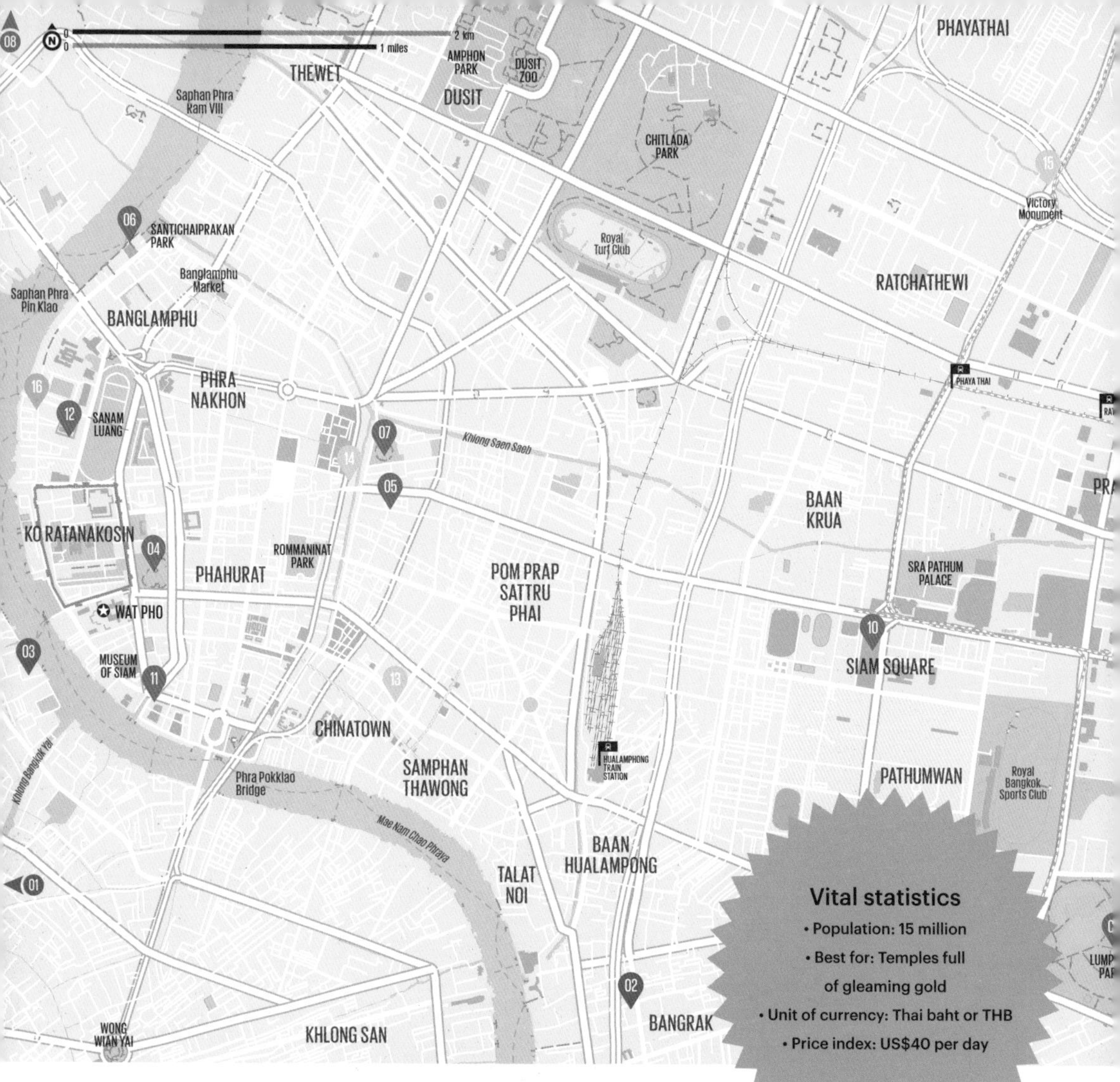

Vital statistics

- Population: 15 million
- Best for: Temples full of gleaming gold
- Unit of currency: Thai baht or THB
- Price index: US$40 per day

BANGKOK

All that glitters is gold in Bangkok, where every turn reveals another shimmering chedi *(shrine) or gleaming Buddha. The good news is that you don't have to be rich to see these treasures; in Thailand's City of Angels, you can eat like a king and see the sights on a shoestring.*

01 Baan Silapin Artist's House
Hidden away on a Thonburi *klorng* (canal), this historic wooden house is home to traditional puppeteers, who are training the next generation in this ancient Southeast Asian art form. Every afternoon from 2pm the black-clad puppetmasters bring Thai legends to life; it's nostalgic and atmospheric. *Wat Thong Sala Ngam, Soi 28, Th Phet Kasem; 10am-6pm; free.*

02 The Bangkokian Museum
The pocket-sized Bangkokian is a hidden jewel in a city where most of the treasures are proudly on display. Spread over a series of dolls' house-like homes are rooms full of personal belongings that look as if the owners stepped through the front door to pick up some noodles in 1960 and never came back. *273 Soi 43, Th Charoen Krung; 10am-4pm Wed-Sun; free.*

03 Wat Arun
The small entrance fee at Wat Arun delivers priceless experiences. Approached from the river, the towering *prangs* (Khmer-style towers) of the Temple of Dawn look like carved stone; up close, they reveal themselves to be gardens of mosaic flowers in broken Chinese porcelain. Dip your head respectfully to the *yaksha* (guardian giants) as you enter the statue-filled gardens. *watarun.net; off Th Arun Amarin; 8am-6pm; 50B.*

04 Aerobics at Saranrom Park
After a few seafood feasts, many visitors to Bangkok feel like they might benefit from a little exercise. Why delay? Every evening, Saranrom Park fills with the sound of grunts and pop beats as free open-air aerobics classes roll into motion. All welcome; leotards optional. *Bounded by Th Ratchini, Th Charoen Krung & Th Sanam Chai; park open 5am-9pm; free.*

05 Ban Baat
Thailand's monks need freight-loads of begging bowls *(bàht)* for collecting alms for the poor, and this tiny urban village keeps the traditional bowl-making art alive. Jump off the *klorng* boat at Tha Phan Fah and you'll hear the tap, tap, tap of metalworkers hammering bowls together from eight leaves of different metals, representing the eightfold path of Buddhism. *Soi Ban Baat; 8am-5pm; free.*

06 Chao Phraya Express Ferry
For about the price of a bowl of rice, you can board Bangkok's most atmospheric vantage point on a budget river cruise. The best time to ride the ferry is at dusk; join the monks waiting at Tha Phra Athit pier and cruise past some of Krung Thep's landmark monuments, refreshed by balmy evening breezes. *chaophrayaexpressboat.com; Th Phra Athit Pier; 9.30am-10pm; 10-40B.*

07 Golden Mount (Wat Saket)
Low-rise Ko Ratanakosin and Banglamphu are big on bucket lists but short on viewpoints from where they can be seen. That's where the Golden Mount comes in. Just east of the Democracy Monument, this artificial mountain is crowned by a looming golden *chedi* terrace and offers bird's-eye city views. *Off Th Boriphat; 7.30am-5.30pm; free.*

MASSAGE ON THE CHEAP

Massage is part of the culture in Bangkok, but finding a legitimate budget massage among the pricey spas and dodgy operators can be something of a challenge. Our tip is head to source – Wat Pho (*Th Sanam Chai; 8.30am-6.30pm*) is both an astonishing temple and the spiritual home of Thai massage and traditional Thai medicine. At the famous massage school you can get a relaxing 30-minute pummelling from monastery-trained practitioners in one of the pavilions within the temple or in the training facility without, all for a wallet-pleasing 260B.

BOOZE AND DON'TS

Exploring Bangkok can be thirsty work, but a bottle of Chang beer can cost more than a meal, and wine and spirits can empty your wallet in a heartbeat. Follow the lead of locals and stock up on refreshments at the nearest 7-Eleven, saving posh sit-down drinks for special occasions. Your hotel balcony is the best spot for an impromptu drinks party; public drinking is frowned upon, and banned in parks and religious sites, including the grounds of monasteries.

08 Ko Kret Island

Bangkok's tiny Burmese enclave feels like a country village, smuggled into the northern suburbs and secreted inside a loop of the Chao Phraya River. Founded in 1722, this miniature community of potters follows an 18th-century pace of life. Wander boardwalk lanes past potters' studios to a tiny, wonky riverside *chedi* in the Mon style. At weekends there's a bustling (rather unpleasantly so) market. *Nonthaburi; 24hr; free.*

09 Lumphini Park

Before Bangkok erupts into life each morning, a more gentle awakening takes place in Lumphini Park, where old-timers gather to practise t'ai-chi before an audience of monitor lizards and the odd jogging octogenarian. For a few precious hours the city seems to float in a bubble of calm, before revving engines break the illusion. *Bounded by Th Sarasin, Th Phra Ram IV, Th Witthayu & Th Ratchadamri; 4.30am-9pm, free.*

10 MBK Center Moo·ay tai

Moo·ay tai (Thai boxing) is a sport for connoisseurs, which may explain the steep price tags that accompany tickets at the stadiums. No matter: boxing fans on a budget can get in on the action for free every Wednesday at 6pm, when boisterous bouts fill an open-air ring in front of Bangkok's favourite teen fashion mall. *Th Rama I; from 6pm Wed; free.*

11 Pak Khlong Talat Flower Market

Flowers aren't just for special occasions here; locals sweeten the air with perfumed blooms as part of their daily routine. At festivals and celebrations, though, flower-arranging goes into overdrive, with outrageous floats of flowers and banana leaves for processions

ONE-DAY FREE PASS

Start off the day by taking a 7am meditation class at Wat Mahathat; you'll need that sense of inner calm as you navigate the backpacker crowds to reach Tha Phra Athit pier, embarkation point for the Chao Phraya Express Ferry (p023). Ride the river on to Tha Ratchawong pier, then stroll up to Tha Yaowarat in Chinatown for lunch. It's only a short hop north to the lanes of Ban Baat (p023), then watch the sunset on top of the Golden Mount (p023). Suitably uplifted, wander across the *klorng* for a bowl of the city's best *pàt tai* at Thip Samai.

and home shrines. If nothing else, the market has to be the most fragrant spot in the city. *Th Chakraphet; 24hr; free.*

12 Wat Mahathat meditation classes

While the crowds mob the cloisters of Wat Pho, you'll find a little Buddhist serenity nearby at Wat Mahathat, where local worshippers outnumber selfie-takers and tour guides. Three-hour meditation classes run daily by donation, and the *wí·hăhn* (main chapel) is ringed by shady Buddha-filled cloisters so you can find space for inner reflection. *3 Th Maha Rat; meditation classes 7am, 1pm & 6pm; free.*

13 Chinatown street eats

Everyone knows the best food in Bangkok is served up on the street, and Chinatown is the top table in town. On the *sois* (side streets) along *Tha Yaowarat*, slippery noodles coil like snakes, fish swim in rivers of sweet chilli, prawns dive into sizzling sauces and crabs caper in curry seas. It's Bangkok's tastiest, most diverse street-food feast at bargain prices. Happy eating! *bangkok.com/chinatown; Th Yaowarat; 5-11pm; dishes 30-50B.*

14 Thip Samai

Forget the insipid, greasy *pàt tai* sold on Tha Khao San; people in the know make a beeline for Thip Samai to consume bowl after bowl of 'Ghost Gate Noodles' – the best *pàt tai* in Bangkok, and by extension, the world. Thip Sami is low-key, local and delicious, as the queues attest. *313 Th Mahachai; 5.30pm-1.30am, closed on alternate Wed; mains 25–120B.*

15 Victory Monument boat noodles

Most of the soup vendors who used to ply their trade along Bangkok's *klorng* have long since hung up their paddles, but you can still find the delicious 'boat noodle soup' that made them famous on a narrow alleyway north of the Victory Monument, at prices so low locals order three bowls at one sitting. *Off Th Phaholyothin, Victory Monument; 11am-6pm; noodle soup from 11B.*

16 Amulet Market

Thai Buddhists have been trading religious amulets for centuries. Collectors congregate at the amulet-stacked stands that dot the pavement along Tha Maha Rat, haggling over particularly sought-after Buddhist tablets, votive objects and oversized phallic symbols. Look out for committed aficionados, struggling to stand under the weight of all their amulets. *Th Maha Rat; 7am-5pm; free.*

17 Chatuchak Weekend Market

Leaving practically every other market in Thailand in the shade, Chatuchak is not so much a market as a city of stalls. In this maze of alleyways, you can haggle for antique lacquerware, bargain for chopsticks, negotiate for Thai silk and hill-tribe silver, or just sip cocktails in a back-alley bar watching the mayhem unfold. Weekends were made for this! *chatuchak.org; Th Phahonyothin; 9am-6pm Sat + Sun; admission free.*

18 Rot Fai Market

An abandoned rail yard seems just the right setting for a market devoted to everything retro. Stalls at Rot Fai are stacked high with pre-loved biker jackets, vintage Vespas and mid-century Bakelite and melamine. Mobile bars in flip-top VW campers and armies of young Thai hipsters stocking up on retro threads just add to the carnival atmosphere. *facebook.com/taradrodfi; Soi 51, Th Srinakharin; 6pm-midnight Wed & Fri-Sun; admission free.*

ARTS & CULTURE · MUSIC & FILM · SPORTS & LEISURE · FOOD & DRINK · FESTIVALS & EVENTS

BĚIJĪNG

A true megacity, Běijīng's thoroughfares are heaving with history and often enveloped in the aroma of sizzling street eats. Prices have risen recently, and few visitors will leave without splurging a few dollars to explore the Forbidden City and the Summer Palace, but there's plenty to see for free.

01 798 Art District

Běijīng's best contemporary art galleries blossom amid the concrete skeleton of a decommissioned military factory built by East Germany. Wandering the Bauhaus buildings of 798 Art District, where Maoist slogans still adorn arches, is interesting, but don't miss the **Beijing Tokyo Art Projects** (BTAP) (*tokyo-gallery.com; 10am-6pm Tue-Sat Apr-Oct, 10am-5pm Nov-Mar; free*) and **UCCA** (*ucca.org.cn; 10am-7pm; free Thu*). *Dà Shānzi; cnr Jiuxianqiao Lu & Jiuxianqiao Beilu; free.*

02 Běijīng Museum of Natural History

There are 200,000-plus items to explore in this collection, from creepy crawlies and a live aquarium to prehistoric monsters. The stars of the dinosaur exhibit are *Mamenchisaurus jingyanensis*, a 26m-long lizard that stomped around China in the late Jurassic, and the skull of a huge prehistoric elephant-like beast that once roamed Asia. Book free tickets a day in advance. *bmnh.org.cn; 126 Tianqiao Nandajie; 8.30am-5pm Tue-Sun; free.*

03

09

10

OLYMPIC FOREST PARK
0
5 km
0
2.5 miles
WUDÀOKOU
10d
10c
01
Xiba River
Běijīng Normal University
LIUYĪN PARK
RENDINGHU PARK
QINGNIÁN HÚ PARK
DÌTÁN PARK
HAIDIĀN
Běijīng Jiaotong University
Xihai Lake
Liangma River
14b
GHOST ST (GUI JIE)
ZIZHÚYUÁN PARK
07
SANLITÚN EMBASSY AREA
06a
ZHĀNGMĀMA
15
14a
08b
CHĀOYÁNG
XICHÉNG
Běihǎi Lake
05
XIDAN
XICHÉNG
JǏNGSHĀN PARK
TUÁNJIÉHÚ PARK
IMPERIAL GARDEN
09a
12b
Zhōnghǎi Lake
Forbidden City
17
12a
RÌTÁN PARK
10a
09b
13b
03
Nánhǎi Lake
Oriental Plaza
10b
04
TIAN'ANMÉN SQUARE
XICHÉNG
Yinshui Qu
BĚIJĪNG TRAIN STATION
Tonghui River
06b
DASHILAR
BĚIJĪNG WEST TRAIN STATION
Vital statistics
• Population: 20 million
• Best for: Cheap eats and ancient culture
• Unit of currency: Chinese yuan ¥ or CWY
• Price index: US$80 per day
16
NIU JIE SNACK STREET
02
TEMPLE OF HEAVEN PARK
LÓNGTÁN PARK
11
BĚIJĪNG AMUSEMENT PARK
TÁORÁNTÍNG PARK
BĚIJĪNG SOUTH TRAIN STATION
08a

03 Capital Museum

Discover the history and culture of Běijīng, including its folk traditions, in this contemporary museum housed in a modern building. Galleries include a brilliant batch of ancient Buddhist statues, an excellent exhibition of ornate Chinese porcelain, a collection of cultural relics from the Peking Opera and displays of ancient bronzes, jade, calligraphy and paintings. Recover with a cuppa (¥15) in the second-floor teahouse. *capitalmuseum.org.cn; 16 Fuxingmenwai Dajie; 9am-5pm Tue-Sun; free.*

04 National Museum of China

Delve into 5000 years of state-approved Chinese history, art and culture here, through permanent exhibitions including the excellent 'Ancient China', which spans prehistory to the Qing Dynasty. The 'Road of Rejuvenation' describes how China descended into semi-feudalism after the 1840 Opium War, before embracing Marxism and marching off on the road to 'national happiness and prosperity'. Present passports at the ticketing centre before 3.30pm. *en.chnmuseum.cn; 16 East Chang'an Ave; 9am-5pm; free.*

05 Běihǎi Park

Its history spanning five dynasties, this tranquil 1000-year-old imperial island park boasts Buddhist temples, swirling dragon motifs, lovely landscaping, picturesque pavilions and lakefront views. Emperors once retreated to the waterlily-filled ponds of the Jingxin Room (Quieting Heart Room) – a garden within a garden – for reflection and relaxation. *beihaipark.com.cn; 1 Wenjin St, Xichéng; 6am-8.30pm Apr-May & Sep-Oct, 6am-10pm Jun-Aug, 6am-8pm Jan-Mar & Nov-Dec; admission high/low season ¥10/5.*

BĚIJĪNG

ONE-DAY FREE PASS

One of the world's biggest public squares, Tiān'ānmén Sq sprawls across 440,000 sq metres (73 football pitches), yet there is nowhere to sit down. Fortunately, there's plenty to see for free, including the Monument to the People's Heroes (10-storey obelisk), the Great Hall of People, the National Museum of China, and the Chairman Mao Memorial Hall (a mausoleum containing Mao's waxy-looking embalmed body). The square is patrolled by Segway-riding police, and each morning, during the flag-raising ceremony, soldiers march through the Gate of Heavenly Peace and cross the square, taking exactly 108 paces per minute, in strides that are precisely 75cm long.

06 Hútòng hiking

Beneath Bird's Nests and high-rises, Běijīng's beating heart can still be heard in the hútòngs – labyrinth-like ancient laneways. Enjoy this increasingly endangered experience by exploring the alleyways around the Drum Tower (such as **Nanluoguxiang,** 6a) and in Dashilan, directly south-west of Tiān'ānmén Square, looking for narrow **Qianshi Hútòng** (6b; *off Zhubaoshi Jie*). Or check out the imperial hútòng courtyards, once home to royal eunuchs, to the north-east of Jǐngshān Park. *24hr; free.*

07 Lake Houhai

Wild swimming isn't the first activity you think of in Běijīng, but going for an early morning splash is a ritual for some residents of this supercity, who dive into the icy embrace of Lake Houhai whatever the weather. Unsurprisingly, temperatures can be demanding – the lake freezes solid in the bitter Běijīng winter, when you can skate around it instead – but it's an interesting spectator sport. *24hr; free.*

08 Market trends

Sack the **Silk Market** (*14 Dongdaqiao Lu; 9.30am-9pm*), which is an overrated tourist trap where you must elbow your way through crowds haggling for fake labels to reach the hard-nosed silk vendors on the third floor – and head instead to the sprawling outdoor **Muxiyuan Fabric Market** (8a; *23 Dahongmen Lu, Fengtái district; 8am-5pm*) and tourist-light **Tiān Yì Goods Market** (8b; *158 Di'anmen Waidajie; 9am-7.30pm*) for much better bargains. *Admission free.*

09 Non-forbidden city

It costs to go past the Meridian Gate and enter the **Palace Museum** (9a; ¥40–60), but you can appreciate its imperial enormity for free. Approaching from Tiān'ānmén Sq, stroll under the Mao portrait and gawp at the outer courtyard. Then explore **Zhōngshān Park** (9b; adult ¥3), once part of the imperial city but now with open-access to the public, where the pavilions and temples include the 1421 Altar of Earth and Harvests. *24hr; free.*

10 Ogle big pants and a bird's nests

Běijīng boasts extraordinary contemporary architecture, including the 234m-high **CCTV Headquarters** (10a; *32 Dongsanhuan Zhonglu*), which locals call Dà Kùchă ('Big Pants'), because it resembles trousers, and the curvy **National Centre for the Performing Arts** (10b; *2 West Chang'an Ave*). You can do paid tours of the **National Stadium** (10c; Bird's Nest) and **National Aquatics Centre** (10d; Water Cube) (*both at the Olympic Sports Centre*), but the best view is free, after dark, when they're illuminated with solar-generated power. *24hr; free.*

11 Pānjiāyuán Market

Sharpen your haggling skills and dive into the crowded and cacophonous chaos of Pānjiāyuán Market, where about 3000 dealers and 50,000 treasure-hunters do battle over ownership of *yìshù* (arts), *gōngyì* (crafts) and *gǔwán* (antiques). The best place in Běijīng for a bargain, here's where you'll discover everything from Cultural Revolution retro memorabilia to Middle Kingdom keepsakes. Weekends are best. *Caveat emptor*, obviously. *West of Pānjiāyuán Qiao; 8.30am-6pm Mon-Fri, 4.30am-6pm Sat + Sun; admission free.*

12 Temple of the Sun

In the early morning, you'll see citizens old and young performing t'ai-chi exercises in Běijīng's beautiful parks, like a slow-motion flash mob. In **Rìtán Park** (12a), you'll also find an altar originally built by a Ming Dynasty emperor in 1530, and used for offering ritual sacrifices to the sun. The Temple of the Moon is on the other side of the city, in **Yuetan Park** (12b). *Rìtán Park; 6am-9pm; free.*

13 **Bar with a view**

Access to the **CCTV Tower Observation Deck** (13a) costs an elevated ¥70, but you can get a window seat in the **Atmosphere Bar** (13b; *until 2am daily*) of the Shangri-La on the 80th floor of the China World Trade Centre, and drink in the views for the price of a beer. Of course, if a classic Běijīng pea-souper descends, you'll see nothing – but at least you'll have ¥70 beer money.

14 **Happy hour**

Booze will quickly bust your budget, particularly if you're fond of European beers. Stick to local lagers and explore backstreet bars for better bargains. **Sanlitún Bar Street** (14a; *Chaoyang District*) is good – look out for **Mojito Man** (*43 Sanlitún N St*), where mojitos cost ¥15. Elsewhere, popular little **El Nido** (14b; *59 Fangjia Hútòng*) sells Harbin beer for just ¥10 a bottle, and wine (a Běijīng rarity) for ¥25 a glass.

15 **Jīngzūn Peking Duck**

Coming to the place formerly known as Peking and not puckering up to a duck is like skipping the Forbidden City. It's a pricey dish in some touristy restaurants, but this local joint, which is popular with expats, serves a delicious Peking duck with the works for just ¥128. The ambience is excellent here, too, and you have the option to sit outside on the wooden terrace amid glowing red lanterns. *6 Chunxiu Lu; 11am-10pm.*

16 **Mǎliándào Tea Market**

If you're someone who knows your pu-erh from your oolong, then you'll get a kick from a trip to Mǎliándào, where virtually all the tea in China can be seen,

BĚIJĪNG

STREET EATS

Dining out in Běijīng is an adventure in itself and it costs very little to eat exceedingly well in this tasty town. The cuisine of Chinese minority Muslim ethnic groups such as the Hui and Uighur is fantastic, and incredibly cheap; explore Niu Jie snack street for some excellent options. Zhāng Māma (*76 Jiaodaokou Nandajie; 10.30am-10.30pm; mains ¥10-20*) is the place for hot and zingy Sìchuān snacks, especially the chilli-infused broth *málà xiāngguō*. Ghost St (*Gui Jie*), a 1.4km strip that's home to over 150 restaurants, is the best place for a late-night bite, especially if you fancy spicy lobster.

sniffed and sampled. It's mainly aimed at wholesalers, but most vendors will give you a complimentary taste, and then you can sip plenty more brews in teashops. You can get your hands on tea sets here as well, at potentially bargain prices. *11 Măliándào Lu; 8.30am-6pm; admission free.*

17 Wángfŭjĭng snack street

Adventurous foodies will find that there isn't much they can't chomp in China, particularly on this busy pedestrianised lane behind an ornate *paifang* (ancient arch) north-east of Tiān'ānmén Sq. Here you'll discover dishes from deep-fried scorpions and starfish to skewered seahorses, plus less challenging offerings from around China, such as *zhájiàngmiàn* (Běijīng noodles in fried bean sauce) and spicy Sìchuān soups like *málà tang. West off Wángfŭjĭng Dajie; 9.30am-10pm; most dishes ¥10.*

18 Běijīng International Kite Festival

Cast your eyes to the sky in order to watch for free this annual two-day celebration of a traditional Chinese pastime that stretches back hundreds of years. Over the weekend, some incredibly colourful and frequently complex creations are floated into the big blue above Běijīng, including antique kites, and the free-flying and anarchic aerodynamic action attracts enthusiasts from all over the world. *Běijīng Garden Expo, Fengtai District + Olympic Green, Tongzhou District; Apr; free.*

- **Most hostels and coffee shops offer free wi-fi. You won't get Facebook, Twitter or Gmail, but Skype and WhatsApp work.**
- **Běijīng's subway system now has English signs and announcements. Most journeys cost ¥3 to ¥6.**
- **Buses are challenging, but they're a good way to get your bearings and with a Běijīng Transportation Smart Card (*travelchinaguide.com/cityguides/beijing/transportation/smart-card.htm*) fares are half price (¥1).**
- **7-Elevens sell booze, perfect for picnics in Běijīng's parks.**
- **If you over order the food when you're eating out, ask the service staff to *dăbāo* – box up the leftovers.**

ARTS & CULTURE | MUSIC & FILM | SPORTS & LEISURE | FOOD & DRINK | FESTIVALS & EVENTS

BEIRUT

BEIRUT

Once known as the 'Paris of the East', the modern-day capital of Lebanon has evolved over the years into a culturally complex and exciting city where eastern influences effortlessly coexist with those from the west, and where history resonates as powerfully and seductively as anywhere in the magical Middle East.

04

01 American University of Beirut Archaeological Museum

This museum in the landscaped grounds of Beirut's most prestigious university showcases a collection that is modest in size but great in quality. Highlights include a collection of Phoenician artefacts (coins, glass, steles) and moving memorial portrait busts from Palmyra dating from the 2nd to 3rd centuries AD. *aub.edu.lb/; Bliss St, Hamra; 9am-5pm Mon-Fri winter, 9am-4pm summer; free.*

02 Beirut Central District (BCD)

It's taken over a quarter of a century to recover from the battering it took in the Civil War, but an inspired programme of urban restoration has re-endowed Beirut's Downtown district with the sophistication beloved of the 1960s jet set. Wander the streets around Place de l'Etoile to see buildings dating from the Ottoman and French mandates, archaeological ruins and a swathe of historic mosques, synagogues and churches. *24hr; free.*

03 Sursock Museum

Beirut has a cutting-edge contemporary arts scene, and this recently reopened museum is one of the jewels in its crown. Housed in an ornate 1902 mansion that has been given the renovation of a lifetime courtesy of architects Jean-Michel Wilmotte and Jacques Aboukhaled, it offers both temporary exhibitions and a permanent collection of modern and contemporary art. *Rue Sursock, Achrafiye; 10am-6pm Wed & Fri-Mon, noon-9pm Thu; free.*

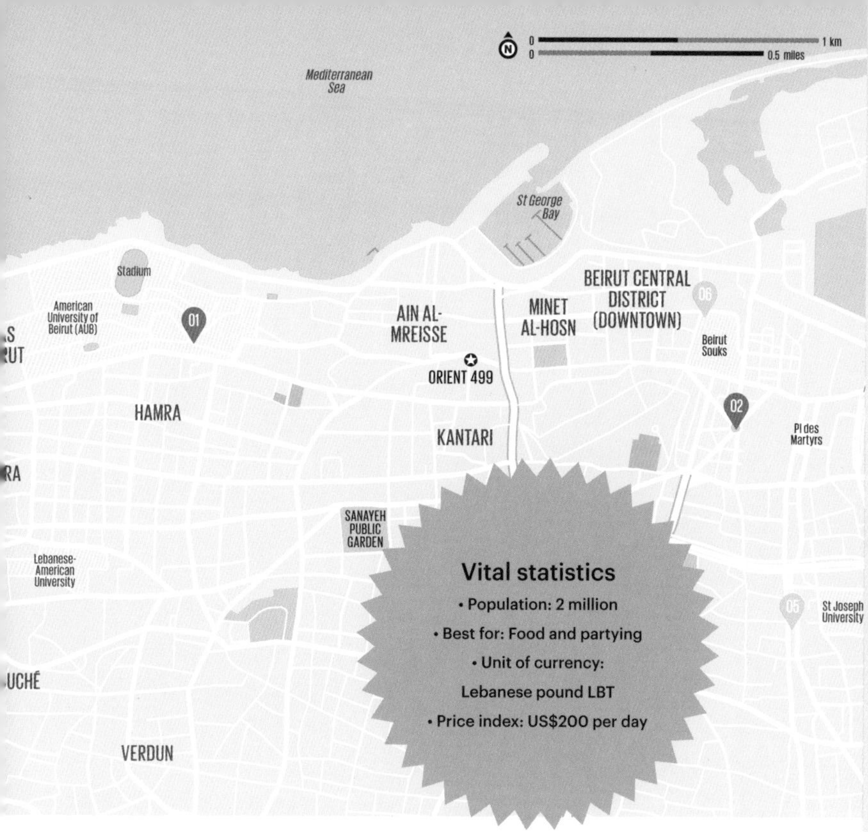

Vital statistics

- Population: 2 million
- Best for: Food and partying
- Unit of currency: Lebanese pound LBT
- Price index: US$200 per day

04 Corniche

In warm weather, a sunset stroll along Beirut's waterfront corniche is the city's signature experience. Start at the Zaitunay Bay marina and wander east towards the iconic Pigeon Rocks, passing a string of sybaritic beach clubs along the way. You'll enjoy peerless people-watching opportunities and can reward yourself near the end with a coffee at local institution, **Al-Rawda Cafe** *(Chouran St; 7am-midnight)* next to the wonderfully retro Luna Park funfair.

05 Beirut Falafel Strip

Once best known as part of the infamous Green Line that separated warring East and West Beirut, these days Beshara al-Khoury St is a place that brings Beirutis together for its fabulous falafel joints. The oldest is **Falafel Sahyoun** (*falafelsahyoun.com; St 17; 10am-11pm*), established in the 1930s, and others include **Falafel Tabboush** (*St 17; 10am-midnight*) and **Arax** (*Al Maliyah Building, St 17; 10am-midnight*). *About LBT3000-13,500.*

06 Souk el Tayeb Farmers' Market

This Saturday-only event certainly lives up to its name, which translates as 'The Good Market'. Located in front of the Beirut Souks in the Downtown district, it was established in 2004 to bring fractured communities together through the sharing of food, traditions and hospitality, and has been going strong ever since. Small-scale farmers (many organic), artisan food-makers and local craftsfolk sell fresh produce, tasty snacks and handicrafts. *soukeltayeb.com; Beirut Souks; 9am-2pm Sat; admission free.*

MADE IN BEIRUT

Lebanon is known throughout the Middle East for the excellence of its cuisine, but the local handicrafts are an equally compelling – if lesser known – drawcard for those visiting the country. The quality of local designer clothing, textiles and homewares is impressive and prices are eminently affordable, making this a shopping destination par excellence. Head to drop-dead-gorgeous designer shop Orient 499 (*499 Omar Daouk St, Mina El Hosn; 10.30am-7pm Mon-Sat*) or handicrafts hub L'Artisan du Liban (*Centre Saint Antoine, Rue Gouraud, Gemmayzeh; 9.30am-7pm Mon-Fri, 9.30am-5pm Sat*) to score an enviable array of souvenirs, or just to admire the great handiwork on display.

ASIA'S BEST SUNSETS WITHOUT THE PRICE TAG

01

MANILA BAY – THE PHILIPPINES

Pollution and geography conspire to create great beauty over Manila Bay, setting for some of Asia's most spectacular sunsets. Get there early and stake out a viewing spot near the funfair at Mall of Asia, Manila's answer to Santa Monica Pier. *Seaside Blvd, Manila; free.*

02

SARANGKOT – NEPAL

With its mirrored lake and mountain canopy, Pokhara was made for stunning sundown spectacle. For maximum oohs and aahs, head for Sarangkot on the ridge above Phewa Tal for the evening light show over Mt Machhapuchhare and the Annapurna mountains. *Npr30.*

03

TSIM SHA TSUI EAST PROMENADE – HONG KONG

Sunset comes with an after-dinner show at Hong Kong's Tsim Sha Tsui Promenade. Stroll along the Ave of the Stars (hello there Jet Li, howdy Jackie Chan), then grab a waterfront seat ready for sunset and the Symphony of Lights. *Salisbury Rd, Hong Kong; free.*

04

TOKYO METROPOLITAN GOVERNMENT BUILDING – JAPAN

Sunsets over cities really need to be seen from above; the challenge is finding a viewing deck without a monster entry fee. Enter the Tokyo Metropolitan Government Building, offering gratis sunset views from the 45th floor. *2-8-1 Nishi Shinjuku, Tokyo; free.*

05

07

05

U BEIN BRIDGE – MYANMAR
Some landmarks are best seen as silhouettes, and U Bein Bridge is one of them, being at its most photogenic as the sun dips over Taungthaman Lake. In the final hours of daylight, the world's longest teak bridge throngs with monks, bikes and locals going about their picturesque business. *Amarapura; free.*

GOLDEN TEMPLE – INDIA
Pilgrims mob the Golden Temple whatever the time of day, but a special magic hovers over the most sacred shrine to Sikhism at sunset, when the elegant, gold-encrusted Harmandir Sahib glows like an ember on a mirror sea. *Amritsar; free.*

07

JIMBARAM BEACH – BALI
Sunset, sand, seafood – what's not to like about Jimbaran Beach? Grab a table on the foreshore, order grilled ocean prawns, squid, barracuda, snapper and mud crabs and feast all your senses as the western sky gets a repaint from the setting sun. *Bali, Indonesia; free.*

WEST LAK E – CHINA
The poet Su Shi was waxing lyrical about Huangzhou West Lake in the 11th century, and a thousand years has fortunately done little to diminish the spot's charm. Pick a viewing point by a willow-pattern bridge and let the sunset float you across the centuries. *Huangzhou; free.*

ARTS & CULTURE MUSIC & FILM SPORTS & LEISURE FOOD & DRINK FESTIVALS & EVENTS

DELHI

Delhi offers a seductive glimpse of all of India in miniature. Inexpensively explore ancient Mughul monuments and elegant architect-designed avenues or check out the colour and chaos of the old city. Enjoy spending time and attention on sights as much as your hard-earned cash? Feel free to do so here!

01 Be a bookworm

Keep cool, cultured and caffeinated at a Full Circle Bookstore. These air-conditioned bookshops with cafes are a browser's heaven, due to their local, often cheap, editions of Indian and international writers, good history sections, meet-the-author events and laid-back coffee shops. *fullcirclebooks.in; Khan Market* (1a)*: bookstore & cafe 9.30am-9.30pm; Greater Kailash 1* (1b)*: bookstore 10am-8pm, cafe 9.30am-8.30pm; admission free.*

06

02 Indian National Trust for Art and Cultural Heritage (INTACH)

Take a walk in the past with INTACH. Led by passionate historians and popular with Delhi-ites as well as tourists, these weekend walks are a good way to see the city through the eyes of its residents, and areas less likely to be on an independent traveller's sightseeing itinerary, such as Mehrauli Archaeological Park. Online registration required. *intachdelhichapter.org/heritage_walks.php; various locations; check website for details; Rs 100.*

03 Evenings at India International Centre (IIC)

Set in leafy surrounds, the IIC is a great place to experience classic and contemporary performances, productions and presentations. It buzzes with energy as (depending what's on) scholars rub shoulders with trendy types, and locals mingle with visitors before and after gigs. Most events are open to the public and there is also a massive library. *iicdelhi.nic.in; 40 Max Mueller Marg; free.*

PLENTY OF DOUGH

Abhijit Menon-Sen draws a detailed mud-map of Chandni Chowk, where the Old Famous Jalebi Wala (*Dariba Kalan, Chandni Chowk; 10am-9pm; Rs 45 per 100g*) has been a feature of Delhi since his childhood. "Look for the crowd on this corner," he says. So what's a *jalebi*? "It's a deep-fried squiggle of dough soaked in tooth-jarringly sweet syrup. They're best when just fried, so if you have to wait for more, either the *lassi-wallah* opposite or the jewellery shops in the lane are both acceptable distractions. But don't get so distracted that you then miss the next batch!"

04 Hang out with flying foxes

In the huge trees that line Janpath, Delhi's soundest sleepers ignore the never-ceasing flow of traffic below. Also known as fruit bats, the flying foxes snooze upside down during daytime, coming and going in wheeling clouds at dawn and dusk. (And beware below – an animal turning itself the right way up is a sure sign poo is on the way!) *Janpath, near Janpath Circle; during daylight hours; free.*

05 Lodi Gardens

At any time of the day, join the crowd of laughing yogis, canoodling couples, dog-walkers, squirrel-feeders, serious runners, elderly strollers, casual cricketers or family picnickers that frequent this idyllic 36-hectare city park. All activity takes place against a fabulous backdrop of landscaped gardens, crumbling tombs and Mughul monuments (and, in the ancient trees, some of the best birdwatching in Delhi). *Enter at South End Rd; 6am-8pm October-March, 5am-8pm April-September; free.*

06 Breakfast tea Delhi-style

Drink tea at sunrise with *chai-wallahs* in old Delhi and watch the world awaken. Yawning drivers unfurl themselves from cycle-rickshaws, street-dwellers tidy their sidewalk patches, street-sweepers get busy and street-sellers hawk their goods. Head for a sweet-smelling fug of sugared tea and scalding milk, sit on a bench with a cuppa and, along with the locals, prepare for the day ahead. *Outside Red Fort, north of main entrance; dawn; tea from Rs 10.*

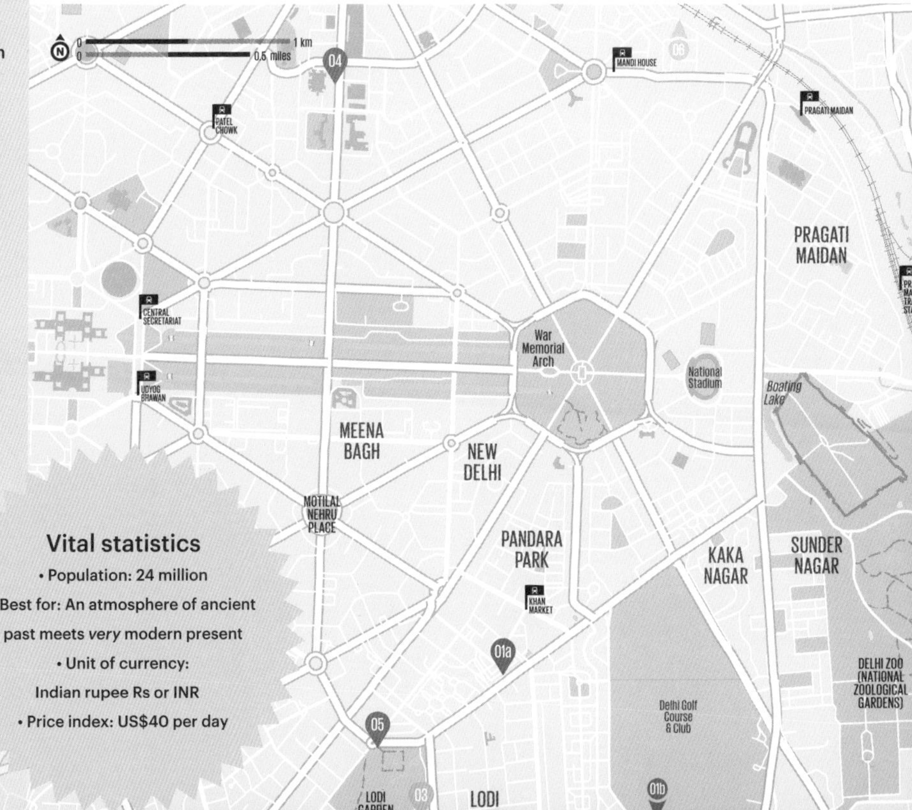

Vital statistics

- Population: 24 million
- Best for: An atmosphere of ancient past meets *very* modern present
- Unit of currency: Indian rupee Rs or INR
- Price index: US$40 per day

ARTS & CULTURE MUSIC & FILM SPORTS & LEISURE FOOD & DRINK FESTIVALS & EVENTS

DUBAI

At first glance, flashy Dubai looks decadent and indecently expensive, but beneath the excesses of the modern metropolis lies a once-modest pearl-trading settlement, still visible between the behemoth buildings and monstrous malls. Even in the new city there are things to do and see cheaply or for free.

DUBAI

01 Ayyam Gallery

Since it was founded in 2006, the impressive Ayyam Gallery – which operates across two blue-chip venues in Dubai and runs a third gallery in Beirut – has showcased brilliant contemporary art by emerging artists from the Middle East. Check the website for details of exhibitions, which are typically free to access and usually thought-provoking. *ayyamgallery.com; Gate Village Bldg 3, DIFC & Unit B11, Alserkal Ave, Al Quoz.*

02 Camel Museum

Beit Al Rekkab (House of Camels) celebrates camels and the role these 'ships of the desert' play in Arabic history, culture and literature. When Dubai was just a creek-side settlement, camels were everything to the Bani Yas Bedouin, from beast of burden and status symbol to provider of milk and medicine (camel urine can cure ulcers and alopecia, apparently), racing animals as well. *Al Shindagha Historic Village; 8am-2pm Sun-Thu; free.*

02

06

05

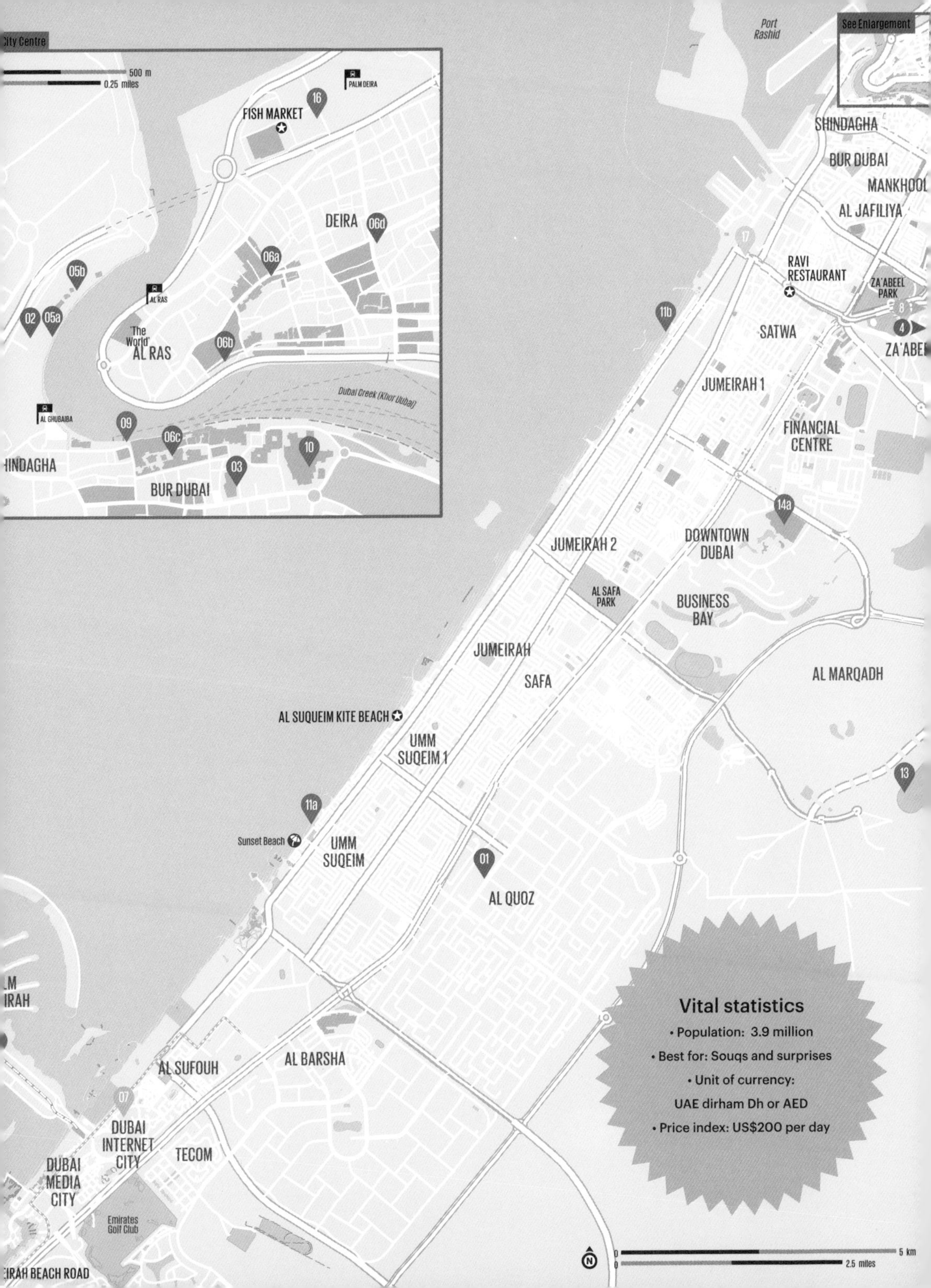

Vital statistics

- Population: 3.9 million
- Best for: Souqs and surprises
- Unit of currency: UAE dirham Dh or AED
- Price index: US$200 per day

03 Dubai Museum

Al Fahidi Fort, completed in 1787, is the oldest structure in this ever-evolving city – and the former palace and prison now houses Dubai Museum. Inside, you can learn about Dubai's past as a pearl-trading settlement and witness the incredible scale of change since 1960, when the modern metropolis began erupting from the sand. Items include instruments and weapons, and displays incorporate souqs, *dhows* and pearl-diving. *Al Fahidi St; 8.30am-8.30pm Sat-Thu, 2.30-8.30pm Fri; Dh3.*

04 Jaddaf *dhow*-building yard

Nothing quite says Arabia like a *dhow* – the iconic sailing vessels that have plied the waters around the peninsula for hundreds of years. These ships are still made by hand in a traditional boat yard in Jaddaf, across the water from Dubai Festival City. Watch artisans working their magic with teak and sheesham wood – using just hammer, saw, chisel, drill and plane – as they have done for time immemorial. *Free.*

05 Sheikh Saeed Al Maktoum House

The former home of the current Emir of Dubai's grandfather, this palace is now a museum (5a) where a fantastic photography display tells the tale of Dubai's metamorphosis from Bedouin settlement to modern metropolis. The building itself is an architectural gem and has an ingenious inbuilt pre-air-conditioning cooling system. Nearby, find the **Heritage and Diving Villages** (5b), both of which are free-entry displays exploring Dubai's pearl-diving history. *Al Shindagha Heritage Village, Bur Dubai; 8am-8.30pm Sat-Thurs, 3-9.30pm Fri; adult/child Dh3/1.*

09

06

THE LOCAL'S VIEW

"The souqs in Karma, Deira and Bur Dubai sell food and clothes cheaply, and you can find amazing Asian food there for next to nothing. My favourite is Pakistani Ravi Restaurant (*Shop 245, Al Dhiyafa Rd, Satwa; 5am-3am*), which serves the best curry in town. We're in a desert, but the green parks only cost Dh4 to enter and have running tracks, barbecues and spaces for playing football and picnicking. Jumeirah Beach Road has lots of public beaches and Al Suqueim Kite Beach has a view of the seven-star Burj al Arab Hotel." – Dave Spours, graphic designer

06 Souq look

Embrace authentic Arabia in Dubai's souqs, beginning at the all-glittering **Gold Souq** (6a; *Sikkat Al Khail St; 10am-1pm & 3-10pm*) and the **Spice Souq** (6b; *btwn Baniyas Rd, Al Ras Rd & Al Abra St; 9am-10pm Sat-Thu, 4-10pm Fri*). Also worth a look are **Bur Dubai Souq** (6c; *btwn Bur Dubai waterfront & Ali bin Abi Talib St*) and the **Covered Souq** (6d; *btwn Al Sabkha Rd, 107th St & Naif Rd*). *Admission free.*

07 Indie screen scene

Not everyone in Dubai likes blockbusters in characterless multiplexes. The Scene Club meets monthly to screen the cream of world cinema, discuss the films' themes and provide a networking platform for people interested and involved in independent filmmaking. These sessions typically take place in the main auditorium of the conference centre in Dubai Knowledge Village – just join the group online and register for a free ticket. *thesceneclub.com; free.*

08 Rooftop cinema

Free films are screened under the stars every Sunday at a rooftop cinema amid the gardens that top Dubai's Egyptian-themed mall. The movies start rolling at 8.30pm, but rock up early to bag yourself a beanbag and a prime spot. Popcorn, hotdogs and beverages are available at Dubai's standard scary prices, but at least the flick is free. *pyramidsrestaurantsatwafi.com; Pyramids Rooftop Gardens, Wafi Mall, Oud Metha Rd; from 8.30pm Sun; free.*

09 *Abra* (cadabra)

Be magically transported into traditional Dubai by hopping aboard a little *abra* (water taxi), and crossing to the Deira side of the creek. The north bank is traditionally the scene of frenetic activity, as sea traders arrive from the Persian Gulf and unload their cargoes – but the boat trip itself, on a crowded motorised *dhow*, is the most memorable experience. Although do take care when stepping aboard. *Dubai Creek; Dh1.*

10 Al Fahidi Historic District

Whenever the futuristic glitz of the modern city loses its shine, go for a head-clearing wander through this historic 'hood, formerly known as Bastakia, and take a peek at Dubai's past. This traditional Arabic area was settled by wealthy pearl traders and textile merchants from Bastak, Iran, in the late 19th-century, and its winding alleyways are now home to galleries in restored houses, bustling cafes and cool boutique hotels.

11 Beach life

If you're not staying in a hotel based at a beach, you can either pay to use beach parks, or hit the free public beaches, which generally have fewer facilities. **Burj Beach** (11a) is gratis, with good views of Burj Al Arab, and **Jumeirah Beach** (11b) has a new 14km-long corniche running through it, which is perfect for running or walking. Public beaches have barbecues that cost about Dh5 to use. *24hr; admission free.*

12 Take a yoga class

The augmented reality of life in Dubai's air-conditioned cityscape may leave you in need of some mental readjustment. If so, consider stretching out to the voluntary Friends of Yoga organisation, which runs free yoga classes every day at 5.30am and 7.30pm at 13 locations around the UAE, including Deira Creek, Bur Dubai Creek, Zabeel Park, JLT Park and Internet City. Register online to find the nearest session. *friendsofyogaglobal.org; free.*

13 Horse racing at Meydan Racecourse

The sport of kings isn't exclusively reserved for sheiks, and it doesn't necessarily come at a princely price. Arrive early to get free access to the general-admission area of Meydan Grandstand, and watch thoroughbreds in action. Seats with good views are available, and it's possible to see the horses in the Parade Ring from the sides of the apron. *www.dubaiworldcup.com; Nad Al Sheba; Nov–Mar; free.*

14 Mall crawl

Dubai boasts many impressive consumer cathedrals, some of which are more like amusement parks than shopping centres. In **Dubai Mall** (14a; *thedubaimall.com; Financial Centre Rd; 10am-11pm Sun-Wed, 10am-midnight Thu-Sat*), you can freely view 30,000 sea creatures in an epic aquarium, and get views of 830m-high Burj Khalifa, the world's tallest building. **Ibn Battuta Mall** (14b; *ibnbattutamall.com; Sheikh Zayed Rd; 10am-10pm Sun-Wed, 10am-midnight Thu-Sat*) offers themed sections decorated like China, Spain, India, Persia, Egypt and Tunisia. *24hr; admission free.*

15 Palm Jumeirah

Even if your budget doesn't quite extend to staying in one of the eye-wateringly expensive hotels that dot the Palm Jumeirah, you can still go island hopping on this artificial archipelago that blooms out into the Persian Gulf. Walk up the tree for free, or you could splash just a little cash on a return ticket for the **monorail** (*palm-monorail.com; Dh25*) that runs right along the trunk of this man-made marvel.

16 Pehlwani wrestling

Every Friday, shortly before sundown, crowds of construction workers amass in the sandlot behind the fish market in Deira to watch – and participate in – contests

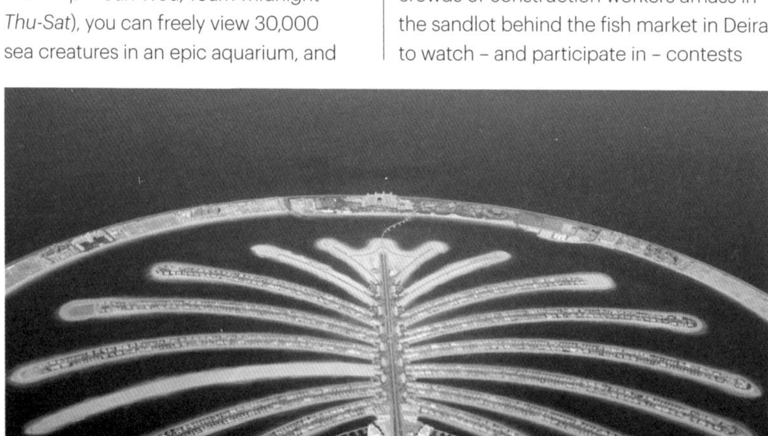

ONE-DAY FREE PASS

The perfect antidote to downtown Dubai is a stroll along the creek, through the city's historic quarters. Start by wandering the labyrinthine alleys of Al Fahidi (p041). Go past the modern Grand Mosque, where non-Muslims are permitted into the minaret only, then practise your haggling in Bur Dubai's souqs (p041). Continue along the creek to explore Al Shindagha's heritage villages (p040), or catch an *abra* (p041) across to Deira, where more souqs await. Continue along Corniche Rd to find the frenetic food and fish market, where the fruits of the Persian Gulf – including sharks – are diced daily.

of strength and skill. Pehlwani wrestling is a traditional sport in Southeast Asia (from where most of the labourers hail) that sees two loincloth-clad men attempting to knock each other down. Crowds are excitable, but friendly – dress modestly. *Deira; 5pm Fri; free.*

17 2nd of December

The name may have changed to 2nd of December (to honour the UAE's National Day), but you can visit the street formerly known as Al Dhiyafah Rd at any time to treat your taste buds to a smorgasbord of cheap street food. Expats mingle with manual workers and tourists, inhaling the aromas and chomping dishes from Iran, India, Lebanon and Africa. *24hr; admission free.*

18 Street nights

A community-based celebration of street culture, this award-winning festival embarks on an annual mission to entice people out of Dubai's colossal air-conditioned malls and into the open, using live music, a line-up of street-food-style restaurants and the largest gathering of artists in the UAE, who get busy turning walls and fences into a canvas. Keep an eye on the website for details of the next event. *streetnights.ae; free.*

TIP BOX

• When shopping for bargains and street food – whether in the souqs (p041), the fish market or along 2nd of December St – keep cash (including small-denomination notes) handy, and haggle hard for knick-knacks.

• If you're in town for a while, copy the locals and pick up the Entertainer books/app (*theentertainerme.com/tryapp; Dh450*), which gets you 2-for-1 deals at restaurants, cafes, theme parks, spas etc, and can be worth the initial outlay even during a holiday if you use it extensively.

• Dubai's population of expats operate a recycling system through Dubizzle (*dubizzle.com*) a classifieds site with an extensive 'free stuff' section.

ARTS & CULTURE MUSIC & FILM SPORTS & LEISURE FOOD & DRINK FESTIVALS & EVENTS

HONG KONG

Hong Kong gives as good as it gets, and enjoying it doesn't have to cost a fortune; with a rich imagination, the city can be as much a pauper's playground as it is a tycoon's. As an added bonus, nature's free wildernesses are just a cheap and easy bus-ride away.

01 Affordable Art Fair

If you like art with all the works (wine, sleek staff to answer questions), this is the cheapest option. And it's good. You'll see thousands of original works, including ones by big names like Nobuyoshi Araki. Prices are in the HK$1,000 to HK$100,000 range, inexpensive by art-world standards, as is the entry fee. *affordableartfair.com/hongkong/; locations vary; May; admission HK$160.*

02 'Free Wednesdays' at museums

Admission is free every Wednesday at several museums (*museums.gov.hk*). The museums of **History** (2a; *100 Chatham Rd S; 9.30am-12.45pm, 2-5pm Mon-Fri, 9.30am-noon Sat*) and **Heritage** (2b; *1 Man Lam Rd; 10am-6pm Mon & Wed-Fri, 10am-7pm Sat + Sun*) will teach you about Hong Kong. **Flagstaff House Museum of Tea Ware** (2c; *hk.art.museum; 10 Cotton Tree Dr; 10am-6pm Wed-Mon*) and the **Railway Museum** (2d; www.*heritagemuseum.gov.hk; 13 Shung Tak St; 9am-6pm Wed-Mon*) are always free.

Vital statistics

- Population: 7.2 million
- Best for: Food, and making the most of the proximity between city and country
- Unit of currency: Hong Kong dollar HK$ or HKD
- Price index: US$150 per day

03 Para Site Art Space

One of Hong Kong's (and indeed Asia's) oldest and most active indie art institutions, Para Site has built a reputation for being at once critical and adventurous when it comes to curation and mixing media. Exhibitions are edgy and tend to grapple with contemporary urban-related topics. They will leave you stroking your chin, in a good way (we hope). *para-site.org.hk; 22nd fl, Wing Wah Industrial Bldg, 677 King's Rd; noon-7pm Wed-Sun; free.*

04 PMQ

It may tout itself as an 'art hub' but Police Married Quarters (PMQ) is about local design with a commercial bent. The shops, which are mostly homewares and fashion, are worth a peek even if you're not buying anything. And there's always a decent exhibition on in one of the studios. The wide corridors and breezy courtyards are pleasant. *pmq.org.hk; 35 Aberdeen St, Soho; site 7am-11pm, shops 11am-7pm; free.*

05 Cantonese Opera at Temple Street Night Market

You don't have to know Cantonese opera to enjoy the show here. Hong Kong's liveliest night market is abuzz with hawkers, fortune-tellers and aromas from open-air restaurants. Just stop by for a while and let the cymbals, the singing, and the stylised gestures work on your senses. Who knows, years from now hearing these exotic strains once more may trigger happy memories of your Hong Kong trip. *Temple St, Yau Ma Tei; 6-11pm; free.*

06 Music at Sense99

Occupying a flamboyant apartment with red walls, chandeliers and fake chesterfields, this speakeasy comes alive

THE LOCALS' VIEW

"Pharmacies and wet markets are cheaper than supermarkets. Upstairs shops and cafes charge less than street-level ones." – Angela Chan, novelist

"The cheapest way to the airport is by MTR to Tung Chung, then change to a bus. Public swimming pools are HK$17 a swim. Supermarkets have different prices on different days. Monday is cheapest at Parkn Shop; look out for yellow labels for clearance items. Most supermarkets have a shelf of reduced-price products." – Janine Cheung, barrister

"Film festival (*hkiff.org.hk*) screenings are cheaper than commercial ones. For performing arts, choose shows by smaller companies and avoid the big arts festivals." – Gérard Henri, cultural critic

every weekend for an unpretentiously artsy crowd. Drums and an electric guitar sit at the ready for jam sessions on the upper floor. Depending on your luck, participants could be professional musicians, drunken friends, or you. Remember to bring your instrument. *sense99.com; 2nd & 3rd fls, 99 Wellington St; 9pm-4am Fri + Sat; free.*

07 Street Music Concert Series

These concerts are the ideal balance of professional curation and fizzy spontaneity. Genres range from indie rock to Cantonese opera. You're bound to like something, even if it's just the captivating atmosphere. Concerts happen monthly at the **Arts Centre** (7a; *2 Harbour Rd, Wan Chai; 5.30-8pm, 3rd Sat*), **Comix Home Base** (7b; *7 Mallory St, Wan Chai; 3-4.30pm, 4th Sun*) and **Blue House** (7c; *72 Stone Nullah Ln; 7.30-9pm, 2nd Thu*). *hkstreetmusic.com; free.*

08 Visage One

Hair salon by day, jazz den by night, Visage has the vibe of a secret society. Nobody knows which acts are going to be playing; nobody cares, because everyone trusts Benki, the owner. But come Saturday, followers trickle into the venue, reverently taking up seats behind the musicians, on the stairs, in the shampoo chair, and await the drop of the first note. *Po Lung Bldg, 93 Hollywood Rd, Soho; 8.30-11.30pm Sat; free.*

09 Hiking the MacLehose Trail

Secluded bays, volcanic rocks, cloud-cloaked peaks and ancient villages are but some of the stunning and varied sights along the 100km-long MacLehose Trail. The 10-section path begins at Pak Tam Chung in Sai Kung in the east, winds past country parks and ends in Tuen Mun in the west. Most sections have exits from which public transport can whisk you to the nearest town within an hour. *hiking.gov.hk; 24hr; free.*

10 Horse racing at the Happy Valley Racecourse

For HK$10 you can spend an evening enjoying the city's most popular spectator sport at a floodlit horse-racing track. Just cheer along with the crowd as hooves thunder towards the finishing line or up the game by betting. Either way, bring your own grub (and booze) if you don't want to pay through the nose to keep your stomach happy. *hkjc.com; Wong Nai Chung Rd, Happy Valley; 7.30-10.30pm Wed, Sep-Jun; HK$10.*

11 Ping Shan Heritage Trail

Precolonial and contemporary rural Hong Kong sit side-by-side along this 1km trail. You'll pass by a dozen historic buildings belonging to the powerful Tangs, founders of this sprightly five-century-old village. The handsome ancestral hall has been the venue for banquets and fashion shows (William Tang is a designer). Tsui Sing Lau is Hong Kong's oldest surviving pagoda. *Ping Shan, Yuen Long; halls & pagoda 9am-1pm & 2-5pm; closed Tue; free.*

12 Hong Kong-style barbecue

The key to this cheap and cheery activity is pre-marinated meat (pork chops, chicken wings, sausages), vegetables and, of course, marshmallows. You'll also need two-pronged tridents known as 'BBQ forks', paper plates (or lettuce leaves for a green alternative), charcoal and a lighter. Pick these up at a supermarket, then head to a beach or country park and claim a barbecue pit. It's easy. The challenge is starting the fire...

13 Khalsa Diwan Sikh Temple

It's not a food bank but Hong Kong's largest Sikh temple hands out free vegetarian meals (*from 11.30am-8.30pm*) to anyone passing through its gates, regardless of their 'faith, caste, colour or country of origin'. In return for the meal of *dal* or *sabzi*, you can volunteer to wash the dishes. Sunday prayer sessions (*9am-1.30pm*) and daily prayers (*6am-8.30am, 6.30pm-8pm*) are also open to everyone. *khalsadiwan.com; 371 Queen's Rd E, Wan Chai; free.*

14 Cheung Chau Bun Festival

You may have heard of this mad century-old scramble – during which participants scale a tower that is covered with 'good luck' buns and try to pocket as many of the treats as possible – just one of many re-enactments of a Qing-dynasty ritual on Buddha's birthday. Another of these, the Parade of Floats, features children dressed up as deities or, increasingly, politicians; rituals that once drove away pirates addressing ideological concerns. *cheungchau.org; locations & dates vary; free.*

15 Dragon Boat races

Watching dragon boats against a backdrop of decorated fishing junks, with people burning hell notes and casting them into the water, is a rich experience. There are two to four races a month from March to October. Among the most spectacular are those in Stanley and Tai O at the Dragon Boat Festival, and in Lamma and Po Toi on Tin Hau's Birthday. *hong-kong-traveller.com; locations & dates vary; free.*

16 Fire Dragon Dance at Mid-Autumn Festival

Over three nights during this festival, a 67m-long straw dragon decorated with 70,000 glowing incense sticks is paraded by hundreds of hot-blooded males in the affluent Causeway Bay neighbourhood of **Tai Hang** (16a; *taihangfiredragon.hk; free*). The smoky ritual commemorates the time some 100 years ago that the dance was

HONG KONG

THRIFTY COMMUTING

The tram (*hktramways.com*) and the Star Ferry (*www.starferry.com.hk*) are precious pieces of Hong Kong's mobile heritage. Combine rides on the two with walking for a green, scenic and affordable way to explore the city. For a flat fare of a paltry HK$2.30, the world's largest fleet of still-operating double-decker streetcars (c. 1904) lets you travel as far as you like over 16km of track on Hong Kong Island. The 12-minute ride aboard the Star Ferry (c. 1880) with its postcard-perfect views of Victoria Harbour will only set you back HK$2.50.

© Keith Mulcahy | 500px

performed under the same full moon to end a plague and a typhoon. Another fire dragon dances in **Pok Fu Lam Village** (16b; *hong-kong-traveller.com; free*). Go early; it gets crowded.

17 Freespace Happening, West Kowloon

Why not spend an idle Sunday chilling with some of the young movers and shakers of Hong Kong's cultural circle? This newborn monthly event features a kaleidoscope of activities that includes live music, film, dance, parkour and handicrafts among many others. Just pack a picnic and a Frisbee; there's more than enough in the way of lawn and expansive sea views to go around. *westkowloon.hk; Nursery Park, West Kowloon Promenade; 2-7pm, 2nd Sunday of the month; free.*

18 Hungry Ghosts Festival

To appease roaming spirits during the seventh lunar month when the gates of hell are believed to be unbolted, people make food and faux-money offerings by the roadside, while neighbourhood communities set up bamboo scaffolds to host religious ceremonies (both Buddhist and Taoist) and Chinese opera performances. The month-long Hungry Ghosts festivities end when a paper effigy of the God of Hades is burnt, clenched fist, bulging eyes and all. *discoverhongkong.com; free.*

16

CUT-PRICE TOURS

These heritage sites offering free English tours are well worth a visit:

- **Asia Society (*asiasociety.org*), a US-founded institution, now stages top-notch exhibitions.**
- **Mei Ho House Youth Hostel (*yha.org.hk*) and museum were once grassroots housing destroyed by fire.**
- **Tai O Heritage Hotel (*taioheritage hotel.com*) guarded the coast against pirates.**
- **Galleries at Jao Tsung-I Academy (*jtia.hk*) explain its uncanny history.**

Venues you can visit only by joining a tour:

- **North Kowloon Magistracy (*visitscadhk.hk*), now a school.**
- **Tsz Shan Monastery (*tszshan.org*), an antiquity-inspired modern monastery.**
- **Join any tour to enter Chinese medicine clinic, Lui Seng Chun (*scm.hkbu.edu.hk*) for a look. On free consultation days, doctors take your pulse *gratuit*.**

 ARTS & CULTURE MUSIC & FILM  SPORTS & LEISURE FOOD & DRINK FESTIVALS & EVENTS

MUMBAI

India remains a relatively inexpensive place to travel, but Mumbai – home of Bollywood and the country's biggest, busiest, richest and most cosmopolitan metropolis – is probably the priciest place to visit. However, there are plenty of budget options in the old-Bombay mix of tricks, which offer spice without the price.

01 British India

Gargoyle-spotting is free at the Victorian **Chhatrapati Shivaji Terminus** (1a), the world's busiest railway station. Nearby, the **Gateway of India** (1b) – a basalt arch built to mark King George V's 1911 visit – is a people-watching spot, especially during March's Elephanta Festival. Boats depart here to the UNESCO -listed **Elephanta Caves** (*Rs250*), 1300-year-old hand-carved cave temples.

02 Kala Ghoda Art

While entry to the **National Gallery of Modern Art** (*ngmaindia.gov.in; 11am-6pm Tue-Sun; Rs500*) costs, Kala Ghoda also boasts **Jehangir Art Gallery** (2a; *jehangirartgallery.com; Mahatma Gandhi Rd; 11am-7pm; free*), with work by modern Indian artists. In January/February, **Kala Ghoda Festival** (*kalaghodaassociation.com; free*) is a nine-day celebration of art and multiculturalism. Nearby, **Project 88 Gallery** (2b; *project88.in; BMP Building, NA Sawant Marg, Colaba; 11am-7pm Tue-Sat; free*) shows more cutting-edge work.

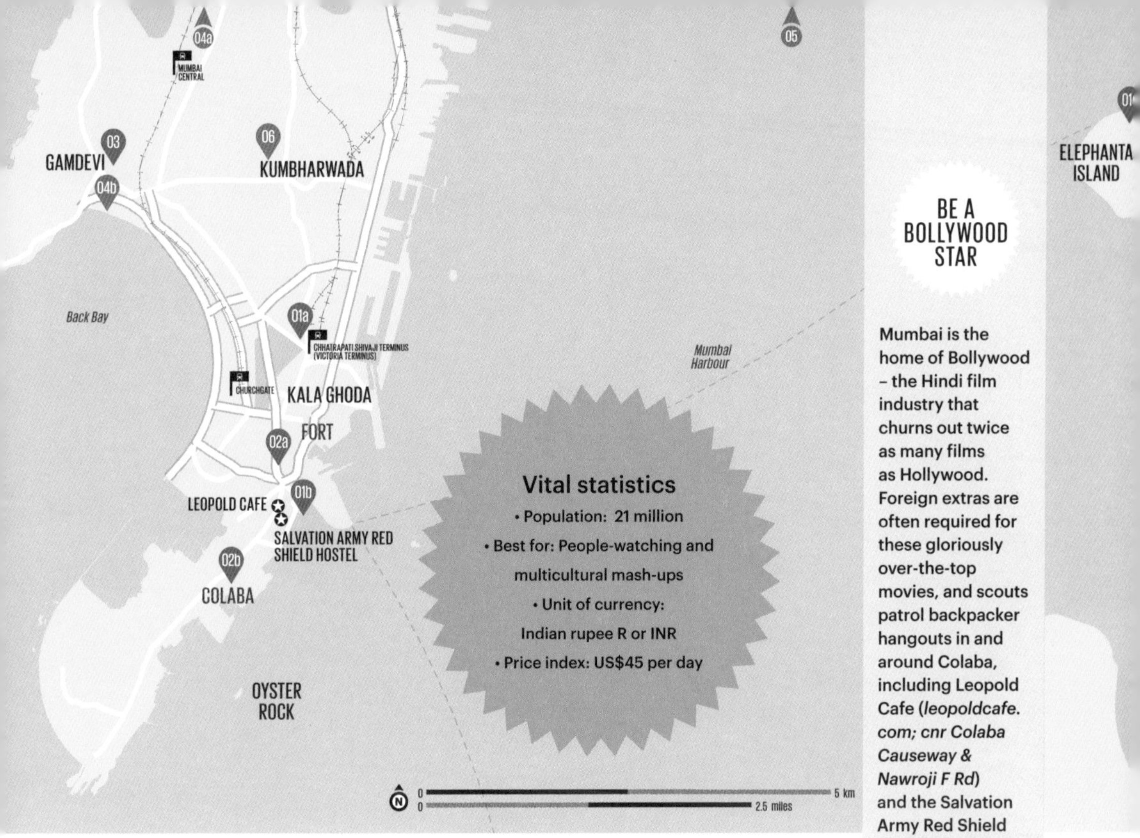

MUMBAI CENTRAL
GAMDEVI
KUMBHARWADA
Back Bay
CHHATRAPATI SHIVAJI TERMINUS (VICTORIA TERMINUS)
CHURCHGATE
KALA GHODA
FORT
LEOPOLD CAFE
SALVATION ARMY RED SHIELD HOSTEL
COLABA
OYSTER ROCK
Mumbai Harbour

ELEPHANTA ISLAND

Vital statistics

- Population: 21 million
- Best for: People-watching and multicultural mash-ups
- Unit of currency: Indian rupee R or INR
- Price index: US$45 per day

03 Mani Bhavan

Mahatma Gandhi was a regular visitor to Mumbai, and when in town he stayed here, developing *Satyagraha*, the philosophy of non-violent resistance. Now the building is a museum, with displays, photos and letters written by Gandhi. *gandhi-manibhavan.org; 19 Laburnum Rd, Gamdevi; 9.30am-6pm; free.*

04 Bombay beaches

The Island City has several beaches worth exploring. **Juhu Beach** (4a), north of the city, is less busy, but central **Chowpatty Beach** (4b) is more interesting, crowded with cricket-playing families, vendors and dancing monkeys. From October to March, Hindus flock here to celebrate Ganesh Chaturthi by dunking effigies of the elephant-headed multi-armed god into the sea. *24hr; free.*

05 Sanjay Ghandi National Park

The 'lungs of Mumbai', the world's biggest national park within city limits, isn't free, but it's cheap (*Rs33*) and easy to access. Visit to go boating, see waterfalls and wildlife, and explore the 1000-year-old Kanheri Caves (*Rs100*), carved into a ravine by Buddhist monks. *sanjaygandhinational park.net; 7.30am-6pm.*

06 Thieves Market

Singular souvenirs can be picked up for a steal at the chaotic, cacophonic Chor Bazaar (Thieves Market), where vendors flog everything from Bollywood posters to Raj-era knick-knacks. Perusing the treasure and trash on show here is an essential Mumbai experience (just keep your wallet somewhere safe). *Mutton St; 11am-7.30pm Sat-Thu; admission free.*

BE A BOLLYWOOD STAR

Mumbai is the home of Bollywood – the Hindi film industry that churns out twice as many films as Hollywood. Foreign extras are often required for these gloriously over-the-top movies, and scouts patrol backpacker hangouts in and around Colaba, including Leopold Cafe (*leopoldcafe.com; cnr Colaba Causeway & Nawroji F Rd*) and the Salvation Army Red Shield Hostel (*Ormiston Rd*) where you can register your interest at reception. Exercise caution if approached while alone, but scams seem rare. It makes for a memorable experience, and your wages may cover the cost of a tour of Film City (*mumbaifilm citytours.com; Goregaon; 10am-5pm; tours from Rs600*).

1 SRI SAGAR - INDIA

The south-Indian dosa (crepe) is a way of life, and Bengaluru's were voted best in the world. It's worth braving the queues for Sri Sagar's thick benne dosa (butter dosa). *Margosa Rd, Malleswaram, Bengaluru; 7am-9pm; dosas from Rs30.*

3 TALAT CHANG PHEUAK NIGHT MARKET - THAILAND

Chiang Mai gourmands head straight for the night markets. At Talat Chang Pheuak, the Cowboy Lady's stall serves the finest kôw kăh mŏo (stewed pork leg with rice) in the north. *Th Mani Nopharat, Chiang Mai; 5pm-midnight; dishes from 30B.*

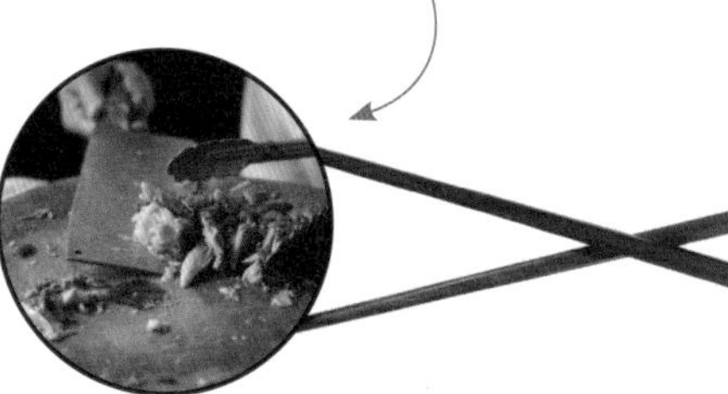

2 JOO HOOI CAFE - MALAYSIA

Penang without laksa is like Batman without Robin. When trawling George Town for this hawker treat, swing into Joo Hooi for one of the island's best bowls. *Cnr Jln Penang & Lebuh Keng Kwee, George Town; 11am-5pm; mains from RM3.*

7 KIMLY - CAMBODIA

Kep-sur-Mer was where Cambodia's colonial masters came to feast on the finest crabs in the Mekong Delta; the French are gone, but the crabs remain, served an incredible 27 ways at this veteran seafood restaurant by the Crab Market. *Crab Market, Kep; 9am-10pm; dishes from US$2.50.*

ASIA'S BEST CHEAP GOURMET GRUB

Inside every budget traveller lies a secret gourmet. Lucky, then, that some of Asia's finest food is served for discount prices down on the street.

6 WARUNG IBU OKA – BALI

If you thought suckling pig was just for 16th-century monarchs, think again. In Indonesia, roast babi guling is food for the people, and Warung Ibu Oka serves roast-pork plates for rupiah-saving prices. *Jl Suweta, Ubud, Bali; 10am-4pm; mains from 50,000Rp.*

5 LIN HEUNG TEA HOUSE – HONG KONG

Finding discount dim sum is a challenge in Hong Kong, but Wellington St's Lin Heung is as old school as they come: steamers on trollies, sulky service and delicious, inexpensive dim sum that makes it all worthwhile. *160-164 Wellington St, Hong Kong; 6am-11pm, dim sum to 3.30pm; dim sum from HK$12.*

8 NASI KANDAR PELITA – MALAYSIA

Malaysia gets a double dip thanks to its fabulous Mamak hawker food; at Nasi Kandar Pelita, a meal of exquisite roti *canai* (fried flatbread with daal and chicken curry) will set you back pennies. *149 Jln Ampang, Kuala Lumpur, 24hr, RM2-8*

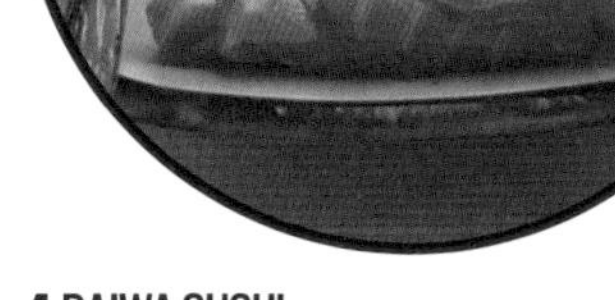

4 DAIWA SUSHI – JAPAN

Sampling sushi at source is de rigueur on a trip to Tokyo, and sashimi is sliced straight from the day's catch at Daiwa Sushi, where set-menu lunches are ocean-fresh and (by Tokyo standards) friendly on the pocket. *Bldg 6, 5-2-1 Tsukiji Chūō-ku, Tokyo; 5am-1.30pm Mon-Sat; sushi sets from ¥3500.*

ARTS & CULTURE | MUSIC & FILM | SPORTS & LEISURE | FOOD & DRINK | FESTIVALS & EVENTS

SHÀNGHĂI

Modern China's showpiece city is where fashionistas shop and moneyed Chinese magnates seal their deals. But with its ample free museums, parks and art galleries – not to mention eminently affordable street-food markets and no-frills dumplings joints – a visit to sleek, chic Shànghăi doesn't have to break the bank.

01 M50

Shànghăi's best-known arts enclave is this trend-setting complex of industrial buildings down graffiti-splashed Moganshan Road. It may not be as provocative as some of Běijīng's edgier art districts but it's still well worth poking your nose around the artists' studios, and there are plenty of good places in which to sip coffee and slurp noodles should you run out of steam. *50 Moganshan Rd; most galleries 10am-6pm daily; free.*

02 Shànghăi Museum

Arguably the best museum in China (it contains more than a million objects) this striking collection of Middle Kingdom masterpieces showcases the craft of a millennia – from ancient bronzes and religious sculptures through to some of China's finest examples of ceramics, paintings, jade, coins and calligraphy. Note, only 8000 people are allowed in each day, so don't arrive too late. *www.shanghaimuseum.net/en/; 201 Renmin Ave; 9am-5pm, last entry 4pm; free.*

06

03 Fùxīng Park

Designed by the French in 1909, leafy Fùxīng Park is a delightful place in which to escape the heat of the sun and the incessant noise of the mind-boggling traffic. During the early morning in particular the park fills with dancers, card-players, people walking backwards and t'ai-chi practitioners. Find a bench under a wutong tree, and see how some of Shànghăi's residents really unwind. *South Shaanxi Rd, Xintiandi; 5am-6pm; free.*

ONE-DAY FREE PASS

Start the day in People's Park (*West Nanjing Rd; 6am-6pm, 6am-7pm Jul-Sep; free*), then head to the Shànghǎi Museum. Grab a simple lunch at nearby Yang's Fry Dumplings (*97 Huanghe Rd; 6.30am-8.30pm; 4 dumplings ¥6*), then walk via East Nanjing Rd (*most shops 10am-10pm*) – Shànghǎi's most famous shopping strip – to the quirky Post Museum (*250 North Suzhou Rd; 9am-5pm Wed, Thu, Sat & Sun; free*); don't miss the views from the rooftop garden. Saunter along the iconic Bund, then follow your nose to Yunnan Rd Food Street (*South Yunnan Rd*) for barbecued lamb skewers and ice-cold beer.

04 The Bund (Wàitān)

The ultimate symbol of concession-era Shànghǎi, this grandiose riverside sweep of former banks and trading houses makes for one of China's standout city strolls. The art-deco and neoclassical buildings now house boutiques, hotels and restaurants, but it's the pedestrian-friendly, elevated promenade that's the place to be: early morning, watch locals practising t'ai-chi; early evening, return for a spectacular neon-lit cityscape. *East Zhōngshān No 1 Rd; 24hr; free.*

05 Tiánzǐfáng

To focus your wanderings in the graceful French Concession district, head to this charming tree-lined pocket of traditional *lòngtáng* alleys, interspersed with wi-fi cafes, cool bars and restaurants, art shops and excellent small boutiques selling everything from ethnic embroidery and hand-wrapped pu-erh teas to retro dinnerware. Families still reside in many of the buildings here, lending the area a community atmosphere. *tianzifang.cn; Taikang Rd; 24hr; free.*

06 Qibao Ancient Town

If big-city brashness is getting to you, ride the subway out to the attractive canal-side *guzhen* (ancient town) of Qibao, which dates from the far-off Northern Song Dynasty (AD 960-1127). You can skip the ¥45-ticket, which gains you entry into specific buildings, and instead simply drift around the network of lanes and arched bridges as you size up street vendors for potential snacks. *2 Minzhu Rd; sights 8.30am-4.30pm; free.*

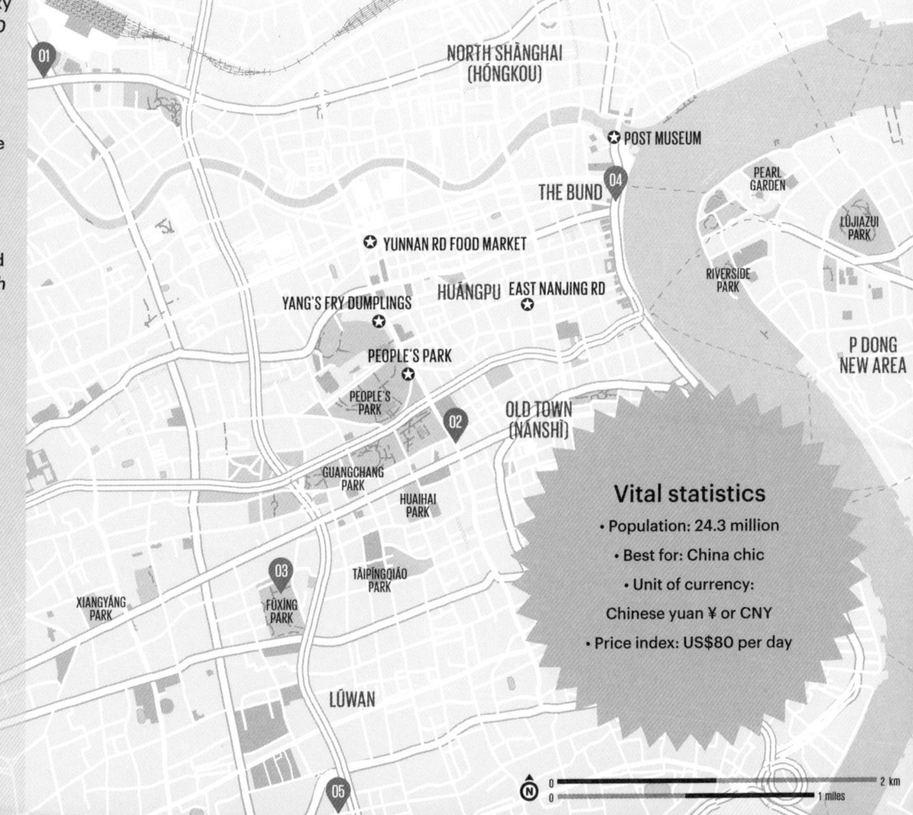

Vital statistics

- Population: 24.3 million
- Best for: China chic
- Unit of currency: Chinese yuan ¥ or CNY
- Price index: US$80 per day

ARTS & CULTURE · MUSIC & FILM · SPORTS & LEISURE · FOOD & DRINK · FESTIVALS & EVENTS

SINGAPORE

It might be one of the world's most expensive cities, but once you've nailed the priciest part – finding somewhere to sleep – you'll be surprised to discover how far your Singapore dollars can stretch. From green spaces to a kaleidoscope of temples, many attractions won't cost you a cent.

01 Baba House

One of Singapore's best-preserved Peranakan heritage homes, Baba House offers a fascinating window into the life of an affluent Straits-Chinese family living in Singapore a century ago. The only way in to this sumptuously restored 1890s-era house is on a guided tour, which is excellent and free. Bookings are essential. *nus.edu.sg/cfa/museum/about.php; 157 Neil Rd; free tours 2pm Mon, 6.30pm Tue, 10am Thu, 11am Sat; free.*

06

05

02 Buddha Tooth Relic Temple

This five-storey Buddhist temple houses what is reputedly the enlightened one's left canine tooth, which was recovered from his funeral pyre in Kushinagar, northern India. You'll find the relic inside a 420kg solid-gold stupa in a dazzlingly ornate room. Swing by the third-floor museum for more relics, and check out the huge prayer wheel in the rooftop garden. *btrts.org.sg; 288 South Bridge Rd; 7am-7pm with relic-viewing 9am-6pm; free.*

02

FARRER PARK FIELDS
LITTLE INDIA
NS23
SRI VEERAMAKALIAMMAN TEMPLE
HOUSE OF TAN TENG NIAH
TEKKA CENTRE
ISTANA PARK
MT EMILY PARK
ABDUL GAFOOR MOSQUE
06
KAMPONG GLAM
EW17
04
FORT CANNING PARK
Alexandra Canal
FORT CANNING PARK
F.CLUB
THE PADANG
07
03a
03c
NE2/EW16
MARINA PROMENADE
Esplanade Jetty
Singapore River
TIONG BAHRU PARK
HENDERSON PARK
15
PEARL'S HILL CITY PARK
Marina Bay
03b
CÉ LA VI
08
WONDER FULL
09
05
02
13
CHINATOWN
14
BOON TAT STREET
01
TANJONG PAGAR
Tanjong Pagar Plaza
MARINA SOUTH
SPOTTISWOODE PARK
RAEBURN PARK
SINGAPORE RAILWAY STATION
HarbourFront
Keppel Harbour
Vital statistics
• Population: 5.5 million
• Best for: Mouth-watering hawker food and cultural big-hitters
• Unit of currency: Singapore dollar S$ or SGD
• Price index: US$130 per day
PULAU BRANI
Causeway Bridge
Resorts World
Selat Sengkir
Serapong Golf Course
Strait of Singapore
SENTOSA ISLAND
Palawan Beach
12
Buran Darat
0
2 km
0
1 miles

03 Free art tours

Several Singaporean hotels have excellent art collections that are also accessible to non-guests, from the **Pan Pacific's Public Art Space** (3a; *panpacific.com; 7 Raffles Blvd; free*) to the artworks that are integrated into many of the public areas of **Marina Bay Sands** (3b; *marinabaysands.com; 10 Bayfront Ave; free*). Art lovers are truly spoiled at **The Ritz-Carlton, Millenia Singapore** (3c; *ritzcarlton.com; 7 Raffles Ave; free*), where anyone can take the tour of its collections, which range from Dale Chihuly glass-blowings to Frank Stella installations.

04 National Museum of Singapore

The queen of Singapore's vibrant museum scene is located in a grand, neoclassical 19th-century building. Be sure to check out its magnificent restored rotunda, which includes 50 carefully crafted pieces of stained glass. In addition to the museum's permanent displays showcasing Singapore's history and culture, many special exhibitions hosted here are also free of charge and free one-hour tours are also on offer. *nationalmuseum.sg; 93 Stamford Rd; 10am-6pm; free.*

05 Sri Mariamman Temple

Singapore's oldest Hindu temple (incongruously located slap-bang in the middle of Chinatown) features a technicolour 1930s *gopuram* (tower) above the entrance, the key to the temple's South-Indian Dravidian style. A shrine to the goddess Mariamman takes pride of place inside. Every year in October, the temple hosts the Thimithi festival, when devotees queue to walk over the burning coals with their bare feet. *heb.gov.sg; 244 South Bridge Rd; 7am-noon & 6-9pm; free.*

12

09

THRIFTY COMMUTING

As if Singapore's excellent public transport network wasn't good value already, the cost of a standard journey by metro or bus drops from S$S1.40 to S$0.79 when using a pre-loaded EzyLink card (*ezlink.com.sg; available from the airport, most rail stations and 7-Eleven stores*), but if you're planning to make a lot of trips over a couple of days, consider opting for a Tourist Pass, which allows unlimited bus and rail travel for S$10 (one day), S$16 (two days) and S$20 (three days), plus a refundable S$10 deposit for the card.

06 Sultan Mosque

Designed in the Saracenic style and topped by a golden dome, Singapore's largest mosque looks as if it could have been plucked from a sequence from Disney's *Aladdin*. The present building was built in 1928 – on the site of the 1825 original. Cloaks can be borrowed for free at the entrance if you would like to have a peep inside. *sultanmosque.org.sg; 3 Muscat St; 10am-noon & 2-4pm Sat-Thu, 2.30-4pm Fri; free.*

07 Esplanade – Theatres on the Bay

Topped with a spiky roof that has been compared to everything from flies' eyes to two upturned *durians*, Singapore's S$600-million entertainment centre offers a non-stop programme of international and local performances, including a number of free outdoor shows. Check the website for upcoming events, and if you manage to save some dough by catching a freebie, then consider treating yourself to a pre-show tipple at the rooftop bar, Orgo (*orgo.sg; 6pm-1.30am*). *esplanade.com; 1 Esplanade Dr; some free performances.*

08 Movies by the Bay

Due to a fantastic year-round climate for outdoor entertaining, Singapore was made for watching movies under the stars. One of the best free-film nights is the long-running DBS Movies by the Bay, with screenings held on the promenade by Shoppes by the Bay, usually on the third Friday and Saturday of each month. Early birds even get complimentary popcorn! *dbsmoviesbythebay.com; next to Shoppes by the Bay, Marina Bay; free.*

09 Gardens by the Bay

This eco-fantasyland of space-age bio-domes, hi-tech trees and whimsical sculptures really has to be seen to be believed. Although the indoor conservatories and Supertree-top skyway are chargeable, arguably the coolest thing to see here is free: time your visit for 7.45pm or 8.45pm to see the Supertrees twinkle and glow for the spectacular Garden Rhapsody light-and-sound show. *gardensbythebay.com.sg; 18 Marina Gardens Dr; outdoor gardens 5am-2am; admission free.*

10 Haw Par Villa

If this ultra-kitsch ode to Chinese mythology dreamed up by Aw Boon Haw, the entrepreneurial creator of the medicinal salve Tiger Balm, isn't the weirdest 'theme park' on earth, it's gotta come close. Swing by this curious garden to giggle at its garish statues and dioramas, each recounting Chinese folk stories, and the Ten Courts of Hell, a gruesome vision of the underworld. *262 Pasir Panjang Rd; 9am-7pm; free.*

11 Singapore Botanic Gardens

Escape the city for an afternoon to admire this lush, botanical wonderland peppered with lovely lakes, rolling lawns and themed gardens. It's free to explore this beautiful UNESCO World Heritage site, although it's worth considering forking out S$5 for entry to the National Orchid Garden (*8.30am-7pm*) – the largest showcase of tropical orchids on earth – as well. *sbg.org.sg; 1 Cluny Rd; gardens 5am-midnight; main gardens free.*

12 Sentosa Island Beaches

Entrance fares to most of Sentosa's big-name attractions (such as Universal Studios and SEA Aquarium) can soon add up, but it's (almost) free to laze the day away on the island's beaches. Choose

SINGAPORE

from busy **Siloso** (which is packed with eateries and bars) on the island's northwest, more chilled-out **Tanjong** to the south, and **Palawan Beach**, where there are free paddling pools (perfect for kids) in the middle. *sentosa.com.sg/en/beaches; 24hr; pedestrian entry to Sentosa Island S$1.*

13 **Maxwell Food Centre**

A fantastic spot in which to savour some of the city's famous street-food staples, Maxwell Rd is one of Singapore's most accessible hawker centres. There are dozens of stalls to choose from, but some of the enduring favourites include Tian Tian Hainanese Chicken Rice, Fried Sweet Potato Dumpling and Maxwell Fuzhou Oyster Cake. Hint: if there's a queue for the food, it's a good bet. *Cnr Maxwell & South Bridge Rds; 8am-10pm; dishes from S$2.50.*

14 **Satay Street**

Each night, the street next to Telok Ayer Market (also known as Lau Pa Sat hawker centre) is blocked to traffic and transformed into an open-air restaurant lined with sizzling barbecues and dubbed Satay Street. Order a dozen satay sticks doused in delicious peanut sauce and a jug of Tiger beer for the ultimate budget feast. *Boon Tat St; 7pm-1am Mon-Fri, 3pm-1am Sat & Sun; satay costs approximately S$0.60 per stick.*

15 **Tiong Bahru bakery cafes**

The trendiest neighbourhood in Singapore is brimming with fashionable cafes, coffee shops and boutiques. Top off a morning spent window-shopping by indulging in a sinful pastry and a perfectly brewed coffee (*about S$8 for both*) from either **Tiong Bahru Bakery** (*tiongbahrubakery.com; 252 North Bridge Rd; 8am-10pm*), **Drips Bakery Café** (*drips.com.sg/dripsbakery; 82 Tiong Poh Rd; 11am-9.30pm Sun-Thu, 11am-11pm Fri + Sat*) or **Plain Vanilla Bakery** (*plainvanillabakery.com; 1D Yong Siak St; 11am-8pm Mon-Fri, 9am-8pm Sat, 9am-6pm Sun*).

FREE DRINKS!

Booze is particularly pricey in Singapore, but you can drink cheaply (and sometimes even for free) if you know where and when to go. Most bars offer a daily happy hour, starting anywhere from noon until 9pm. Deals range from 'two-for-one' drinks to S$8 and S$10 cocktails and pints. Ladies' night deals (usually on Wednesdays) are among the best, with free entry and one drink at Cé La Vi (*celavi.com; 1 Bayfront Ave*) and a free bottle of vodka if you bring four of your girlfriends with you to f.Club (*f-club.sg;* Clarke Quay).

SINGAPORE

16 **Chingay**

On the 22nd day after Chinese New Year, Chingay delivers Singapore's biggest and best street parade – a flamboyant multicultural affair featuring lion dancers, floats and other cultural performers. You'll need to purchase tickets in advance for a good seat in one of the viewing galleries, but it's still possible to watch the parade gratis from the roadside barriers around the CBD circuit. *chingay.org.sg; CBD; Feb; public spectators free.*

17 **Singapore Food Festival**

If there's one thing Singaporeans are passionate about it's food, so it's no surprise the city hosts an annual celebration of all things edible. The 10-day culinary extravaganza includes tasting events, special dinners and food tours across Singapore. Most command a small fee (usually covering tastings) but check the programme for free events where complimentary sample dishes are offered to early birds. *yoursingapore.com; various locations; Jul-Aug; some free events.*

18 **Singapore International Film Festival**

Singapore's largest and longest-running film event focuses on showcasing both groundbreaking international films as well as providing a global platform for the best of Singaporean cinema. Screenings are held at multiple venues across the island, including **Marina Bay Sands** (p058), **Shaw Theatres Lido** (*shaw.sg; 350 Orchard Rd*), **National Museum of Singapore** (p058) and **The Arts House** (*theartshouse.sg; 1 Old Parliament Lane*). Check the website for information on freebies. *sgiff.com; various locations; Nov-Dec; some free screenings.*

Start by exploring the laneways of Little India (*24hr; free*), taking in Sri Veeramakalimman Temple (*141 Serangoon Rd; 5.15am-12.15pm & 4-9.15pm; free*), the Abdul Gafoor Mosque (*41 Dunlop St; free*) and the House of Tan Teng Niah (*7 Kerbau Rd; 24hr; free*). Lunch at the Tekka Centre (*cnr Serangoon & Buffalo Rds; 7am-11pm; dishes S$2-10*) then take the metro to Clarke Quay for a stroll around Fort Canning Park (*nparks.gov.sg; 24hr; free*), or to Chinatown. Enjoy a satay feast on Boon Tat Street, then watch the light-and-water show Wonder Full (*Event Plaza at Marina Bay; 8pm & 9.30pm, plus 11pm Sat & Sun; free*).

ARTS & CULTURE | MUSIC & FILM | SPORTS & LEISURE | FOOD & DRINK | FESTIVALS & EVENTS

TOKYO

Tokyo gets a bad rap for being expensive, but it isn't justified. Many of the top sights are actually free, but it's more than that: just wandering the city is a dazzling experience. Come for the contemporary architecture, head-turning fashion or the delicious bowls of noodles around every corner.

01 Arashio Stable

Even most locals don't know this, but a few sumo stables – where the wrestlers live and train – allow visitors to watch morning practice. At the friendliest stable, Arashio, you can spectate through the window, giving you a much closer look than you'd get at a tournament. Check the website for a practice schedule and rules for visitors. *arashio.net; 2-47-2 Hama-chō, Nihombashi, Chūō-ku; 7.30-10am; free.*

02 Diver City Tokyo Plaza

In front of this mall (standard issue, but great food court) is an 18m-tall model of a Gundam robot from the anime of the same name. You don't need to know the series to appreciate that a giant robot is an excellent photo op. From 6pm to 11pm it's lit up, and looks extra impressive against the skyline. *1-1-10 Aomi, Kōtō-ku; free.*

03 Omote-sandō

It's harder to hate on luxury boutiques when they come in such stunning packages as the ones that span

Vital statistics

- Population: 37.8 million
- Best for: All-encompassing urban experience
- Unit of currency: Japanese yen ¥ or JPY
- Price index: US$135 per day

the zelkova tree-lined boulevard Omotesandō. The shops, all of them completely different, are designed by big names in contemporary architecture, including the Japanese Pritzker Architecture Prize-winners Itō Toyō and the duo behind SANAA, Sejima Kazuyo and Nishizawa Ryūe. The whole street is like a walk-through showroom. *Jingūmae, Shibuya-ku; 24hr; free.*

04 Tokyo Metropolitan Government Building

Despite the dry-sounding name, the capital building is a fantastic double freebie: it's an impressive piece of modern architecture by Japan's late, great Tange Kenzō and, way up on the 45th floor, there is a free observatory. On a clear day you can see Mount Fuji in the west. In the evening, Tokyo's twinkling lights stretch to the horizon. *2-8-1 Nishi-Shinjuku, Shinjuku-ku; 9.30am-10.30pm; free.*

05 Imperial Palace

Smack in the middle of the city is the home of Japan's emperor. Free tours of the forested grounds run twice daily (*10am & 1.30pm, Mon-Fri*). More enjoyable, however, is being free to roam around the East Garden (*9am-5pm, closed Mon & Fri*) or take advantage of the free bicycle rentals available on Sundays (10am-3pm), which you can use to cycle around the outer moat. *1 Chiyoda, Chiyoda-ku; free.*

06 Jakotsu-yu

Visiting an *onsen* (natural hot spring) is high on the Japan bucket list. But you needn't journey far or pay extortionate resort prices: this humble public bathhouse uses natural spring water and even has a lantern-lit outdoor bath. Splurge (¥*200*) on admission to the sauna; towels and toiletries are extra, the former

11

18

SUMMER FESTIVALS

Summers in Tokyo are hot and sticky but the abundance of free festivals more than makes up for it. First, there are the firework displays that happen at regular intervals around the city – the biggest is the Sumida River fireworks (*sumidagawa-hanabi.com/index_eg.html*) on the last Saturday in July. There are also parades with folk dancing and sweaty men (and some women) chanting and heaving portable shrines through the streets. Bonus: wherever there is a festival there are *yatai* (food stalls) serving up cheap treats such as *yakisoba* (fried noodles) and *okonomiyaki* (savoury pancake). *For a list of events, see gotokyo.org.*

available to hire. Included in the cost: a totally local experience. *1-11-11 Asakusa, Taitō-ku; 1pm-midnight Wed-Mon; adults/children/infants ¥460/180/80.*

07 Meiji-jingū

An oasis in the urban jungle, this grand Shintō shrine is cloistered in a wooded grove (and feels about five degrees cooler than everywhere else in summer). To reach it, you walk along a gravel path under towering wooden *torii* gates. The shrine is wooden, unadorned and is a popular setting for traditional weddings and rites – which you might spot if you're lucky. *1-1 Yoyogi Kamizono-chō, Shibuya-ku; dawn-dusk; free.*

08 Roppongi Hills

OK, this is a high-end mall, but of the benevolent sort: public artworks, such as a Louise Bourgeois' spider sculpture, adorn the grounds. There's also a landscaped garden that's perfect for a picnic (cheaper food vendors are in the basement) and an amphitheatre that holds free events, like morning t'ai-chi, in summer. The complex is a love-it-or-hate-it piece of postmodern architecture. *6-11-1 Roppongi, Minato-ku; building open 7am-11am; admission free.*

09 Sensō-ji

With its five-storey pagoda, cauldron of smoky incense and rickshaws parked out the front, this millennium-old Buddhist temple is a bit ham-fisted with its old-Japan feel, but is a must-see all the same. Lining the main path are a dozen different snack vendors selling delicious inexpensive goodies like *age-manjū* (deep-fried stuffed buns). After dusk, when the crowds thin out a little, the grounds are illuminated. *2-3-1 Asakusa, Taitō-ku; 24hr; free.*

10 Shibuya Crossing

A big part of Tokyo's appeal is its dense, urban quality: getting swept up in the crowd, marvelling at the logistic efficiency, blinking back at that neon. No other place in the city packages this experience quite as neatly as Shibuya Crossing, Tokyo's most famous intersection. At peak hours, more than a thousand people cross with each light change. Go in the evening when the neon is bright. *Shibuya-ku; 24hr; free.*

11 Yoyogi Park

Of all Tokyo's parks, this is the most fun. The landscaping is haphazard, wild along the fringes; there are no 'keep off the grass' signs here. On sunny weekends, all sorts gather for picnics, Frisbee, drumming and dancing. The plaza across the street hosts free festivals on weekends during summer, including many hosted by the city's ethnic communities. *2-1 Yoyogi Kamizono-chō, Shibuya-ku; 24hr; free.*

ONE-DAY FREE PASS

If it's a Saturday or Sunday, start early with a visit to the UNU Farmers' Market (*5-53-7 Jingūmae, Shibuya-ku; 10am-4pm Sat & Sun*), where you can get coffee and brunch from one of the food trucks. Then head to Omote-sandō (p062) – to check out the contemporary architecture – followed by a stroll up the pedestrian alley (and teen fashion-mecca) Takeshita-dōri. On the other side of Harajuku Station is the peaceful sanctuary, Meiji-jingū (p065). From here it's a short walk to Yoyogi Park (p065) where, with any luck, there will be a festival happening (complete with food stands).

12 Forest Beer Garden

In summer, gardens and department store rooftops around the city host outdoor beer gardens. Of these, Forest Beer Garden holds the biggest party – it seats up to 1000 – and also consistently offers the best deal: a two-hour all-you-can-eat barbecue buffet coupled with all-you-can-drink beer. It may be wise to wear loose-fitting trousers… *14-13 Kasumigaoka-machi, Shinjuku-ku; 5pm-10pm Mon-Fri, noon-10pm Sat & Sun, Jun-Sep; dinner course women/men ¥3800/4100.*

13 Isetan Department Store

The basement food hall (known as *depachika* in Japanese) in this fancy department store includes outlets from some of the country's top restaurants and confectioners. You can easily put together a pretty spectacular meal of sushi, dumplings, *tonkatsu* (fried pork cutlet) sandwiches and cake for approximately US$20 per person. Then take it upstairs to eat it on the roof garden. *isetan.mistore.jp; 3-14-1 Shinjuku, Shinjuku-ku; 10am-8pm; admission free.*

14 Katsu Midori Sushi

Run by famed Tokyo sushi shop **Sushi-no-Midori** (*sushinomidori.co.jp*), this is the city's best *kaiten-zushi* (conveyor-belt sushi, sushi-train or sushi-go-round) restaurant. It is pricier than most, but is still a bargain for the quality. It's always crowded, meaning all the plates making the rounds are fresh; you can also order directly from the chefs. Best visited at off-peak hours. *8th fl, Seibu Department Store, 21-1 Udagawa-chō, Shibuya-ku; 11am-11pm; plates ¥100-500.*

15 Ore no Kappō

The growing Ore no chain is a boon to budget gourmands: you get all the top-notch nosh of a high-end restaurant without the white tablecloth service – a compromise that means you also get

05

cut-rate prices. Ore no Kappō specialises in Japanese haute cuisine (there are other branches doing French and Italian), with a menu overseen by a Michelin-starred chef. *oreno.co.jp; 8-8-17 Ginza, Chūō-ku; 3-11pm; dinner around ¥4000.*

16 Sagatani

This noodle joint quite possibly wins the prize for offering Tokyo's best cheap meal: fresh, stone-ground *soba* (buckwheat) noodles are made daily and served on bamboo trays. Delicious noodles with a side of *goma* (sesame) dipping sauce costs just ¥380, and you can wash it down with a ¥150 beer. Located in nightlife district Shibuya, Sagatani is popular at all hours of the day. *2-25-7 Dōgenzaka, Shibuya-ku; 24hr; noodles from ¥280.*

17 Tsukiji Market

By the time you read this, Tokyo's wholesale fish market – one of the city's most popular attractions – will have probably settled into its new home in Toyosu. However, the 'outer market', the collection of vendors selling everything from sushi to boots that sprung up around the old market, will remain. The rumours are that the city plans to transform it into a green market. *tsukiji-market.or.jp; 4-10-16 Tsukiji, Chūō-ku; 5am-2pm; admission free.*

18 Hanami

When the cherry blossom blooms in early spring, the whole of Tokyo goes into party mode. Popular parks, such as Yoyogi Park (p065), Ueno Park and Inokashira Park, fill with revellers who bring tarps to lay out under the trees, barbecues, and sometimes even turntables and speakers. Entry to the parks is free; beer and snacks from the nearest convenience store are optional (but are highly recommended). *24hr; late Mar-early Apr; free.*

THE LOCALS' VIEW

"Try nice *kaiseki* (haute cuisine) restaurants at lunchtime since they usually have cheaper courses than at dinner. Also, you can get cheap tickets to Tokyo Disneyland after 6pm on weekdays." – Kanae, product manager

"Shop on the *shōtengai* (high street with locally owned stores) instead of at retail stores. If you're lucky, the owner may give you an *omake* (freebie)." – Mari, communications worker

"At most big train stations, there is a shop called Kaldi that sells cheap imported foods like curry paste, coconut milk, wine and cheese. It's great for picnic food and snacking." – Stephanie, therapist

EUROPE

ARTS & CULTURE · MUSIC & FILM · SPORTS & LEISURE · FOOD & DRINK · FESTIVALS & EVENTS

AMSTERDAM

Like an heirloom bracelet passed through generations, Amsterdam offers a diverse array of ancient charms happily coexisting side by side with modern acquisitions, each with its own fascinating story. Altogether the city exudes a uniquely Dutch urban exoticism. Fortunately there's plenty of admiring that can be done for free.

01 Houseboat Museum

Living on a canal is not uncommon for Amsterdammers, and you'll inevitably become curious about houseboats' interiors. Too shy to ask? Just head to this quaint converted boat that was built around 1914. Used first as a freighter then a family home, it's now set up to give an idea of how we'd function in a 2-bed residence undulating on water. *houseboatmuseum.nl; Prinsengracht 296; see website for season-varying hours; €4.50.*

Vital statistics

- Population: 1.6 million
- Best for: Art, design and history, with no less than 44 museums and 7000 monuments, there's a lot to behold in this culture-packed city
- Unit of currency: Euro €
- Price index: US$180 per day

02 Lunchtime Concerts at the Concertgebouw

Indulge your auditory senses at the stately Concertgebouw. The neoclassical 1888 structure is as impressive as its renowned acoustics. It offers free 12.30pm concerts featuring orchestral, chamber music and emerging musicians in the Main Hall or Recital Hall on Wednesdays (except July and August): proof that highbrow culture needn't come at a cost. *concertgebouw.nl; Concertgebouwplein 10; free.*

03 Bloemenmarkt (Flower Market)

Flowers liven up the brown buildings and North Sea skies of Amsterdam. Experience this juxtaposition via a leisurely canal-side stroll through the floating flower market. From azaleas to tulips and exotic flora, the 150-year old Bloemenmarkt provides an authentic Amsterdammer no-cost experience. Take-home bulbs and kitschy souvenirs aren't much more. *Singel btwn Koningsplein and Muntplein; 9am-5.30pm Mon-Sat, 11am-5.30pm Sun; admission free.*

04 Canal Walk

The city's canals offer a glimpse of 17th-century Amsterdam, its water-bound culture and unparalleled beauty, for free. The Canal Ring's charms are particularly evoked in the evening, when the lanterns are lit and the reflections of the footbridges' golden lights twinkle on the water. Amble along concentric Prinsengracht, Keizersgracht, Herengracht and Singel canals and take in the Reguliersgracht, which runs perpendicular and offers picturesque views at the intersections. *24hr; free.*

05 Swimming at the Zuiderbad

An atmospheric swim seems fitting in a water-bound city, and there's no need to stray far from the Museumplein or to pay a lot, thanks to the pristinely maintained Zuiderbad. The water is warm (27°C) and the pool, operating since 1912, features a pretty mosaic fountain. Take a few memorable laps in the ambience of the spacious, light-filled art deco building (c 1897). *amsterdam.nl/sport/sport-amsterdam/zwembaden/zuiderbad; Hobbemastraat 26; €2.75-3.60.*

06 Amsterdam Cheese Museum

You have probably noticed that cheese is a staple in the daily Dutch diet. This quaint little shop and educational centre is filled to the rafters with massive cheese wheels (and slightly smaller rounds). Take a one-stop dairy tour through the Netherlands, learning how the cheese is made and tasting its many regional varieties, then ham it up in traditional costume for photo ops. *cheesemuseumamsterdam.nl; Prinsengracht 112; 9am-7pm daily; free.*

FREE UP YOUR SATURDAYS

Spend Saturday morning in Jordaan's Noordermarkt (*jordaanmarkten.nl; 9am-4pm; free*) and Lindengracht Market (*9am-4pm; admission free*). Tram to Plantage using an iamsterdam card (*iamsterdam.com; 24/48/72hr cards €49/59/69*), which includes public transport and admittance to attractions. Explore the Verzetsmuseum (*verzetsmuseum.org; Plantage Kerklaan 61; 11am-5pm; entrance with iamsterdam card*) or Hortus Botanicus (*dehortus.nl; Plantage Middenlaan 2a; 10am-5pm; iamsterdam card*), then head to the Brouwerij 't IJ microbrewery (*brouwerijhetij.nl; Funenkade 7; bar 2-8pm, English-language tours 3.30pm; tours €4.50*).

ARTS & CULTURE | MUSIC & FILM | SPORTS & LEISURE | FOOD & DRINK | FESTIVALS & EVENTS

ATHENS

Bargains already abound in this friendly Greek capital that's navigating its way through a political and financial crisis. From street art to historical wonders, Athens' charms will both surprise and educate. While coffee is expensive by Europe's standards, you'll be thrilled to otherwise discover your euros go a long way.

01 Embros Theatre

Culture vultures should head for this multipurpose artistic hub, which is run on community donations by a group of theatre artists and theorists called the Mavili Collective. Try some Latin dancing, Cuban salsa, or see a play or an exhibition. When your exertions are done, settle down in the chill-out area and chat to locals about its fascinating history. *embros.gr; King Palamedes 2, Psirri; times vary: check online calendar; free.*

02 Freeday bike ride

Cycling in Athens is generally pretty hopeless since there is no cycleway infrastructure to speak of and the roads are gridlocked. But come Friday night, traffic stops (with the help of police and volunteers) for this four-hour peloton that anyone of any ability can join, just BYO bike. Glide serenely and safely through the usually pollution-ridden streets with a thousand other like-minded night-riders. *facebook.com/freedayride; departs Agion Asomaton Sq; 9.30pm; free.*

03 Kavouri Beach

It's hot, you want a swim, but you aren't interested in paying to paddle in circles in an urban pool that's full of people. Panic not, help is at hand, just a 30-minute drive out of the city. The gorgeous Attica coastline offers million-dollar views, and although some of the beaches along here charge admission, Kavouri is yours for the taking. Dive in. *Western shore of Vouliagmeni headland; 24hr; free.*

THIS IS MY ATHENS

To get shown around the city for free by a local volunteer on your very own customised tour, submit your request online at least 72 hours before your trip, tell them the sorts of things you do/ don't want to do and you'll be matched up with the best Athenian for the job. And there's no pressure at all to tip.

04 Lykavittos Hill

Want to see the Acropolis without paying a fee? Scale Lykavittos Hill, the highest point in Athens (277m), for a bird's-eye view. There's a funicular *(8.45am-midnight Fri-Wed, 10.30am-midnight Thu, every 30 min; €7 return)* originating at the same point as your ascent on foot, but there's some smug triumph in getting a workout. Dawn or sunset offers the most spectacular photo ops and cooler temperatures. *Depart Ploutarchou St; 24hr; free.*

05 National Gardens

Grab some picnic supplies in Pláka and weave your way through the district's winding streets to this idyllic 15-hectare sanctuary of green. There are ducks, a kids' playground, and a little zoo! Or just spread your picnic blanket under some date palms with a frappé, some olives, feta or whatever *mezedhes* take your fancy, and enjoy the peace and the cool. *Cnr Leoforos Vasilissis Sofias & Leoforos Vasilissis Amalias, Syntagma; 7am-dusk; free.*

06 Parliament Building and Changing of the Guard

Even if you're not usually into pomp and ceremony, when in a new city, if there's some cultural high-kicking going on, you need to get yourself in among it. Here, every hour on the hour, you can watch the changing of the (guards) of the Tomb of the Unknown Soldier (Mnimeio Agnostou Stratiotou), all impeccably attired in short kilts and pom-pommed shoes. *Plateia Syntagmatos; 24hr, on the hour; free.*

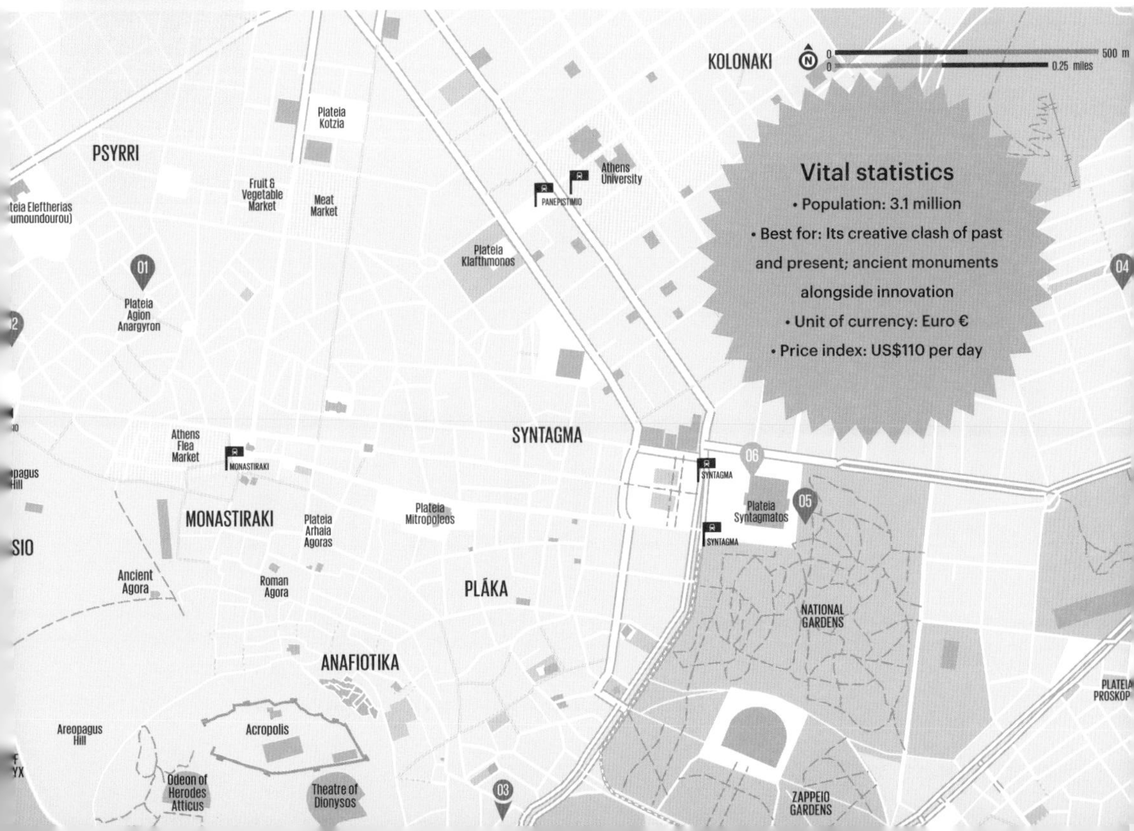

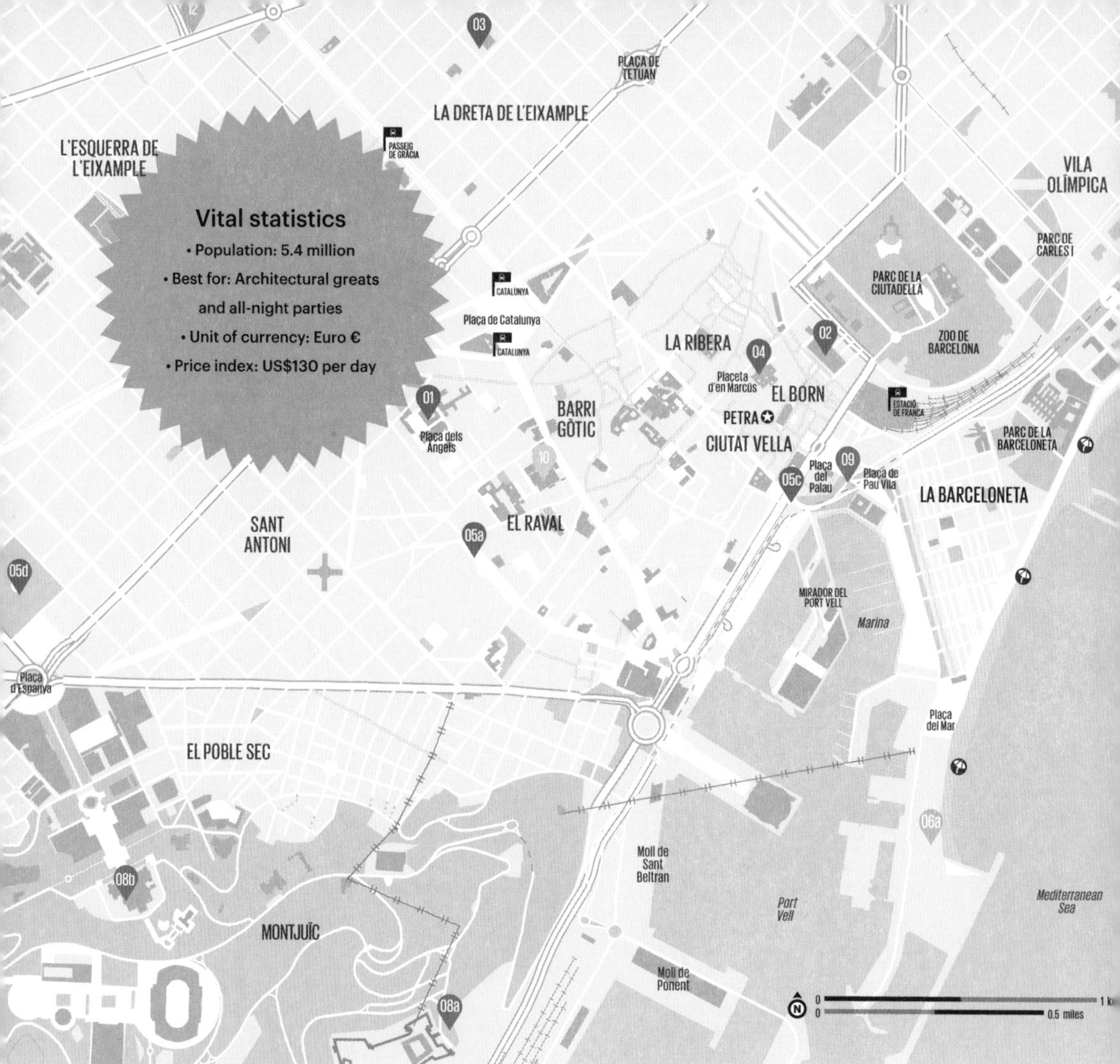

BARCELONA

Barcelona is the perfect mix of seaside town meets cosmopolitan city. It has the beach, the eternal good weather and a reputation for partying till dawn that merges seamlessly with its stunning modernist architecture and world-class gastronomy. Add to that its very moderate pricing and you'll never want to leave...

SPORTS & LEISURE

FOOD & DRINK

FESTIVALS & EVENTS

01 Centre de Cultura Contemporània de Barcelona

An innovative cultural space, the CCCB offers everything from exhibitions, debates and film nights to courses and lectures along a general theme of urbanisation and contemporary culture. A visit is always thought provoking, while the courtyard itself is pretty spectacular to behold and features a huge mirrored wall. *cccb.org; Montalegre 5; 11am-8pm daily, closed Mon (except holidays); free for everyone 3-8pm Sun, reduced rates available at other times.*

02 El Born Centre Cultural

This converted market building, used for exhibitions, is a spectacular structure and a landmark of Catalan Modernism. However, what takes centre stage is the politically charged history of its subterranean ruins, testament to the destruction wrought by Spanish King Philip V after Barcelona's painful defeat in the 1714 War of Succession. *elborncentrecultural.barcelona.cat/; Plaça Comercial 12, 10am-8pm Tue-Sun Mar-Sep, 10am-7pm Tue-Sat Oct-Feb, 10am-8pm Sun; free, admission to exhibitions €4.20-6.00.*

03 Modernist Architecture

The town is littered with impressive works by modernist greats such as Gaudí, Domènech i Montaner and Puig i Cadafalch, whose enchanting fairy-tale-like facades can be seen and revered from a street view (which sure beats standing in the queues). The highest concentration of these works is in the Eixample district, in the area known as the Quadrat d'Or (the Golden Square). *Free.*

04 Museu Picasso

This museum provides an insightful look into the formative years of Picasso's early life. It's well worth a visit, not only to see the evolution of a budding genius (via more than 3500 works) but also to observe his experience of the city. Get there early. *museupicasso.bcn.cat; Carrer Montcada 15-23; 9am-7pm Tue-Sun, 9am-9.30pm Thu, closed Mon (except holidays); free first Sun of the month & every Sun after 3pm.*

05 Public/Street art

Barcelona has a wealth of public art to marvel at and explore, including Fernando Botero's fat cat (5a) on Rambla del Raval; *Peix*, the giant stainless-steel fish sculpture (5b) on the waterfront designed by Frank Gehry; and Roy Lichtenstein's iconic 15m-high *El Cap de Barcelona* (5c) at Port Vell. There's

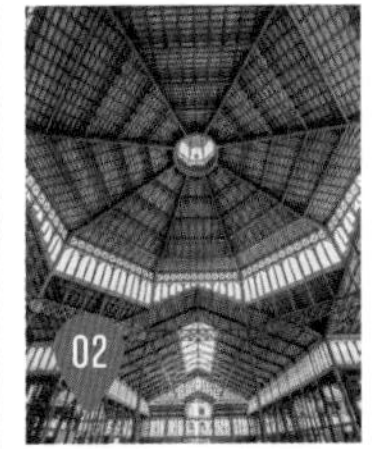
02

04

09

08

BARCELONA

MENU DEL DIA

Some say Franco invented it to improve productivity by giving workers an incentive not to go home for lunch. Others say it was designed for visitors, when tourism was rapidly developing on the Mediterranean coast. Whatever the reason, the menu del dia is loved by all who stumble across its high-value plates. It's a two- to three-course set lunch that costs around €7 to €12. Our favourite is Petra (*Carrer dels Sombrerers 13, 1.15-4pm & 8.30-11pm Mon-Thu, 1.15-4pm & 9pm-midnight Fri-Sat; Menu del Dia €6.75-12.25*) for its fresh flavours and kitsch design, including utensils transformed into lights.

also plenty to satisfy Miró enthusiasts, including the *Woman and Bird* (5d) sculpture in Parc de Joan Miró. *24hr; free.*

06 Flicks al Fresco

There's nothing quite like watching a movie under the night sky and Barcelona's balmy weather makes this easy all through the summer months. You have your choice of venues: the scenic square of **CCCB** (1; Gandules' Outdoor Cinema Season – see p075) or the open beach of **San Sebastian** (6a; Cinema Lliure a la Platja; *cinemalliure.com; Platja de Sant Sebastià; Thu & Sun, Jul-Aug*). Movies can be slightly hit-and-miss independent productions but are usually conversation-starters nonetheless. *See websites for times; free.*

07 Swing Events

Swing has taken off in Barcelona in a big way and free events and classes (most in Catalan) have popped up all over the city. These are friendly affairs where anyone can join in and try their luck on the dance floor. Some courses and lessons cost a little money, but we're only talking a few euros for what is sure to be a fun-filled session. *swingmaniacs.com or bcnswing.org; check websites for venues, times and prices.*

08 Montjuïc Hill

Take the funicular (public transport tickets valid) or simply hike to the top for awe-inspiring views of the city, charming gardens and a host of interesting sights. Some are paid-entry, otherwise there's free access to the **Castell de Montjuïc** (8a; *Ctra de Montjüic; 10am-8pm daily*), one-time fortress of the city. The fresco-filled **Museu Nacional d'Art de Catalunya** (8b; *Palau Nacional; 10am-8pm Tue-Sun*) is free the first Sunday of the month and Saturdays after 3pm.

THE LOCAL'S VIEW

"My name is Llibert Figueras (*@llibertf*), I'm the executive producer at Sauvage.tv, where we shoot commercials. I'm 35, born and raised in Barcelona, a Catalan and in love with the city. For me, Barcelona's charm lies in the balance it offers between extremes, which makes living and working here a delight. One of my favourite free activities is to walk on the beach. It clicks something inside that connects me with the city. Since we are in a sun-blessed, warm country, we've adopted a street lifestyle. From terraces to winding streets, Barcelona is a lovely place to wander around."

09 The beach and waterfront

Barcelona's famed waterfront and artificial beaches provide a breezy break from the crowded, winding historic centre. Join the many joggers and cyclists on the palm-lined boardwalk dotted with overflowing but expensive *chiringuitos* (beach bars), or search for your own patch of sand on its many beaches. From the crowded Barceloneta district to the nudist Platja de la Mar Bella, there's sure to be something to suit everyone. *24hr; free.*

10 Mercado de la Boqueria

An oldie but a goody, this lively city market is one of Barcelona's chief attractions and provides a happy onslaught of the senses, with an abundance of jostling tourists and myriad different smells and colours. It has everything, from fruit and veg to glistening seafood and startling butchers' displays. Choose the cheap smoothies and picnic-perfect deli goods for a tasty, thrifty lunch. *Les Rambles 91; 8am-8.30pm Mon-Sat; admission free.*

11 Festes de la Mercè

Originally held in honour of the city's patron saint La Mercè, this 500-event fiesta now just seems like a good excuse for the city's biggest annual party. What everyone is waiting for is the Castellers (human towers), the Correfoc (a fire run featuring a dragon whose flames come terrifyingly close to bystanders), and the Gigantes, a parade of giant royals and other notable characters. *spanish-fiestas.com/festivals/festes-merce; Sep; free.*

12 Festa Major de Gràcia

It's like a wild street party attended by groovy grandmas, angsty teenagers, gawping tourists and everyone in between, festooned with expert crafters' stalls and packed with free events and concerts. That's the only way to describe the city's biggest street festival, which revolves around a themed competition of street decoration and for one week a year transforms this quiet local neighbourhood into party central. *festamajordegracia.cat; Gràcia district; Aug; free.*

EUROPE'S BEST NATIONAL PARKS

Yours to keep: a free pass to Europe's best bits – areas enshrined as national parks, where the only entry requirement is a sense of adventure.

JOTUNHEIMEN – NORWAY

'Home of the Giants', this park contains the country's 29 highest mountains, including 2469m-high Galdhøpiggen. In Norway everyone enjoys *allemannsretten* – free access to the countryside, including national parks. Backcountry hiking routes here include the Besseggen Ridge. *jotunheimen.com; Norway; free.*

BAVARIAN FOREST/ŠUMAVA – GERMANY / CZECH REP

This wild utopia is where Bavaria meets Bohemia in Europe's largest forest. Over 10,000 animal species inhabit these woods, with their hiking, cross-country skiing and cycling trails. Wild camping allowed. *nationalpark-bayerischer-wald.de; free.*

BRECON BEACONS – WALES

This dark-sky reserve is home to the moody Black Mountains and magical Coed-y-Rhaeadr (Wood of the Water), where cascades include Sgwd-y-Eira (the Snow Waterfall) on the River Hepste, with a path leading right behind the curtain of water. *breconbeacons.org; free.*

VATNAJÖKULL – ICELAND

Europe's biggest national park covers 12 per cent of Iceland's entire surface area and is home to the continent's most powerful waterfall – the mighty Dettifoss. Visitors come to go glacier-hiking and ice-caving on the country's largest ice cap. *vatnajokulsthjodgardur.is; free.*

GRAN PARADISO – ITALY

On the flanks of Italy's highest peak, 4061m-high Gran Paradiso, alpine ibex prance about like they own the place. Once the hunting ground of King Victor Emmanuel II, this stunning park is now the preserve of hikers, climbers and cross-country skiers. *pngp.it; free.*

CAIRNGORMS – SCOTLAND

Britain's largest NP occupies a vast plateau punctuated by five of the country's highest peaks, including 1309m-high Ben Macdui, haunt of Am Fear Liath Mòr (spectral beast), and several bothies (free mountain shelters). Not for the faint-hearted... *cairngorms.co.uk; free.*

LE PARC NATIONAL DES PYRÉNÉES/ORDESA Y MONTE PERDIDO – FRANCE/SPAIN

Separated only by the Pyrénées, these twin parks share fantastic fauna, including Europe's largest raptor, the lammergeier (bearded vulture). Hundreds of hiking trails wend through the valleys and wild camping is possible in France. *parc-pyrenees.com; free.*

OLYMPUS – GREECE

In Greek mythology the peaks and gorges of Olympus housed the 12 Olympian gods. Nowadays, golden eagles look down from the heavens, while the hills are home to wolves, wildcats, and walkers exerting themselves in the original Olympic theatre. *www.olympusfd.gr; free.*

OULANGAN KANSALLISPUISTO – FINLAND

Sitting on the Finland/Russia border, this stunning park is home to hundreds of reindeer and the multi-day Karhunkierros trail, a 50-mile week-long trek during which hikers can stay for free in huts along the way. *luontoon.fi/en/oulanka; Lapland, free.*

Illustration | Patrick Hruby

ARTS & CULTURE | MUSIC & FILM | SPORTS & LEISURE | FOOD & DRINK | FESTIVALS & EVENTS

BERLIN

Berlin is a bon vivant feasting on the smorgasbord of life, never taking things – or itself – too seriously. Over 25 years after the fall of the Wall, the German capital continues to tempt with its creativity, culture and cosmopolitan outlook, all wrapped up in a surprisingly affordable package.

01 East Side Gallery

It's ironic that Berlin's must-see tourist attraction is one that no longer exists: the Berlin Wall. Thankfully there's the East Side Gallery, a 1.3km-long fragment of the barrier that's been smothered in street art to become the longest open-air gallery in the world. As you walk along, reflect upon what life must have been like during the Cold War. *eastsidegallery-berlin.de/; Mühlenstrasse btwn Oberbaumbrücke & Ostbahnhof; 24hr; free.*

02 Berlin Wall Memorial Exhibit

The Gedenkstätte Berliner Mauer offers a great primer on what the border strip actually looked like and how it impacted the lives of people on both sides of it. It extends along 1.4km of the original course of the Wall and includes a recreated death strip, original Wall segments, a documentation centre, a memorial chapel and several information stations. *berliner-mauer-gedenkstaette.de; Bernauer Strasse 111 btwn Schwedter Strasse & Gartenstrasse; 8am-10pm; free.*

03

10

16

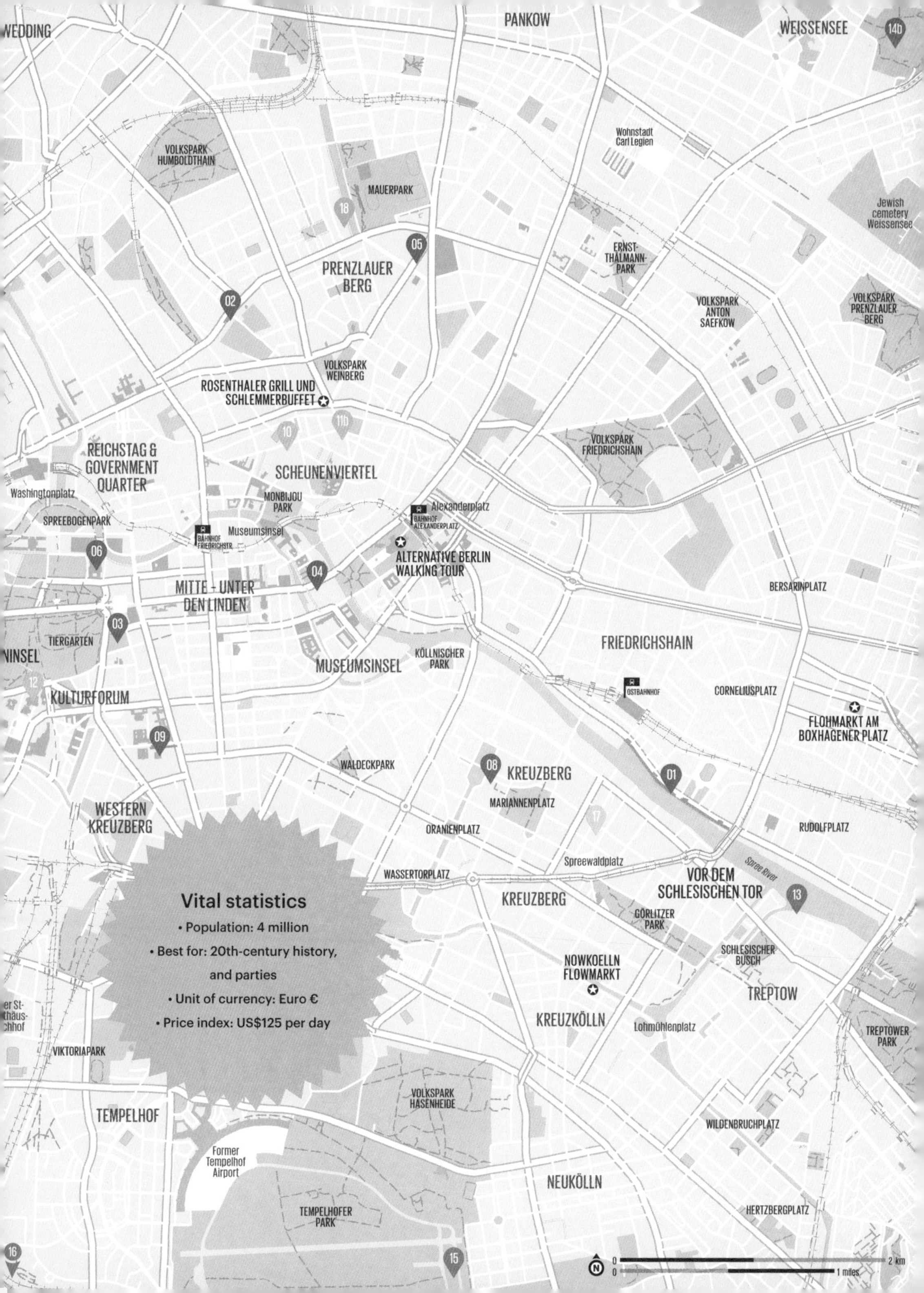

WEDDING
PANKOW
WEISSENSEE
14b
Wohnstadt Carl Legien
VOLKSPARK HUMBOLDTHAIN
MAUERPARK
18
Jewish cemetery Weissensee
05
ERNST-THÄLMANN-PARK
PRENZLAUER BERG
02
VOLKSPARK ANTON SAEFKOW
VOLKSPARK PRENZLAUER BERG
VOLKSPARK WEINBERG
ROSENTHALER GRILL UND SCHLEMMERBUFFET
10
11b
VOLKSPARK FRIEDRICHSHAIN
REICHSTAG & GOVERNMENT QUARTER
SCHEUNENVIERTEL
Washingtonplatz
MONBIJOU PARK
Alexanderplatz
BAHNHOF ALEXANDERPLATZ
SPREEBOGENPARK
BAHNHOF FRIEDRICHSTR
Museumsinsel
ALTERNATIVE BERLIN WALKING TOUR
06
04
MITTE - UNTER DEN LINDEN
BERSARINPLATZ
03
TIERGARTEN
INSEL
KÖLLNISCHER PARK
FRIEDRICHSHAIN
MUSEUMSINSEL
12
OSTBAHNHOF
CORNELIUSPLATZ
KULTURFORUM
FLOHMARKT AM BOXHAGENER PLATZ
09
WALDECKPARK
08
KREUZBERG
01
MARIANNENPLATZ
WESTERN KREUZBERG
17
ORANIENPLATZ
RUDOLFPLATZ
Spreewaldplatz
Spree River
WASSERTORPLATZ
VOR DEM SCHLESISCHEN TOR
KREUZBERG
13
Vital statistics
• Population: 4 million
• Best for: 20th-century history, and parties
• Unit of currency: Euro €
• Price index: US$125 per day
GÖRLITZER PARK
SCHLESISCHER BUSCH
NOWKOELLN FLOWMARKT
TREPTOW
KREUZKÖLLN
Lohmühlenplatz
VIKTORIAPARK
TREPTOWER PARK
VOLKSPARK HASENHEIDE
TEMPELHOF
WILDENBRUCHPLATZ
Former Tempelhof Airport
NEUKÖLLN
TEMPELHOFER PARK
HERTZBERGPLATZ
16
15
0
2 km
0
1 miles

03 Holocaust Memorial

Feel the presence of uncounted souls as you meander through the maze that is Berlin's Memorial to the Murdered Jews of Europe. The vast site consists of 2711 concrete slabs of varying height arranged in a claustrophobic grid that you are free to explore at will. A subterranean information centre provides heart-wrenching context. *stiftung-denkmal.de/en/home.html; Cora-Berliner-Strasse 1; memorial 24hr, information centre 10am-8pm Apr-Sep, 10am-7pm Oct-Mar, closed Mon; free.*

04 Humboldt-Box

Berlin's biggest building project is actually a blast from the past: the reconstruction of the baroque Prussian royal city palace that was destroyed by the East German government in 1951. To be known as Humboldtforum, the behemoth is due for completion in 2019. Pop by the futuristic Humboldt-Box to bone up on the project and sneak a preview of the museums and the cultural institutions it will host. *humboldt-box.com; Schlossplatz 5; 10am-7pm; free.*

05 Photoautomaten

Forget about iPhone selfies in front of the Brandenburg Gate; your true Berlin hipster moment comes courtesy of a coin-operated photo booth. For a measly €2, you and your BFFs get to mug for an invisible camera, then wait for the machine to spit out a strip of four black-and-white passport-size pictures. There are booths all over Berlin, including one on Kastanienallee. *For locations see photoautomat.de; 24hr; €2.*

06 Reichstag Dome

While Germany's politicians hammer out policies in the plenary hall, you can keep an eye on them from the top of their office building, the Reichstag. A lift whisks you to the roof of this Prussian-era building to let you drink in great city views and walk inside the glass-and-mirror dome designed by Norman Foster. Advance registration is required.

ONE-DAY (ALMOST) FREE PASS

Buy a *Tageskarte* or public transport day ticket (*€6.90 to €7.40*) and hop on bus 100 at Bahnhof Zoo (*Hardenbergplatz 11*) to be whisked past such sights as the Reichstag and Museum Island. At Alexanderplatz, join the 11am donation-based walking tour by Alternative Berlin Tours (*alternativeberlin.com*) to get a primer on Berlin's subculture. Hungry? Rosenthaler Grill und Schlemmerbuffet (*Torstrasse 125; 24hr; dishes €2.80-7*) offers the city's best kebabs. Walk it off in the Scheunenviertel, the Jewish quarter that is now a charismatic warren of indie boutiques and cafes. Wrap up the evening on the dance floor of Clärchens Ballhaus.

bundestag.de/htdocs_e/visits/kuppel; Platz der Republik 1; 8am-midnight, last entry 10pm, every 15 min; free.

07 Sachsenhausen Concentration Camp

Just outside Berlin proper, the Nazis built Sachsenhausen, one of the most notorious concentration camps on German soil. Tens of thousands of the 200,000 prisoners perished behind its sinister gates between 1936 and 1945. Now a memorial, gripping exhibits in original sites like the infirmary barracks and the execution area tell their stories and keep the memory alive. *stiftung-bg.de/gums/; Strasse der Nationen 22, Oranienburg; 8.30am-6pm Mar-Oct, 8.30am-4.30pm Nov-Feb; free.*

08 Street Art in Kreuzberg

Graffiti and street art have been part of Berlin's creative DNA since the 1970s, especially in Kreuzberg, a veritable outdoor canvas for international and local talent. Among the best-known works is Victor Ash's US-Soviet space race-inspired *Astronaut/Cosmonaut*, ROA's five-storey-tall *Nature Morte* depicting animal carcasses, and Blu's bizarre *Pink Man* – a creature composed of hundreds of naked writhing bodies. *Everywhere; 24hr; free.*

09 Topographie des Terrors

Hitler, Himmler, Göring, Goebbels – the mere mention of the most odious of Nazi Germany sends shivers down one's spine. This morbidly fascinating documentation centre shines the spotlight on Third Reich leaders and their henchmen and stands in the very spot from where the regime's most fearsome institutions – including the Gestapo and the SS central command – once orchestrated their unspeakable reign of terror. *topographie.de; Niederkirchnerstrasse 8; 10am-8pm; free.*

10 Clärchens Ballhaus

The Golden Twenties live on in this grand Weimar-era ballroom clad in shimmering tinsel. Nightly, everyone from hipsters to grannies cut cool figures on the well-worn parquet dance floor as DJs stack the decks with classic swing, tango, mambo, jive and other sounds of yesteryear. Come earlier for low-cost lessons. *ballhaus.de; Auguststrasse 24; from 9pm Mon-Thu & 3-6pm Sun; free.*

11 Jazz Jams

There's plenty of free music in bars and pubs around town, but on

BERLIN

18

Saturday nights, jazz fiends flock to the jam session at the **A-Trane** (11a; *a-trane.de; Bleibtreustrasse 1; free from midnight Sat, €5 before*), a minuscule club which has a stage that's been graced by a roll call of greats including Wynton Marsalis. On Wednesday evenings, the equally respected **b-flat** (11b; *b-flat-berlin.de; Rosenthaler Strasse 13; from 9pm Wed; free*) hosts its own free-flow event.

12 Lunchtime concert at the Philharmonie

Instead of just stuffing your tummy, why not feed your ears with a lunchtime foyer concert played by some of the meister musicians of the Berliner Philharmoniker, one of the world's top classical orchestras. The weekly performances lure hundreds of culture-hungry fans, so arrive early to stake out a good spot in the mustard-yellow Philharmonie, the city's landmark

13

THE LOCAL'S VIEW

"To save on fruit and veg, I hit the farmers' markets just before closing when lots of the vendors drop their prices. Drinks in pubs increase costs so instead I grab some beers at a kiosk and hang out in the park or by the river. Yes, it's legal! Some clubs don't charge a cover just after opening, so I get my hand stamped and come back when the party's in full swing. I prefer cheaper indie cinemas to the expensive multiplexes, except on 'Kinotag' when they too have ticket deals, usually Tuesdays." – Susanne Kreisel, Berliner

concert hall. *berliner-philharmoniker.de; Herbert-von-Karajan-Strasse 1; 1pm Tue Sep-Jun; free.*

13 Badeschiff

Summers in Berlin wouldn't be the same without the Badeschiff, a mega-cool urban beach club built around a river barge-turned-swimming pool and moored in the Spree River. Splash around in the daytime and stay to sip sunset cocktails with a great view of the fairy-tale-like bridge Oberbaumbrücke. In winter, Badeschiff is all covered up and turned into a toasty sauna-cum-bar chill zone for hipsters. *Eichenstrasse 4; 8am-midnight May-Sep (weather permitting); €5.*

14 Chilling by a lake

If you're wondering where all the locals are on a hot summer weekend, look no further than the nearest lake. They'll be keeping cool right there in the sand or beneath trees, cold brewski in hand. Favourite swimming holes include the idyllic **Krumme Lanke** (14a; *free*), the circular **Weisser See** (14b; *from 9am; free*) and the vast **Strandbad Wannsee** (14c; *8am-9pm Sat & Sun, vary Mon-Fri; €5.50*), whose 1.3km-long beach has lured water rats for over a century.

15 Kicking back in Tempelhof Airport

It was the venue for Orville Wright's (1871–1948) early flights, the first Zeppelin landing, Lufthansa's first scheduled flight and the Berlin Airlift. Today, historic Tempelhof Airport is a vast park and playground where you can cycle, skate or kiteboard across the smooth tarmac, fire up a barbecue or simply check out a hippie-style urban gardening project. *Enter on Oderstrasse, Columbiadamm or Tempelhofer Damm; dawn-dusk; free, guided tours €16.50.*

16 Royal splendours in Park Sanssouci

In Potsdam, **Sanssouci Park** (*potsdam-park-sanssouci.de/home.html; Zur Historischen Mühle 1, Potsdam; 8am-dusk; free*) is what happens when a king has good taste, bulging coffers and access to the finest artists. Frederick the Great (1712–86) masterminded this royal summer retreat, whose rococo pads can be admired while strolling around the park. Must-sees: **Sanssouci Palace** (*Maulbeerallee; 10am-6pm Tue-Sat Apr-Oct, 10am-5pm Nov-Mar; €8*) and the **Chinese Tea House** (*10am-6pm Tue-Sun May-Oct; €8*).

Street Food Thursday at Markthalle Neun

The mother of all Berlin's street food markets hasn't lost a step since bursting on to the scene in 2013. Join food fans on Thursday nights in a gorgeously restored 19th-century Kreuzberg market hall to feast on such global flavour explosions as New Zealand meat pies, Taiwanese burgers or Korean tacos. It's all best paired with a good pint of local Heidenpeters craft beer. *markthalleneun.de; Eisenbahnstrasse 42/43; 5-10pm Thu; admission free.*

18 Sundays in the Mauerpark

The premium time for visiting the Mauerpark is on a Sunday, when this scrawny patch of green reclaimed from the Berlin Wall death strip erupts into a wacky carnival. Forage for treasure at the flea market, then grab a beer and find your favourite street performer, watch aerosol-wielding Picassos testing new tags or clap along to live-on-stage performers or crazy crooners at the outdoor karaoke. *Bernauer Strasse; 10am-midnight; free.*

Flea markets are like urban archaeology: you need patience and luck, but, oh the thrill when unearthing treasure! Here are our top picks:

- **Flohmarkt am Mauerpark (*Bernauer Strasse; 8am-6pm Sun*): the 'mother of all markets' for retro threads and local designers.**
- **Boxhagener Platz (*Boxhagener Platz; 10am-6pm Sun*): mostly locals offloading their spring cleaning.**
- **Berliner Trödelmarkt (*berlinertroedelmarkt.com; Strasse des 17. Juni 110-114; 10am-5pm Sat & Sun*): antiques, bric-a-brac and arts and crafts.**
- **Nowkölln Flowmarkt (*nowkoelln.de; Maybachufer; 10am-5.30pm every other Sun Mar-Nov*): hipster-heavy local-designer market.**

ARTS & CULTURE · MUSIC & FILM · SPORTS & LEISURE · FOOD & DRINK · FESTIVALS & EVENTS

BRUGES

It's easy to see why Bruges is so popular, with romantic scenery around every cobblestone-lined canal and quaint square. There's the fine art, even finer chocolate and beer, and while prices soar to capitalise on the tourist trade, you can dodge the touts and make this UNESCO-listed city your own.

01 Onze-Lieve-Vrouwekerk (Church of Our Lady)

A must-visit for art lovers, this 13th-century church boasts the tallest tower in Bruges and is home to Michelangelo's marble *Madonna and Child* (1504), which was purchased and donated by a local merchant, making this church the only place to house a Michelangelo piece outside Italy during the artist's lifetime. There are also lovely works by other artists in the apse. *Mariastraat; 9.30am-4.30pm Mon-Sat, 1.30-4.30pm Sun; free.*

02 Arentshof

If you haven't had enough romantic bridge action at **Minnewater**, then take a stroll over the one at this pretty park. Nicknamed 'Lovers' Bridge', apparently it's where most locals have their first kiss, aww. The canal views are priceless, so long as it's not just you ogling kissing couples. There are several attractive sculptures by artist Rik Poot to admire if things get awkward. *7am-10pm Apr-Sep, 7am-9pm Oct-Mar; free.*

03 Begijnhof

You will be craving a tranquil escape in Bruges and, praise be, this 13th-century garden complex is the very thing. You don't have to be a single or widowed woman either, although that's precisely who this serene, tree-filled courtyard originally accommodated. Spring is the ideal time to visit, when the garden is a sea of golden daffodils, but any time of the year will be aesthetically pleasing for a serene stroll. *Wijngaardstraat; 6.30am-6.30pm; free.*

ST-JAKOBS-PLEIN
Muntplein
06
Markt
Burg
05
Hulden-vettersplein
Simon Stevinplein
KONINGIN ASTRIDPARK
Guido Gezelle-plein
02
'tZand
01
HOF ARENTS
GODSHUIS ST-TRUDO
…denpoort
Beursplein
Minnewater
Walplein
03
04
MINNEWATER PARK
0 500 m
0 0.25 miles

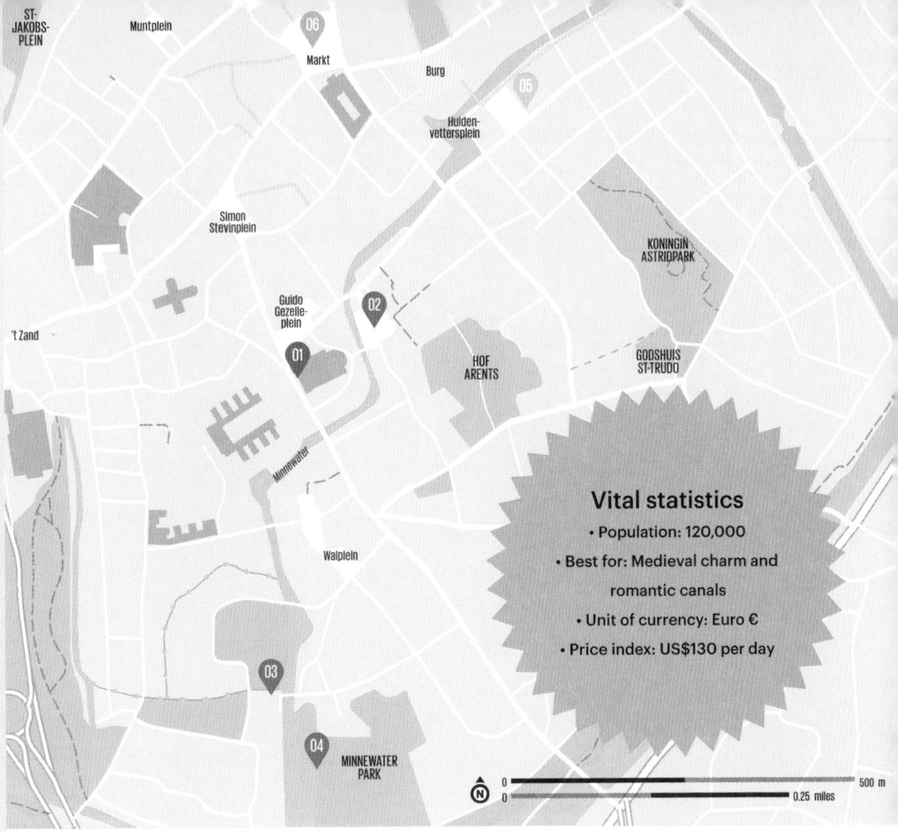

Vital statistics

- Population: 120,000
- Best for: Medieval charm and romantic canals
- Unit of currency: Euro €
- Price index: US$130 per day

LEGENDS OF BRUGES

Not many tours in Bruges are free, unless you're guiding yourself and, let's face it, do you know as much as a local? Here, for absolutely nothing, you get two hours to hear about the city's history, and experience free chocolate, beer tastings, and discounts on waffles and bike hire, as well as receiving a personal tour of the city centre. Bargain! Tips are appreciated, though not compulsory and, as you might expect from a free walkabout, groups can be large. *legendsofbruges.com; in front of statue at Grote Markt; 9.45am and 2.30pm Tue & Thu-Sun, 2.30pm Mon & Wed; free.*

04 Minnewater

If you're heading for somewhere that you know means 'Lake of Love', hopes are going to be high. And yes, the park around this one-time dock-turned-lake makes a very picturesque spot for a picnic. According to legend, if you walk over the lake's bridge with someone special you'll experience eternal love. With this kind of pressure, we say pack some champagne and strawberries – who knows what might happen. *Free.*

05 Vismarkt

Going strong since 1821, Bruges' fish market, held on weekdays in a colonnaded arcade, is ideally located for a bit of people-watching, not to mention seafood-browsing. At weekends, stalls sell bric-a-brac and antiques. You're sure to work up an appetite, so pop into cafe **Gouden Karpel** (*dengoudenkarpel.be/*) for a takeaway crab sandwich (*from €4*), grab a bench by the Groenerei Canal, and watch the action. *Steenhouwersdijk; 7am-1pm Tue-Fri; free.*

06 Markt

It is nonsense to think that you need to purchase an overpriced waffle, *frites* or a ticket for a horse-and-carriage ride to appreciate the grandeur of Bruges' market square and the town's neo-Gothic architecture. To minimise the crowds and maximise your enjoyment, come to the market at dawn or at night, when the 83m-high Belfort (bell tower) is illuminated. Wednesday's food market is a fantastic way to sample local cheeses, meats, breads and so much more. *the-markt.com/wednesday-market.html; 10am-1pm; free.*

 ARTS & CULTURE  MUSIC & FILM SPORTS & LEISURE FOOD & DRINK FESTIVALS & EVENTS

BUDAPEST

It's not hard to fill your time with freebies in Budapest; days can be spent just wandering the streets admiring the architecture. Once tired of that, head to one of the markets and monuments or, for the cost of a few drinks, spend an evening in an atmospheric ruin pub.

03

01 Heroes' Square

A symbolic spot in Budapest, Hősök tere is an impressive site and provides a vantage point from which there are fantastic views straight down Andrássy út, the city's charming UNESCO-listed leafy boulevard. In the square is the 36m-high Millenary Monument – with the Archangel Gabriel standing atop – as well as the Heroes' Monument, a stone cenotaph dedicated to those who gave their lives for the freedom of Hungary. *24hr; free.*

02 Kerepesi Cemetery

The 56-hectare National Graveyard was established in 1847. It contains around 3000 impressive gravestones and tombs, including those of many prominent Hungarians. The cemetery is very well preserved and it's definitely worth spending a little time wandering through. Pick up a free map from the conservation office at the entrance and don't miss the Workers Movement Pantheon. *VIII Fiumei út 16; 7.30am-5pm, 7.30am-8pm May-Jul, 7.30am-7pm Apr & Aug; free.*

03 Gellért Hill

Give yourself a workout by scaling Gellért Hill. Your reward? Stunning city views, best at sunrise or sunset. You'll also find the Citadella fortress up here, which was built by the Habsburgs after the War of Independence (1703–11) but never saw a battle, as well as **Liberty Monument** (1947) – the 14m-high lady with the palm frond standing as a tribute to the Soviet soldiers who died liberating the city in 1945. *24hr; free.*

04 Margaret Island

Smack bang in the middle of the Danube, largely pedestrianised Margaret Island is a 2.5km-long retreat attracting hordes of locals and tourists on hot summer days. There are many activities on offer here: some, such as the swimming pools, bicycle hire, bars and cafes, will require you to flash the Forint, but it doesn't cost a thing to wander the gardens and visit the medieval ruins. *24hr; admission free.*

05 Budapest's markets

Whether you're browsing for knick-knacks or drooling over delicacies, a visit to one of the many markets is a great cheap excursion. Most well known is **Nagycsarnok** (5a; *Great Market, IX Vámház körút 1-3, 6am-5pm Mon-Fri, 6am-3pm Sat*), where you can grab paprika and traditional souvenirs. Otherwise try **Esceri Piac** (5b; *XIX Nagykőrösi út, 8am-4pm Mon-Fri, 5am-3pm Sat, 8am-1pm Sun*) – one of Central Europe's largest flea markets. *Admission free.*

06 Ruin pubs

What dive bars are to NYC, ruin pubs are to Budapest. Housed in rundown abandoned houses (*rom-kocsmák*) and courtyards where you can drink away the night, these bars are typically kitted out with retro decor. As their popularity has grown, some chic permanent establishments are starting to appear alongside the more shabby pop-up pubs that started the trend. *Venues change frequently, so check ruinpubs.com for details. Admission free.*

SHOES ON THE DANUBE

This is a sobering memorial dedicated to the Hungarian Jews who were ordered to remove their footwear before being shot and thrown into the Danube by the fascist Arrow Cross Party during WWII. The monument consists of a motley display of 60 pairs of cast-iron shoes and boots lining the west bank of the river between Széchenyi István tér and Parliament. The moving display was created by sculptor Gyula Pauer and film director Can Togay in 2005. ***V Antall József rakpart; 24hr; free.***

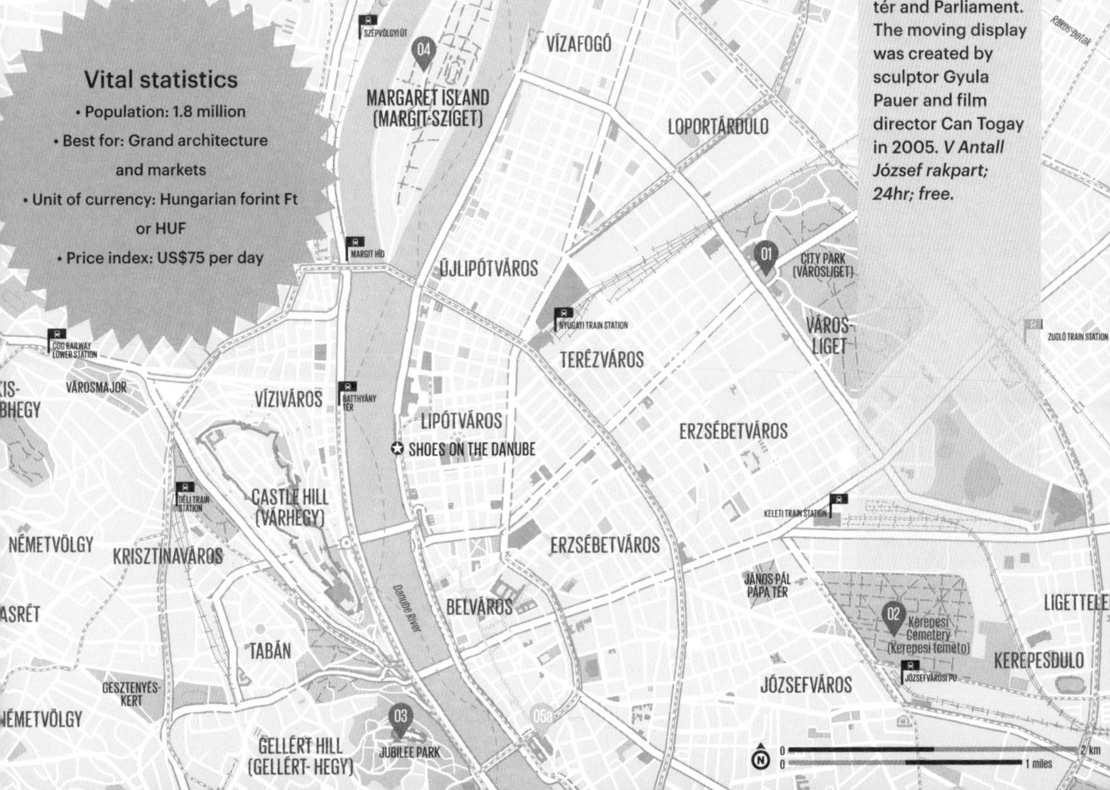

Vital statistics

- Population: 1.8 million
- Best for: Grand architecture and markets
- Unit of currency: Hungarian forint Ft or HUF
- Price index: US$75 per day

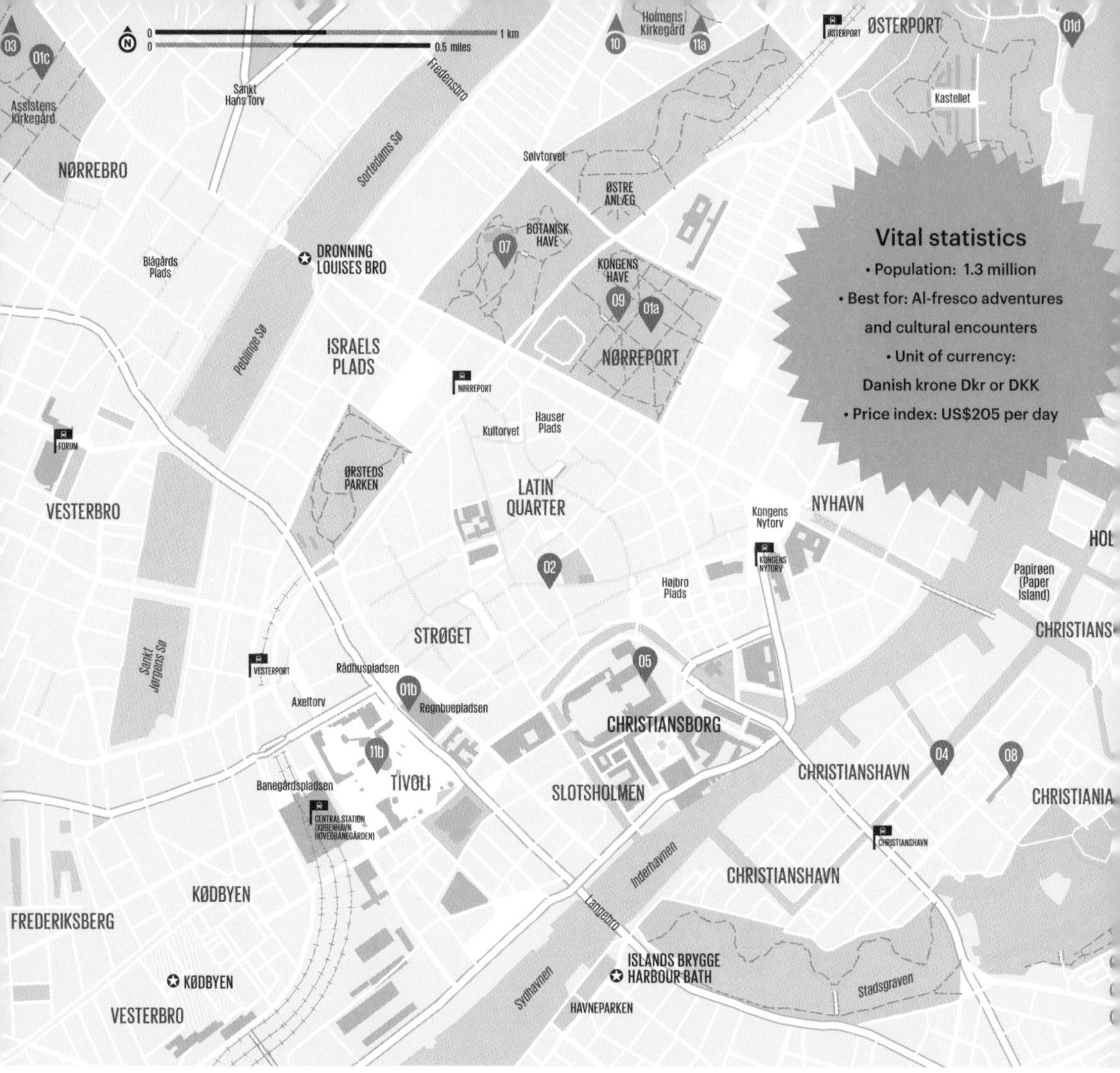

COPENHAGEN

Like a lot of Scandinavian destinations, Copenhagen has a reputation as a wallet-wrecking place to visit – yet it was recently declared the happiest place on the planet by the Earth Institute, and we have a suspicion that free access to loads of attractions helps put a smile on locals' faces.

01 Hans-free foot tour

Hans Christian Andersen was born in central Denmark, but lived in Copenhagen. Statues of the author stand in **Kongens Have** (1a; p093) and outside the **City Hall** (1b; *Rådhuset; 1599 København V*), and he's buried in **Assistens Churchyard** (1c; *Kapelvej 4*). However, children and adult Hans fans will want to visit Copenhagen's most photographed sight: **The Little Mermaid** (1d; *mermaidsculpture.dk*) on her lonely granite perch in the harbour. *24hr; free.*

02 Making connections

In Lego's homeland, blockheads can make a pilgrimage to the toy's birthplace in Billund, 260km west of Copenhagen, and pay to enter Legoland (*299Dkr*). Or they could visit Copenhagen's **Lego store** (*lego.com; Vimmelskaftet 37; 10am-6pm Mon-Thu & Sat, 10am-7pm Fri, 10am-5pm Sun*), to freely enjoy the 'Living Room' creative arena, see huge models and learn facts (there are 915,103,765 ways to combine six eight-stud Lego bricks). *Free.*

03 Open-air Museum

At a sprawling site just outside the city you can explore pre-Industrial Revolution Scandinavia at one of the world's biggest open-air museums. The 50 original buildings range from windmills to a poorhouse, and are occupied by people dressed as peasants and millers explaining how Denmark evolved from 1650 to 1950. *natmus.dk/museerne/frilandsmuseet; Kongevejen 100, 2800 Lyngby; 10am-4pm Tue-Sun May-Jun & Aug-Oct, 10am-5pm Jul-Aug; free.*

04 Royal Danish Naval Museum

Housed in an old navy hospital, this museum tells the country's seafaring history and has model boats dating to the 1600s. Recreations range from sailing vessels to the Spækhuggeren (Killer Whale), which offers a taste of the claustrophobic conditions a 33-man crew of the submarine would endure. *natmus.dk/museerne/orlogsmuseet; Overgaden Oven Vandet 58; noon-4pm Tue-Sun; free.*

05 Tårnet of Christiansborg Palace

Shooting out from the top of Christiansborg Palace – former regal residence of Denmark's monarchy, and current home of the country's parliament – the 106m-tall Tårnet (Tower) is Copenhagen's highest vantage point. As a gift to the people of the city, the government has made access free. Crowning the islet of Slotsholmen, it offers a cracking view across the city's rooftops. *taarnet.dk; Christiansborg, 1218 København K; 11am-9pm Tue-Sun; free.*

02

THE LOCAL'S VIEW

"In summer, socialising outdoors is cheap. We're lucky to have free swimming spots around the harbour, such as the Islands Brygge's Harbor Bath (*7am-7pm Mon-Fri Jun-Aug; free*), and lots of great picnic spots. Locals call Dronning Louises Bro (a bridge across the lakes) Copenhagen's 'longest bar'; there are benches all the way along, and the sunny eastside is a really popular hangout, where people drink beer and listen to music. Kødbyen – formerly the Meatpacking District – is now an ubercool area with great street food, and somewhere you can buy beverages." – Per Munch, journalist

Beach-bumming and sea-swimming

Visitors to Copenhagen can build castles on Blue-Flag beaches at **Amager Strandpark** (6a; *amager-strand.dk; free*), a reclaimed island with 4.6km of sand and lagoons for swimming and kayaking. Serious swimmers head into the deeper waters of Øresund's **Helgoland sea bath** (6b; *10am-6pm 23 Jun-31 Aug; free*). A second lido, **Kastrup Søbad** (6c; *taarnby.dk/oplev-taarnby/idraetslivet-i-taarnby/kastrup-soebad; opening times vary; free*), is further south. Both offer segregated pools where swimwear is optional...

Botanical Garden

Behind Rosenborg Castle, these 10-hectare gardens boast a fine collection of 13,000 horticultural wonders, housed in a complex of 27 historical greenhouses, including a special air-conditioned one for recreating the frigid conditions preferred by Arctic flora. The 1874 Palm House stands 16m tall and has a cast-iron spiral staircase leading to an upper passageway. *botanik.snm.ku.dk; Øster Farimagsgade 2 B, 1353 København K; 8.30am-6pm Apr-Sep, 8.30am-4pm Oct-Mar; free.*

Freetown Christiania

Free-spirited, this semi-autonomous, self-governing, eco-oriented commune has been attracting non-conformists and artists since the early 1970s, when squatters moved into the abandoned 41-hectare military camp and started building an alternative neighbourhood. There have certainly been issues, but collective businesses, DIY-built homes, communal eateries, beer gardens and music venues have survived and thrived. Tours (*Jun-Aug daily, Sep-Jun weekends; Dkr40*) run from the main entrance on Prinsessegade. *christiania.org; free.*

TIP BOX

- Copenhagen's new bike-share programme (*bycyklen.dk*) costs Dkr25 per hour for casual use, and this is a very cycle-friendly city.
- Don't fork out for an expensive touristy boat trip – take the standard commuter ferry (harbour bus).
- Visit Tivoli Gardens (right) on Fridays to catch regular free pop/rock concerts.
- Many museums are free on Wednesdays, but it's worth buying a Copenhagen Card (*copenhagencard.com; Dkr359–799/24–120 hr*) when visiting lots of the city's big attractions.
- Copenhagen is famous for its gourmet restaurants, but one of the best meals in town is a wiener from a *pølsevogn* (sausage wagon).

09 King's Garden

The most central of Denmark's trio of tree-covered royal gardens surrounds **Rosenborg Castle**, home of the crown jewels. The castle costs Dkr90 to enter, but the gorgeous gardens are free, and offer regal levels of relaxation. Sunbathe, picnic or hunt down sculptures, including the 400-year-old *The Horse and the Lion*, featuring a human-faced lion chomping a horse. *kongernessamling.dk; Kongens Have; Øster Voldgade 4A; 7am-11pm, 7am-5pm winter; free.*

10 The Deer Park

Just north of the city, you'll find the vast woodland of Jægersborg Dyrehave, sprawled across 1000 hectares of green wilderness. Amid copses of 400-year-old trees, around 2000 red and fallow deer range free, as can you. Locals flock to this forest park to enjoy hiking, biking, jogging and picnicking, and in the middle of it you'll discover the world's oldest amusement park, **Bakken**. *Dyrehaven, 2930 Klampenborg; 24hr; free.*

11 Thrills and spills

The planet's oldest amusement park, **Bakken** (11a; *bakken.dk; Dyrehavsbakken; entry free Mar-Aug, multi-ride wristband Dkr249, half price Wed*), was founded in 1583. Situated in the Deer Park, it's easily reached by public transport and features Ferris wheels and ancient rollercoasters. In the city, explore another historic amusement park, **Tivoli Gardens** (11b; *tivoli.dk; Vesterbrogade 3; 11am-11pm Sun-Thu, 11am-midnight Fri-Sat; Dkr99*), which inspired Walt Disney to create Disneyland.

12 Copenhagen Jazz Festival

During the 1960s and 1970s, several influential American jazz artists settled in Copenhagen, and the city became the jazz capital of Europe, with a vibrant local scene revolving around the legendary **Jazzhus Montmartre**. Now, every summer, the city transforms into one huge jazz club, with 1315 concerts over 10 days across 100 venues, many of them in the open and for free. *jazz.dk/cphjazz/forside; Jul, see website for details.*

EUROPE'S BEST WILD SWIMMING

Forget paying to go to the pool – plunge in at the deep end with these European al-fresco aquatic adventures.

BAGGY POINT – ENGLAND
Swim through several secret sea caves at this delightful Devonshire dipping spot, including one tide-swept tunnel hidden from lily-livered landlubbers. Wildlife along this part of the coast includes seals, dolphins and porpoises. *nationaltrust.org.uk/baggy-point; North Devon, England; free.*

UPPER LETTEN RIVER POOL, RIVER LIMMAT – SWITZERLAND
An urban oasis during the summer swelter, this 400m-long swimming canal in the fast-flowing river Limmat is a spot that attracts hundreds of swimmers. There's a 2m diving board, plus a bar and beach volleyball fields. *zuerich.com; Zürich, Switzerland; 9am-8pm May-Sep; free.*

PURCARACCIA CANYON – CORSICA
The hike to the pools in this canyoning hotspot is demanding, but worth the effort. Swim in – and slide between – a series of pools fed by crystal-clear mountain water, and enjoy an infinity pool teetering on a waterfall edge. *wildswim.com/cascades-de-purcaraccia-corsica; Quenza, Corsica; free.*

LAKE BOHINJ – SLOVENIA
The Julian Alps offer top-class swimming, including the lovely-but-costly Lake Bled lido. However, travel down the road to Triglav NP's Lake Bohinj and discover wilder scenery for free. The Sava Bohinjka River provides a chilly thrill for flow-swimming fans. *tnp.si/national_park; Triglav National Park, Slovenia; free.*

LAKE WALCHEN – GERMANY
Bavaria is blessed with a batch of brilliant bathing spots, and this deep alpine lake in the mountains south of Munich is one of the most spectacular. Gravel beaches surround the mineral-rich turquoise water, and there are offshore islands to explore. *Near Kochel, Germany; free.*

LAC D'ANNECY – FRANCE
Heated by subterranean hot springs, this Alpine lake is unsurprisingly popular. Many beaches charge during the summer, but Plage d'Albigny à Annecy-le-Vieux and Plages des Marquisats are free. Wilder spots can be found too – some with great cliff jumps. *lac-annecy.com; Haute-Savoie, France; free.*

LAGO DI FIASTRA – ITALY
Camp beneath mountains on the north shore of this stunning beach-lined lake, and slide into the embrace of its gin-clear water. Take a snorkel – there's much to explore, including a rumoured submerged village. *lagodifiastra.it; Monti Sibillini NP, Italy; free.*

LOCH LOMOND – SCOTLAND
You need a brave heart to swim in Scotland, but this beautiful loch – Britain's biggest puddle – might tempt you in. This is the home of the annual Great Scottish Swim (and also, apparently, a monster – albeit one without the celebrity status of its Loch Ness cousin). *lochlomond-trossachs.org; Loch Lomond & The Trossachs NP, Scotland; free.*

Illustration | Owen Gatley

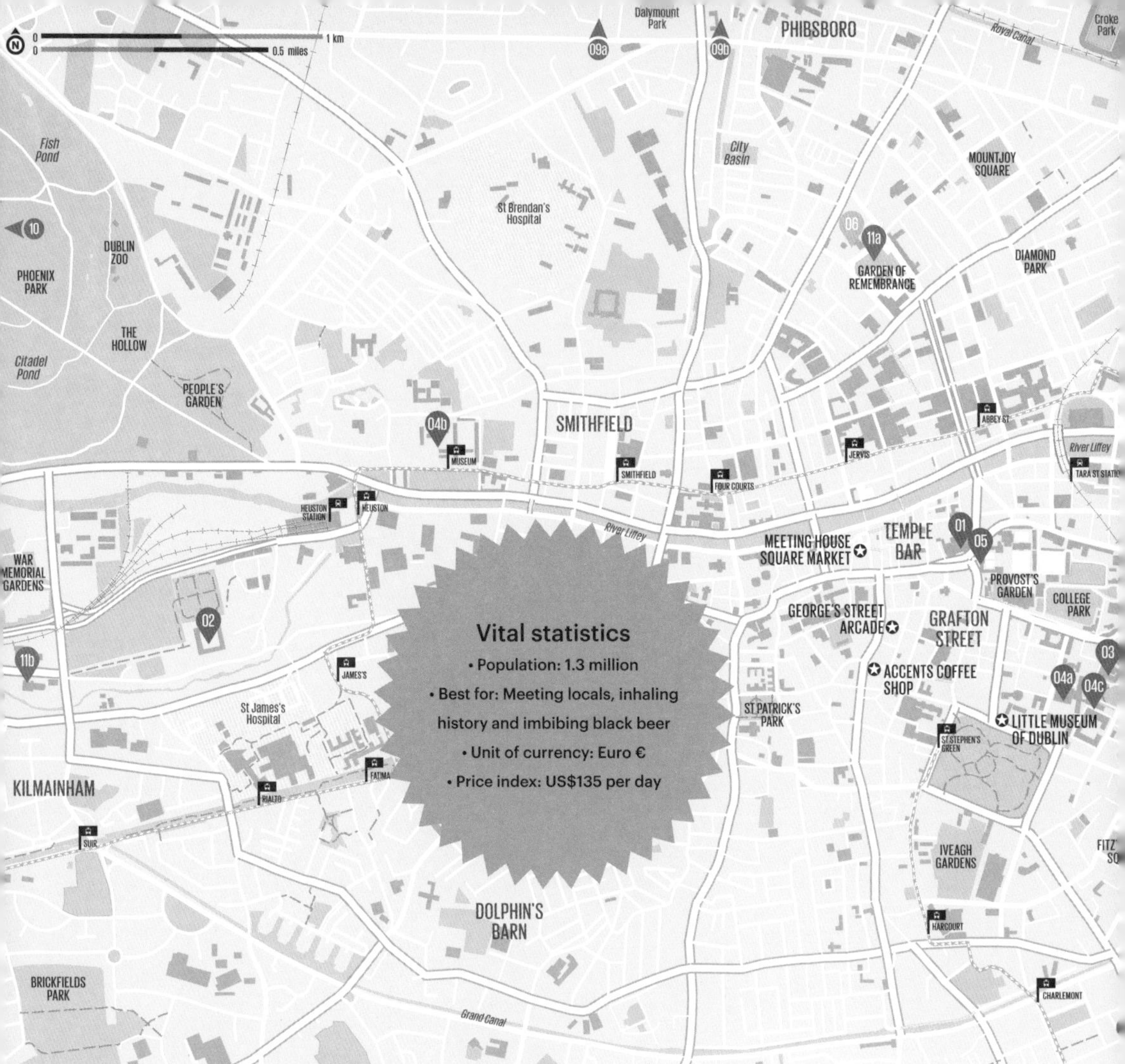

DUBLIN

Ireland's capital is a charismatic and occasionally confounding city, where high culture and light-hearted craic go hand-in-hand, and history is literally etched into every corner. Locals are generous of spirit and garrulous by nature, and in the legendary public houses, the iconic black stout runs freely... but rarely cheaply.

01 Bank of Ireland/Irish Houses of Parliament

Behind the tellers there's a tale to be told here. This 1733 Palladian pile was the world's first purpose-built parliament building. Its design inspired Washington's House of Representatives, but after the 1801 Act of Union, the British insisted the interior be altered to prevent future notions of independence. The House of Lords survived, however. Ask to enter the ornate chamber. *College Green; 10am-4pm Mon-Fri, free tours 10.30am Tue; free.*

02 Irish Museum of Modern Art

A former hospital, the building that now nurses Ireland's premier collection of modern art was founded in 1684. The structure was based on Les Invalides in Paris, which helps to explain the formal facade and elegant courtyard, both completely incongruous with the current contents: 3500 artworks by Irish and international artists, including a tableau of fruit made from wet toilet paper. *imma.ie; Royal Hospital, Kilmainham; 11.30am-5.30pm Tue-Fri, 10am-5.30pm Sat, noon-5.30pm Sun; free.*

03 National Gallery of Ireland

Packed to the rafters with Irish art, Dutch masters, Italian Baroque and works from all the major European schools, this oasis of culture and calm in the midst of Georgian Dublin has 15,000 paintings and sculptures to get your eyes around. Admission costs nothing, you can borrow audioguides and drawing kits, and also attend free lectures, tours and workshops. *nationalgallery.ie; Merion Square; 9.15am-5.30pm Mon-Wed, Fri & Sat, 9.15am-8.30pm Thu, 11am-5.30pm Sun; free.*

04 National Museum of Ireland

This mighty museum explores Ireland's heritage via four million objects spread across four sites. The Irish Folklife division is in Mayo, but the remaining three are in Dublin: **Archaeology** (4a; Kildare St), where you'll explore prehistoric Ireland and Viking-era Dublin; **Decorative Arts & History** (4b; Collins Barracks), including a display about the 1916 Uprising; and **Natural History** (4c; Merrion St), with its Irish elk skeleton. *museum.ie; 10am-5pm Tue-Sat, 2-5pm Sun; free.*

05 Trinity College Dublin

Swan around the beautiful green grounds and cobbled squares of Trinity College, Ireland's top university, which dates back to 1592. An air of erudition pervades the place, and if you laze on the grass, undergrad-style, for long enough, you might even absorb some knowledge

08

WRITERS' WALK

On a self-guided stroll through Dublin, you'll meet the city's most celebrated authors, immortalised as effigies in the surroundings that inspired them. Poet Patrick Kavanagh sits on a bench contemplating the Grand Canal, while Oscar Wilde sprawls on a rock in Merrion Square, facing his childhood home. Nearby, playwright George Bernard Shaw waits outside the National Gallery he loved. Cross the Liffey to find *Ulysses* author James Joyce on the corner of O'Connell and North Earl Sts. Further north, on the banks of the Royal Canal, Brendan Behan occupies a bench near Mountjoy Prison, where he spent time.

by osmosis. The list of former students includes Oscar Wilde, Samuel Beckett, Jonathan Swift and, er, Courtney Love. *tcd.ie; College Green, Dublin 2; 7am-midnight; free.*

06 Sunday concerts

From September to June, a series of free, live musical performances take place in the Sculpture Gallery at **The Hugh Lane**. The Sundays @ Noon gigs began in 1975, and feature the classical talents of both Irish and international musicians. The wider gallery (*10am-6pm Tue-Thu, 10am-5pm Fri + Sat, 11am-5pm Sun; free*) houses Francis Bacon's studio plus contemporary art. *hughlane.ie; Dublin City Gallery The Hugh Lane, Parnell Sq; free.*

07 Bike about

Dublin is a great cycling city, but if you've forgotten your bike, don't stress, just borrow one. Dublinbikes has more than 100 stations around the city, with at least 15 rental bikes at each. A three-day pass costs €5, after which the first 30 minutes is free on every bike (incremental charges apply thereafter). For a cheapskate challenge, try biking around the city in sub-half-hour hops. *dublinbikes.ie; €5 plus time-based charges.*

08 Forty Foot

This deep-water wild-swimming spot on Dublin Bay is where locals have been plunging into the icy embrace of the Irish Sea for 250 years. 'Snotgreen' and 'scrotumtightening' is how Joyce describes the sea in *Ulysses* – but it's actually very clean. He's right about the temperature, though. The well-maintained area has a changing spot. Come on the DART (train), which runs along Dublin's scenic coast. *outdoorswimming.ie; Sandycove; free.*

THE LOCAL'S VIEW

"Saturdays begin with a cup of Dublin Smog tea in Accents Coffee & Tea Lounge (*accents-lounge.com; 23 Stephen St Lower, Dublin 2; 10am-11pm Mon-Sat, 12.30-10pm Sun*). Then I often wander through George's Street Arcade (*georgesstreetarcade.ie*), perusing the vintage clothes and jewellery shops, before ducking into the Little Museum of Dublin (*littlemuseum.ie; 15 St Stephen's Green; 9.30am-5pm Fri-Wed, 9.30am-8pm Thu; €5*). Later, I hit the food market in Temple Bar, for some street eats. The Meeting House Square market (*meetinghousesquare.ie; 10am-4.30 pm Sat; admission free*) has a wonderful selection of organic produce, and buskers provide great entertainment." – Deirdre Quinn, volunteer

09 Glasnevin Cemetery

Ireland's most significant graveyard, **Glasnevin Cemetery** (9a) is the final resting place for all the big names from the country's past, from politicians and poets to writers and revolutionaries. Entry is unrestricted, and you can nose around for free (paid guided tours are also available). Afterwards, have a life-affirming black pint next door in **John Kavanagh's** (9b; Prospect Sq), known as 'the Gravediggers'. *glasnevintrust.ie; Finglas Rd, Dublin 11; 9am-9pm; free.*

10 Phoenix Park

Although walled, this expanse of greenery just to the west of Dublin city centre feels utterly wild. Hundreds of free-range deer run and rut around this 709-hectare park, which also contains **Dublin Zoo**. The zoo has an entry fee, but like the deer, visitors are free to roam (not rut) around the rest of the park, to picnic lakeside at the **Furry Glen**, and see 15th-century **Ashtown Castle**. *phoenixpark.ie; 24hr; free.*

11 Walk the line

A small city full of intriguing blink-and-you-miss-them corners and characters, Dublin is best discovered at walking pace, so skip the tour bus. Follow the Dubline, a walking route from **Parnell Sq** (11a), through the centre to historic **Kilmainham Gaol** (11b). You can get the most out of your walk by downloading the free Dublin Discovery Trails App, which consists of a series of self-guided walking trails that spiral off the main Dubline. *dubline.ie; 24hr; free.*

12 City of a Thousand Welcomes

A warm welcome is guaranteed with this brilliantly innovative concept. Register on the City of a Thousand Welcomes website before your trip to Ireland, and they'll send you a free guide to the city and pair you with a volunteer city ambassador. When you arrive, your ambassador will invite you to their favourite pub or cafe for a free pint or cuppa, and tell you about their city. *cityofathousandwelcomes.com; free.*

ARTS & CULTURE | MUSIC & FILM | SPORTS & LEISURE | FOOD & DRINK | FESTIVALS & EVENTS

EDINBURGH

A castle-dominated medieval city built around a long-extinct volcano, Auld Reekie is famous for festivals, including the Fringe and Hogmanay, which erupt annually sending red-hot streams of entertainment flowing on to the streets. A tourist mecca, it can be pricey, but the bonhomie is free, as are many attractions.

01 Gratis galleries

Edinburgh's excellent free galleries include the **Scottish National Gallery** (1a; *The Mound; 10am-5pm Fri-Wed, 10am-7pm Thu; free*), which houses works by greats (Raphael, Rubens, Cézanne) and local artists. The **Scottish National Gallery of Modern Art** (1b; *75 Belford Rd; 10am-5pm; free*) has Hockney paintings and sculptures by Duane Hanson, while the **Scottish National Portrait Gallery** (1c; *1 Queen St; 10am-5pm Fri-Wed, 10am-7pm Thu; free*) contains many famous faces. *nationalgalleries.org*

02 Museum Mile

The Royal Mile offers four fantastic free museums: **The Writers' Museum** (2a; *Lady Stair's Close; 10am-5pm Mon-Sat, noon-5pm Sun Aug only; free*), celebrating Scottish scribes; the **Museum of Childhood** (2b; *42 High St; 10am-5pm Mon-Sat, noon-5pm Sun; free*); the **Museum of Edinburgh** (2c; *142 Canongate; 10am-5pm Mon-Sat, noon-5pm Sun Aug only; free*); and **People's Story** (2d; *163 Canongate; 10am-5pm Mon-Sat, noon-5pm Sun during Festival only; free*). *edinburghmuseums.org.uk.*

03 Welcome to Holyrood

Due to the recent success of the Scottish National Party, politics is the new rock 'n' roll in Scotland. Fittingly, the Scottish Parliament sits in an award-winning but eyebrow-raising building by Catalonian architect Enric Miralles. Visit for free to learn about Scotland's political

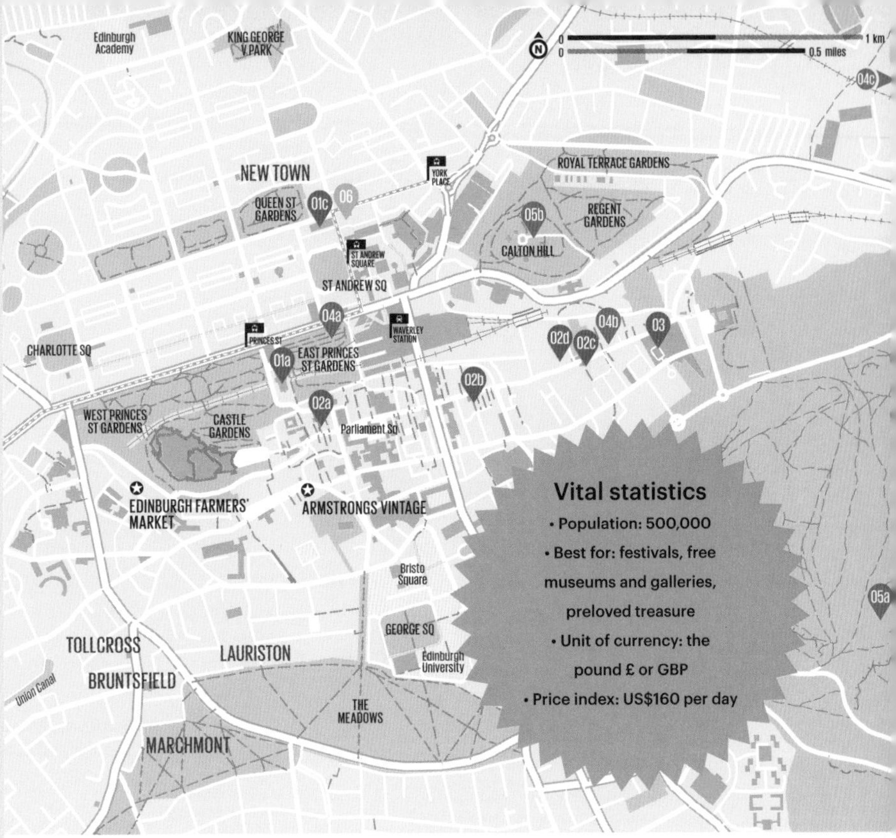

Vital statistics

- Population: 500,000
- Best for: festivals, free museums and galleries, preloved treasure
- Unit of currency: the pound £ or GBP
- Price index: US$160 per day

THE LOCAL'S VIEW

"As a university city, we have loads of great second-hand bookshops and vintage stores, including Armstrong's (*armstrongsvintage.co.uk; 83 The Grassmarket; 10am-5.30pm Mon-Fri, 10am-6pm Fri-Sat, noon-6pm Sun*), an Edinburgh institution. Treasures await discovery in the charity shops around George Sq and in upmarket Morningside in the city's south. Many restaurants – particularly once you escape the tourist drag and enter the neighbourhoods – do good lunch deals and allow BYOB (bring your own bottle) in the evenings. Fresh food can be found around the castle, at the Saturday morning Edinburgh Farmers' Market (*edinburgh farmersmarket.co.uk; Castle Tce; 9am-2pm Sat; admission free*)." – Cate Nelson-Shaw, Edinburgher

history and see livc debates, or take a tour. *scottish.parliament.uk; Canongate; 10am-5pm Mon-Sat; free.*

04 Garden parties and wild swimming

On sunny days, thousands enjoy the bucolic embrace of **Princes Street Gardens** (4a; *Princes St; opening times vary; free*), while **Dunbars Close** (4b; *Canongate; 24hr; free*) is a hidden haven. Others build mini Edinburgh castles on **Portobello Beach** (4c; *24hr; free*), where swimmers shiver in North Sea swell. True bravehearts can join the **Loony Dook** (4d; *24hr; free*), a New Year's Day dip in the Firth of Forth at South Queensferry.

05 Sister Vistas

To view one of Europe's prettiest capitals, make the one-hour ascent to **Arthur's Seat** (5a; *24hr; free*), a volcanic peak that dominates Edinburgh's eastern skyline and has a 2000-year-old hill fort. For a gentler jaunt, scale 143 steps to the brow of **Calton Hill** (5b; *24hr; free*), where an unfinished Acropolis-style edifice overlooks the Athens of the North.

06 Festival Frenzy

Each August, Edinburgh explodes with a season of events including a **Book Festival** (*edbookfest.co.uk*), **Military Tattoo** (*edintattoo.co.uk*) and the world-famous three-week-long **Edinburgh Fringe** (*edfringe.com*). All this action means cheap accommodation is scarce, but street entertainment and open-entry events are everywhere. Outside August, grab a slice of free Sunday-afternoon comedy at **The Stand** (6; *thestand.co.uk; 5 York Pl*) where an improvisation show cures hangovers with humour.

ARTS & CULTURE

MUSIC & FILM

SPORTS & LEISURE

FOOD & DRINK

FESTIVALS & EVENTS

GENEVA

GENEVA

Think big and have a ball in Geneva – it will be deeply satisfying, we promise. This city on the Swiss shore of Lake Geneva is one of the world's most expensive. Summer is best, when free cultural thrills abound beneath the snow-white eye of Mont Blanc. Not a bad backdrop!

01 CERN

Blow your mind with a free guided tour of the laboratory where the World Wide Web was born in 1989. Blow it still further with a gander at the Large Hadron Collider, the world's most massive machine, which accelerates protons down a 27km-long circular tube to create new matter from the resulting collisions. Incredible but true. *cern.ch; Meyrin; guided tour 11am Mon-Sat & 1pm Mon, Tue, Thu & Fri; free.*

02 Aubes Musicales @ Bains de Paquis

Each morning in the balmy summer months, while the rest of the city sleeps, a mixed crowd of music-lovers, revellers and the culturally curious gather at the city's vintage 1930s swimming baths on a jetty in the lake for a clandestine concert at dawn. Jazz, Latin, classical Bach, French chansons...any sound goes, and the atmosphere is spellbinding. *bains-des-paquis.ch; Quai du Mont-Blanc; 6am Jul-Aug; admission and coffee free.*

04

03 La Barje

This waterside vintage caravan with its bright, candy-striped paintwork radiates energy and outdoor buzz. Drinks and snacks are cheap (profits help young people in difficulty), but it's the catchy line-up of free gigs, concerts and street theatre that steals the show. Grab a front-row seat on the grassy riverbanks of the Rhône and chill in style. *labarje.ch; Promenade des Lavandières; 11am-midnight Mon-Fri, 3pm-midnight Sat & Sun Apr-Sep; free.*

ONE-DAY FREE PASS

Snap Geneva's L'horloge Fleurie (*Quai du Général Guisan; free*), then explore Cathédrale St-Pierre (*saintpierre-geneve.ch; Pl du Bourg-de-Four 24; 10am-7.30pm; free*). Picnic in Terrasse Agrippa d'Abigné (*24hr; free*), then hit the lake for art at Cité du Temps (*citedutemps.com; Pont de la Machine 1; free*) and a swim at L'amarr@GE (*10am-8pm Sun-Wed, to 9pm Thu-Sat May-Sep; adult/child Sfr2/1*). Dine at Buvette des Bains (*buvettedesbains.ch; Quai du Mont-Blanc*) and watch films by starlight at CinéTransat (*cinetransat.ch; Parc de la Perle du Lac; free*).

04 Jet d'Eau

Splash out beneath Geneva's iconic pencil fountain, which shoots up water 140m into the air at the incredible velocity of 200km/h. Dash beneath it along the pier and know there are seven tonnes of water in the air at any one time. And what goes up has to come down... *Quai Gustave-Ador; 10am-4pm mid-Nov–Feb, 10am-dusk Mon-Thu, 10am-10.30pm (with illuminations) Fri-Sun Mar, Apr & mid-Sep–Oct, 9am-11.15pm daily (with illuminations) May–mid-Sep; free.*

05 Parc des Bastions

Challenge a local to a game of chess in Parc des Bastions. A constant crowd lingers around the giant chessboard watching the duel in this well-manicured city park. When you tire of kings and queens, stroll through local history: a statue of Red Cross co-founder Guillaume-Henri Dufour is here, as are John Calvin and his Protestant Reformer mates in nightgowns ready for bed! *Promenade des Bastions; 24hr; free.*

06 Firework Finale to the Fêtes de Genève

No expense is spared when it comes to the fireworks display that marks the conclusion of the city's Fêtes de Genève in the summer, and it is watched by half a million people. A fortnight of free concerts and cultural events climax with a spectacular hour of pyrotechnics above Lake Geneva, accompanied by music and fired with Swiss precision from floating bases on the water. *fetes-de-geneve.ch; Jul-Aug; free.*

Vital statistics

- Population: 600,000
- Best for: Lakeside action
- Unit of currency: Swiss franc Sfr or CHF
- Price index: US$150 per day

ARTS & CULTURE   MUSIC & FILM   SPORTS & LEISURE   FOOD & DRINK   FESTIVALS & EVENTS

HELSINKI

Brand new by European capital standards, 200-year-old Helsinki's walkable downtown – filled with design boutiques and parks – is easy to enjoy on the cheap. In summer, Finns pack the seaside beaches, islands and cafes. Nurse a drink at a beer garden, where the locals let loose under the midnight sun.

01 Design District

The epicentre of modernist Finland is the downtown Design District, where **flagship stores** (*Pohjoisesplanadi Street; 10am-8pm weekdays, 10am-5pm Sat + Sun; admission free*) from globally recognised brands like Iittala, Marimekko and Aarikka line Esplanadi Park. Browsing the 200 design studios, art galleries and clothing and jewellery boutiques can feel like hip (and free) museum-hopping. Bonus: the district runs down to **Sinebrychoff Park** (*hel.fi; Blvd 40*), where there are sometimes free performances.

02 Kiasma Contemporary Art Museum

This museum is worth a visit just for the architecture alone. The curved modernist glass building, opened in 1998, was designed so that seasonal light could play with the building's interior space. The museum features a rotating gallery of contemporary art and multimedia exhibits, an aspirational gift shop and a cafe. *kiasma.fi; Mannerheiminaukio 2; 10am-5pm Tue & Sun, 10am-8.30pm Wed-Fri, 10am-6pm Sat; adults €12, free 1st Fri of month.*

03 Temppeliaukion

Finished in 1969 and known as the Rock Church, the bedrock Lutheran church's copper dome tops a skylight ring of narrow windows, bathing the interior with ethereal light. Plan your visit accordingly: a near-constant stream of organ music or free concerts show off the surprisingly excellent acoustics.

HELSINKI

Vital statistics

- Population: 1.2 million
- Best for: Modern art- and design-lovers
- Unit of currency: Euro €
- Price index: US$190 per day

Lutherinkatu 3; generally 10am-5pm when church is not in session; free.

04 Suomenlinna Island

Hop on a ferry to the UNESCO site that dates to 1748, when Finland was a Swedish colony. Explore the fortress, sunbathe, or take advantage of free events, exhibits and museums. There are a dozen restaurants and bars and a hostel. *suomenlinna.fi; Port of Helsinki; ferry tickets from Helsinki's kauppatori to Suomenlinna's main quay one way/return €2.50/5, 15 minutes, three times hourly, less frequent in winter, 6.20am-2.20am.*

05 Take a sauna

The most Finnish thing you could do in Helsinki is not only free, but ubiquitous and requires nothing. Literally, nothing. Not even clothing. Almost every building in the country comes with at least one sauna, and that includes hotels, inns and hostels. Most public places have two, so you and your naked brethren or sisters will sweat it up separately, in temperatures that average 70–90ºC. *Prices vary.*

06 Hakaniemi Market Hall

Out of reindeer skins, ammonium chloride liquorice or squeaky cheese? Get these and other typical Finnish foodstuffs as well as traditional souvenirs and handicrafts of the non-edible variety at the two-storey Hakaniemi Market Hall. Skip expensive Finnish restaurants and make a cheap meal out of local delicacies like reindeer meatballs, salmon soup, or, yes, squeaky cheese (*leipäjuusto*) with cloudberry jam. *hakaniemenkauppahalli.fi; Hämeentie 1a; 8am-6pm Mon-Fri, 8am-4pm Sat; admission free.*

THE LOCAL'S VIEW

"Typically, Finns spend Friday evenings hanging out at Sinebrychoff Park (*Blvd 40; free*). The best places for drinking are Trillby & Chadwick (*Katariinankatu; 4pm-12.30am Tue-Thu, 4pm-1.30am Fri + Sat*) or Ateljee Bar (*Sokos Hotel Torni, Yrjönkatu 26; 2pm-1am Sun-Tue, 2pm-2am Wed + Thu, 12pm-2am Fri + Sat*). You can find cheap meals on one of four 'Restaurant Days', when locals build food stands in the streets and parks. What I love most are the free music events – intimate outdoor parties thrown by the techno label Dept. Music, or the Kallio Block Party in August." – Jenni Salonen, filmmaker, Veli Creative

EUROPE'S BEST FREE MUSEUMS AND GALLERIES

Museum-mooching can be a pricey pursuit, but there's no need to dust the cobwebs off your wallet to enjoy these esteemed collections.

01

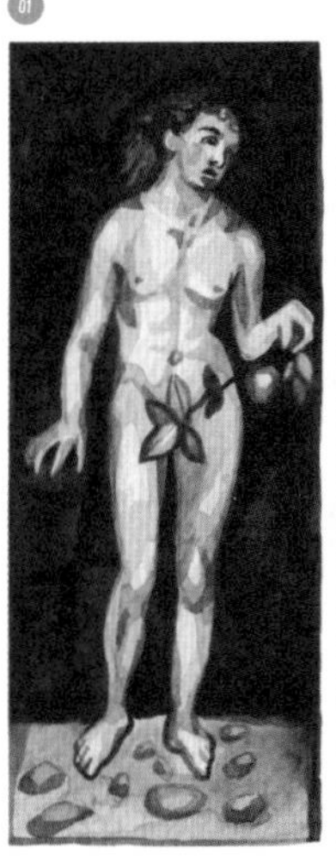

02

01 THE PRADO – SPAIN

Formerly a royal collection, this feast of fine art is now free every evening. One of the world's greatest galleries, it boasts paintings by Goya, Raphael, Rubens and more. *museodel-prado.es; Paseo del Prado, Madrid, Spain; free 6-8pm Mon-Sat & 5-8pm Sun.*

02 SCHUTTERSGALERIJ – NETHERLANDS

One of the world's only 'museum streets', this walk-through gallery mixes historic portraits with a sprinkling of Dutch Masters, some amusing modern artwork and a 350-year-old statue of Goliath. *amsterdammuseum.nl; Kalverstraat 92, Amsterdam, Netherlands; 10am-5pm; free.*

BERLIN WALL MEMORIAL – GERMANY

This poignant museum preserves the last surviving piece of the wall, tells the story of the ghost station of Nordbahnhof S-Bahn, and relates tales of horror, heroism and hope on Bernauer Strasse. *berliner-mauer-gedenkstaette.de; Bernauer Strasse 119, Berlin, Germany; 8am-10pm; free.*

GORKY HOUSE-MUSEUM – RUSSIA

In the Ryabushinsky Mansion – a 1906 art-nouveau house designed by Fyodor Shekhtel and gifted to Maxim Gorky in 1931 – you can tiptoe through the life of one of Russia's most famous writers. *museum.ru/M402; Malaya Nikitskaya ul 6/2, Moscow, Russia; 11am-5.30pm Wed-Sun; free.*

03 BRISTOLIAN STREET ART – ENGLAND

Free-range chin-strokers can enjoy some of the world's best modern street art in Bristol. In Banksy's home town, the al-fresco scene is sensational, with public spaces splattered with murals and installations by guerrilla artists. *bristol-street-art.co.uk; Bristol, England; 24hr; free.*

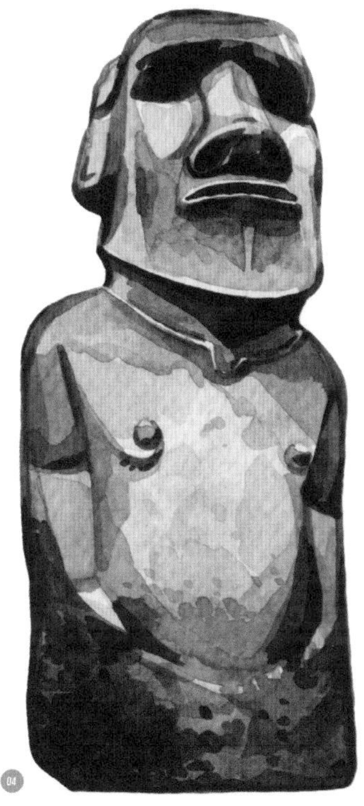

MUSÉE CARNAVALET – FRANCE

History meets art in this peculiarly Parisian institution, where 100 Tardis-like rooms transport visitors through time, via paintings and artefacts from the City of Light's illuminating past. *carnavalet.paris.fr; 16 Rue des Francs-Bourgeois, Paris, France; 10am-6pm Tue-Sun; free.*

04 ROYAL DANISH ARSENAL MUSEUM – DENMARK

This ensemble ranges from samurai swords to a WWII German V-1 flying bomb, via various guns and spiky things. The cache was begun in 1604, by warlord King Christian IV. *natmus.dk/museerne/toejhusmuseet; Tøjhusgade 3, 1220 Copenhagen, Denmark; free noon-4pm Tue-Sun.*

05 BRITISH MUSEUM – ENGLAND

London's full of famous freebies, but this mothership museum, packed with souvenirs pinched during Blighty's globe trotting heyday, is tops. You'll never get around in one day – just come back. *britishmuseum.org; Great Russell St, London, England; 10am-5.30pm Sat-Thu, 10am-8.30pm Fri; free.*

Illustration | Holly Exley

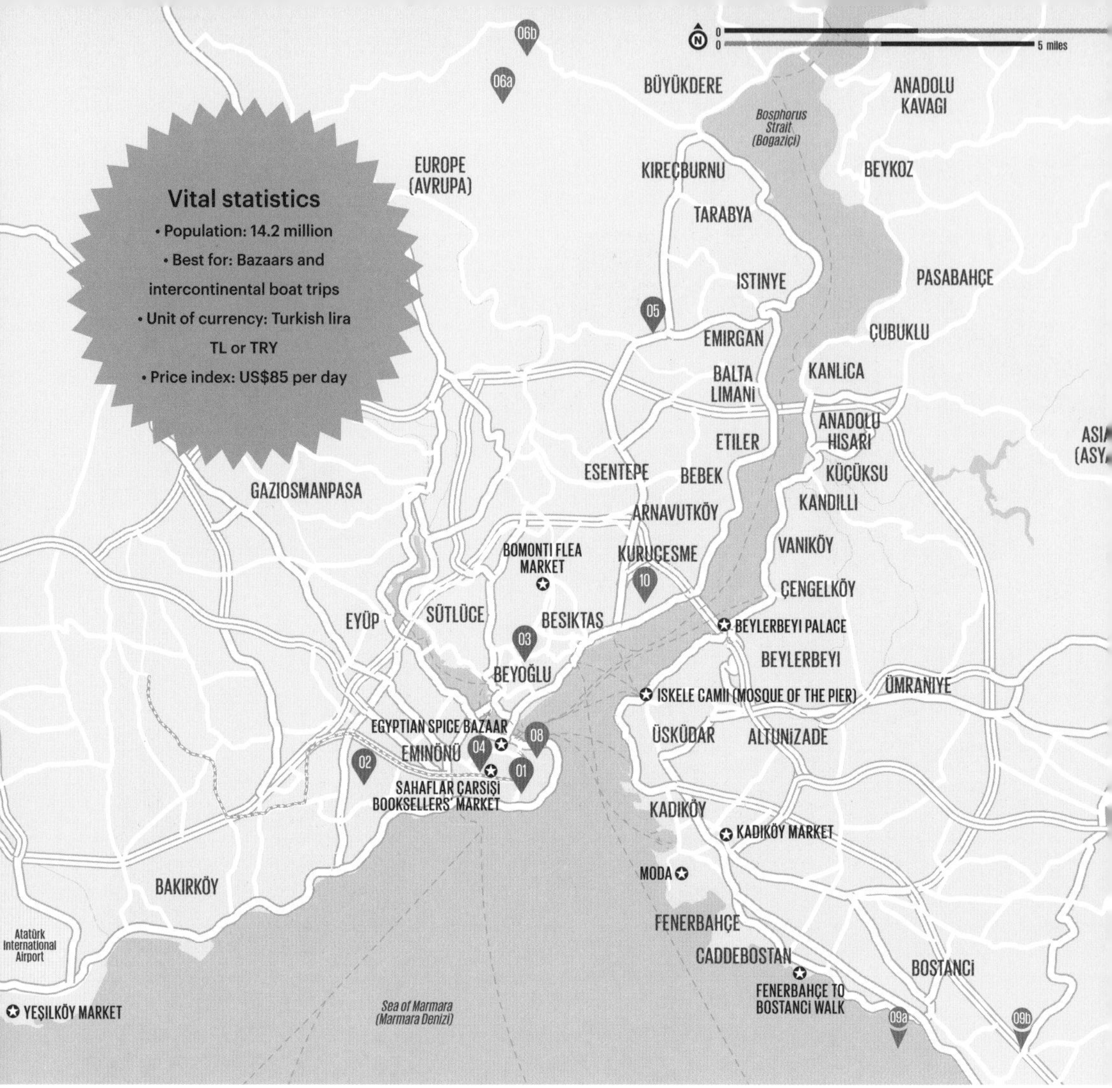

İSTANBUL

Straddling the Bosphorus, with one foot in Asia and the other in Europe, İstanbul is a cultural whirlpool where west meets east. Silk Road traders, meandering merchants and bargain-hunting travellers have hustled and haggled in the bazaars for centuries, and even when your budget's tight, there's plenty to delight.

01 Blue Mosque

The stunning 400-year-old Sultanahmet Camii was built by Sultan Ahmet I to rival the Hagia Sophia. The mosque's moniker derives from the 20,000 blue tiles that flow across its cascading domes. Avoid prayer time, which happens five times a day, including sunrise and nightfall (listen for the *ezan* being chanted from the six minarets), and observe etiquette explained on the website. *bluemosque.co; 9.30am-5.30pm, except during prayers; free.*

02 Dancing dervishes

Experience a tradition that UNESCO describes as one of the Masterpieces of the Oral and Intangible Heritage of Humanity, by witnessing a Sema ceremony performed by the Contemporary Lovers of Mevlana Association each Thursday evening. After watching the dancers (often called whirling dervishes) you can join a Q&A session with the mystics to find out more about the ancient Sufi ceremony. *emav.org/emav/silivrikapi-mevlana-cultural-center; Silivrikapı Mevlana Cultural Center, Mevlânakapı Mah; 7.30-11pm Thu; free.*

03 Doğançay Museum

This modern art museum, housed in a super-narrow 150-year-old five-storey building in bustling Beyoğlu, displays a cool collection of work by Burhan Doğançay and his father Adil Doğançay, two of Turkey's most important painters. Five decades of artistic expression is exhibited, including Doğançay junior's graffiti-inspired work. If you're here from 3pm to 5pm you'll even score complimentary afternoon tea. *dogancaymuseum.org; Balo Sokak No: 42, Beyoğlu 34335; 10am-6pm Tue-Sun; free.*

04 Grand Bazaar

It's free to visit the world's biggest and busiest market, and up to 400,000 people daily explore the 61 colourful covered streets and narrow alleyways that make up İstanbul's Grand Bazaar, perusing 3000 shops and chomping cheap eats. Travellers have been rubbing lamps and thumbing through trinkets for bargains here for 600 years, and it's not unusual to receive a free cuppa from enthusiastic carpet sellers. *grandbazaaristanbul.org; 9am-7pm Mon-Sat; admission free.*

05 The Elgiz Museum

Turkey's original contemporary art museum features a privately owned collection, which includes an impressive swag of works by international names like Tracey Emin and Jan Fabre, and local

02

ON THE EASTSIDE

Don't make the mistake of overlooking Asian İstanbul. A Bosphorus boat crossing is an essential experience, and the enigmatic east bank offers plenty to see for free. Start by exploring the happening 'hood of Moda, with its cafes, theatres, bookstores and record shops, and then saunter along the seaside sahil yolu promenade from Fenerbahçe to Bostancı. Have a nose at Beylerbeyi Palace (former summerhouse of the sultans) and the 16th-century İskele Camii (aka Mosque of the Pier and Mihrimah Sultan Mosque) in Üsküdar, commissioned by Süleyman the Magnificent's daughter Mihrimah Sultan. *24hr; free.*

talent including Ömer Uluç and Princess Fahrelnissa Zeid. It stands incongruously amid the high-rises of the Maslak business district, and has an open-air terrace, used as an exhibition platform for sculptors. *Beybi Giz Plaza 34398 Maslak; 10am-5pm Wed-Fri, 10am-4pm Sat; free.*

06 Belgrade Forest

This 5,500-hectare woodland (6a) to the north of İstanbul is populated by deer, boar, snakes and the odd wolf. A former royal hunting ground, it takes its name from the thousands of Serbs who ended up here after being ejected from Belgrade in 1521. Visit during the week for reduced-rate entry to the fantastic **Atatürk Arboretum** (6b; *Sarıyer Köyü; 4TL 8am-sunset Mon-Fri, 10TL weekends*), containing thousands of plants.

07 Bosphorus boats

Sipping tea while cruising the busy Bosphorus Strait – a 32km umbilicus between the Black Sea and the Sea of Marmara – is an unmissable experience. While they're not the bargain they once were, **İDO** (*ido.com.tr*) Fast Ferry and Sea Bus services remain a cheap alternative to touristy cruises. Keep your eyes peeled: three dolphin species live in the strait and they often surf boats' bow waves.

08 Gülhane Park

On the Bosphorus' beautiful banks, this great green garden is a leafy retreat offering İstanbulians a bit of welcome breathing space and the occasional live concert. In a former life, it was part of the neighbouring Topkapı Palace, home to four centuries worth of Ottoman sultans, including the long-ruling Süleyman the Magnificent (1520–66), who lived here with his harem, protected by eunuchs. *Cankurtaran Mh; dawn-dusk; free.*

MAGICAL MARKETS

Beyond the giant jumble of the Grand Bazaar (p109), there are many more markets to explore in this old Silk Road terminus. Istanbul's photogenic Egyptian Spice Market (*misircar sisi.org; Misir Çarsisi, Eminönü; 9am-7pm Mon-Sat, 10am-6pm Sun*) has been doing colourful business since 1663. Visit Asia for a taste of non-touristy fresh-food and cheap-clothes trading at Kadiköy (*Tue & Fri*), or seek shade beneath chestnut trees with tobacco-chewing intellectuals at the 15th-century booksellers' market, Sahaflar Çarşısı (*Beyazıt Mh; daily*). The Bomonti Flea Market is a smorgasbord of treasure and trash, while Yeşilköy (green village) offers better-quality gear, fantastic tea, and greenery.

09 Princes' islands

For just TL3 per leg, explore the Sea of Marmara's car-free Adalar ('the Islands'). From Kabataş, ferries provide views of Topkapı Palace, Hagia Sophia and the Blue Mosque (starboard), and Üsküdar and Haydarpaşa (port) en route to Kadıköy, before heading to the Islands. Hop off at **Heybeliada** (9a) – for pine groves, beaches and Hagia Triada Monastery – and beautiful **Büyükada** (9b) to see the Splendid Palace Hotel. Check the timetable at *ido.com.tr*.

10 Yıldız Park

Once walled off and reserved exclusively for Sultan Abdülhamid II and other regal residents of Yıldız Palace, this pretty park is now a public oasis in the middle of the city. A favourite picnicking spot for locals, it offers old Ottoman houses, flower-fringed walking trails, lovely lakes, picturesque pavilions and even an outdoor gym for burning off some of those delectable döners. *Yıldız Mh; 24hr; free.*

11 International İstanbul Jazz Festival

What began in 1984 as an offshoot of a broad cultural celebration (the İstanbul Festival) evolved into a major jazz jamboree encompassing many genres (rock, pop, blues, reggae), and has attracted top acts from Miles Davis and Dizzy Gillespie to Massive Attack, Björk and Lou Reed. Free events, like 'Jazz in the Parks', happen alongside ticketed ones. *caz.iksv.org/tr; Jul.*

12 İstanbul Film Festivals

Every November, the **İstanbul International Short Film Festival** (*istanbulfilmfestival.com*) presents an expertly curated collection of 20-minute-or-less short films to enthusiastic audiences at numerous city venues. Films screen three times daily (with English subtitles), entry is free and you can join workshops and Q&A sessions with filmmakers. In spring, the **Mountain Films Festival** (*dagfilmfest.org*) showcases new adventure films, with talks and exhibitions. *See websites for details.*

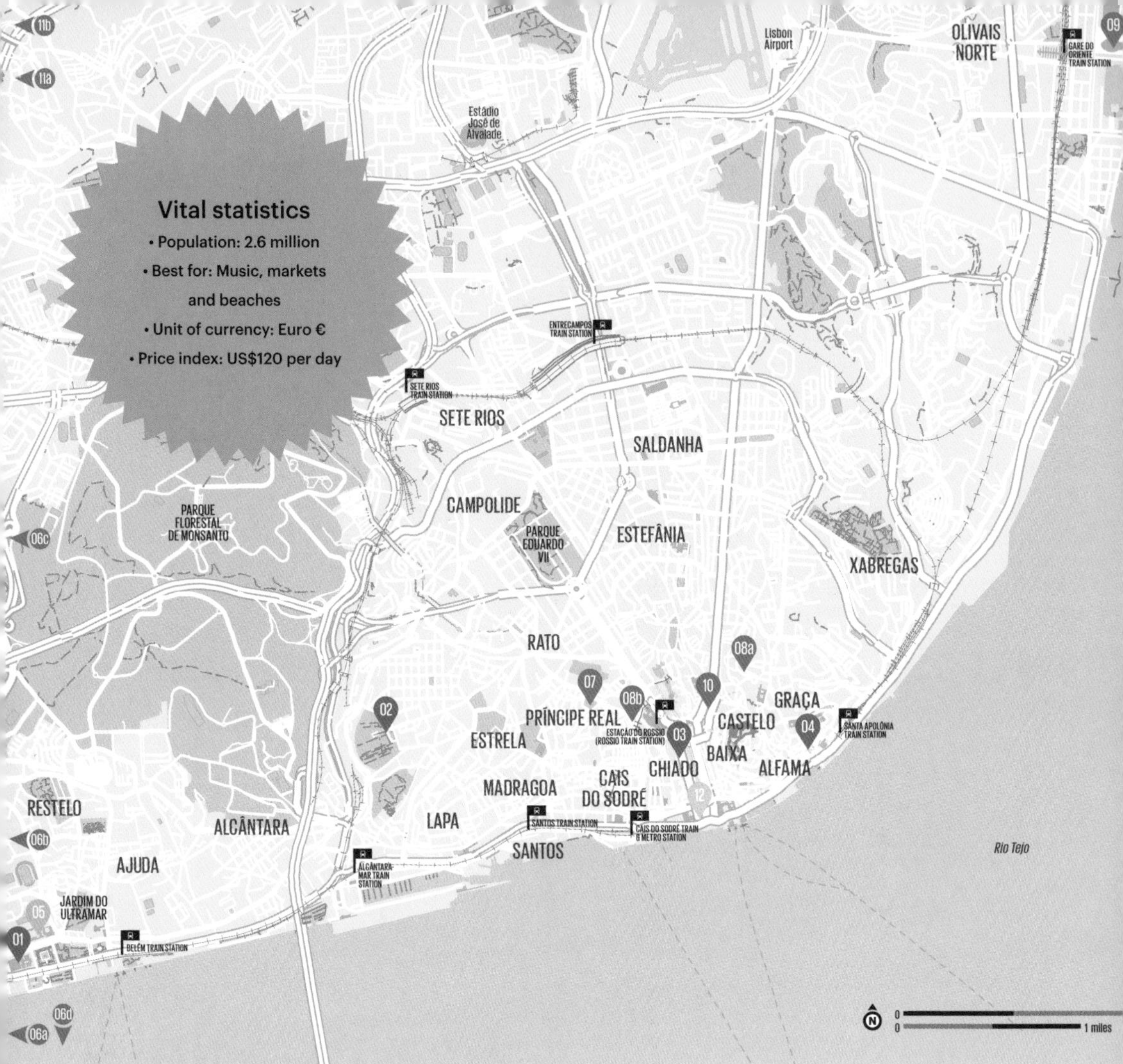

LISBON

On the wild western periphery of Europe, Lisbon is the only capital on the continent to be blessed with ocean-stroked beaches and urban surf breaks, which guarantee a degree of free fun in themselves. But the bargains don't ebb with the tide there's more to explore in this Iberian metropolis.

ARTS & CULTURE MUSIC & FILM SPORTS & LEISURE FOOD & DRINK FESTIVALS & EVENTS

01 Berardo Collection Museum

With more than 1000 works by the likes of Bacon, Dalí, Picasso, Pollock and Warhol, this cool cache of contemporary art, valued at €316 million, includes a broad swathe of European and American conceptual art, spanning surrealism to hyper-realism, minimalism to pop art. Don't miss the vintage posters in the ace advertising art display. *museuberardo.pt; Centro Cultural de Belém, Praça do Império; 10am-7pm; free.*

02 Cemetery of Pleasures

When their time's up, Lisbon's leading lights are buried here, beneath the cypress trees in Cemitério dos Prazeres (the intriguing name derives from the nearby neighbourhood of Prazeres – 'Pleasures'). Statues of the deceased stand amid house-like funerary chapels in this city of the dead. For the living, the cemetery offers breathtaking views across the Alcântara valley and the Tagus river. *Praça São João Bosco; 9am-5pm, 9am-6pm May-Sep; free.*

03 Elevador de Santa Justa

Unsurprisingly, *A Cidade das Sete Colinas* (the City of Seven Hills) has some steep climbs. Bypass the Carmo Hill hike by hitching a lift in this street elevator, designed by an apprentice of Gustave Eiffel, which features ornate neo-Gothic iron arches and wonderful wooden carriages. Dedicated tickets (€5 return) are a rip-off, but the elevator is part of Lisbon's public transport network, so one-day metro/bus tickets are valid. *Baixa district; 7am-11pm.*

04 Mosteiro dos Jerónimos

Building began on this UNESCO-listed beauty in 1501 – bankrolled by Manuel I, whose coffers were overflowing with spice cash after Vasco da Gama (interned inside) discovered a sea route to India – but it took a century to complete. Entry is free once a month, or just go gargoyle-spotting around the Gothic masterpiece. *mosteirojeronimos.pt; Praça do Império 1400-206; 10am-5.30pm Tue-Sun; €10, free 1st Sun of month.*

05 Fantastic Fado

Lisbon is famous for fado – the city's signature soundtrack, featuring guitars, mandolins and a 'Fadista' singing a melancholic muse – the Iberian blues. Fado might be found anywhere, but for guaranteed auditory pleasure book a table at **Mesa de Frades** (*Rua dos Remédios 139A; 7pm-2am Mon-Sat*) formerly a chapel, now an azulejo-tiled restaurant. You'll need to pay for food, but the fado is free and goes on late.

01

03

11

05

LISBON

06 Beaches and breaks

Lisbon arguably boasts Europe's best urban beaches. The sandy arcs west of Lisbon, on the Tagus estuary's northern bank, are the most accessible. With gentle surf, soft sand and good train services, **Praia de Carcavelos** (6a) is popular for people-watching and castle-building, and **Praia de Tamariz** (6b) in Estoril is another hotspot. Surfers should explore **Praia do Guincho** (6c), to the north, and **Costa da Caparica** (6d) in the south.

07 Jardim do Príncipe Real

This tranquil 19th-century Romantic-style garden hosts a weekly **market** (*9am-2pm Sat*), featuring organic food, craftwork (handbags and jewellery) and antiques. The park's focal point is the century-old Mexican cypress – a giant parasol for collectives of card-playing locals, some almost equalling the tree in their antiquity. There's also a large octagonal lake, an aqueduct and the subterranean **Museu da Água Príncipe Real** (*10am-5.30pm Wed-Sat; €2*). *Jardim França Borges; 24hr; free.*

08 Lookout!

The city of seven hills serves up a septuplet of *miradouros* (viewpoints). The highest is **Miradouro da Senhora do Monte** (8a), Our Lady of the Hill, where a tile panel explains that you're looking out over São Jorge Castle, Mouraria, Carmo Convent and the Sea of Straws in the Tagus river estuary. Another cracking vista is served up at the **Miradouro de São Pedro de Alcântara** (8b) reached via **Elevador da Glória**.

09 Parque das Nações

Portugal's Park of the Nations flowered during the 1998 World Fair, which was themed around the 500th

THRIFTY COMMUTING

An alternative to expensive bus tours is the canary-yellow Eléctrico 28e (*€2.50*), which rattles from Praça Martim Moniz to Campo de Ourique via Lisbon's loveliest sights. It gets packed, so go early. Lisbon's commuter ferries also provide riverside vistas far more cheaply than tourist cruises. Ferries (*€2.65*) cross the Tagus from Cais do Sodré, Terreiro do Paço and Belém, providing great views of both banks, including Belém Tower. Combined tickets (*transporteslisboa.pt; €6/24hr*) cover buses, metro, the Santa Justa escalator and the city's funiculars. Lisboa Cards (*visitlisboa.com; €18.50*) are valid on public transport and get you into museums and attractions.

09

12

anniversary of Vasco da Gama's arrival in India. The free-access outdoor arena sprawls for 5km along the Tagus, and features include erupting 'volcano' fountains, wildly impressive al-fresco urban art, a world-leading **Oceanário** (*oceanario.pt; Esplanada Dom Carlos I; 10am-8pm; €16*), cable cars (*€5.90 return*) and the soaring sail-like **Vasco da Gama Tower**. *portaldasnacoes.pt; park admission free.*

10 Praça Martim Moniz

Named after a knight who was killed in the 1147 siege of Lisbon, this vibrant square is the centrifugal point of Lisbon's magical multicultural area. Here, under the watchful eye of Castelo de São Jorge, locals from various backgrounds sip beers, do yoga, play ball games, chomp cheap and very cheerful international cuisine, and dance to DJs (*3pm-midnight Thu + Fri*) At the weekend, the **Fusion Market** features stalls selling just about everything from *empadão* (casserole) to aphrodisiacs.

11 Sintra-Cascais Natural Park

Stand on the westernmost point of mainland Europe and peer off the precipitous cliffs of **Cabo da Roca** in Sintra-Cascais Natural Park, just outside Lisbon. The lighthouse is an evocative sight. Slightly further north, the super-sized free attractions continue with dinosaur tracks wandering up the chalky south cliff behind **Praia Grande**. The 60 fossilised footprints are 100 million years old, and were left by Megalosaurus and Iguanodons. *24hr; free.*

12 Wine tasting

Portugal is better known for port than wine (the clue's in the name), but can the country produce a decent drop of vino? Judge for yourself in the tasting rooms of **ViniPortugal**, ruddy face of the Association of the Portuguese Wine Industry, where you can try out 12 wines from different regions of the country. *viniportugal.pt; Sala Ogival, Terreiro do Paço; 11am-7pm Tue-Sat; admission free, tasting costs €2 per four wines.*

ARTS & CULTURE MUSIC & FILM SPORTS & LEISURE FOOD & DRINK FESTIVALS & EVENTS

LONDON

The original Big Smoke may have cleaned up its environmental act, but it's not unusual to witness visitors choking on the prices charged for food, drink and basic services. London is one of the world's greatest cities, though, and if you avoid the traps, there's plenty to see for free.

01 Grant Museum of Zoology
Ever wondered what male mammal skeletons would look like if prudish Victorian curators hadn't removed their penis bones? Find out in London's last university zoological museum. There are 68,000 specimens from around the Animal Kingdom here, including the thylacine (Tasmanian tiger) and dodo. After hours, the museum comes to life with evening events, including film nights and open-mic sessions. *ucl.ac.uk/museums/zoology; Rockefeller Building, 21 University St, WC1E; 1-5pm Mon-Sat; free.*

02 Highgate Cemetery
London's most famous heritage-listed graveyard/de facto nature reserve houses numerous dead celebrities – from Karl Marx and Malcolm McLaren to George Eliot and Douglas Adams – along with 170,000 others. The west section is only accessible via guided tours (costly), but visitors can explore the east cemetery; there's a charge, but it's not too – ahem – stiff. *highgatecemetery.org; Swain's Lane,*

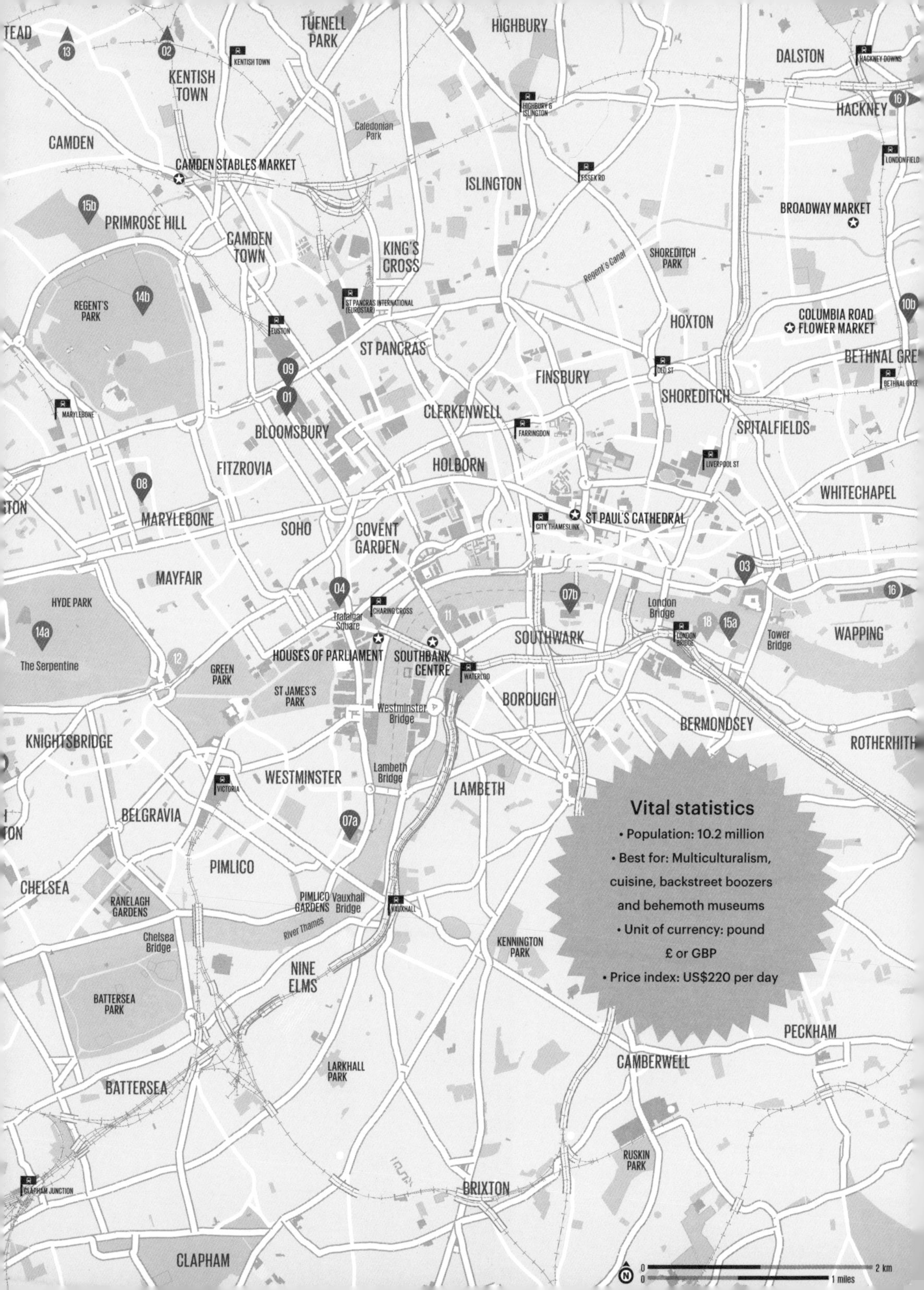

Vital statistics

- Population: 10.2 million
- Best for: Multiculturalism, cuisine, backstreet boozers and behemoth museums
- Unit of currency: pound £ or GBP
- Price index: US$220 per day

N6; 10am-5pm Mon-Fri, 11am-5pm Sat + Sun; over-18s £4.

03 London Wall

Before paying a small fortune to break into the Tower of London, head across the road to check out the remains of a structure that pre-dates the Tower by a thousand years. This is the best-preserved section of the Roman wall that once encircled the city. Archaeologists believe the defensive pile was built circa AD 200, 150 years after Boadicea sacked the city. *www.english-heritage.org.uk; Tower Hill, EC3N; 24hr; free.*

04 National Gallery

It started with three-dozen paintings in 1824 – now you can gawp at more than 2300 works from the world's finest brush- and chisel-wielding artists, from medieval times to the early 20th century. Highlights include Monet's water lilies, Van Gogh's sunflowers, Rembrandt's portraits, Constable's renditions of pre-Industrial England and myriad masterpieces from da Vinci, Michelangelo, Raphael, Rubens, Turner, Cézanne... the list just goes on. *nationalgallery.org.uk; Trafalgar Square, WC2N; 10am-6pm Sat-Thu, 10am-9pm Fri; free.*

05 Natural History Museum

The tsunami of fury that was unleashed by the announcement that 'Dippy', the iconic (but replica) diplodocus standing in the Natural History Museum's entrance hall, is to be replaced with a whale skeleton in 2017 reveals how beloved this institution is. Every British child visits this building at least once, and so should you – it's worth it for the high-Victorian architecture alone, never mind the 80 million items. *nhm.ac.uk; Cromwell Rd, SW7; 10am-5.50pm; free.*

CYCLE OR STROLL

Our top tip for seeing London is to travel overland, under your own steam. Grab a Santander Cycle (*tfl.gov.uk/modes/cycling/santander-cycles; free first 30mins, £2 per 30mins thereafter*) and download routes from the website. Better still – walk. Strolling is free and London's streets are full of surprises. There are several self-guided walks (*tfl.gov.uk/modes/walking/*), but one of the originals remains the best; even if you only do the central section of the 15-mile Jubilee Walkway (*tfl.gov.uk/modes/walking/jubilee-walkway*), you'll pass along the Southbank and see the Tate Modern, Houses of Parliament, the London Eye, St Paul's Cathedral, HMS Belfast, Trafalgar Square and Tower Bridge.

06 The Science Museum

This cathedral dedicated to the worship of scientific thought and the technical achievements of humanity attracts around 3.3 million people each year. The collection of 300,000 objects spans everything from aircraft to microchips, with highlights including Stephenson's 'Rocket' (early steam engine), a full-size replica of the 'Eagle' moon-lander from 1969, and the 'Clock of the Long Now', designed to keep time for 10,000 years. *sciencemuseum.org.uk; Exhibition Rd, SW7; 10am-6pm Sat-Thu, 10am-10pm Fri; free.*

07 The Tate

This four-venue gallery is home to controversial pieces and experimental work, such as the 4D Sensorium, which combines visuals with smells, sounds and tactile elements. Two of the gallery's four UK sites are in London: **Tate Britain** (7a; *Millbank, SW1P; 10am-6pm*), displaying British art from 1500 to the present day, and **Tate Modern** (7b; *Bankside, SE1; 10am-6pm Sun-Thu, 10am-8pm Fri + Sat*), which exhibits art from 1900 onwards. *tate.org.uk; free.*

08 The Wallace Collection

There's more in the way of fine art here – including Frans Hals' *The Laughing Cavalier* and works by Rembrandt – but perhaps more interesting is the fine collection of weapons and armour. The impressive arsenal includes a 10th-century sword and firearms that date from the 16th century. There's also a fantastic haul of French furniture, which includes pieces from Marie Antoinette's rooms at Versailles and an oak commode that was once perched upon by Louis XV. *wallacecollection.org; Manchester Sq, W1U; 10am-5pm; free.*

09 The Wellcome Collection

Take a visit to 'the free destination for the incurably curious' and discover how doctors treated people who'd tumbled into the Thames by blowing smoke up their bottoms. Established by 19th-century pharmacist Sir Henry Wellcome, this museum explores the territory where medicine, life and art meet. Among medical curios, you'll find used guillotine blades and Napoleon's toothbrush. *wellcomecollection.org; 183 Euston Rd, NW1; 10am-6pm Mon-Wed & Fri, 10am-8pm Thu, 10am-4pm Sat; free.*

10 Victoria and Albert Museum (V&A)

With a collection of 4.5 million objects filling 145 galleries and spanning 5000 years, the V&A (10a) is the world's greatest art-and-design museum. It's a mind-meltingly eclectic mix, from paintings, sculptures and photographs to textiles and oriental crockery. The museum also runs the **Museum of Childhood** (10b; *vam.ac.uk/moc; Cambridge Heath Rd, E2; 10am-5.45pm; free*), housing the UK's biggest collection of toys and games. *vam.ac.uk; Cromwell Rd, SW7; 10am-5.45pm Sat-Thu, 10am-8pm Fri; free.*

11 Mediatheque

The British Film Institute's Southbank den is full of big- and little-screen gold. There's an exhibition space, cinema screens and bars, but don't miss Mediatheque, where you can simply park yourself in front of a widescreen computer and access thousands of documentaries, films and TV programmes. Book ahead on the website or just turn up, but be aware that the booths are limited. *bfi.org.uk/mediatheque; BFI Southbank, SE1; 11am-11pm Mon-Thu, 11am-11.30pm Fri + Sat; free.*

12 The Vault

Squirrelled away in a secure room (a former Coutts Bank vault), London's original Hard Rock Cafe keeps a hoard of musical memorabilia, including Kurt Cobain's sunglasses, a guitar strummed by Jimi Hendrix and a US Army shirt worn by John Lennon. Access is granted for nowt if you buy a burger and fries. *hardrock.com/cafes/london; Hard Rock Cafe, 150 Old Park Lane; 11.30am-12.30am Mon-Thu, 11am-1am Fri + Sat, 11.30am-10.30pm Sun; admission free.*

13 Hampstead Heath's Ponds

This oasis in north London has been a wild-swimming spot for decades. There are three ponds in all: male (complete with diving board), female and mixed (which gets very busy during the summer). Facilities include changing and sunbathing areas. These are the only outdoor-swimming arenas in Britain open and lifeguard-patrolled 365 days a year. The city views are stunning, and nearby Golders Hill Park has a deer enclosure. *cityoflondon.gov.uk/things-to-do/green-spaces/hampstead-heath/swimming; 7am-dusk; £2 per day.*

14 Parklife

Inner-city parks are London's lungs of London. Millions of people come to sunbathe, boat, swim and picnic around the Serpentine in **Hyde Park** (14a; *royalparks.org.uk/parks/hyde-park; 5am-midnight; free*) or to hear soapbox oratory at Speaker's Corner, and the free-entry Winter Wonderland (*November to January*) features fabulous festive shenanigans. A couple of miles away, **Regent's Park** (14b; *www.royalparks.org.uk/parks/the-regents-park; 5am-8pm; free*) boasts a fantastic flower garden, and near the inner circle is the hidden entrance to idyllic St John's Lodge Garden.

15 Project Awesome

See London at sunrise with beads of hard-earned sweat on your brow by joining a free group run/exercise session. Project Awesome meets at 6.30am three

"Bargains galore lie hidden in plain sight on London's supposedly mean streets. Hungry? Hit Camden Stables Market (*camdenmarket.com; Camden High St, NW1; 10am-6pm; admission free*) or Hackney's Broadway Market (*broadwaymarket.co.uk; E8; 9am-5pm Sat; admission free*) just after closing, when street-food vendors shift their remaining stock at knocked-down prices. Sunday's Columbia Road Flower Market (*columbiaroad.info; Columbia Rd, E2; 8am-3pm Sun; admission free*) has the added attraction of live music. London sways to many free beats: head north to Kilburn for un-themed-Irish-pub experiences, or poke an ear into a big art-centre foyer for something more classical." – Colin Gallagher, civil servant

LONDON

times a week: Wednesday at The Scoop by Tower Bridge (15a), Friday at Primrose Hill (15b), and Monday at a mystery location. Sessions are inclusive of all fitness levels and everyone is invited for coffee afterwards. Join the Facebook, Twitter or Instagram groups for updates. *projectawesomelondon.com; free.*

16 Walk the Line

Think outside the square and follow the Line instead. This self-guided contemporary- and modern-art walk – the first of its kind in the city – roughly traces the Greenwich Meridian line, from the O2 and the regenerated Greenwich Peninsula across to Queen Elizabeth Olympic Park, with sculptures by artists including Damien Hirst, Martin Creed, Gary Hume and Eduardo Paolozzi pointing the way. Interactive maps are on the website. *the-line.org; free.*

17 Cabmen's Shelters

Free food is rare in London, but you can get cheap chow if you know how – follow that taxi! Cabmen's Shelters were introduced in the 19th century to provide hansom-cab drivers with some bargain bites. Thirteen of the green shelters survive and they still serve super-cheap tucker to cabbies and as take-away to anyone else. Try a full-English breakfast sandwich (£2.80), with an honest-guv 50p cuppa. *24hr.*

18 More London Free Festival

This annual series of free events hijacks the South Bank of the River Thames for four months of summer action comprising of everything from live music and fringe theatre performances to children's entertainment and screenings of flicks in the Scoop – a 1000-seat concrete amphitheatre near Tower Bridge. The big screen on site broadcasts major sporting events such as Wimbledon and the Tour de France. Events take place year-round along the South Bank, which is also the atmospheric location for a Christmas market. *morelondon.com; The Scoop; Jun-Sep; free.*

SURF THE SOUTHBANK

On the banks of the River Thames, the Southbank Centre is a vortex of cultural activity, but when summer hits it blooms into a honeypot attraction for connoisseurs of al-fresco action too. The Queen Elizabeth Hall Roof Garden is an outdoor oasis, with a wildflower meadow, mini allotments and a woodland garden – all with killer views. The Square hosts weekly markets with street food, and the Riverside Terrace regularly features live performances. People cavort in the jumping jets of Jeppe Hein's 'Appearing Rooms' fountain, and at river level there's an urban beach. *southbankcentre.co.uk; Belvedere Rd, SE1; 10am-10pm Jun-Sep; admission free.*

EUROPE'S BEST FREE WALKING TOURS

Yes, that's right, a guided city stroll, for free (apart from the discretionary tip at the end).

ALTERNATIVE BERLIN – GERMANY

See all the great gritty bits of the German capital: street art, skateparks, artist squats, multicultural neighbourhoods, graffiti galleries, day raves, flea markets and more. *alternativeberlin.com; 11am, 1pm & 3pm.*

RUNNER BEAN TOURS – SPAIN

Architect Gaudí made a big mark on Barcelona; this freebie walk focuses solely on him, from his first masterpiece, Palau Güell, to his unfinished magnum opus, the Sagrada Família. *runnerbeantours.com; 11am (& 4.30pm, summer).*

NENO & FRIENDS – BOSNIA & HERCEGOVINA

Let Neno and Merima show you the must-see attractions of Sarajevo, accompanied by a personal and passionate take on the country's history, politics and thriving cultural scene. *sarajevowalkingtours.com; 10.30am, Apr-Oct.*

BRUSSELS GREETERS – BELGIUM

This goes one step further than a regular gratis city tour – hook up with these volunteers in advance to arrange a bespoke freebie, based on your interests – history, football or *frites*. Tips not required.*brussels.greeters.be.*

NEW ROME FREE TOUR – ITALY

What we like about this is its timing. Leaving the Spanish Steps at 5.30pm for a scoot around key sites (Temple of Hadrian, Pantheon, Trevi Fountain), it's good for solos who'd like evening company. *newromefreetour.com; 5.30pm.*

BELGRADE WALKING TOURS – SERBIA

Start with the Downtown Tour for an intro to the Serbian capital, then join the Zemun Tour (3pm, Saturdays), which focuses on the narrow streets of this old neighbourhood. *belgradewalkingtours.com; 11am & 4pm.*

FREE WALKING TOUR.COM – POLAND

Choose the classic Old Town Tour; moving Jewish Kraków; pickle- and pierogi-filled Foods of Kraków; or late-night Macabre Kraków. *freewalkingtour.com/krakow; 10am & 3.30pm, Mar-Oct (Old Town tour – others vary).*

LJUBLJANA FREE TOUR – SLOVENIA

Meet a yellow-dressed guide at the Pink Church for a tour of the Slovene capital – both its main sites and the secret bits only a local can divulge. *ljubljanafreetour.com; 11am.*

FREE WALK ZÜRICH – SWITZERLAND

If you think lakeside Zürich is all cold corporate finance, join the Zürich West tour, which lifts the lid on the city's grungier side – from factories-turned-theatres to the red-light district. *freewalkzurich.ch; 3pm.*

BATH GUIDES – ENGLAND

The Mayor of Bath's Honorary Guides have been running free tours of the Georgian city for 80 years. Tours start outside the Pump Rooms. *bathguides.org.uk; 10.30am & 2pm Sun-Fri, and 7pm Tue-Thu May-Sep, 10.30am Sat.*

ARTS & CULTURE MUSIC & FILM SPORTS & LEISURE FOOD & DRINK FESTIVALS & EVENTS

MADRID

Life in Madrid courses through the streets day and night with peculiarly Spanish passion. This is also one of Europe's high-culture capitals with a peerless portfolio of art galleries. This combination of riotous fun and artistic sensibility is Madrid's gift to the world, and much of it can be enjoyed for free.

01 Caixa Forum

Architecture that makes abundant use of rusted wrought iron and a hanging garden that climbs storeys above Madrid's grandest boulevard; exhibitions on the cutting edge of photography and pop culture; and one of the best gift shops to grace any of Madrid's galleries. Welcome to Caixa Forum, a dynamic cultural experience and the Spanish capital's most striking example of zany contemporary architecture. *Paseo del Prado 36; 10am-8pm; admission free, exhibitions from €4.*

02 Centro de Arte Reina Sofía

Picking up where the Prado stops, the Reina Sofía rushes headlong into 20th-century Spanish art. There are dozens of modern masters here, but the big three dominate: Pablo Picasso, Joan Miró and Salvador Dalí. Picasso's *Guernica* is perhaps the highlight. Time it right for free entry. *museoreinasofia.es; Calle de Santa Isabel 52; 10am-9pm Mon & Wed-Sat, 10am-7pm Sun adult/concession €8/free, free 1.30-7pm Sun, 7-9pm Mon & Wed-Sat.*

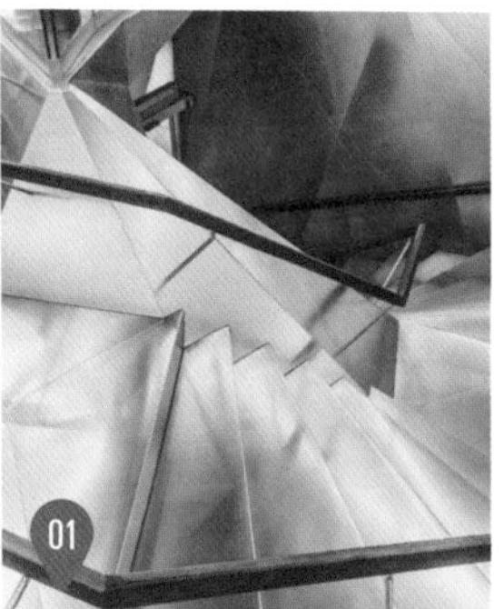
01

14

10

0
2 km
0
1 mile
Universidad Complutense
COMPLEJO AZCA
Vital statistics
• Population: 6.45 million
• Best for: A dead heat between artistic excellence and beguiling street life
• Unit of currency: Euro €
• Price index: US$125 per day
PARQUE DE SANTANDER
ARAPILES
RÍOS ROSAS
CASTELLANA
CHAMBERÍ
ARGÜELLES
TRAFALGAR
SALAMANCA
LAS VENTAS
07
ALMAGRO
JARDINES DE MARÍA EVA DUARTE DE PERÓN
15
CONDE DUQUE MALASAÑA
03
RECOLETOS
GOYA
PARQUE DE LA MONTAÑA
PLAZA DE ESPAÑA
JARDINES DE DESCUBRIMIENTO
CHUECA
RECOLETOS
RECOLETOS
PRÍNCIPE PÍO
JUSTICIA
PARQUE FUENTE DEL BERRO
11
CAMPO
12
CAMPO DEL MORO
Plaza de la Armería
CENTRO
PARQUE DEL BUEN RETIRO
SOL
06
Estanque
16
14
13
08
BARRIOS DE LAS LETRAS
RETIRO
LOS AUSTRIAS
10
04
PARQUE DE ROMA
LA MORERÍA
09
JERÓNIMOS
PLAZA DE LA PAJA
CALLE CAVA BAJA
JARDINES DE LAS VISTILLAS
HUERTAS
01
JARDÍN DE LOS PLANTELES
17
LA LATINA
REAL JARDÍN BOTÁNICO
ATOCHA
02
LAVAPIÉS
EL RASTRO
JARDÍN DEL RASTRO
ATOCHA TRAIN STATION (ESTACIÓN DE ATOCHA)
Estadio Vicente Calderón
Río Manzanares

03 Museo de Historia
Madrid's historical story is wonderfully told at this restored museum. The city's most elaborate doorway, an 18th-century baroque confection raised by Pedro de Ribera, opens on to a collection that includes Goya's *Allegory of the City of Madrid*, some hilarious caricatures of Napoleon and, in the basement, a brilliant scale model of Madrid in 1830. *madrid.es/museodehistoria; Calle de Fuencarral 78; 11am-2pm & 4-7pm Tue-Fri, 10am-2pm & 4-7pm Sat & Sun; free.*

04 Museo del Prado
The Prado (as it's known to its friends) is truly world class. Come here for Goya and Velázquez, or for Flemish masters such as Rubens and Rembrandt. And on no account miss Bosch's hallucinatory *Garden of Earthly Delights*. To pay not a cent for the privilege, come in the last two hours before closing time. *museodelprado.es; Paseo del Prado; 10am-8pm Mon-Sat, 10am-7pm Sun; adult/child €14/free, free 6-8pm Mon-Sat & 5-7pm Sun.*

05 Ermita de San Antonio de la Florida
Art galleries are one thing, but this fine little hermitage (also known as Panteón de Goya) down by Madrid's Río Manzanares shelters one of the city's most remarkable sights. Lavish murals painted by Goya in 1798 adorn the ceiling, while the master himself is buried beneath the altar (mysteriously minus his head). *sanantoniodelaflorida.es; Glorieta de San Antonio de la Florida 5; 10am-8pm Tue-Sun, hours vary Jul & Aug; free.*

06 Museo Thyssen-Bornemisza
This privately owned collection is many visitors' favourite gallery in

07

11

SAVVY SNACKING

Madrid can be an expensive place in which to eat out, but there are some strategies for keeping costs down. To start the day, take full advantage of hotel breakfasts or, if they're not included in your room price, head for the local bar where a croissant and coffee will rarely break the bank. All Madrid restaurants and most bars will offer a lunchtime menú del día, a three-course meal for a fraction of à la carte prices. In between meals, in some bars you'll also get a small (free) tapa when you buy a drink.

Madrid. Its genius is to gather all of the European masters down through the centuries right up to the present day, all under one roof. We challenge you to find any of the continent's greats who aren't represented. Best of all, it's free on Mondays. *museothyssen.org; Paseo del Prado 8; 10am-7pm Tue-Sun, noon-4pm Mon; adult/child €10/free, free Mon.*

07 Plaza de Toros Monumental de Las Ventas

The epicentre of Madrid's bullfighting world, Las Ventas boasts a stirring Mudéjar exterior that mimics a Moorish architectural style and a suitably coliseum-like, four-storey-high, 25,000-seat arena surrounding the broad sandy ring. If you're unable to stomach a live bullfight but remain curious, the **Museo Taurino** (*9.30am-2.30pm Mon-Fri, 10am-1pm Sun Mar-Oct, 9.30am-2.30pm Mon-Fri Nov-Feb; free*) is crammed with memorabilia. *las-ventas.com; Calle de Alcalá 237; 10am-5.30pm; see website for ticket prices.*

08 Casa Pueblo

Free live jazz forms the centrepiece of this fabulous bohemian bar in the heart of the Barrio de Las Letras. But they didn't build their century-old reputation on music alone: there's everything here from cakes and cocktails to clusters of thirty-somethings earnestly discussing the political conspiracies of the day. Only the drinks aren't free. *Calle de León 3; 5pm-2am Mon-Thu, 5pm-3am Fri, 3pm-3am Sat, 3pm-2am Sun; admission free.*

09 Jazz Bar

It was back in the 1920s that Madrid first acquired its reputation as a European jazz capital par excellence and it's still a fabulous destination for enthusiasts.

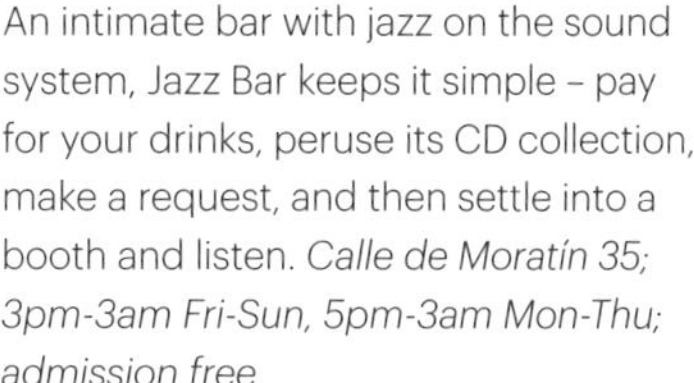

An intimate bar with jazz on the sound system, Jazz Bar keeps it simple – pay for your drinks, peruse its CD collection, make a request, and then settle into a booth and listen. *Calle de Moratín 35; 3pm-3am Fri-Sun, 5pm-3am Mon-Thu; admission free.*

10 Popular

In the heart of the hip-and-happening Huertas district, Populart is a fabulous (and free) jazz venue. The music is top-notch, with classic jazz, Latin, blues and swing all being part of the mix. Compay Segundo and the Canal Street Jazz Band should give you an idea of how good it gets here. *populart.es; Calle de las Huertas 22; 6pm-2.30am Sun-Thu, 6pm-3.30am Fri & Sat, concerts 10pm; admission free.*

11 Jardines del Campo del Moro

These pretty gardens beneath the palace have all the grace and scale that onc associates with European royal playgrounds. The Moor's Field is also rich in significance: a 12th-century military victory here kept Madrid in Christian hands and the city was never again taken. The elegant **Fuente de las Conchas** is the perfect late-afternoon vantage point. *patrimonionacional.es; Paseo de la Virgen del Puerto; 10am-8pm Apr-Sep, 10am-6pm Oct-Mar; free.*

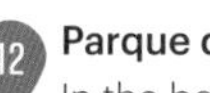

12 Parque del Buen Retiro

In the beating heart of Madrid, El Retiro is an oasis of green and one the Spanish capital's favourite playgrounds. Abundant greenery, the glorious iron-and-glass Palacio de Cristal, a statue of the devil, Madrid's oldest tree and enough space for the city's weekend crowds to freely frolic make this a very Madrid experience, especially late on a Sunday afternoon. *esmadrid.com/informacion-turistica/parque-del-retiro; Plaza de la Independencia; 6am-midnight May-Sep, 6am-11pm Oct-Apr; free.*

13 **Plaza de Santa Ana**

If you were to try to understand the secret of Madrid's street life in a single place, Plaza de Santa Ana would be a fine choice of venue. Watched over by appealing architecture, brought to life by iconic bars, and filled with stories of artists, movie-makers and bullfighters, Santa Ana is the starting point of so many epic Madrid nights and a worthy destination in its own right. *24hr; free.*

14 **Plaza Mayor**

Many a visitor has fallen in love with Madrid at this beautiful square. Down through its history, the plaza – a stirring example of Madrid's very own Madrid Baroque architectural style – has hosted bullfights, royal weddings, the beatification of saints and the trials of the Spanish Inquisition. To really understand its allure, join the locals on the cobblestones and watch Madrid's endlessly entertaining street life pass by. *24hr; free.*

15 **El Rincón de Jerez**

There's nowhere else quite like this in Madrid. After dinner, at 11pm from Tuesday to Saturday, they turn off the lights, spark candles and sing *La Salve Rociera*, a song with deep roots in the flamenco and Catholic traditions of southern Spain. It will send chills down your spine. And the food's not bad either! *elnuevorincondejerez.es; Calle de Rufino Blanco 5; 1-4.30pm & 7pm-midnight Tue-Sat, 1-4.30pm Sun Sep-Jul; raciónes (tapas) €7-13.*

16 **Mercado de San Miguel**

This converted belle-époque iron-and-glass produce market showcases all that's good about eating out in Madrid. The stalls, most of which serve wine and tapas, combine the traditional and the innovative, those twin pillars of

MADRID CARD

Keeping sightseeing and other costs down is made easier if you buy the Madrid Card (*madridcard.com; 24/48/72/120hr €47/60/67/77*) and are willing to follow a fairly intensive programme while in town. After your initial outlay, you're covered for public transport, walking tours and entry to more than 50 museums in and around Madrid (including the major art galleries, Real Madrid's Estadio Santiago Bernabéu and the Palacio Real), as well as receiving discounts in a number of restaurants, shops, bars and car rental companies.

MADRID

Spain's culinary revolution, and yes, you have to pay to sample most of them, unfortunately. But it's the irresistible buzz that accompanies the eating here that's the real drawcard. *mercadodesanmiguel.es; Plaza de San Miguel; open 10am-midnight Sun-Wed, 10am-2am Thu-Sat; admission free.*

17 El Rastro

One of the largest flea markets in Europe, El Rastro is a Sunday-morning Madrid institution. In a skein of streets where La Latina segues into Lavapiés, the market's numerous stalls offer up both junk and treasure in pretty much equal measure, from cheap clothes and luggage to antiques and old flamenco records. It makes sense to dig deep. Later, follow the locals to **Calle Cava Baja** for tapas. *Calle de la Ribera de los Curtidores; 9am-3pm Sun; admission free.*

18 Fiesta de San Isidro

Annually, on 15 May – and, in time-honoured Madrid tradition, on numerous days either side of that date – the Spanish capital celebrates its patron saint, San Isidro, with non-stop processions, parties, bullfights and plenty of free concerts. Locals of all ages don their regional dress, and the night before the actual day itself is one of Madrid's biggest parties, which continues happily until dawn and beyond. *esmadrid.com; see the website for locations & times; free.*

17

ONE-DAY FREE PASS

Begin in the Plaza de la Paja in La Latina neighbourhood, one of Madrid's oldest. The medieval streetscape continues in nearby Calle Cava Baja, one of Madrid's best tapas streets, before you climb to the Plaza Mayor. Stop for cheap snacks and street food at the Mercado de San Miguel, then catch the Metro across town to the Parque del Buen Retiro (p127). By late afternoon, choose between the Museo del Prado or Thyssen-Bornemisza (both p126), then climb the Huertas hill for free live jazz at Populart (p127).

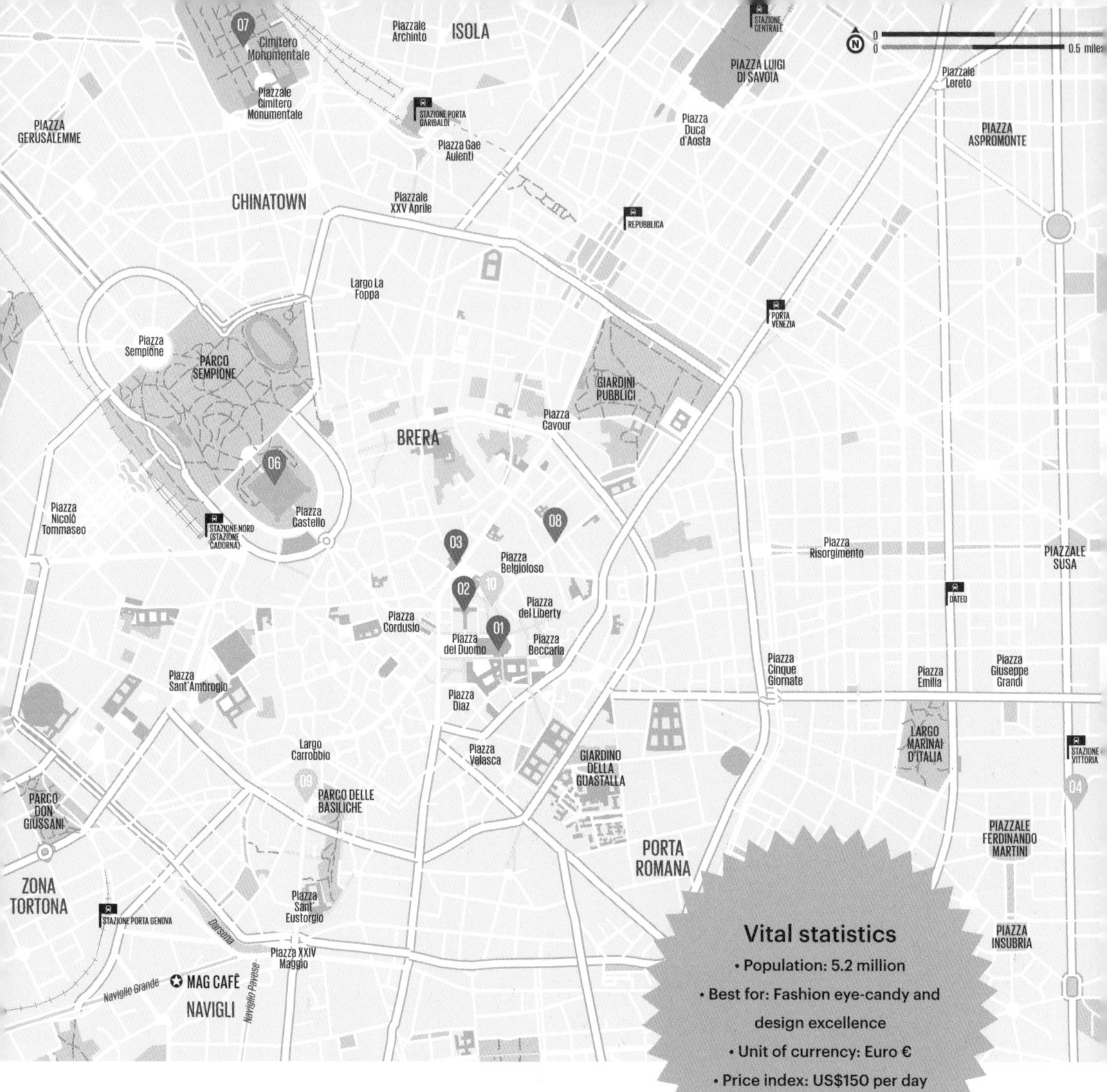

Vital statistics

- Population: 5.2 million
- Best for: Fashion eye-candy and design excellence
- Unit of currency: Euro €
- Price index: US$150 per day

MILAN

Welcome to the well-heeled world of Italy's most glamorous city. Lauded as a world-class fashion, design and financial centre, it's where impeccable taste meets lavish wealth. Understandably, it can get pricey. Yet delve deeper and you'll find a Milan of hidden courtyards and local haunts, which cost next to nothing.

ARTS & CULTURE | MUSIC & FILM | SPORTS & LEISURE | FOOD & DRINK | FESTIVALS & EVENTS

01 Duomo

You can't miss the striking marbled cathedral at the heart of Milan, which took six centuries to complete. Its awesome size and the extravagant detail of its filigree spires and statues (each one different from the next) along with its crowning glory, the golden Madonnina, captures your attention, especially around sunset when the facade takes on its famous pinkish hue. *duomomilano.it; Piazza del Duomo; visitors 8am-8pm, last ticket 7pm; €2.*

02 Galleria Vittorio Emanuele II

This is among the world's oldest shopping centres and also one of the most elegant, with its neo-classical features, vaulted arcades and soaring glass and cast-iron roof. Admire its iconic stores such as the art-nouveau Camparino and the original Prada shop. Otherwise you can spin your heel on the testicles of the mosaic bull, which according to legend brings good luck. So they say... *Piazza del Duomo; 24hr; free.*

© Santiago Fernández | 500px

03 Teatro alla Scala

Overflowing with old-world charm (think chandeliers and a gold-and-crimson interior), a night at this world-famous theatre is not easily forgotten. Tickets can be fairly pricey, but on the day of the performance 140 gallery tickets can be bought for as little as €7 (depending on the show, see *teatroallascala.org* for details). The view won't be the best you could get, but if you're there just for the experience it's well worth going. *Via Filodrammatici 2; performance times vary.*

04 Macao

This centre for art and culture was started by a network of people in the arts and entertainment industry, as well as a number of students, lefties and other advocates of a free space for culture and dialogue within the city. Macao is situated in an art-nouveau ex-slaughterhouse, and the centre has a cheerful renovated squat vibe, promoting everything from movies to dance nights and concerts. *macaomilano.org; Via Caposile 68; free or by donation.*

05 Mazurka Klandestina Milano

Imagine a secret rendezvous in candlelight, where people dance accompanied by a violin against the backdrop of beautiful and imposing public spaces, such as the city Stock Exchange. This is elegant resistance by an underground movement that began in Milan and is all about reclaiming symbolic places of power with traditional dance. *See the group's Facebook page for more details.*

06 **Castello Sforzesco**

One of the biggest castles in Europe, this imposing red edifice played a pivotal role in the city's history: from being a Visconti fortress then the residence of the Sforza dynasty, and today as a cultural institution. Tour its museums (*free Tuesdays after 2pm and in the last hour*) to delve into Milan's past, then stroll in the park (*6.30am-nightfall*). *milanocastello.it; Piazza Castello; 7am-6pm, 7am-7.30pm daylight savings; free.*

07 **Cimitero Monumentale**

Built according to the winning design of Carlo Maciachini in 1866, this cemetery is awe-inspiring rather than lugubrious. It houses a who's who of Milan's elite, with grand sculptural tombs attesting to the glory of its industrialist dynasties. Enter through the *Famedio* (Temple of Fame), the spectacular marble neo-medieval-style building that houses tombstones of the city's most honoured denizens. *Piazzale Cimitero Monumentale, 8am-6pm Tue-Sun, closed Mon except holidays; free.*

08 **Quadrilatero della Moda**

No visit to Milan is complete without a trip to this Mecca of power fashion houses, one of the most revered fashion districts in the world. Framed by four streets (hence the name) – **Via Montenapoleone**, **Via Manzoni**, **Via della Spiga** and **Corso Venezia** – it's everything you imagined and more: stunning cobblestoned streets, fabulously decadent stores and extreme fashionistas. All worthy of an eye-popping few hours' wandering. *24hr; free.*

09 **Colonne di San Lorenzo**

Nothing is more Italian than relaxing in public spaces and nothing is more

APERITIVO

This time-honoured ritual may not have started in Milan, but nowhere is it more popular. A beloved after-work or pre-dinner affair, it occurs between 6pm and 9pm and essentially involves a light buffet or plate of Italian snacks that can be had for the price of a drink. Most bars offer their own variation (*around €8 to €15*). Those on the Navigli are the most scenic, but also the most touristy. We recommend Mag Cafè (*Ripa di Porta Ticinese 43; aperitivo daily 5.30-9.30pm*) for its speakeasy ambience, excellent cocktails (*€8*), and traditional plate of *formaggi* (cheese) and *salumi* (cold meat).

CYCLING MILAN

Milan is a great city to explore by bike: it's small, flat, and inside the city centre there's not much traffic. Additionally its bike-sharing service (*bikemi.com*) allows you to ride for free (at least for the first 30mins), by registering for weekly or daily subscriptions. We recommend a late-night ride through the city centre to experience it as it was truly meant to be: crowd-free and marked by stunning buildings. Otherwise cycle along the canal known as the Naviglio Grande, where old meets new, and *casa di ringhiera* (charming working-class housing from the 1900s) are interspersed with modern bars.

natural for young locals than enjoying a late-night tipple among the Roman ruins of Colonne di San Lorenzo. You'll find a young crowd here, from international students to young professionals and local lefties. Drinks can be bought at numerous nearby bars or from colourful street vendors such as 'Becks Man', who is easily identifiable by his big sombrero. *Corso di Porta Ticinese; 24hr; drinks €3-6.*

10 Panzerotti Luini

The queue says it all. This place is a much-loved institution for the street food *panzerotti*, fried bread containing both savoury and sweet fillings. It's all in that soft oily bread, and the secret of its recipe has been handed down since 1949. Go for the classic, *mozzarella y pomodoro* (mozzarella and tomato) and you won't be disappointed. *luini.it; Via Santa Radegonda 16; 10am-3pm Mon, 10am-8pm Tue-Sat; classic €2.50.*

11 Ii Aperti

Want to peek into a converted monastery dating back to the 4th century? Only once a year will you get chance to do so, when the doors to the imposing palazzos of the old, rich Milanese families open to reveal their secret inner courtyards. The time and place of the event changes every year so check online for details: *adsi.it; yearly; free.*

12 Fuorisalone

The **Salone del Mobile** (*salonemilano.it*), a six-day paid-entry furniture and design trade fair, is the largest of its kind. Fuorisalone is the umbrella term for the awe-inspiring festival of free design events that takes over the city during the same period. It includes everything from hi-tech installations by big brands to edgy indie design, along with swanky free parties galore. *fuorisalone.it; early Apr; free.*

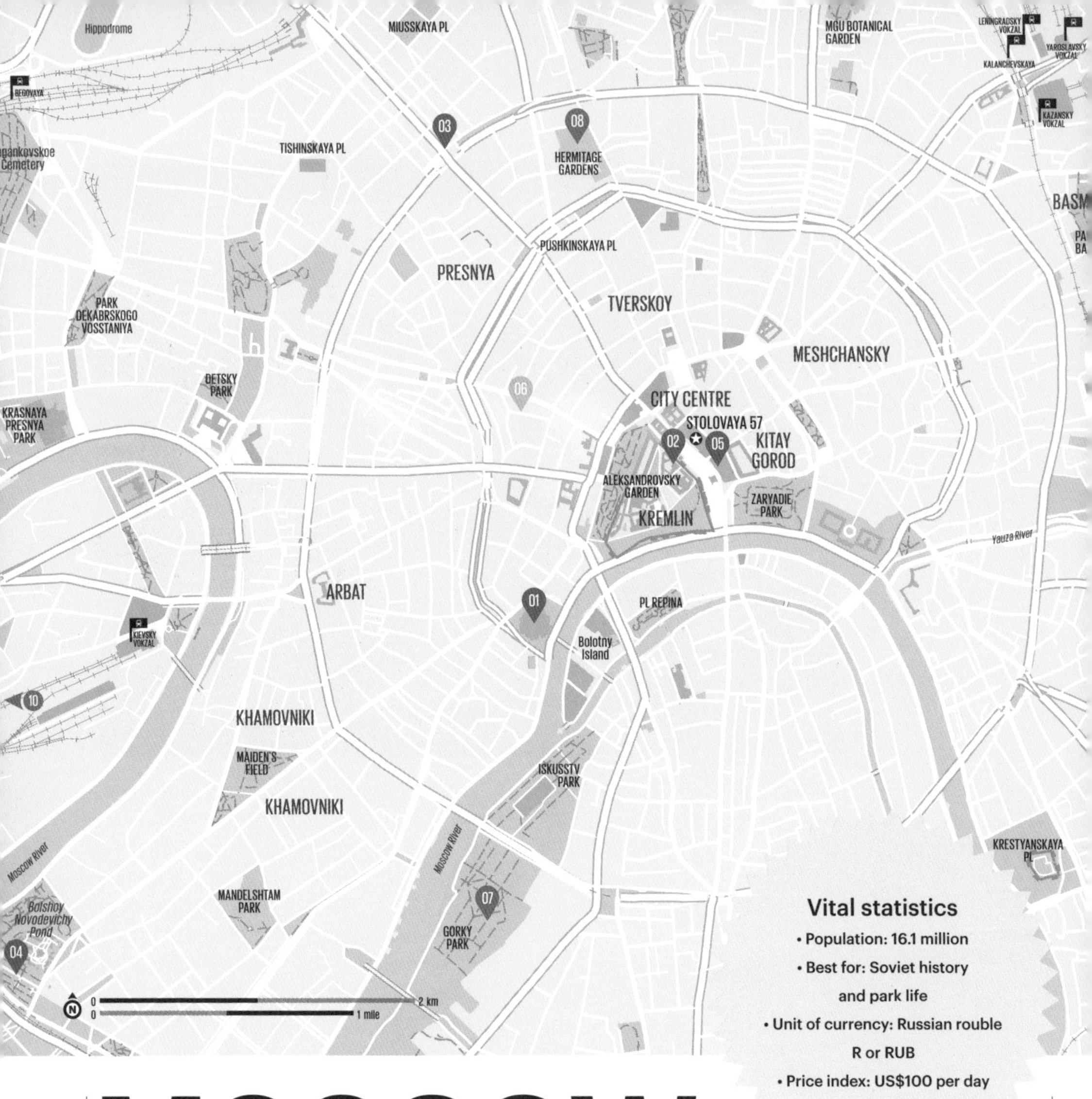

Vital statistics

- Population: 16.1 million
- Best for: Soviet history and park life
- Unit of currency: Russian rouble R or RUB
- Price index: US$100 per day

MOSCOW

While Moscow has had a long-held reputation as one of the priciest cities in the world, it's not all bad news for budget travellers these days. You can keep the roubles in check with plenty of green spaces, epic outdoor monuments, markets, free museums and cheap traditional grub on offer.

ARTS & CULTURE | MUSIC & FILM | SPORTS & LEISURE | FOOD & DRINK | FESTIVALS & EVENTS

01 Cathedral of Christ the Saviour

Standing on the bank of the Moscow River, the shining gold domes of the Cathedral of Christ the Saviour are spectacular to admire from outside and even more impressive inside. It's free to stand in awe, neck craned to take in the fresco-covered dome interior. And don't miss the artwork, *Christ Not Painted by Hand* by Sorokin in the ground-level chapel. *xxc.ru; ul Volkhonka 15; 1-5pm Mon, 10am-5pm Tue-Sun; free.*

02 Lenin's Mausoleum

All it'll cost you to see Lenin's Mausoleum is time spent queueing – and some sleepless nights if you're easily spooked. The embalmed Lenin has been lying at the base of the Kremlin Wall since 1924. Arrive early and be ushered into the dark tomb where you can catch a glimpse of him on your way past and out the exit. *lenin.ru; Red Square; 10am-1pm Tue-Thu, Sat & Sun; free.*

03 Moscow metro art

Riding Moscow's metro will not only transport you from A to B but also into a world of opulence, history, Soviet memorials and some of the best artwork to be found this far underground. For the price of a metro ticket, you can tour the stations and take in everything from the art-deco central hall of Mayakovskaya to the mosaics of past military heroes at Komsomolskaya. *Metro open 5.30am-1am.*

04 Novodevichy Cemetery

Pay nothing but your respects to some of Russia's who's whos at

Novodevichy Cemetery. During Soviet times it was used for those not deemed worthy of Kremlin status, but these days it's known as one of the most elite resting places in Moscow. Wander past tombs for luminaries such as Chekhov, Bulgakov and Stanislavsky and more controversial figures including Stalin's wife and former president Boris Yeltsin. *Luzhnetsky pr 2; 9am-5pm; free.*

05 Red Square

An iconic historical sight, the Red Square lives up to one's lofty expectations when approaching it for the first time. The vast rectangular space will stop you in tracks as your eyes set themselves to panoramic trying to greedily squeeze every bit of architectural wonder into view – from the grand scale of the red-brick Kremlin walls to the bright candy-coloured onion domes of St Basil's cathedral. *Krasnaya pl; free.*

MOSCOW

TAKE A FREE TOUR OF MOSCOW

There are plenty of tours on offer in Moscow to help get you better acquainted with the city and a few of these come at no cost at all. Some of the best picks for free tours in the city include the Moscow Greeter Tours (*moscowgreeter.ru*) run by volunteer local residents, and the insightful Moscow Free Tour (*moscowfreetour.com*) – a two-hour guided walk hosted by some lovely ladies who show you around the Red Square area on their highly informative tour.

06 Moscow Tchaikovsky Conservatory

This concert venue, and one of Russia's finest music education institutions, is a must if you're a classical music-lover. Although tickets can be costly, if you're lucky you can time your visit to coincide with some of the free performances that are occasionally held in the conservatory – an incredible experience. Check the website to see which concerts you can attend for free. *mosconsv.ru; ul Bolshaya Nikitskaya 13; free.*

07 Gorky Park

For a closer look at Muscovites at leisure, head to the expansive, once rundown fun fair Gorky Park, where just about any activity goes. Summer is the best time for watching skaters whizz by, ping-pong players battling it out, hipsters throwing back burgers at pop-up food joints, couples taking a pedal-boat rides on the lake and others playing traditional dancing games or learning how to salsa. *park-gorkogo.com; Krimsky Val 9; 24hr; free.*

08 Hermitage Gardens

To mix with Moscow's coolest, pop into the small, tucked-away Hermitage Gardens. Offering manicured lawns, benches and a peaceful setting, this is the ideal spot in which to wind down after a hard day's sightseeing. You've got a pick of several bars and kiosks, but for penny-pinchers you can't beat a picnic on the grass so stock up on foodie treats en route. *mosgorsad.ru; ul Karetnyy Ryad 3; 24hr; free.*

09 Kolomenskoe Museum Reserve

The 14th-century Kolomenskoe Museum Reserve comprises 4 sq km of parkland just two metro stops from central Moscow. This UNESCO World Heritage site and former ancient royal country seat is a complex of churches and centuries-old gates. The highlight of the reserve is the **Ascension Church**, rising from the front gate overlooking the river. *mgomz.com; metro Kolomenskaya; grounds 8am-9pm, sights 10am-6pm Tue-Sun; free apart from Great Wooden Palace (R400).*

DINE FOR LESS

Stick to a budget in Moscow by familiarising yourself with old-school cafeterias, where you can fill up on traditional Russian dishes for next to nothing. These buffet-style places allow you to indulge in dishes such as herring in a fur coat (herring, beets, carrots and potatoes), borscht and *pelmeni* (dumplings) knocked back with a shot of vodka. Top picks are Stolovaya 57 (*3rd fl, GUM, Krasnaya pl 3; 10am-10pm; mains R200-300*) in the GUM department store on the Red Square, and the chain Grabli (*grably.ru*), which has locations across the city, including one opposite the Contemporary History Museum.

06

03

10 Park Pobedy

The sightseeing at Park Pobedy starts in the metro – check out the mosaics before you ascend from the depths of the station. Once outside, you find yourself standing in front of this sprawling complex, which celebrates the triumph of the Great Patriotic War, dominated by the 141.8m-high obelisk. The endless fountains and monuments are free to wander around but the museum will cost you. *Kutuzovksy pr; dawn-dusk; free.*

05

11 VDNKh

For a surreal, cheap day out, head for this Soviet-style theme park. Exit the station to behold a staggering view of a 100m-high titanium obelisk of a rocket, built in 1964 to commemorate the launch of *Sputnik 1*. Check out cool space paraphernalia in the **Cosmonautics Museum** (*R200*) before exploring the rest of this huge park, which features over-the-top decorative fountains, Soviet monuments and palatial pavilions. *119 Prospect Mira; 9am-11pm; free.*

12 Izmaylovsky Market

The first thing you will see when arriving at Izmaylovksy is the faux Tsar's palace, which might have you turning on your heel. But carry on into the market where the kitsch doesn't stop but there's also a great collection of souvenirs. Browsing is free, or buy cheap gifts, whether it's a fur hat, matryoshka dolls, cosmonaut gear or a bizarre Putin anything. *izmailovsky-park.ru; Izmayalovskoye shosse 73; 10am-8pm; admission free.*

MOSCOW

STINGE HENGE

If the gift shop, fences and entry fees at Stone Henge leave you stone cold, explore these free-to-see rock stars instead.

POULNABRONE DOLMEN – IRELAND

Balanced on the breathtakingly bleak Burren on Ireland's western flank, this elegantly poised dolmen (portal tomb) is 5000 to 6000 years old. Although there are half-hearted ropes (to discourage half-hearted climbers) you can walk freely around it. *County Clare, Ireland; 24hr; free.*

TRETHEVY QUOIT – ENGLAND

Perched on a promontory overlooking the confluence of two streams, this quoit (portal dolmen/tomb) was built between 3700 BC and 3300 BC, probably to house bones – although the acidity in the earth has long since eaten the evidence. *www.english-heritage.org.uk; Bodmin Moor, England; 24hr; free.*

DOLMEN DE MANÉ KERIONED – FRANCE

Carnac is covered with hundreds of standing stones and dolmens. The main site charges €6 for tours (except in winter, when access is free), but nearby Dolmen de Mané Kerioned (three dolmens and small menhirs, all dating to c 3500 BC) is free year-round. *carnactourism.co.uk; Carnac, France; 24hr; free.*

DOLMEN DE MENGA – SPAIN

A behemoth burial mound, the chamber of this 25m-long tumulus – built around 3000 BC with 32 megaliths – was found to contain hundreds of skeletons when it was opened in the 19th century. *www.museosdeandalucia.es/culturaydeporte/museos/CADA; near Antequera, Málaga, Spain; 24hr; free.*

GRIMSPOUND & DRIZZLECOMBE – ENGLAND

Beautiful, desolate Dartmoor is littered with Neolithic and Bronze Age cairns and stone circles, all free for hikers to discover. Notable sites include Grimspound near Widecombe-in-the-Moor and Drizzlecombe's towering menhirs. *english-heritage.org.uk; Dartmoor, England; 24hr; free.*

POSKÆR STENHUS – DENMARK

Denmark's largest surviving round barrow/henge boasts 23 stones, including an 11.5-tonne capstone, which has stood on its neighbours' shoulders since it was balanced there c 3300 BC. Look through the Poskær burial chamber at dawn on the spring equinox to see the sunrise. *visitdjursland.com; Porskærvej 10, Denmark; 24hr; free.*

RING OF BRODGAR – SCOTLAND

Probably Britain's best-preserved stone circles, 27 of the original 60 megaliths at this 4000-year-old site still stand. Measuring 104m across, the ring remains an enigma – used for astronomy possibly, or religious rituals. *historic-scotland.gov.uk; Mainland, Orkney, Scotland; 24hr; free tours daily Jun-Aug, Thu rest of year.*

BRYN CELLI DDU – WALES

The 'Mound in the Dark Grove' is a 5000-year-old Neolithic chambered tomb and henge, designed to precisely align with the rising sun during the summer solstice, when a shaft of light penetrates the passageway and illuminates the inner burial chamber. *cadw.gov.wales; Anglesea, Wales; 10am-4pm; free.*

OSLO

Paying for lunch and a beer can cost a pretty penny in this pretty city and you might well end up screaming like an Edvard Munch painting after getting your bill – but with a little knowledge there's plenty to do in Norway's cool capital that doesn't cost a krone.

01 Akershus Fortress

Once the abode of kings and seat of government, this medieval fortress overlooking Oslofjord has a storied history. When the old town burned down in the 17th century, a new metropolis was built around the ankles of Akershus. The views from battlements over modern-day Oslo are spectacular making this a great place to explore. *7am-9pm; free.*

Building-Hopping

Several of Oslo's prominent buildings can be explored with a self-guided walk, including the **Opera House** (2a; *operaen.no; Bjørvika; 10am-8pm Mon-Fri, 11am-6pm Sat, noon-6pm Sun*). Tours cost 100Nkr but you can freely visit the roof for views over Oslofjord. Also check out the artwork at the **Rådhuset** (2b; *oslo.kommune.no; Fridtjof Nansens plass; 9am-6pm; free*); there's a carillon concert at 1pm on the first Wednesday of the month.

03 Museum-Mooching

Visit Oslo on a Sunday and you'll discover all Norway's national cultural collections are free, including those at the **National Gallery** (3a; Universitetsgata 13; 11am-5pm), home of Edvard Munch's *The Scream* and *Madonna*, plus paintings by Cézanne and Manet; the **Museum of Contemporary Art** (3b; Bankplassen 4; noon-5pm), the **Museum of Decorative Arts and Design** (3c; St Olavsgate 1; noon-4pm) and the **National Museum – Architecture** (3d; Bankplassen 3; noon-5pm). *All nasjonalmuseet.no.*

© Felipe Rodriguez; Cole Nyquist | 500px

OSLO

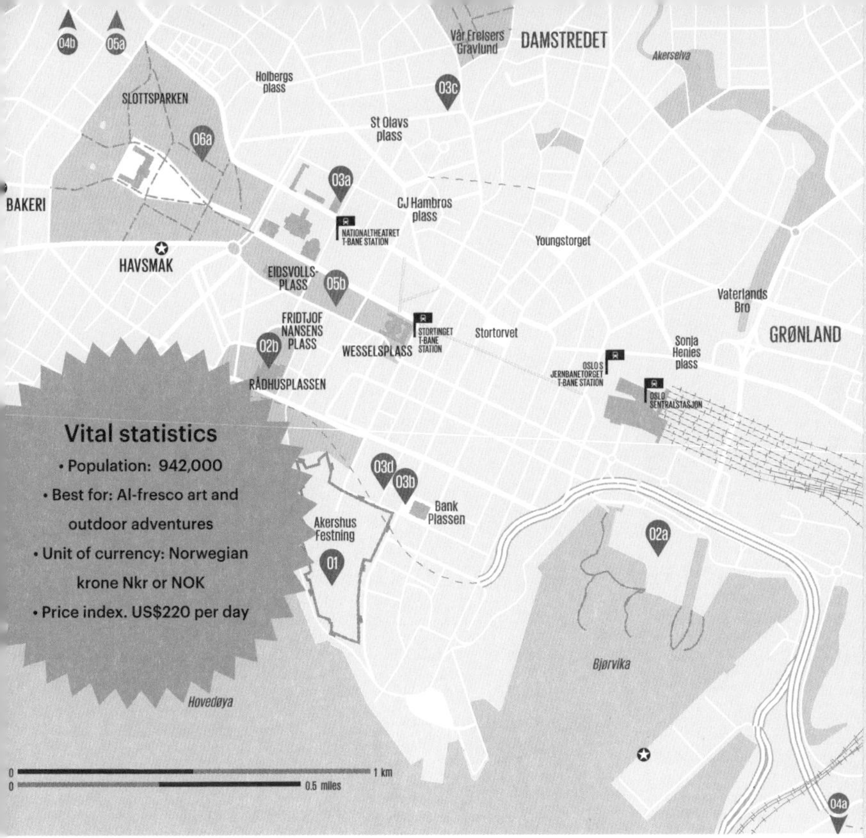

Vital statistics

- Population: 942,000
- Best for: Al-fresco art and outdoor adventures
- Unit of currency: Norwegian krone Nkr or NOK
- Price index. US$220 per day

04 Sculpture Culture

Wander through **Ekeberg sculpture park** (4a; *ekebergparken.com; Kongsveien 23; 24hr; free*) admiring its 31 stone effigies, representatives of European art from the last 130 years. Clamber around the climbing park, feast on fantastic views of the city, and create your own version of Munch's *Scream*. In the northwest of the city, visit **Vigelandsparken** (4b; *vigeland.museum.no; Majorstua/Frogner; 24hr; free*) the world's largest single-artist sculpture park, with 212 works by Gustav Vigeland.

05 Al-fresco Adventures

A mere 20 minutes from the city, **Nordmarka forest** (5a) has plenty of trails to explore by walking, running or riding in summer, or on cross-country skis during winter (rent or BYO skis). There are urban swimming beaches at the city's outskirts and across the islands (see right), and free-to-use ice-skating rinks in the centre during winter, including **Spikersuppa Skating Rink** (5b; *Karl Johan; 11am-9pm; free, skate rental 100Nkr per day*).

06 Picnic at the Palace

The free-access **Palace Park** or **Slottsparken** (6a; kongehuset.no; 24hr; free) is a popular picnicking and people-watching spot for locals and visitors, who often coincide their sandwich-munching with the Changing of the Guard (1.30pm daily). Another awesome al-fresco eating spot is the **Botanical Garden** (6b; *nhm.uio.no; Sars gate 1; 7am-9pm Mon-Fri, 10am-9pm Sat + Sun mid-Mar–Sep, 10am-5pm rest of year*) in Tøyenparken (next to the Munch Museum), which contains 7500 species of plants.

THE LOCAL'S VIEW

In summer, go swimming at the islands. Public transport tickets are valid on standard ferries, and Langøyene has free camping. There's also a beach at Tjuvholmen, and the Sørenga sea bath by the Opera House has a floating sauna! In winter, take the subway to Frognerseteren and rent a sled at Korketrekkeren (akeforeningen.no; Holmenkollveien; 10am-9pm Mon-Fri, 9am-9pm Sat, 10am-6pm Sun, winter; 100Nkr per day). For cheap eats, enjoy free jam and butter when you buy bread rolls at Åpent Bakeri (several locations), and Havsmak (havsmak.no; Henrik Ibsens gate 4; 11am-midnight Mon-Fri, noon-midnight Sat) does takeaway soup for 79Nkr.

– Lars Moastuen, Oslovian

 ARTS & CULTURE  MUSIC & FILM  SPORTS & LEISURE  FOOD & DRINK  FESTIVALS & EVENTS

PARIS

Paris is one of the world's great free cities. For the price of a drink, you can spend hours on a cafe terrasse watching the eternal theatre of the place unfold. If you're able to drag yourself away, there are countless other free sights in this Paris of priceless glamour.

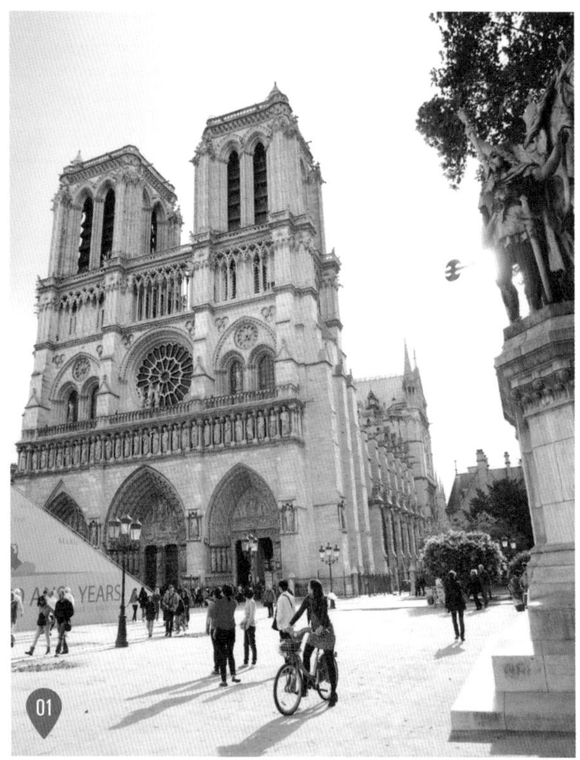

01 Cathédrale Notre Dame de Paris
Believe it or not, entry to this masterpiece of French Gothic architecture, one of the world's best-known churches, is free. First, make a circumnavigation of the exterior with its famed flying buttresses; inside, be wowed by the spectacular rose windows. If you want to get nose-to-nose with the gargoyles, there's a fee to climb the tower. *www.cathedraledeparis.com; 6 place du Parvis Notre Dame, 4e; 8am-6.45pm Mon-Fri, 8am-7.15pm Sat + Sun; free.*

02 Cimetière du Père Lachaise
This hillside cemetery is known for celebrity graves, with Jim Morrison's, Oscar Wilde's and Édith Piaf's most visited. There are many others – writers Molière, Proust and Colette and countless revolutionaries and politicians. It's a sculpture garden, historic monument and one of Paris' major sights. *www.pere-lachaise.com; 16 rue du Repos & blvd de Ménilmontant, 20e; 8am-6pm Mon-Fri, 8.30am-6pm Sat, 9am-6pm Sun; free.*

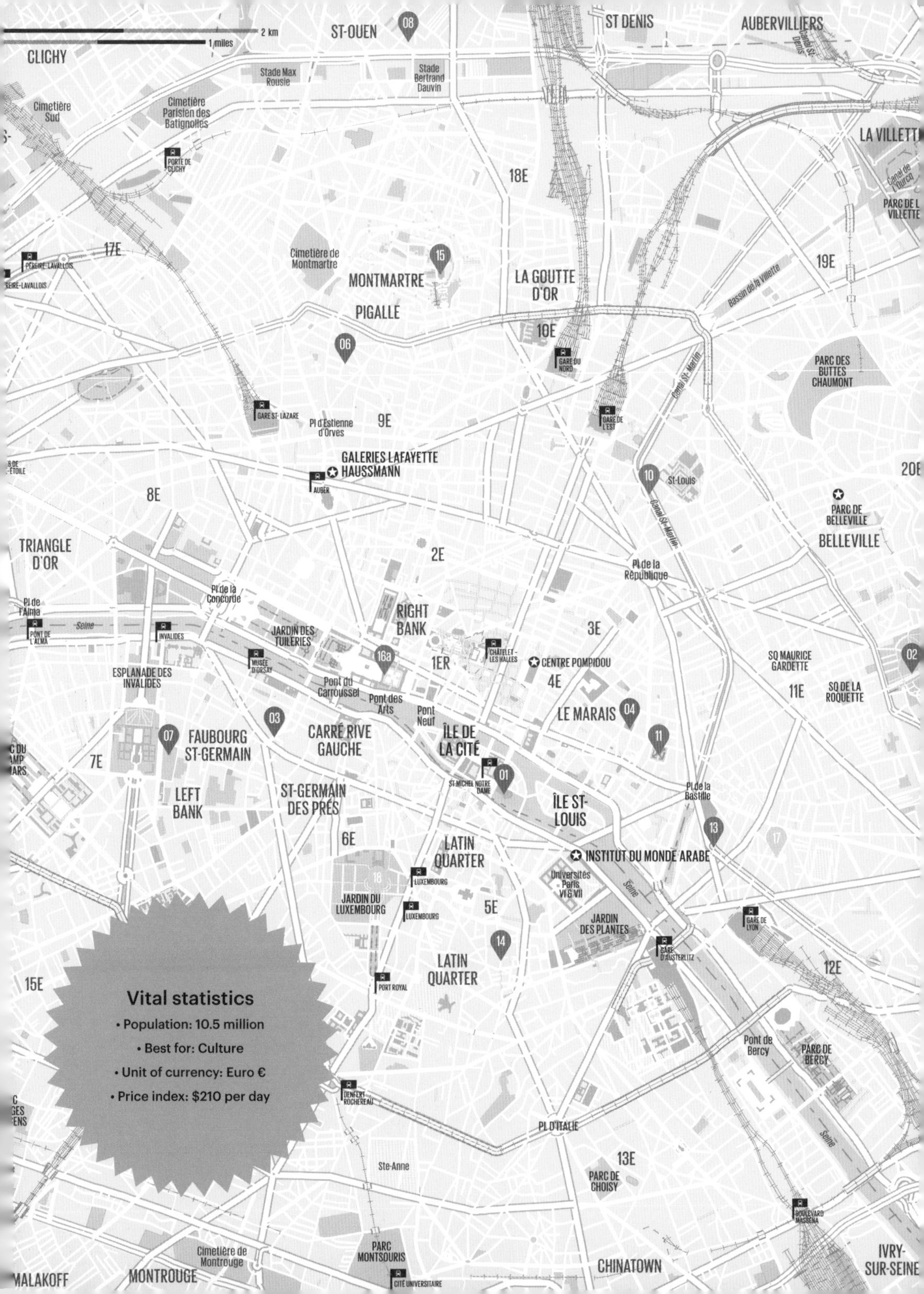

Vital statistics

- Population: 10.5 million
- Best for: Culture
- Unit of currency: Euro €
- Price index: $210 per day

03 Deyrolle

This taxidermy shop dating from 1831 is a veritable museum of natural history. See animals exotic and familiar, great and small, incredibly lifelike and artistically posed (all from zoos, circuses or farms, naturally deceased). And all for sale. If you can't fit a recumbent tiger into your luggage (or budget), pick up a beautifully illustrated vintage poster or a gorgeous arrangement of exotic bugs. *www.deyrolle.com; 46 rue du Bac, 6e; 10am-1pm & 2-7pm Mon, 10am-7pm Tue-Sat; admission free.*

04 Musée Carnavalet

One of the best reasons to visit this museum of Parisian history is its gorgeous setting in two 16th-century *hôtels particuliers*, lavish townhouses built by noblemen of Le Marais. Among its fascinating artefacts and artworks highlights are the painstakingly reconstructed *fin-de-siècle* drawing rooms and baroque interiors, vivid glimpses into how the other half lived in the Paris of the past. *carnavalet.paris.fr; 23 rue de Sévigné, 3e; 10am-6pm Tue-Sun; free.*

05 Musée d'Art Moderne de la Ville de Paris

The beauty of Paris' lesser-known museums: incredible art without the queues. This is among the best, with an outstanding permanent collection of 20th-century artworks, and art-deco furniture and objects. Standouts are Raoul Dufy's *La Fée Electricité* – a room-sized mural depicting the discovery of electricity – Matisse's *La Danse* and a collection of Robert Delaunay's masterpieces. *mam.paris.fr; 11 av du Président Wilson, 16e; 10am-6pm Tue-Wed & Fri-Sun, 10am-10pm Thu; free.*

FANTASTIC FREE VIEWS

Looking out over the City of Lights as night falls: priceless. Montmartre may be a top spot, but it is crowded and you'll get more peaceful vistas from the top of Parc de Belleville. The view along the Seine from the terrace of the Institut du Monde Arabe (www.imarabe.org; 1 place Mohammed V, 5e; 10am-6pm Tue-Thu, 10am-9.30pm Fri, 10am-7pm Sat + Sun) is one of the best of Notre Dame, and costs only a cup of coffee. The top-floor terrace at Galeries Lafayette (haussmann.galerieslafayette.com; 40 blvd Haussmann, 9e; 9.30am-8pm Mon-Sat, 9.30am-9pm Thu) looks out over Opéra Garnier and the Grands Blvds. ***Free.***

06 Musée de la Vie Romantique

Walk through the paved courtyard of this 1830 *hôtel particulier* (grand townhouse) and into the artistic life of 19th-century Paris. Chopin, Delacroix, Ingres, Liszt and others frequented Ary Scheffer's Friday-night salons here. The museum features his works and the memorabilia of neighbour George Sand. The artist's workshops, garden and tearoom are beyond charming, then wander around the surrounding *quartier* of Nouvelle Athènes. *vie-romantique.paris.fr; 16 rue Chaptal, 9e; 10am-6pm Tue-Sun; free.*

07 Musée Rodin's garden

It's well worth the museum's admission price (€7) to see the collection of France's greatest modern sculptor. If strapped for cash, however, you can access just the gardens where some of his most celebrated sculptures – *The Thinker, The Burghers of Calais* and others – are dotted throughout the grounds of the 18th-century mansion where Rodin lived and worked. *musee-rodin.fr; 79 rue de Varenne, 7e; 10am-5.45pm Tue & Thu-Sun; €2.*

08 Browse at Marché Paul Bert

The Marché aux Puces (flea market) de St-Ouen, a sprawling complex of interconnected markets, provides many free hours of entertainment. The standout Marché Paul Bert is more museum than shop (with prices to match). Fans of mid-century interior design will be in heaven, but antiques also abound – expect mounted zebra heads and lots of gilt. *marcheauxpuces-saintouen.com; 96 rue Paul Bert, Saint-Ouen; 9am-6pm Sat, 10am-6pm Sun, 11am-5pm Mon; admission free.*

09 Château de Versailles' gardens

While the château at Versailles is truly extraordinary, the crush of people inside can be hard to bear. But the landscaped gardens – meticulously manicured, dotted with elegant statuary and exuberant fountains, and criss-crossed with paths (bikes can be rented) – are divine and free for half the year. Pack a picnic and distance those madding crowds. *chateauversailles.fr; Versailles; 7am-8.30pm; free Nov-Mar, charge Tue, Sat & Sun Apr-Oct.*

10 Chill at Canal St-Martin

You might recognise the iron footbridges and tree-lined quays from the film *Amélie*. From République to Gare du Nord, the canal is *bobo-* (bohemian-bourgeoisie) central – gentrified but a little scruffy, home to the latest hot new neo-bistro or be-seen cocktail bar. You'll find the locals on the banks enjoying an *apéro* or in full picnic mode with blankets,

FIRST SUNDAYS OF THE MONTH

Many of Paris' top museums are free on the first Sunday of every month: Centre Pompidou (centrepompidou.fr; place Georges Pompidou, 4e; 11am-9pm), Musée d'Orsay (musee-orsay.fr; 62 rue de Lille, 7e; 9.30am-6pm), Musée Rodin (p145), Musée de l'Orangerie (musee-orangerie.fr; Jardin des Tuileries, 1er; 9am-6pm) –to name just a few. Other big sights like the Louvre (louvre.fr; rue de Rivoli, 1er; 9am-6pm), Arc de Triomphe (monuments-nationaux.fr; place Charles de Gaulle, 8e; 10am-11pm Apr-Sep, 10am-10.30pm Oct-Mar) and Château de Versailles (chateauversailles.fr; 9am-6pm Apr-Oct, 9am-5.30pm Nov-Mar) are free only some months. For the full list, see parisinfo.com.

baguettes and fabulous French cheese. Join them. *10e; 24hr; free.*

11 Le Marais on a Sunday

This most strollable of *quartiers* comes into its own on *le weekend*, when the streets are traffic-free. Drift along medieval lanes crammed with Renaissance mansions, quirky boutiques, hip cafes, hidden squares and charming restaurants. Don't miss postage-stamp-size **Place des Vosges** or the old Jewish quarter around rue des Rosiers, where you can nab a bargain lunch at **L'As du Fallafel** *(noon-midnight Sun-Thu, noon-5pm Fri; takeaway dishes €5.50-8.50). 4e; 24hr;* free.

12 Ogle the Eiffel Tower

Perched on the bank of the Seine, this most iconic of structures makes a dramatic climax to a riverside stroll – no entry fee required. You can picnic or play *pétanque* in the **Champ de Mars**, the huge park at its foot, and if you're lucky enough to be here on 14 July you're in for the best (free) fireworks display of your life. *Champ de Mars, 7e; 24hr; free.*

13 Promenade Plantée

The inspiration for New York's High Line, this elevated park built on a 19th-century railway viaduct is an unexpected green space floating above eastern Paris. Starting just east of Opéra Bastille in the hip and *non*-nonsense 12e, it unfolds to provide a quite otherworldly urban adventure. Following the full 4.5km takes you to the very edge of central Paris. *12e; 8am-5.30pm Mon-Fri, 9am-5.30pm Sat + Sun winter, 9am-9.30pm summer; free.*

14 Rue Mouffetard

This legendary Latin-Quarter street, one of Paris' oldest, has a gritty glamour. The backyard of **Sorbonne University**, epicentre of intellectuals and revolutionaries, it became the *quartier*

of Hemingway, Joyce and literary lions who flocked here post-WWI. Visit in the morning, when it's a lively neighbourhood market, and relax on a *terrasse* at **Place de la Contrescarpe** – one of Paris' loveliest squares. *Rue Mouffetard, 5e; 24hr; free.*

15 Streets of Montmartre

Visitors flock here for the neo-Byzantine excess of **Sacré-Cœur basilica**, the spectacular views over Paris, or maybe to get their portrait painted by a Picasso-wannabe on **Place du Tertre**. But if you venture just a few streets beyond the crowds of selfie-stick-toting tourists, you'll discover village Montmartre, dotted with shady squares, art-nouveau water fountains and relics of its fabled artistic past – perhaps even a genuine Parisian. *18e; 24hr; free.*

16 Walk from the Louvre to the Arc de Triomphe

This promenade is supercharged with historic sights. From the **Louvre** (16a; rue de Rivoli, 1er) it's an arrow-straight march through the landscaped **Jardin des Tuileries**, the vast **Place de la Concorde** (home of the guillotine during the Reign of Terror) and down the **Champs-Élysées** to Napleon I's **Arc de Triomphe** (16b). So many sights of such magnificence packed into such a small area – Paris at its monumental best. *1er–8e; 24hr; free.*

17 Marché d'Aligre

Browsing is free at this lively market, though if you go at lunchtime you're bound to splurge. From *fruits de mer* to *fromage* and everything in between, it offers hours of delicious entertainment and colourful photo opportunities. For the best-value blowout in town, hit nearby **Le Baron Rouge** *(1 rue Théophile Roussel, 12; 10am-2pm & 5-10pm Tue-Fri, 10am-10pm Sat, 10am-4pm Sun). marchedaligre.free.fr; rue d'Aligre, 12e; 8am-1pm & 4-7.30pm Tue-Sat, 8am-1.30pm Sun; admission free.*

18 Picnic in Jardin du Luxembourg

With its Renaissance gardens, impressive statuary and status as the home of France's Senate, Jardin du Luxembourg is Paris' grandest public park. But for all that magnificence, it gives a warm welcome. Everyone is here – joggers, kids sailing boats on the pond, *pétanque-players*, bookworms enjoying the comfy seating. The people-watching is truly top-notch. Pack a basket and enjoy the most glamorous picnic of your life. *Rue de Vaugirard, 6e; hours vary seasonally; free.*

BROCANTES AND VIDE-GRENIERS

Every weekend, ephemeral little neighbourhood markets pop up all over Paris. For *vide-greniers* (literally, 'empty attics'), entire streets close to traffic so residents can put their unwanted wares on show for a crowd of eager rummagers. It's a yard sale Paris-style, with a festival atmosphere, live music (sometimes) and plenty of food (always). *Brocantes* are more formal affairs, with official antique-sellers setting up displays of lovely precious old things in covered markets – heaven for browsers. You can find a daily agenda for both at brocabrac.fr. *Admission free.*

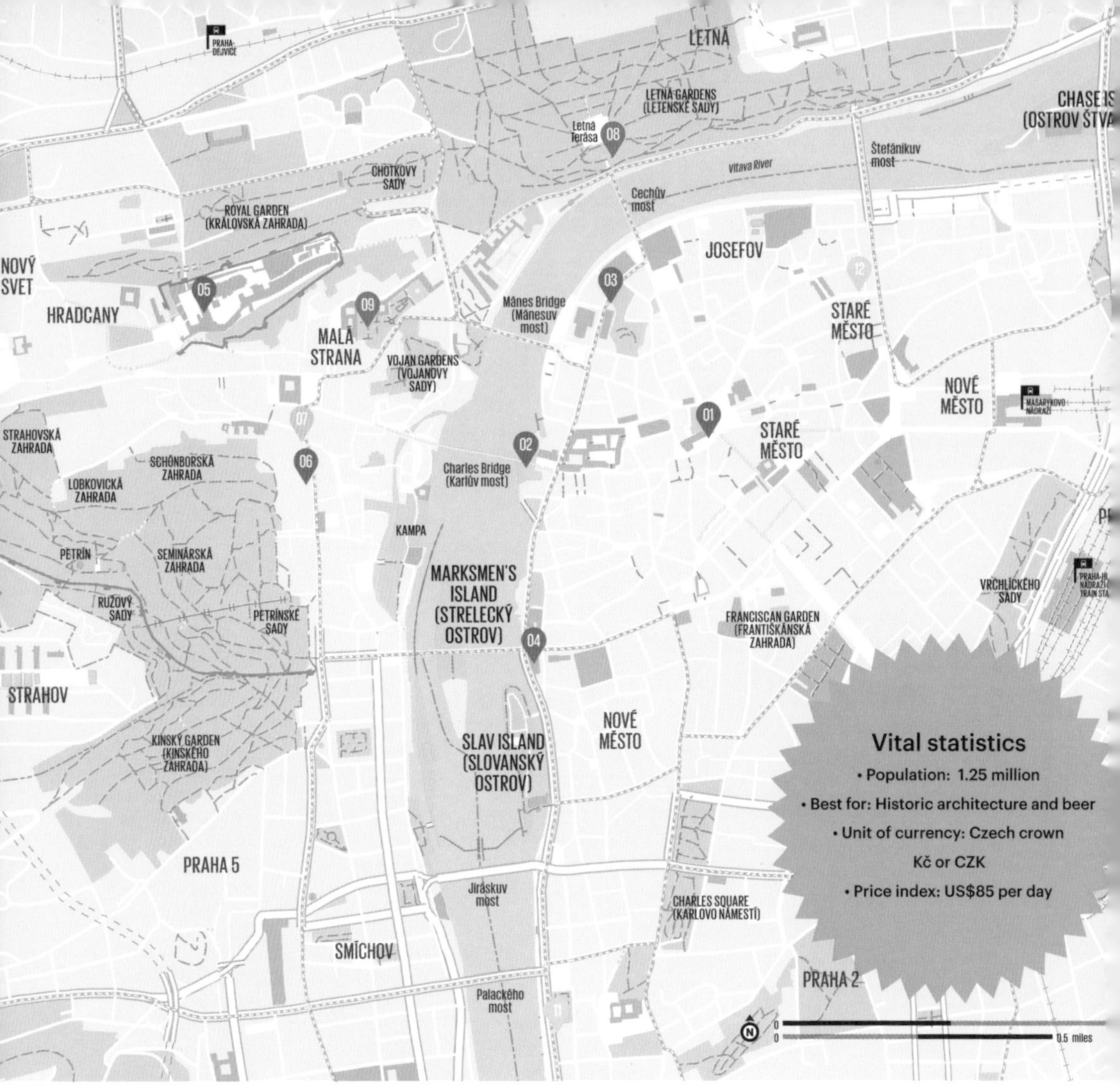

PRAGUE

A quarter of a century after the fall of communism, Prague has emerged as the star of Central Europe. Visitors are lured by the magnificent 14th-century cityscape but end up charmed by the cultural offerings, freewheeling vibe and cheap beer. Prices are still far lower than those of Western Europe.

ARTS & CULTURE MUSIC & FILM SPORTS & LEISURE FOOD & DRINK FESTIVALS & EVENTS

01 Astronomical Clock

Prague's most famous piece of performance art is actually people-free; it's a procession of mechanised marionettes that wow the crowds on the hour from the face of a 600-year-old Astronomical Clock. The ghoulish figures (a skeleton, for one, strikes the hour) are straight out of the Middles Ages. Arrive a few minutes early to secure prime photo-taking real estate. *orloj.eu; Staroměstské náměstí; 9am-9pm; free.*

02 Charles Bridge

It's a no-brainer, but the number-one sight – a 650-year-old Gothic bridge crowned by 30 baroque statues – is free to cross. Shoot for early morning, when the crowds are thinner, and return at night, when the lights, spires and castle combine to magical effect. The tower on the eastern side offers a photo-op worthy of 100 Instagram likes. *muzeumprahy.cz; Karlův most; bridge 24hr, tower 10am-10pm Apr-Sep, 10am-6pm Oct-Mar; tower 90Kč.*

03 Glimpse the Old Jewish Cemetery

Prague's Jewish Museum comprises four historic synagogues and a highly moving burial ground dating from the 15th century that's crammed with hundreds of snaggle-tooth tombstones. It's a must-see destination, but the 300Kč combined-entry ticket can be a budget-buster. It's possible, though, to glimpse the sombre grave-markers for free through a small window on the cemetery's western wall. *jewishmuseum.cz; next to ul 17. Listopadu 2; 24hr; free.*

04 National Theatre

The National Theatre (Národní divadlo) is Prague's most important stage for drama, opera and dance. The best seats in the house are decent value and top out at around 1000Kč for front and centre, but upper-deck and standing-room seats are a steal for what's on offer. Buy tickets at the venue's box office. *narodni-divadlo.cz; Národní třída 4; performances from 7pm; standing-room tickets 110Kč.*

05 Prague Castle

Unforgettably grandiose, Prague castle (Pražský hrad) lords it over the city. Exploring the buildings, including St Vitus Cathedral, can take half a day or longer and cost upwards of 250Kč. The grounds, though, are free and open to the public. Picturesque Golden Lane (Zlatá ulička), a row of miniature houses, is free after 6pm. *hrad.cz; Hradčanské náměstí; 1; grounds 5am-midnight Apr-Oct, 6am-11pm Nov-Mar; grounds free.*

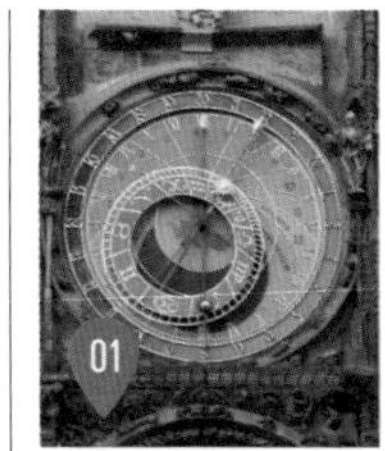
01

03

06

02

PRAGUE

06 **The Infant Jesus of Prague**

This remarkable little wax doll ensconced at the Carmelite Church of Our Lady Victorious in the Malá Strana quarter has been an object of pilgrimage for the Catholic faithful for four centuries. It continues to draw a stream of admirers, and no wonder: the 'infant' is credited with protecting the city from plague, and the destruction of the Thirty Years' War. *pragjesu.cz; Karmelitská 9; 8.30am-7pm Mon-Sat, 8.30am-8pm Sun; free.*

07 **Open Mic at Little Glen's**

There are loads of jazz clubs around town and the level of playing is high. One of the best is Little Glen's (U Malého Glena), named after the club's diminutive expat owner. There's live jazz (for a cover) nightly through the week, but Sundays are special. Local musicians drop by, instruments in hand, for an anything-goes free jam. Come early to grab a seat. *malyglen.cz; Karmelitská 23; from 7.30pm, shows start at 9pm; 150Kč cover, free Sun.*

08 **Letná Gardens**

The Czech capital is known as the 'City of a Hundred Spires' and there's no better place to count them than atop Letná, a long-running ridge of green across the Vltava River north of Old Town. Cross the river at *Čechův* Bridge, climb to a metronome, then walk east or west for breathtaking views. In summer, there's a popular beer garden on the park's eastern edge. *letenskyzamecek.cz; Letenské sady; 24hr; free.*

09 **Wallenstein Gardens**

The stately neighbourhood of Malá Strana is known for its baroque palaces and hidden gardens. The grandest of them all may be the Wallenstein

GETTING AROUND

Walk, walk, walk. Prague's central core is tiny and easily manageable on foot. Indeed, many streets are closed to traffic, and shoe leather may be your only option. For covering longer distances, public transport is cheap and efficient. A 110Kč day pass buys unlimited travel on all trams, metros and buses for 24 hours. Avoid hailing taxis from the street. Cabs are relatively inexpensive, but rogue drivers abound. Instead, ask someone to order a driver for you from a reliable radio-taxi outfit.

Gardens (Valdštejnská zahrada), hidden behind a palace that houses the Czech Senate. Peacocks roam the manicured lawns, and can be glimpsed darting between statues and ponds. A creepy cave wall (grotto) lines the gardens' eastern edge. *www.senat.cz; Letenská; 7.30am-6pm Mon-Fri, 10am-6pm Sat & Sun Mar-Oct, 10am-7pm Jun-Sep; free.*

Beer

A shoo-in for a book on cheap stuff, Czech beer, considered to be among the world's finest, remains Prague's best-value proposition. Normally priced at under 50Kč per half litre, it's cheaper than water and, according to a Czech proverb at least, better for health and attitude. National brewer Pilsner-Urquell remains the gold standard, though quality is high across the board, and there's a budding microbrewing scene to boot. *Bars across the city.*

11 Náplavka Farmers' Market

Prague's favourite farmers' market couldn't have a more picturesque setting: the eastern bank of the Vltava River below the National Theatre. On Saturdays, farmers sell fresh fruit and veg, meats and cheeses. On summer evenings, half the city comes to dangle legs over the water and drink a beer. *farmarsketrziste.cz; Rašínovo nábřeží (nr Palackého náměstí); market 8am-2pm Sat; free.*

12 Lunch at Sisters

Czechs love chlebíčky (open-faced sandwiches), which make for a cheap and filling lunch. You'll find these normally modest slabs of white bread covered with sliced devilled egg or ham at bakeries and butcher's shops. Sisters, however, has taken it to an art form, mixing standard varieties with novelties like herring and wasabi mayo or red beet and mackerel. *chlebicky-praha.cz; Dlouhá 39; 9am-7pm Mon-Fri, 9am-4pm Sat; sandwiches around 35Kč.*

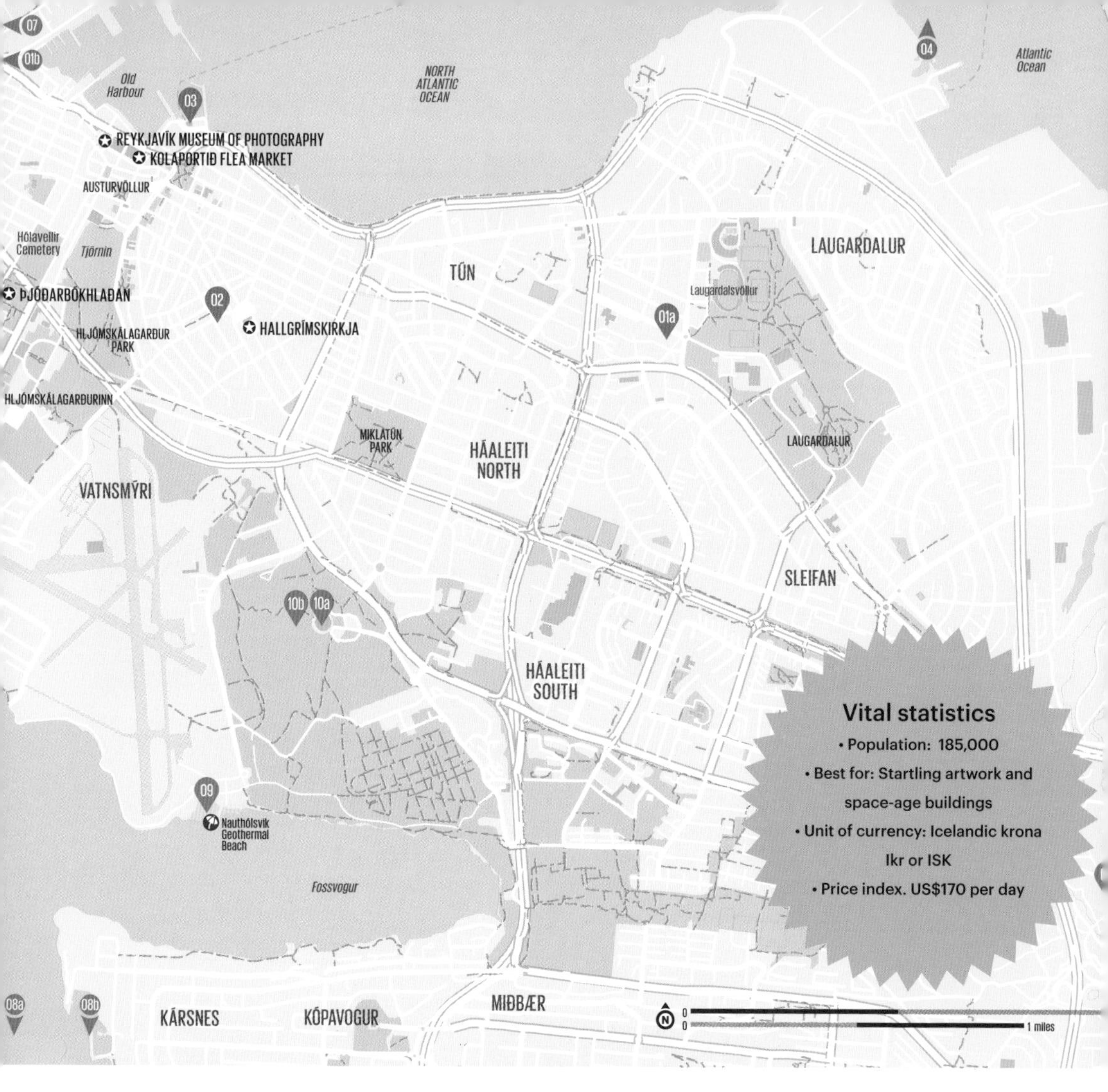

Vital statistics

- Population: 185,000
- Best for: Startling artwork and space-age buildings
- Unit of currency: Icelandic krona Ikr or ISK
- Price index. US$170 per day

REYKJAVÍK

The world's most northerly capital teeters on the top of the globe, presiding over a land of ice and fire. People visit to experience an utterly unique destination – there's no passing trade and Reykjavík doesn't need to tempt with bargains – but intrepid travellers will still unearth treasure aplenty.

 ARTS & CULTURE MUSIC & FILM  SPORTS & LEISURE  FOOD & DRINK  FESTIVALS & EVENTS

01 Ásmundur Sveinsson Sculpture Garden

The former home (1a) of Icelandic sculptor Ásmundur Sveinsson is surrounded by the artist's abstract creations, which are viewable at any time, without paying for the museum (Ikr1200). Sveinsson was inspired by Iceland's landscape and folklore, and his figurative pieces include *Trollwoman*. Enjoy more of his work out in the open around Öskjuhlíð (p155), and outside Reykjavík's University of Iceland (1b; location of *Sæmundur and the Seal*). *artmuseum.is/asmundarsafn; Sigtún; 24hr; free.*

02 Einar Jónsson's Sculptures

Entry to the **Einar Jónsson Museum** costs (Ikr1000), but the garden is free and full of statues by Iceland's first famous sculptor, whose creations feature folkloric and mythological themes. Jónsson's sculptures roam around Reykjavík , with *Outlaws* found by Suðurgata cemetery, an effigy of Iceland's Viking discoverer Ingólfur Arnarson overlooking the harbour, and a statue of the country's independence hero Jón Sigurðsson in Austurvöllur Sq. *lej.is; Eiríksgata 3; 24hr; free.*

03 Harpa

With its waterfront location and gleaming glass-and-steel design, the angular Harpa concert hall and cultural centre is one seriously eye-grabbing piece of architecture. Only half-built when Iceland's economy started melting, its future looked doubtful, but construction eventually continued and Harpa opened in 2011. Tours cost (Ikr1500), but entry to the interior is free, and you might even catch a free show. *harpa.is; Austurbakka 2; 10am-6pm Mon-Fri, 11am-4pm Sat; free.*

04 The Imagine Peace Tower

Yoko Ono's tribute to John Lennon, the Friðarsúlan writes 'Imagine Peace' in 24 languages on clouds above Reykjavík for 61 days each year – 9 October (Lennon's birthday) to 8 December (when he was shot). The geo-thermally powered tower uses 15 searchlights and prisms to beam the hopeful message from a wishing well containing a million written wishes from dreamers around the world, which Ono collected during her *Wish Trees* project. *Viðey Island; Oct-Dec; free.*

05 Elliðaárdalur

An easily accessible but hidden green valley right in the midst of the city, the urban oasis of Elliðaárdalur is found in a fold between the suburbs of Árbær,

01

04

10

03

REYKJAVÍK

Breiðholt and Fossvogur. In its surprisingly bucolic embrace you can explore a forest, follow a river to a waterfall, pick wild berries and go salmon fishing, or just watch wild rabbits running free through the flowers. A perfect picnic spot if the weather is favourable. *24hr; free.*

06 Esja escapades

Azround 10km north of the city, 914m Mt Esja looms large. This imposing edifice is not actually a single mountain, but a range of volcanic peaks; climbing them is a local rite of passage and obligatory for view-hungry visitors. Accessible (if steep) 780m Þverfellshorn has the most clearly marked route and the trailhead is relatively easy to reach on public transport if you don't fancy hiking the whole way. *visitreykjavik.is/mount-esja; 24hr; free.*

07 Grótta Lighthouse

One of the city's most dramatic walks takes free-ranging explorers across a narrow corridor of land to the lighthouse at Grótta. This is an evocative spot, popular with locals, and if you get lucky it's an amazing place to behold the Aurora Borealis. Be sure to time your run right, though, because the footpath disappears when the tide comes in...Or take the number 11 bus to Lindargotu Rd. *Free.*

08 Hafnarfjörður

While most of Reykjavík's attractions charge, just down the road, Hafnarfjörður offers many freebies, including a museum (8a) housing a collection of antique children's toys. Hafnarfjörður is famous for its population of elves and dwarves (seriously). Seek out these and other hidden folk in the Hellisgerði Lava Park *(elfgarden.is; Elf Garden; 1-5pm Tue-Sun summer; free)*, where guided tours *(alfar.is;*

THE LOCAL'S VIEW

You can enjoy a good overview of Reykjavík´s multi-coloured roofscape from the tower of our iconic church, the Hallgrímskirkja, for Isk800. I recommend that you buy local specialities from food trolleys – like Icelandic meat soup, hot dogs, lobster or fish – and enjoy your meal in the beautiful free-access sculpture garden at the Einar Jónsson Museum (p153). I love cycling along the coastline, visiting black-sand beaches, lighthouses, hot springs and the harbour. Don't miss out on local ice cream, which Icelanders enjoy all year, or the hot and relaxing swimming pools scattered around town, which cost around Isk650 to access. – Brynja Ingólfsdóttir, urban planner

2.30pm Tue & Fri summer; 4500Isk) led by elf experts are available.

09 Nauthólsvík geo-thermal beach

Iceland isn't known as a beach destination, but outdoor swimming is surprisingly popular. The city has several thermally heated pools, but Nauthólsvík is the most eccentric option, and it's free. The sometimes snow-covered beach boasts a geo-thermally heated lagoon (15°C to 19°C) and hot tubs (30°C to 39°C), plus showers and changing rooms. Join locals swimming and playing volleyball. *nautholsvik.is; 10am–7pm mid-May–mid-Aug, 11am–1pm Mon-Fri & 11am–3pm mid-Aug–mid-May.*

10 Perlan

From its elevated position atop tree-covered Öskjuhlíð, the Perlan ('Pearl') brings a space-age element to Reykjavík's skyline. Perched on four giant tanks that hold the city's water supply, the great glass dome gently rotates like R2D2's head. Inside you'll find the **Saga Museum** *(sagamuseum.is; 10am-6pm; Isk2000)*, and the pricey **Perlan restaurant** *(perlan.is; 10am-late)* – but access to the balcony is free, and the views across the city are stunning.

11 City Walk

'Free' walking tours are ten a (discretionary) penny nowadays, but this one stands out for its independent and entertaining approach. Historian and Reykjavíkian Marteinn leads the basic City Walk (pay as you please) and a Pubcrawl (10pm-1am; Ikr1000), the cost of which is recouped with reduced-price drinks. Another option is Walk the Crash (2500Isk) with economic historian Magnús explaining Iceland's 2008

financial collapse and the pots-and-pans-revolution recovery. *citywalk.is.*

12 Menningarnótt

Every August, Reykjavík lets down its flaxen hair and celebrates Menningarnótt (Culture Night), which has become Iceland's biggest shindig. Most museums and galleries throw open their doors, pop-up shops and bars erupt, and dance parties, concerts, performances and contests (including the Reykjavík marathon) take place around town. The day ends with fireworks, and many locals open up their houses and invite in people for waffles and drinks. *menningarnott.is; Aug; free.*

EUROPE'S BEST TOURS BY PUBLIC TRANSPORT

Skip pricey tours – instead, embrace the trams, buses and boats that give a more authentic (and cheaper) perspective of a city.

TRAM 28 – LISBON, PORTUGAL

Clatter into Lisbon's steep, tight-packed Alfama aboard a classic yellow tram. The Remodelado streetcars (designed in the 1930s) that work route 28 are the best way to get into the district's medieval alleys, although they can get packed so go early. *Single €2.85, day pass €6.*

TRAM NUMBER 2 – BUDAPEST, HUNGARY

Trundle alongside the Danube, with views up to the spires and turrets of Castle Hill, the Jewish Memorial (sculpted shoes on the riverbank) and grandiose parliament. *Single 350Ft, day pass 1650HUF.*

BOSPHORUS FERRY – İSTANBUL, TURKEY

Travel between Europe and Asia for less than an English pound? Ferries crossing the Bosphorus strait do just that, linking both sides of this continent-straddling city. Sail at sunset to see the minaret-pierced skyline in silhouette. *Single 4TL.*

BATEAU BUS – MONTE CARLO, MONACO

Monte Carlo's electric-powered ferry boats offer a smidgen of water-borne glitz in this razzmatazz harbour. They might not be billion-dollar yachts, but they offer the same views, and leave you with change to spunk at the casino. *Single €2.*

KUSTTRAM – BELGIUM

The 'Coast Tram' skirts Belgium's North Sea shoreline – 68km, from De to Knokke-Heist. Some 68 stops dot the route, enabling a bargain Belgian beach adventure. *Single €3, day pass €5, week pass €20.*

TRANSPORT CARD – GENEVA, SWITZERLAND

Pretty but pricey Geneva can make the impecunious weep. To ease the blow, the city will do you a deal: stay overnight and get a free Geneva Transport Card, covering travel on buses, trams and taxi-boats. *Free.*

MERSEY FERRY – LIVERPOOL, ENGLAND

Hop aboard Europe's oldest ferry service on the 10-minute Seacombe-Pier Head commute, and as the Royal Liver Building's twin towers inch closer, just try to stop yourself bursting into song... *7.20-9.40am, 5-6.40pm Mon-Fri; single £2.50, return £3.*

NUMBER 11 BUS – LONDON, ENGLAND

Ride a regular bus for a squeezed-in-with-the-natives view of the metropolis. Route 11 runs from Fulham to Liverpool Street Station via Chelsea, the Houses of Parliament, Trafalgar Square, St Paul's Cathedral and the Bank of England. *Single £1.50, day pass £5.*

VAPORETTO – VENICE, ITALY

You'll have to forgo the crooning gondolier, but opting for a public vaporetto (water taxi) instead of a private punt will save big bucks, while still offering views of Venice from water level. *Single €7.50, day pass €20.*

Illustration | Owen Gatley

 ARTS & CULTURE  MUSIC & FILM  SPORTS & LEISURE  FOOD & DRINK FESTIVALS & EVENTS

ROME

Rome can be relatively inexpensive for a European capital. The city has free-access ancient historical sites every few blocks (almost all within walking distance), and there's no shame in eating a delectable slice of €3 pizza every night. Museums aren't free, but you could spend all day in just one.

01 Archbasilica of St John Lateran

St Peter's gets most of the fame, but the Archbasilica of St John Lateran is as visually stunning as it is historically fascinating. Built in the 4th century AD, the cathedral survived the Visigoths, the Vandals, an earthquake in the Middle Ages, and several fires. The massive bronze doors are straight from the 2nd century AD Roman Senate. *Piazza di San Giovanni in Laterano 4; 7am-7pm, 7am-6pm in winter; free.*

02 Free Sundays

On the first Sunday of each month there is free access to the **Colosseum** (2a; romancolosseum.org; Piazza del Colosseo; 8.30am-1hr before sunset), **Palatine Hill** (2b; Via di San Gregorio 30 & Via Sacra; 8.30am-1hr before dusk) and the **Roman Forum** (2c; Largo della Salara Vecchia & Via Sacra ; 8.30am-1hr before dusk). Take heed: you are not the only who knows this... *Arrive by 8am for an early spot in the lengthy queue.*

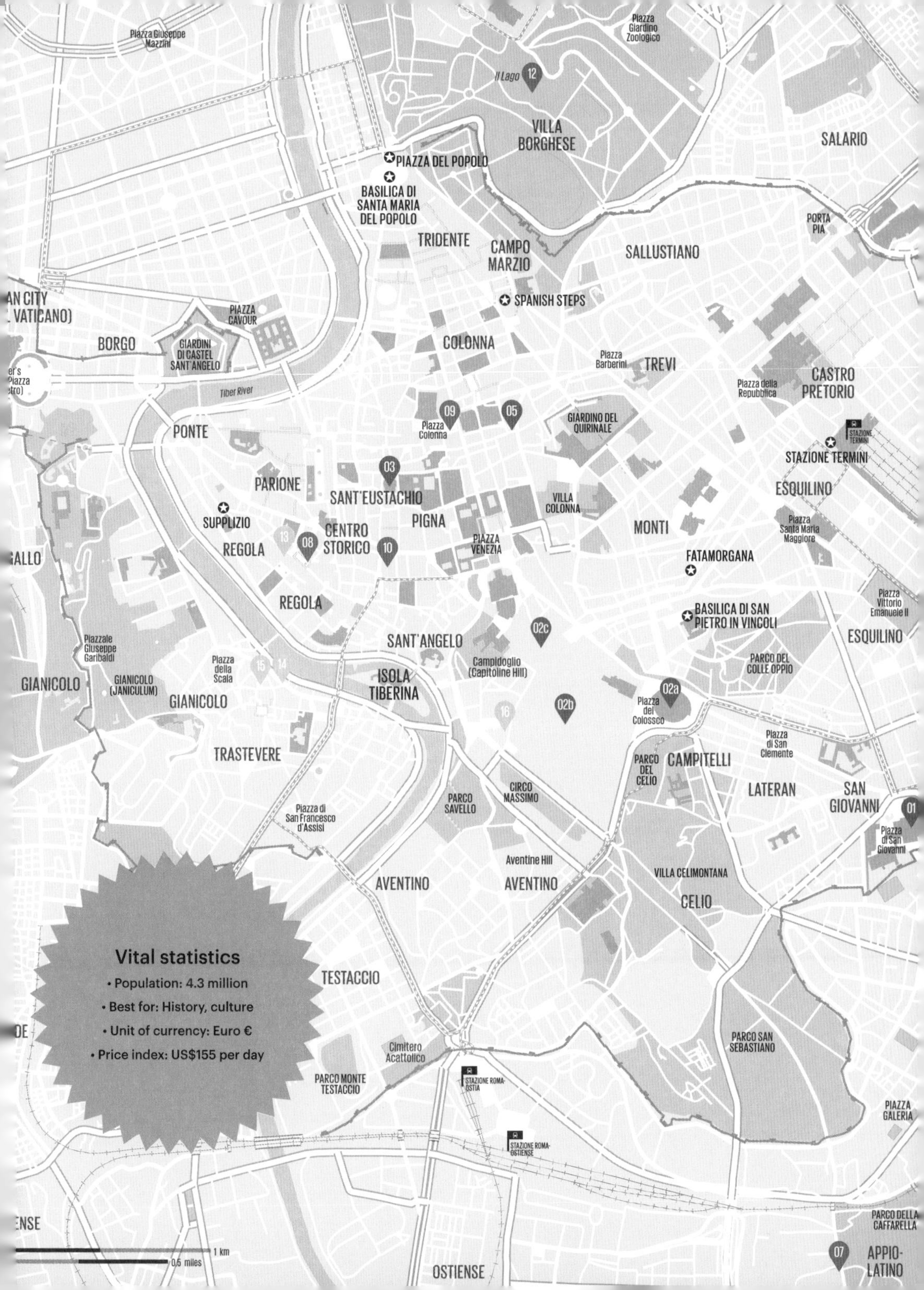

Vital statistics
• Population: 4.3 million
• Best for: History, culture
• Unit of currency: Euro €
• Price index: US$155 per day
PIAZZA DEL POPOLO
BASILICA DI SANTA MARIA DEL POPOLO
VILLA BORGHESE
Il Lago
TRIDENTE
CAMPO MARZIO
SALLUSTIANO
SALARIO
PORTA PIA
SPANISH STEPS
PIAZZA CAVOUR
BORGO
GIARDINI DI CASTEL SANT'ANGELO
Tiber River
COLONNA
Piazza Barberini
TREVI
Piazza della Repubblica
CASTRO PRETORIO
Piazza Colonna
GIARDINO DEL QUIRINALE
STAZIONE TERMINI
PONTE
PARIONE
SANT'EUSTACHIO
PIGNA
VILLA COLONNA
ESQUILINO
SUPPLIZIO
CENTRO STORICO
REGOLA
PIAZZA VENEZIA
MONTI
Piazza Santa Maria Maggiore
FATAMORGANA
BASILICA DI SAN PIETRO IN VINCOLI
Piazza Vittorio Emanuele II
Piazzale Giuseppe Garibaldi
SANT'ANGELO
Campidoglio (Capitoline Hill)
PARCO DEL COLLE OPPIO
GIANICOLO
GIANICOLO (JANICULUM)
Piazza della Scala
ISOLA TIBERINA
Piazza del Colosseo
TRASTEVERE
Piazza di San Clemente
PARCO DEL CELIO
CAMPITELLI
LATERAN
SAN GIOVANNI
Piazza di San Giovanni
PARCO SAVELLO
CIRCO MASSIMO
Piazza di San Francesco d'Assisi
Aventine Hill
AVENTINO
VILLA CELIMONTANA
CELIO
TESTACCIO
PARCO SAN SEBASTIANO
Cimitero Acattolico
PARCO MONTE TESTACCIO
STAZIONE ROMA-OSTIA
STAZIONE ROMA-OSTIENSE
PIAZZA GALERIA
PARCO DELLA CAFFARELLA
APPIO-LATINO
OSTIENSE
1 km
0.5 miles

03 Pantheon

Started during the reign of emperor Marcus Agrippa around 29 BC and reconstructed by more rulers up to AD 202, this grand circular building was used as a church in medieval Christianity. The unreinforced concrete dome is still the largest in the world, and watching the sun stream through the oculus and bounce off the surrounding marble is a near-mystical experience. *turismoroma.it/cosa-fare/pantheon; Piazza della Rotonda; 9am-7.30pm Mon-Sat, 9am-6pm Sun; free.*

04 St Peter's Basilica

Bramante, Bernini, Michelangelo – the list of artists, architects and sculptors who graced the basilica with their craft is long and mighty. While your wait to enter might be longer than the average opera, once you're inside the colossal interior watching light stream through the gilded dome on to the tomb of St Peter, you won't remember the delay. *St Peter's Sq, Vatican City; 7am-7pm summer, 7am-6pm winter; free.*

05 Trevi Fountain

Yes, you will encounter tourist hordes at the Fontana di Trevi, but go anyway. The over-the-top baroque fountain dates back to 1762 and was once the city's terminus for an ancient Roman aqueduct. Legend has it that if you throw a coin in the fountain over your left shoulder using your right hand, you are guaranteed to return to Rome once again. *Piazza di Trevi; 24hr; one tossed coin.*

06 Vatican Museums and Sistine Chapel

Ok, so these are bucket-list Rome destinations, but if you value your time or sanity more than saving on an entrance fee, do not go to the Vatican Museums

THE LOCAL'S VIEW

Try Roman street food such as a *suppli* (fried croquettes) at Supplizio (supplizio.net; Via dei Banchi Vecchi 143; noon-4pm Mon-Sat & 5.30-10pm Mon-Thu, 5.30-11pm Fri & Sat; *suppli* €3-5) or a gelato from a Fatamorgana (gelateria-fatamorgana.it; noon-midnight summer, noon-10.30pm winter; cones/tubs from €2). For free art, enter any church, such as Basilica di Santa Maria del Popolo (Piazza del Popolo; 7am-noon & 4-7pm Mon-Sat, 7.30am-1.30pm & 4.30-7.30pm Sun; free) and Basilica di San Pietro in Vincoli (Piazza di San Pietro in Vincoli 4a; 8am-12.20pm & 3-7pm summer, 3-6pm winter; free).
– Linda Martinez, owner, The Beehive Ho(s)tel

and Sistine Chapel on free Sundays. If you do, then be prepared to arrive early (about 7.30am) or spend two to three hours in line. *vatican.va; St Peter's Sq; 9am-6pm Mon-Sat, last entrance 4pm; free last Sun of month 9am-2pm.*

07 Appian Way

Ever driven on a highway? You can thank Rome and the Appian Way. While the world's first major roads were built to transport soldiers and wartime supplies in 312 BC, these days you'll find locals and tourists strolling under leafy trees. Plan to spend plenty of time here; you'll be passing by dozens of ancient sites, including several creepy burial catacombs (a small entrance fee). *Via Appia Antica; 24hr; free.*

08 Campo de' Fiori

Bring your evening *gelati* to the Campo de' Fiori, where you can sit at the base of the statue of Giordano Bruno and contemplate the existential changes in Rome, and the world. Four hundred years ago, the selfsame philosopher was publicly burned alive for heresy in this square, now filled with tourists and a street market. The vision of a medieval square filled with flowers is still divine. *24hr, free.*

09 Column of Marcus Aurelius

While partaking of your *passeggiata* (evening stroll) stop by the Column of Marcus Aurelius, the 1800-year-old Carrara marble victory statue that honours the former Roman Emperor and Stoic philosopher (and one of the only Roman emperors you'd ever want still governing). While there, tip your hat towards the Palazzo Chigi in the main square; it's the official home to the Prime Minister of Italy. *Piazza Colonna; 24hr; free.*

05

10 Largo di Torre Argentina

Et tu, kitties? Come see where Julius Caesar was assassinated in 44 BC. The sunken square is cordoned off to humans, but there's a feline free-for-all amidst the ruins. If you don't mind a flea or two, you can venture down below; the ruins house a cat sanctuary for the hundreds of stray cats who call the area home. *Via di Torre Argentina; ruins 24hr, cat sanctuary noon-6pm; free.*

11 *Passeggiata* like a local

The *passeggiata* (evening stroll) is the most Italian thing you could possibly do while in Rome. Break out your Gucci bag and Prada shoes and then amble arm-in-arm (or, these days, thumb-on-smartphone) along the fashionable Via del Corso all the way down to the Piazza del Popolo (People's Square). We highly recommend the very fashionable addition of a double-scoop *nocciola* (hazelnut) and *riso* (rice) *gelato. City-wide; early evenings; free.*

12 Villa Borghese gardens

Climb the Spanish Steps to enjoy the view, then escape the tourist chaos at the entrance to the Galleria Borghese art museum by doing as the Romans do: simply stroll through the Villa Borghese's manicured English-style gardens, row boats in the lake past a neo-classical temple, or have a picnic. *Entrances at Piazzale San Paolo del Brasile, Piazzale Flaminio, Via Pinciana, Via Raimondo & Largo Pablo Picasso; dawn-dusk; free.*

13 Forno Campo de' Fiori bakery

While at the Campo de' Fiori admiring the flowers and trying not to imagine a man on the stake, grab a slice of pizza or a piping-hot panino from the Forno Campo de' Fiori. A beloved establishment since 1819, the bakery and pizza-*forno* (oven) joint is the perfect spot to pick up a cheap, quick lunch. *fornocampodefiori.com; Vicolo del Gallo, 14; 7.30am-2.30pm & 4.45-8pm Mon-Sat; pizza slices from €3.*

14 Freni e Frizioni bar

Elegant but casual Freni e Frizioni is a fabulously hip bar in the heart of even hipper Trastevere. Once a mechanic's workshop (hence the name 'brakes and clutches'), it draws bright young things who like to spend a few hours outside in the piazza on a warm evening with friends sipping well-priced cocktails (€7) and nibbling *aperitivos* (€6 to €10, 7pm to 10pm). *freniefrizioni.com; Via del Politeama 4-6; 6.30pm-2am daily.*

15 La Renella restaurant

To stretch your legs and get a view of an utterly charming Roman neighbourhood filled with ancient houses, cobblestone streets and some of Rome's best nightlife, head to Trastevere. Compared to a sit-down meal at any Italian restaurant (average €25 for a full meal), La Renella is a steal. Better yet, it's open practically 24 hours. *Via del Moro 15-16; 7am-2am Tue-Sat, 7am-10pm Sun & Mon; pizza slices from €2.50.*

12

THRIFTY COMMUTING

Skip the overpriced bus tours and explore using public transport with a Roma 24h pass (valid for 24 hours on all bus, tram and metro lines, except for routes to Fiumicino airport; €7). Bus #40 goes from Stazione Termini (Piazza dei Cinquecento) to the Vatican by way of the Torre di Largo Argentina and Piazza Venezia. If you don't fancy hiking to the Villa Borghese Gardens from the Spanish Steps, hop on electric minibus #117. Buy tickets at *tabacchi* (newsstands) and vending machines at main bus stops and metro stations before you travel, and be sure to validate them.

ROME

TIP BOX

Dinner in a restaurant in Rome tends to be pricey, doesn't start until 8pm or later and lasts a looong time. With this in mind, it may be best (and cheaper) to have your main meal at lunchtime, when it is too hot to wander in comfort and anyway some attractions are closed. Take your time so you can properly digest the generally carb-heavy fare. Then, at night, you can grab a slice of pizza, find a lively piazza and finish off with some *gelato*. Or visit a bar with a happy hour and quite possibly a buffet or snacks.

16 **Mercato di Campagna Amica del Circo Massimo**

If Campo de' Fiori feels too touristy, head to this covered market to chat with the farmers and taste local olive oil or honey. Pick up some food and make for one of the many outdoor picnic tables or the nearby Circus Maximus, which despite its history as a grand arena is now a pleasant park. *mercatocircomassimo.it; Via di San Teodoro 74; 9am-6pm Sat, 9am-4pm Sun, closed Aug; admission free.*

17 **Estate Romana festival**

While many Romans leave the city in July and August, the folks who stay or come to visit are rewarded with the wonderful summertime music and art series, Estate Romana, when all of Rome explodes in arts and culture. You'll find outdoor movies, musical acts, street art, concerts and much more. *estateromana.comune.roma.it; check website and social media for updates on times/locations; Jun-Sep; many events free.*

04

08

ARTS & CULTURE MUSIC & FILM SPORTS & LEISURE FOOD & DRINK FESTIVALS & EVENTS

STOCKHOLM

Stockholm is known as style central. Everything here looks a million bucks – so it comes as no surprise that bargains can be hard to find. But they do exist! In fact, some of the city's most defining elements – highlights of its landscape and history – are absolutely free.

STOCKHOLM

01 Medeltidsmuseet

Almost hidden beneath the oldest stone bridge in the city, the Medieval Museum feels like a secret fortress. It was destined to become a parking lot, but excavation crews discovered a stretch of 16th-century city wall and a tunnel leading to the Royal Palace – which now form the core of the artfully displayed multimedia exhibits. *medeltidsmuseet.stockholm.se ; Strömparterren 3; noon-5pm Tue & Thu-Sun, noon-8pm Wed; free.*

02 Riksdagshuset

Take a guided tour of the Swedish Parliament building for an eye-opening lesson in consensus politics. Sweden is governed by 349 representatives of the public; guides explain how the system evolved and works. It's educational, oddly inspiring and much more fun than it sounds! *riksdagen.se; Riksgatan 3; 1hr English tours (max 28 people) noon, 1pm, 2pm & 3pm Mon-Fri late-Jun–Aug, 1.30pm Sat & Sun mid-Sep–late-Jun; free.*

03 Djurgården

One of the 14 islands across which the city is built, Djurgården was originally the royal hunting grounds. These days it consists mostly of quiet parks and leafy trails. The hilly, forested refuge is a mere footbridge away from downtown, and makes an ideal setting for a picnic and a restorative stroll. In warm weather, swim or sunbathe on its sandy beaches. *visitdjurgarden.se/sv/nationalstadsparken; Djurgårdsbron; 24hr; free.*

05

A BREAK FOR LUNCH

Dinner in upscale Stockholm restaurants can be prohibitively expensive, but most places have a daily lunch special at a set price that's typically much more reasonable – which means even budget travellers can try some of the best food in the city if you're willing to do so midday. Look for menus that describe the 'dagens lunch'. It's usually available Monday through Friday, changing daily, and includes salad, bread and coffee with the main dish, making it an affordable way to fill up and try some local specialities.

04 Söder cliffs and Katarina bridge

It's hard to beat the views that await you once you have tramped up the rickety wooden staircases just south of Slussen to the top of the Söder Hills. Take the walkway leading to the historic Katarina lift, then take Maria Trappgränd, a narrow stairway just east of Slussen leading up towards the 500m-long cottage-lined Monteliusvägen; this is also a good picnic area! *Slussen T-bana station; 24hr; free.*

05 Changing of the Guard

If you're in Old Town (Gamla Stan) around noon, you'll hear the drums and marching band that signal the Changing of the Palace Guard. It's a spectacle worth watching, as choreographed guards in uniform bark commands and march in formation. In summer there's usually a military parade leading to the ceremony. *stockholmgamlastan.se/lang_en/se_gora/hogvakten.php ; outer courtyard, Royal Palace; 12.15pm Mon-Sat, 1.15pm Sun in summer, Wed, Sat & Sun only Sep-Apr; free.*

06 Smaka på Stockholm

Sweden's capital is known for its restaurant scene, with boldly experimental chefs making imaginative use of locally sourced ingredients, but dining out tends to blow the budget. Instead of splurging on just one meal, why not instead sample bites from the region's best kitchens (and vineyards, distillers and breweries) at this annual festival of food and drink, held in central Kungsträdgården park. *smakapastockholm.se; Kungsträdgården; first week Jun; 11am-late; free.*

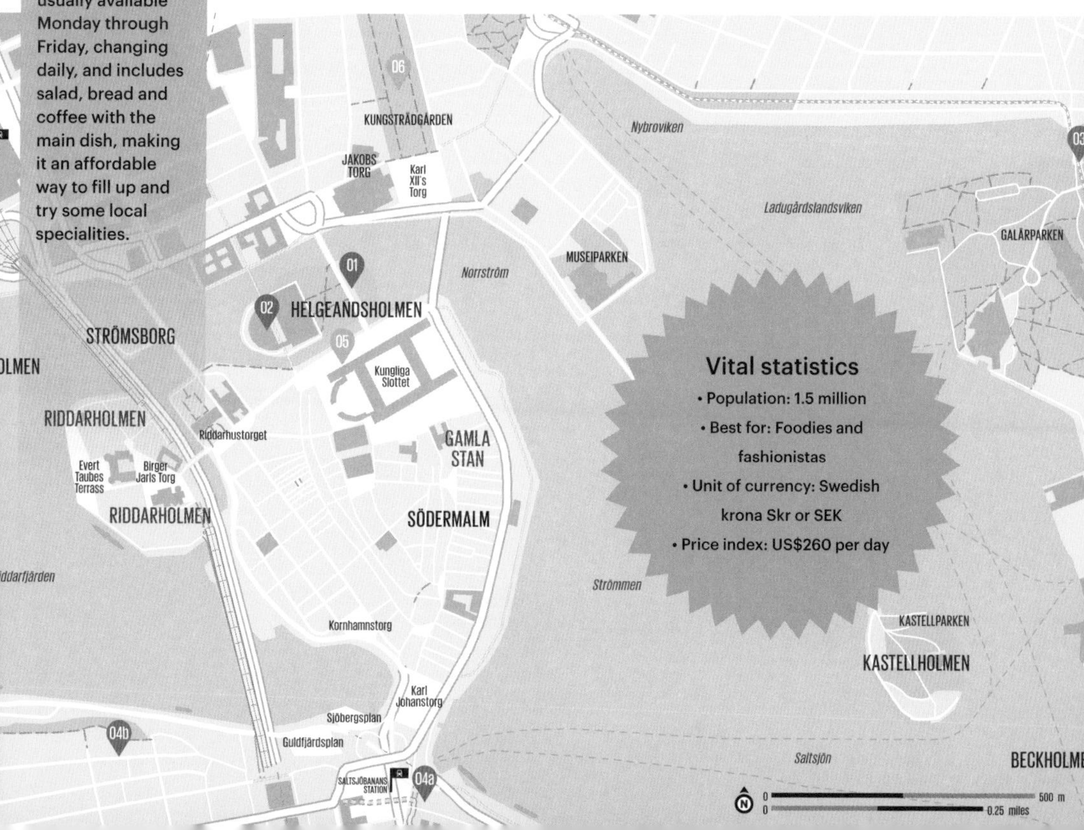

Vital statistics

- Population: 1.5 million
- Best for: Foodies and fashionistas
- Unit of currency: Swedish krona Skr or SEK
- Price index: US$260 per day

ARTS & CULTURE | MUSIC & FILM | SPORTS & LEISURE | FOOD & DRINK | FESTIVALS & EVENTS

VENICE

Venice is the playground of Europe's elite, with five-star hotels, five-course meals and velvet-padded gondolas. But savvy travellers know some of the finest moments are free: glimpses of St Mark's basilica are gratis; Carnival is most fun out on the streets and palaces look best reflected in the Grand Canal.

01 Basilica di San Marco

Venice's byzantine basilica is the apotheosis of the city's self-invention. It took 800 years to build and wrap the bones of St Mark the Evangelist in a golden carapace of mosaics. This is all yours for free, although you can skip the queue by pre-booking (€2). Free tours run at 11am Monday to Saturday (April to October). *basilicasanmarco.it; Piazza San Marco; 9.45am-4.45pm Mon-Sat, 2-5pm Sun summer, 2-4pm Sun winter; free.*

02 DIY architecture tour

While Venice is packed with museums, the real beauty of the city is the city itself: an architectural masterpiece of floating palaces in Istrian stone. Since the 7th century the city's signature flair has evolved into a dazzling composite of styles. Jump on *vaporetto* 1 (every 10 minutes, €7) for a zigzag cruise through a thousand years of history down the Grand Canal to San Marco and the Lido.

03 Isola di San Michele

Surrounded by a high wall and tall cypresses and presided over by Codussi's 1469 pearly white Renaissance church (the first Renaissance church in Venice), San Michele is Venice's island of the dead. Ezra Pound, Sergei Diaghilev and Igor Stravinsky all lie here and music-lovers and architecture buffs come to pay

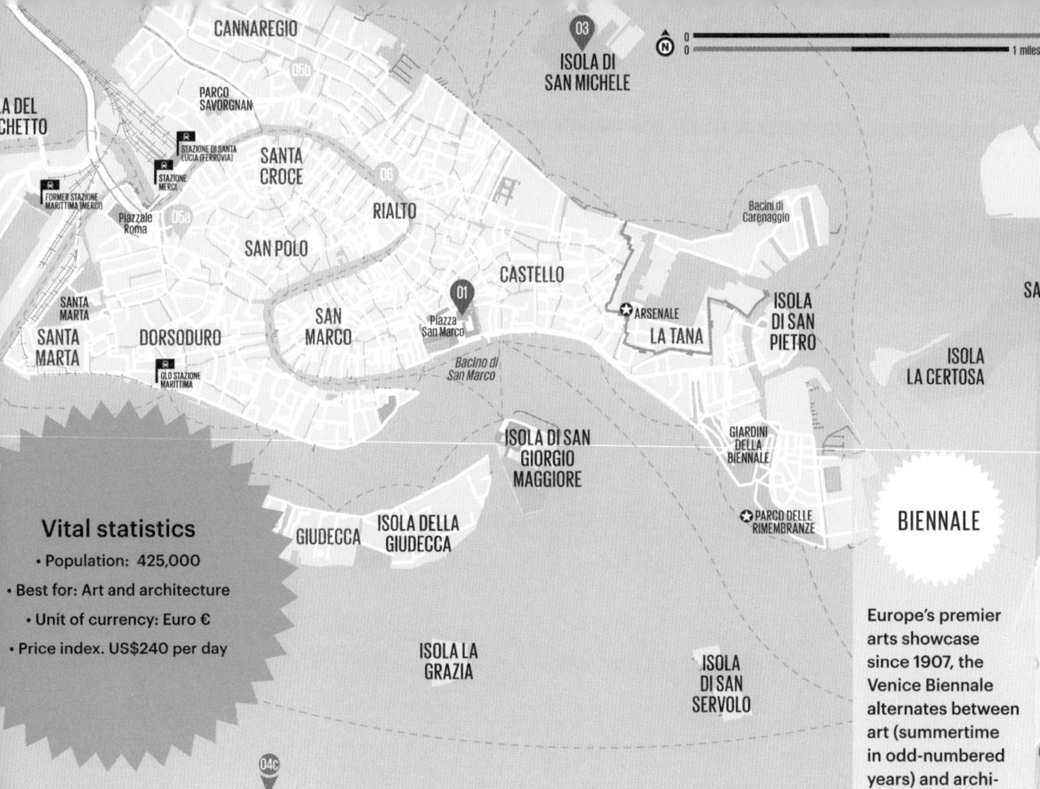

Vital statistics

- Population: 425,000
- Best for: Art and architecture
- Unit of currency: Euro €
- Price index. US$240 per day

their respects and admire the modernist extension and basalt-clad bunker built by David Chipperfield. *7.30am-6pm Apr-Sep, 7.30am-4pm Oct-Mar; free.*

04 Lido beaches

For centuries the bastion of the city, the Lido found a new lease of life in the 19th century as a bathing resort. For years it attracted the *bel mondo* and in September celebrities still flock here for the Film Festival. Mere mortals can make do with the Lido's three free beaches: the **Spiaggia Comunale** (4a), the **San Nicolò beach** (4b) and the **Alberoni** (4c), where Byron raced his horses in 1817. *24hr; free.*

05 Affordable happy hours

Tourists bewail the expense of eating well in this city, but Venetians know better. Instead they opt for *un'ombra* (a 'shade'; a small glass of wine), from as little as €0.60 at **Bacereto Da Lele** (5a; *Santa Croce 183; 6am-2pm, 4-8pm Mon-Fri; 6am-2pm Sat)* and **Cantina Aziende Agricole** (5b; Rio Tera Farsetti; 9am-1.30pm & 5-10pm Mon-Sat), and pair it with *cicheti*, the Venetian version of tapas *(€1 to €4 per plate).*

06 Rialto market

Serving the Empire for over 700 years, the Rialto market and *Pescaria* (fish market) are a part of Venice's living history. Sustainable fishing practices are nothing new in this fish emporium: marble plaques show regulations set centuries ago for the minimum allowable size for lagoon fish. Pay attention to the lagoon seafood here, and you'll better recognise authentic Venetian options on your dinner menu. *Rialto-Mercato, 7am-2pm Tue-Sun, free.*

BIENNALE

Europe's premier arts showcase since 1907, the Venice Biennale alternates between art (summertime in odd-numbered years) and architecture (autumn in even-numbered years). It draws some 300,000 visitors to view contemporary artworks in 30 national pavilions set in the gardens of the Giardini and architectural installations housed in the boat sheds of the Arsenale. While entry to the main event is costly (€30), a mushrooming fringe scene is free and offers access to hidden corners of the city usually out of bounds to the public. At the last count there were over 90 different events to explore. *labiennale.org; free.*

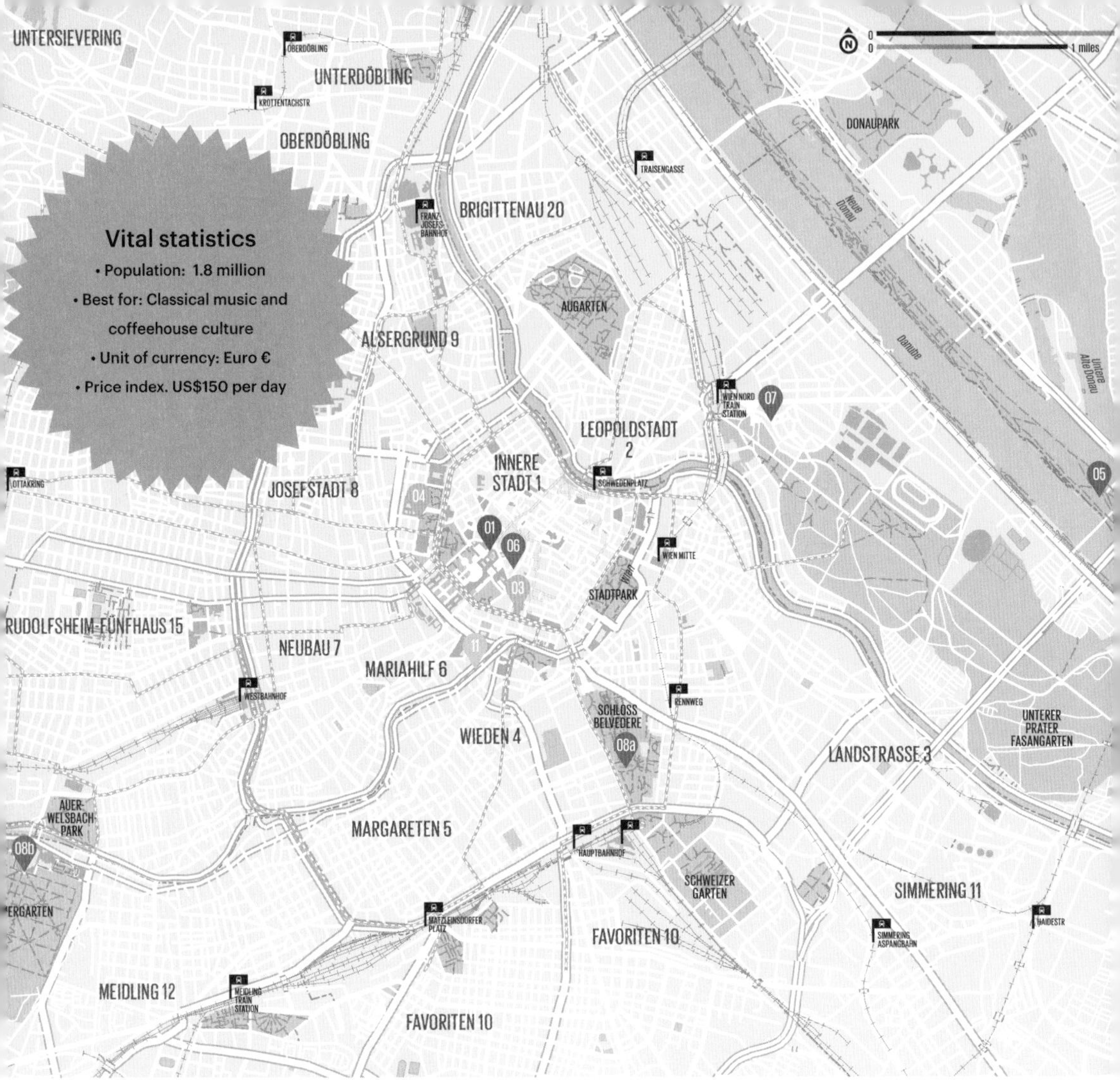

VIENNA

Vienna, with all of its imperial pomp and grandeur, might not seem like a city you can enjoy on a small budget. But dig a little and you'll find free classical concerts, splendid gardens and an historic coffeehouse culture you can enjoy using just the change in your pocket.

01 **Hofburg Imperial Palace**

Once home to the Habsburg rulers, the Hofburg Palace complex is the ultimate symbol of the former imperial power of Austria. Stroll between staggering architecture, a collection of museums, beautiful squares and imperial apartments, and try to imagine what went on at this playground of Austrian royalty. You're free to wander around but there are entrance fees if you want to explore the sights further. *hofburg-wien.at; Michaelerkuppel; 24hr; free.*

02 **Zentralfriedhof cemetery**

Hanging out in a cemetery mightn't seem the best way to spend a holiday, but the Zentralfriedhof is a fascinating place. Stretching over 2.4 sq km and home to roughly three million slumbering residents, this is one of the biggest graveyards in Europe. Stroll through the cemetery and pay respects to big names such as Beethoven, Brahms and Shubert. *Simmeringer Hauptstrasse 232-244; 7am-7pm Fri-Wed, 7am-8pm Thu; free.*

03 **State Opera**

You don't need to spend bucket-loads of cash to see an opera performance at Vienna's glorious State Opera. If you're willing to queue for around an hour and a half in advance, take standing-room seats (better for the circulation anyway) and partial views (it's more about listening than watching, really) then you can be treated to some world-class musical performances at a steal. *wiener-staatsoper.at; Opernring 2; standing-room tickets from €4.*

04 **Summer at Rathausplatz**

To sample the best of the freebies on offer in Vienna, time your trip for summer and make a beeline for the Rathausplatz (City Hall Square). Loads of free events fill up the square here on balmy nights, from free classical concerts and opera performances to food festivals, DJ line-ups and the granddaddy of them all, the immensely popular Musikfilm Festival (filmfestival-rathausplatz.at) – held in the square in July and August. *Free.*

05 **Donauinsel**

Created in 1970, Donauinsel (Danube Island) is the aquatic playground of the city and offers plenty of ways to cool off in summer, whether it's swimming, boating or stripping down to nothing! – parts of the island are designated FKK (Freikörperkultur; free body culture) zones for nudist bathers. If you prefer to keep your clothes on, take to the rollerskating or cycling paths that line the island. *wien.gv.at; Danube Island; 24hr; free.*

03

SAVE AT SAUSAGE STANDS

The city has a culinary scene to match any budget. Street food and markets are dotted around all over the city and your best bet for a 'loose change' meal is a ubiquitous *Würstelstand* (sausage stand). Choose from a range of top-quality sausages for your bread roll, such as a spicy *Debreziner* or a classic *Bratwurst*, then lay on your toppings of choice, from sweet and hot mustards to fried onions and cheese. Tasty!

06 Dorotheum

So you might not have the spare cash to bid on a Monet or an antique coin collection, it doesn't mean you have to miss out on all the fun of the Dorotheum. Though it is one of the largest auction houses in Europe, you can visit to simply admire the building and fantasise (don't bid!) about going home with treasure. *dorotheum.com; Dorotheergasse 17; 10am-6pm Mon-Fri, 9am-5pm Sat; free.*

07 Prater gardens

You can forget whizzing around on white-knuckle rides at the funfair if you're watching your euros, but don't dismiss Prater altogether; this is Vienna's finest parkland. Set over 60 sq km, you've got your pick of picnic spots and plenty of tree-lined boulevards perfect for strolling in. The seasons really show themselves here too; catch blazing chestnut trees in autumn or fluttering blossoms in spring. *prater.at; 1020 Vienna; 24hr; free.*

08 Schloss gardens

Getting inside the mega-posh palaces of Vienna will cost, but you can still put yourself in royal shoes with a drift around the palaces' gardens. The classical French-style gardens of **Schloss Belvedere** (8a; belvedere.at; Rennweg 6; dawn-dusk; free) provide excellent views while the beautifully preserved baroque garden of **Schloss Schönbrunn** (8b; schoenbrunn.at; Schönbrunner Schlossstrasse 47; 6.30am-dusk; free) has paths winding around flowerbeds, classic hedges, Roman ruins and fountains.

09 Wander the Ringstrasse

You don't need to spend a fortune to explore the opulence and grandeur of Vienna; a walk around the Ringstrasse

VIENNA CARD

If museum-hopping is high on your list of things to do in Vienna (as well it should be), pick up a Vienna Card (wien.info) as soon as you arrive to score discounts on tickets to a load of sights and attractions. In addition to the free or reduced entrance fees to top sights, you also get unlimited use of Vienna's underground, trams and buses for a period of 48/72 hours (€18.90/21.90). You can buy the Vienna Card from the airport, tourist information offices and most hotels.

will take you past the city's most stunning architecture and impressive landmarks. This circular boulevard surrounding the Innere Stadt showcases a wealth of 19th-century masterpiece buildings, from the neoclassical facade of Parliament and the stunning State Opera to the majestic Imperial Palace and the domed Kunsthistoriches Museum. *24hr; free.*

10 Coffeehouses

Cafes are a great way to make a few coins go a long way. For the price of a coffee you can linger as long as you like, read the paper and watch the world go by. Vienna is the ultimate city to take advantage of this; the coffeehouse culture is a long-held tradition with a history as rich as the cake. *Coffee €3-5.*

11 Naschmarkt

Dating back to the 16th century, Vienna's massive food market has over 100 stalls stretching for more than 500m along Linke Weinzeile. Here you'll find spices, fruits and vegetables, Middle Eastern street food, cheese, olives, every manner of meat, and traditional kraut in wooden barrels. Grab a falafel or kebab and take in the sounds, sights and smells. *naschmarkt-vienna.com; 06, Linke & Rechte Wienzeile; 6am-7.30pm Mon-Fri, 6am-5pm Sat; admission free.*

12 Save with set-menu meals

Dining out in Vienna can cost a packet but, fortunately, many of the city's restaurants offer something that can help cut back on the costs: Mittagsmenü – *usually a two*-course lunch meal that can be chosen from a set menu. Simply make lunch your main meal of the day and fill up on tasty fare for as little as €10, then grab a *würst* from a *würstelstand* in the evening.

NORTH
AMERICA

MANN
ZEP
FCK

ARTS & CULTURE · MUSIC & FILM · SPORTS & LEISURE · FOOD & DRINK · FESTIVALS & EVENTS

AUSTIN

AUSTIN

In recent times, Austin has grown from being a sleepy college town into a fully fledged destination, with people clamouring to visit (or just showing up with a U-Haul). As a result, prices have risen but it's still a laid-back place where there's plenty to do on the cheap.

03

01 Austin Art Garage

This offbeat and completely non-stuffy gallery owned by two local artists perfectly captures the spirit of the Austin art scene: it's colourful, it's eclectic and it never takes itself too seriously. Come and browse around to catch the vibe, and if you happen to fall in love with the art, there's a good chance you will be able to afford it. *austinartgarage.com; 2200 S Lamar; 11am-6pm Tue-Sat, noon-5pm Sun; free.*

02 Elisabet Ney Museum

Tucked away in a quiet residential neighbourhood, this unassuming miniature castle built in 1892 was the home and studio of sculptor Elisabet Ney. Ney sculpted some of the most notable figures of her time, and her statues can be found at the US Capitol, the Smithsonian and this gem of a museum and art gallery, where she created some of her best work. *304 E 44th St; noon-5pm Wed-Sun; free.*

03 Texas State Capitol

Built in 1888 from sunset-pink granite, this National Historic Landmark is the largest state capitol in the US and a striking centrepiece in downtown Austin. Get a taste of history, government and architecture during the free 45-minute

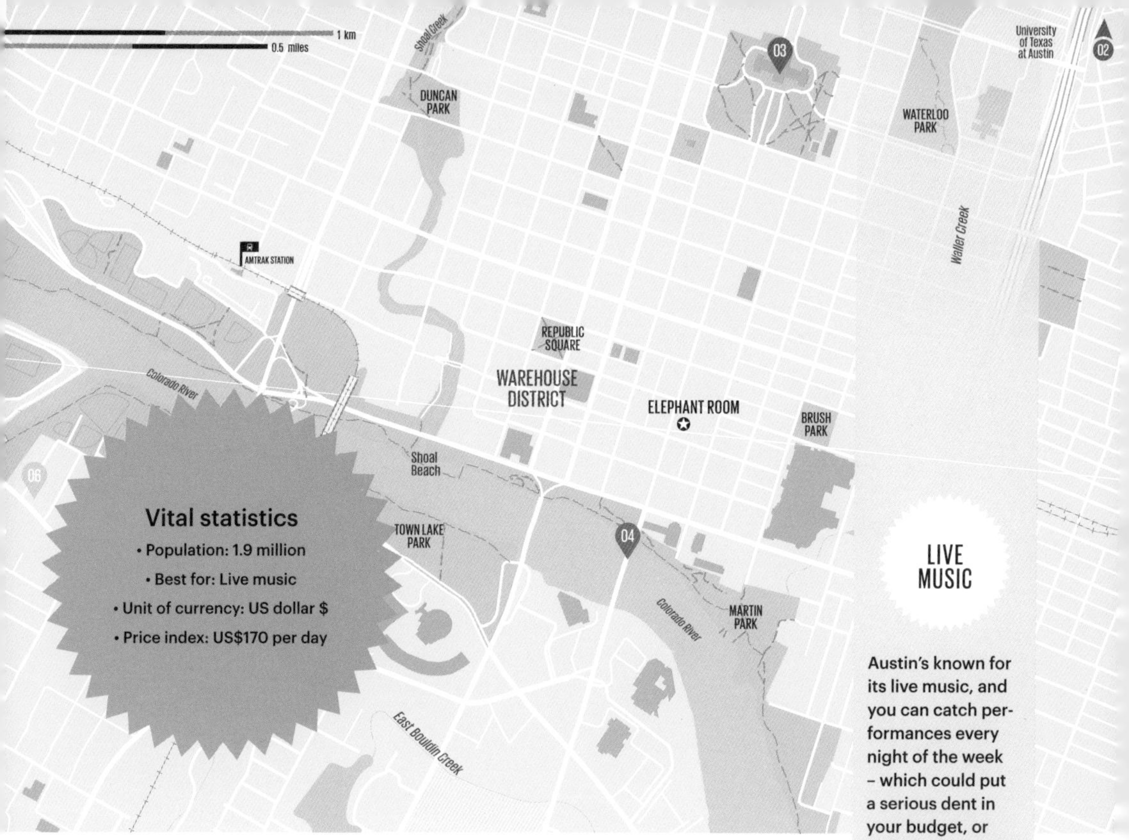

Vital statistics

- Population: 1.9 million
- Best for: Live music
- Unit of currency: US dollar $
- Price index: US$170 per day

tours or, at the very least, drop by to see the rotunda, which creates a whispering gallery with its curved ceilings. *1100 Congress Ave; 7am-10pm Mon-Fri, 9am-8pm Sat & Sun; free.*

04 Bat Exodus

From late March to early November, the largest colony of Mexican free-tailed bats in the US puts on a memorable show every evening, right around dusk. Crowds gather to watch the living funnel cloud of 1.5 million bats, looking like a special effect in a B-movie, as they swarm from under the Congress Avenue Bridge and head off in search of their evening meal. *Congress Avenue Bridge; dusk; free.*

05 Zilker Metropolitan Park

Visit the Japanese Gardens, play a few rounds of disc golf or cool off at Barton Springs Pool, a 3-acre/1.2-hectare swimming hole with the iciest waters this side of the Arctic. Admission is free in the winter and in the early morning, but on hot summer afternoons most people are more than happy to pay the $4 admission fee. *2100 Barton Springs Rd; 5am-10pm Fri-Wed; free, $5 weekend parking.*

06 Chuy's

Millions of students can't be wrong: there's no more affordable way to satisfy your Tex-Mex cravings than with Chuy's free happy-hour nacho car (weekdays 4pm to 7pm). Etiquette dictates you order a beer or margarita, but you won't mind. This is the original location, and it's as kitschy as it was when it first opened in the 1980s. *chuys.com; 1728 Barton Springs Rd; 11am-10pm Sun-Thu, 11am-11pm Fri & Sat; free.*

LIVE MUSIC

Austin's known for its live music, and you can catch performances every night of the week – which could put a serious dent in your budget, or cost nothing at all, depending on how you play it. Check out Continental Club (*continental club.com; 1315 S Congress Ave; till 2am; admission varies*), a local favourite with free shows during happy hour. Or try Elephant Room (*elephantroom.com; 315 Congress Ave; till 2am; free Sun-Thu*) for jazz in a cool, subterranean setting. There's never a cover at Little Longhorn Saloon (*thelittlelonghornsaloon.com; 5434 Burnet Rd; free Tue-Sun*), the most loveable dive bar in town.

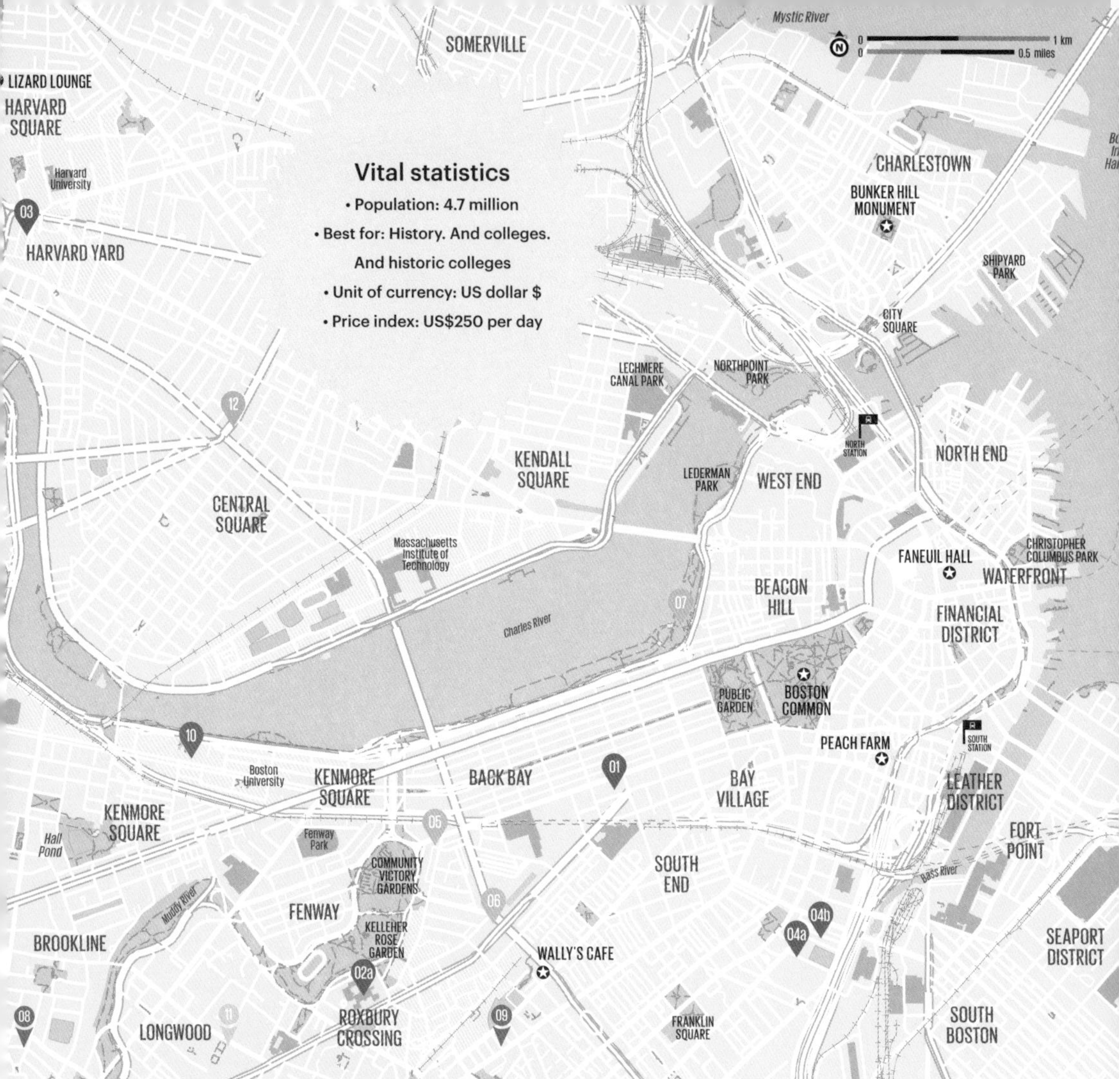

BOSTON

This history of Boston is the history of America. And no single element has influenced this history more than the city's penchant for learning. The educational institutions have been a source of artistic innovation and scientific thought. Plus, the sizeable student population guarantees cheap beer and plenty of free fun.

ARTS & CULTURE | MUSIC & FILM | SPORTS & LEISURE | FOOD & DRINK | FESTIVALS & EVENTS

01 Boston Public Library

Of course it's free, it's a public library. But the BPL is also a mini museum of art and architecture, with murals by John Singer Sargent and Pierre Puvis de Chavannes, sculpture by Augustus Saint-Gaudens and magnificent bronze doors by Daniel Chester French. Grab a brochure and wander around or join the free daily guided tour. *bpl.org; 700 Boylston St; 9am-9pm Mon-Thu, 9am-5pm Fri-Sat, 1-5pm Sun; free.*

02 Free museum nights

Boston's art collections are truly rich. But if you're not, the price of museum admission may seem hefty. Fortunately, both the Museum of Fine Arts and the Institute for Contemporary Art offer completely free admission one evening a week. Ogle some Impressionists at the **MFA** (*mfa.org; 465 Huntington Ave; 4-10pm Wed; free*) on Wednesdays, or ponder the present at the **ICA** (*icaboston.org; 100 Northern Ave; 5-9pm Thu; free*) on Thursdays.

02

03 Harvard University

Since it was established in 1636, dropping the name 'Harvard' rarely fails to impress: this is the country's oldest and most esteemed university. The historic heart of the college is Harvard Yard, where red-brick buildings and leaf-covered paths exude academia. Take a student-led tour to get the skinny on student life, the centuries-old architecture and the infamous 'statue of three lies'. *harvard.edu/visitors; 1350 Massachusetts Ave; check website for details; free.*

04 SoWa Artists Guild

The city's hottest contemporary art scene is in SoWa (meaning So-uth of Wa-shington St). Browse the diverse goods at the seasonal **SoWa Open Market** (*newenglandopenmarkets.com; 460 Harrison Ave; 10am-4pm May-Oct; admission free*), which is packed with stalls selling fun, funky arts and crafts. Or peek behind the scenes at **SoWa First Fridays** (*sowaboston.com; 450 Harrison Ave; 5-9pm first Fri of month; free*), when artists open their studios to the public.

05 Berklee College of Music

Want to get the low-down on modern jazz? Or songwriting, or electronica or world music? The innovative Berklee College of Music is the place to do it. In addition to the bigger-name venues, Berklee offers free concerts in the recital halls, where students, and faculty and visiting musicians share their soul-stirring sounds. These folks have racked up more than 250 Grammys, so it should be good. *berklee.edu/events; free.*

06 **Boston Symphony Orchestra**
Do you like the idea of being able to listen to world-class orchestral music in a magnificent hall, conducted by a passionate young conductor, without breaking the bank? You're in luck, as the Boston Symphony Orchestra offers $20 tickets for patrons under the age of 40. Listeners of any age can queue for the $9 rush tickets, which go on sale three hours before concerts on Tuesday and Thursday evenings as well as Friday afternoons. *bso.org; 301 Massachusetts Ave; prices vary.*

07 **Charles River Esplanade**
Seek out a spot on the Charles River Esplanade, catch a breeze off the river and tune into a free family flick (*sunset Friday, Jul-Aug*) or an orchestral performance (*bostonlandmarksorchestra.com; 7pm Wednesday, Jul-Aug*). If you can't sit still, the Esplanade Association also offers free Zumba (*6pm Tuesday, Jul-Sep*) at the Hatch Shell and yoga (*6pm Wednesday, Jul-Sep*) at Fiedler Field, as well as other free fun fitness activities. *esplanadeassociation.org; free.*

08 **Arnold Arboretum**
The 265-acre/107-hectare Arnold Arboretum is more than just an urban oasis where you can escape crowded city life and wander in peace among some 15,000 exotic trees and flowering shrubs, it also presents an opportunity to learn something for free, as there are guided tours (*10.30am Mon, Thu & Sat, 1pm Sun*), lectures and art exhibitions. Lilac season in early May is a highlight. *arboretum.harvard.edu; 125 Arborway, Jamaica Plain; dawn-dusk; free.*

09 **Blue Hills Reservation**
Encompassing more than 7000 acres (28 sq km), the reservation is the ultimate escape to nature that's close to the city. Some 125 miles (14km) of hiking trails crisscross the hills, including several routes to the summit of Great Blue Hill (194m), which gives fantastic city-skyline views. Swimming and skiing make the

BOSTON

HISTORIC FOOTSTEPS

The fight for American independence began in Boston. The best introduction to this revolutionary history is the Freedom Trail (*thefreedomtrail.org, free*), a 2.4-mile walking tour that winds its way around the city, past 16 historic sites. Just follow the red line from the Boston Common (America's oldest public park) to Bunker Hill (site of a key battle), passing landmark churches, graveyards, meeting houses and museums – many of which are free to enter. If you prefer to be guided, the National Park Service (*nps.gov/bost*) offers free partial walking tours, departing from Faneuil Hall from April to October (times vary).

STUDENT BUDGETS

College kids know how to get the best out of Boston without paying big bucks. If you're hungry and broke, graduate student John Louis recommends Chinatown: "For the best lunch special check out Peach Farm (*4 Tyler St, 11am-3am*) and get a massive quantity of tasty goodness for $4.99. Plus it's in a sketchy Chinatown side-street basement." Bonus! For entertainment, open-mic nights are "sometimes really badass". Louis vouches for the Open-Mic Challenge at the Lizard Lounge (*lizardloungeclub.com; 1667 Massachusetts Ave, Cambridge; 7.30pm Mon; patron/performer $6/3*). The nightly jam session at Wally's Café (*wallyscafe.com; 427 Massachusetts Ave; 6-9pm; free*) is also popular.

Blue Hills a year-round destination – just 14 miles (23km) south of downtown Boston. *695 Hillside St, Milton; dawn-dusk; free.*

10 Judson B Coit Observatory

Star light, star bright, first star I see tonight, wish I may, wish I might, find something free to do tonight. Well, if it's a clear Wednesday night, why not head to the Coit Observatory at Boston University to get involved in some star-gazing? Astronomy club members answer questions and make sure that the telescopes are pointing in the right direction. *bu.edu/astronomy; 725 Commonwealth Ave; 7.30pm Oct-Mar & 8.30pm Apr-Sep; free.*

11 Samuel Adams Brewery

Did somebody say free suds? The beer may not be the most important or enduring legacy of the celebrated patriot and failed brewer Sam Adams; but it's a pretty good one, especially if you are after a cheap afternoon's entertainment. Take a guided tour of the Samuel Adams Brewery to see how the beer is made and sample how it tastes. *samueladams.com; 30 Germania St; 10am-3pm Mon-Sat; donation $2.*

12 Improv Boston

Boston is a really funny place. And by that we do mean funny ha-ha. To cite some famous examples, comedians Conan O'Brien, Jay Leno and Denis Leary all hail from Boston. You can see numerous funny folks (although it's unlikely to be those guys) performing stand-up at Improv Boston at the free late-night weekend Nightcap or at the Sunday-evening, pay-what-you-can People's Show. *improvboston.com; 40 Prospect St, Cambridge; 11.30pm Fri + Sat & 9pm Sun; free.*

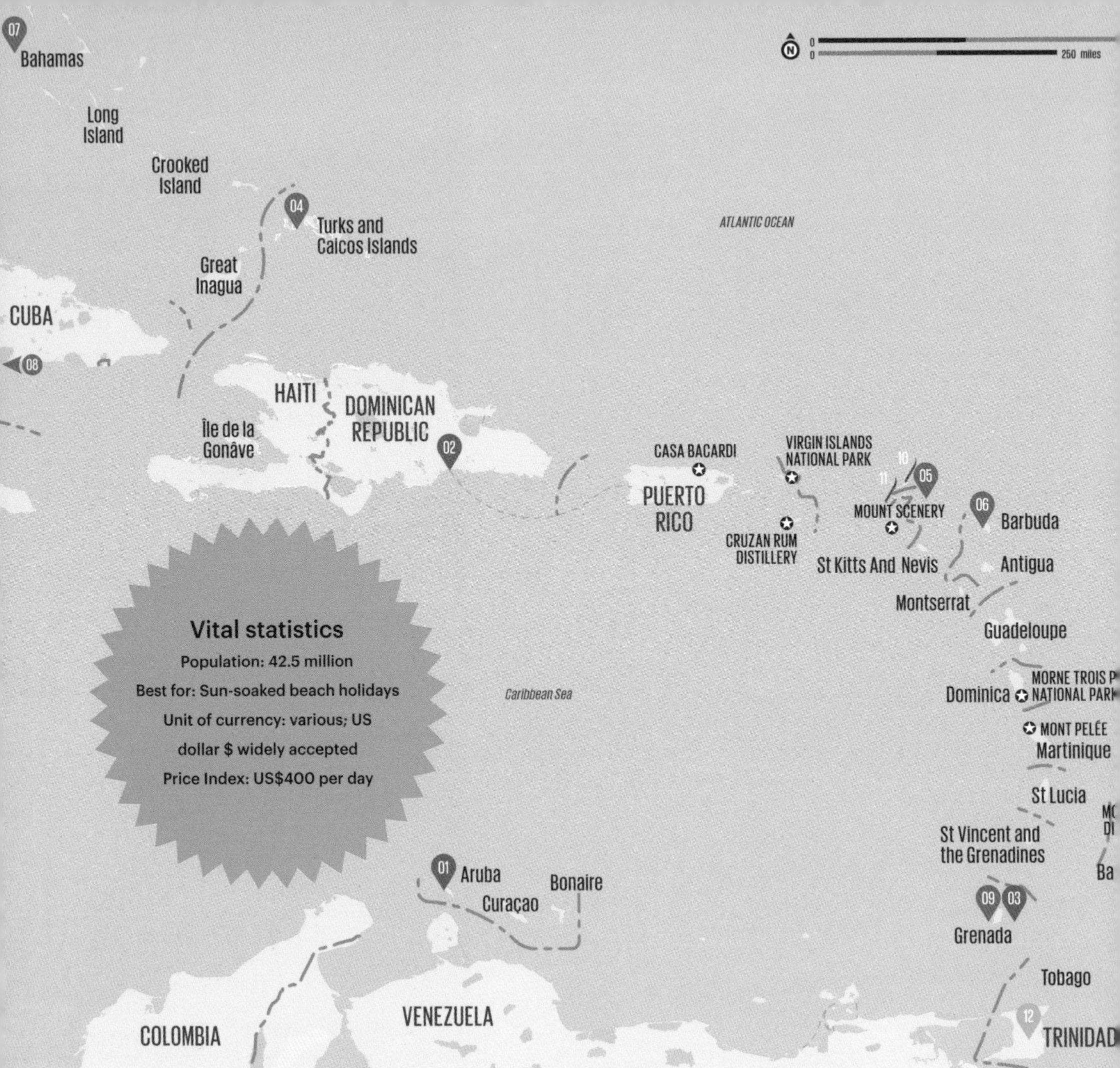

THE CARIBBEAN

Seven thousand islands offer seven million reasons to visit the Caribbean – land of the never-ending holiday. Sure, the region has a reputation for breaking the bank, but vacationers flock here in droves for one thing in particular: the beaches. And the good news is they're all free.

01 Aruba Aloe museum and factory

Brought to Aruba in the mid-19th century, aloe thrived in the scorching Caribbean sun and was quickly perceived as a veritable wonder plant. Soon afterwards, the island was covered in aloe farms and today visitors can take a short tour of the museum and factory to learn about the history and try out some free samples. *arubaaloe.com; Pitastraat 115, Oranjestad; 8am-5pm Mon-Fri, 9am-5pm Sat; free.*

02 Ciudad Colonial, Dominican Republic

Known locally as Zona Colonial, this historic Santo Domingo neighbourhood is the oldest permanent European settlement in the Americas, and has thus been declared a UNESCO World Heritage Site. Explore the churches and chapels bedecked in centuries-old art, and don't miss the Cathedral of Santa María la Menor, the oldest basilica in the 'New World', which overlooks Parque Colon, the city's central square so-named for the eponymous explorer. *24hr; free.*

03 The Carenage, Grenada

Window-shopping costs absolutely zip and there's no better place to do it in all of the Caribbean than along St George's waterfront on the island of Grenada. Known as the Carenage, the stroll-friendly harbourside features historical manses, fleets of brightly coloured little bobbing boats, and a hillside full of striking homes bathed in cheery paint that lead up to a towering stone fort. *St George's; 24hr; free.*

04 Grace Bay, Turks & Caicos

No one can deny the awesomeness of Grace Bay, largely considered the most beautiful beach in the entire Caribbean for its fluorescent blue waters and creamy sand ripped straight from your honeymoon Pinterest board. A gaggle of corporate types have gotten wise to the beach's charms, setting up over-the-top luxury digs along the pearlescent shores, but fortunately access to paradise is still free. *24hr; free.*

05 Happy Bay Beach, St Martin

On an island blessed with top-notch beaches, privacy becomes paramount. Happy Bay fulfils that criterion in spades and is accessible via a path from Friar's Bay. Once you arrive, the beach is usually pretty bare (as are its occupants). There's hardly any boat traffic either, due to the fact that there isn't a large-enough curvature in the cove to block the tidewater from dizzying swells. *sxm-beaches.com; 24hr; free.*

01

TAKE A HIKE

The Caribbean's natural assets extend beyond its beaches – hundreds of volcanic peaks rise from the ocean floor offering soaring vistas and memorable hikes. Never costing more than the price of a minimal conservation fee, the following treks are among the most spectacular: on Saba follow the Sandy Cruz Trail up Mount Scenery (*24hr; free*); explore the trails that wend through the Morne Trois Pitons National Park (*24hr; free*) on Dominica; toe the foothills ringing Mont Pelée (*24hr; free*) in Martinique; and circle through the vast Virgin Islands National Park (*nps.gov/viis/index.htm; park 24hr, visitor centre 8am-4.30pm; free*) on St John.

06 Low Bay, Barbuda

Antigua's low-profile baby brother, Barbuda is widely considered to be the best island for beaches in the whole region. And Low Bay takes the prize as being *the* prime spot, with 17 miles (27km) of unbroken sandy beach that feels more like a low-slung sandbar than a proper bay or cove. Here, you're much more likely to find the beach crowded with birds than with people. *24hr; free.*

07 Pig beach, Exuma, Bahamas

This is the only place in the Caribbean where you can splash around with celebrities and not have to pay a dime, because these stars have no idea they're famous. An overnight Instagram sensation, the pigs of Exuma live in the wild (according to legend they were left by sailors with plans to return for a pork roast) and take a daily dip. *Big Major Cay, Exuma, 24hr; free.*

08 Seven Mile Beach, Grand Cayman

Although its name is a bit of an exaggeration (it's only about five miles long), Cayman's best beach anchors much of the island's tourism industry and is refreshingly free of pedlars. Perfectly manicured and sporting some seriously white sand, Seven Mile has plenty of public access, making it great for walks, jogs and snorkelling in the reefs offshore near the Government House and Marriott hotel. *caymanislands.ky/activities/beaches/sevenmilebeach.aspx; 24hr; free.*

09 Underwater Sculpture Park, Grenada

The world's most unique art gallery is located 6ft under. Under water, that is. Spearheaded by British artist Jason deCaires Taylor, the project seeks to

RUM DEALS

Rum buoyed much of the colonial economy in the Caribbean and several distilleries still pump out the spirit today, offering factory tours that not only shed light on the region's history and the chemistry of the distillation but also get you stinking drunk. Try Casa Bacardí (*visitcasabacardi.com; Carr. 165 Km. 6.2, Cataño; 9am-4.30pm Mon-Sat, 10am-4.30pm Sun; admission US$12*) in Puerto Rico; cruise around the Cruzan Rum Distillery (*cruzanrum.com; 3A Estate Diamond, Frederiksted; 9am-4.30pm Mon-Fri, 10am-2pm Sat-Sun; admission US$8*) on St Croix; or stumble through the Mount Gay Distillery (*mount gayrum.com; Exmouth Gap, Brandons; 9.30am-3.30pm Mon-Fri, admission US$10*) on Barbados.

03

12

raise conservation awareness through compelling sculpture work. Of his sunken pieces, the most striking is *Vicissitudes*, a ring of outward facing children. Admission will cost you a tank of scuba bubbles or, for the more intrepid, a lungful of air. *grenadaunderwatersculpture.com; Molinière Bay, free.*

10 Hungry's, Anguilla

Some Caribbean islands, such as Anguilla, have become the gathering grounds for the rich and famous (Brad and Jennifer's 'break-up house' is located here), but that doesn't mean you have to suffer through a vacation's worth of overpriced meals. Plump for one of the local food vans, such as Hungry's, established in 2004, which swaps white tablecloths for honest-to-goodness local fare including tangy seafood chowder. *hungrysgoodfood.com; The Valley Rd, opposite St Gerard's Roman Catholic Church; breakfast, lunch & dinner; soup US$5.*

11 Sunset Beach Bar, Sint Maarten

In the Caribbean there are probably as many bars as there are beaches, but this is a standout among freeloaders. Located perilously close to the international airport, the outdoor watering hole offers front-row seats as the jumbo jets careen towards the runway. Good news ladies: if you go topless you drink for free. *sunsetsxm.com; 2 Beacon Hill Rd; breakfast, lunch & dinner; beer from US$3.*

12 Trinidad Carnival, Trindad & Tobago

Trinidad boasts the biggest party in all of the Caribbean: carnival blasts across the island on the Monday and Tuesday before Ash Wednesday each year (usually mid-February). Though it costs to partake in the parade itself, it's free to watch the fireworks blast, Soca dancers whirl in colourful headdresses, and steel drums echo from the panyards. *gotrinidadandtobago.com/trinidad/carnival; various locations & times; free.*

CHICAGO

Chicago's cloud-scraping architecture and world-class museums take centre stage when it comes to the city's attractions, and deservedly so. But don't overlook the oddball galleries, rockin' music parties and top-chef diners. Forgive us for saying it, but the Windy City will blow you away with its low-key, cultured awesomeness.

ARTS & CULTURE | MUSIC & FILM | SPORTS & LEISURE | FOOD & DRINK | FESTIVALS & EVENTS

01 American Toby Jug Museum

A Toby jug is a ceramic pitcher shaped like a chubby old guy wearing a tri-cornered hat and 18th-century garb. Over the centuries the jugs took on other personas, say John F Kennedy, Joseph Stalin or a sad-eyed puppy. Approximately 8000 – the world's largest collection – hide in this basement, tours of which are given by the owner. *tobyjugmuseum.com; 910 Chicago Ave, Evanston; 10am-4pm Tue & Thu; free.*

02 Chicago Cultural Center

The block-long landmark building (1897) is a treasure chest of complimentary cultural corkers. Museum-quality art exhibitions, foreign film screenings and lunchtime concerts by jazz bands and electronic dance music DJs lead the roster. There are also two stained-glass domes to admire. On weekends, volunteers step off from here for hour-long walking tours of downtown. *chicagoculturalcenter.org; 78 E Washington St; 9am-7pm Mon-Thu, 9am-6pm Fri & Sat, 10am-6pm Sun; free.*

03 Frank Lloyd Wright Architecture

Sure, you can pay the $17 admission fee to tour **Frank Lloyd Wright's Home and Studio** (*951 Chicago Ave, Oak Park; 9am-5pm*), where the famed architect launched his Prairie Style. Or you can wander around the neighbourhood for free and gawk at other abodes he designed. Ten of them cluster within a few blocks. *Google it, or buy an architectural site map for $4.25 from the studio shop for details.*

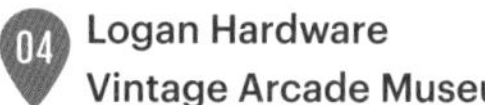

04 Logan Hardware Vintage Arcade Museum

Logan Hardware is a used-record store with a little something extra in its back room: the Vintage Arcade Museum. Buy anything in the shop, and you'll then be let loose on a Donkey Kong, Ms Pac Man, Dolly Parton pinball and 20 other flashing, whirring, beeping games from c 1985. They are all free to play. *logan-hardware.com; 2532 W Fullerton Ave; noon-9pm Mon-Sat, noon-7pm Sun; records from $3.*

05 Money Museum

Pop into the small gallery that is tucked away inside the Federal Reserve Bank of Chicago, and you'll emerge richer than you were when you entered. Literally, since the museum provides a bag of moolah to take home (if only it wasn't shredded...). See cool exhibits on counterfeit bills and snap a photo

CHICAGO

clutching the million-dollar-stuffed briefcase. *cityofchicago.org and look under 'Education'; 230 S LaSalle St; 8.30am-5pm Mon-Fri; free.*

06 National Museum of Mexican Art

Founded in 1982 by Carlos Tortolero, the nation's largest Latino arts centre is criminally overlooked, perhaps because it's in the off-the-beaten path (but easy-to-reach) Pilsen neighbourhood. The museum loads up on skeleton-rich folk art, psychedelic op art, groovy beadwork and politically charged Latino, Mexican and Chicano pieces, as well as featuring events such as ballet, family craft days and guided tours. *nationalmuseumofmexicanart.org; 1852 W 19th St; 10am-5pm Tue-Sun; free.*

07 Second City

Improv comedy began in Chicago, and The Second City is where it happened. Bill Murray, Stephen Colbert, Tina Fey and many more honed their wit here. Shows typically cost about $30, but you can nab a little-known bargain: turn up around 10pm (Friday and Saturday excluded) – after the regular show – and watch a free half-hour improv set. *secondcity.com; 1616 N Wells St; free improv around 10pm Mon-Thu & Sun.*

08 Buddy Guy's Legends

Chicago birthed the electric blues, and the ace place to hear the amped-up grooves is Buddy Guy's Legends. Evening shows cost $10 to $20, but musicians wail for free during lunchtime and dinner sets. OK, you probably should buy something (a drink or meal), as the club is also a Cajun restaurant, but there's no minimum charge. *buddyguy.com; 700 S Wabash Ave; free sets noon-2pm Wed-Sun & 6-8pm daily.*

TIP BOX

• The website of the Chicago Park District (*chicago parkdistrict.com*) lists all kinds of free events, from movies to live music to theatre – that take place in green spaces citywide.

• Hot Tix (*hottix.org*) sells same-week drama, comedy and performing arts tickets for half price (plus a service charge of about $4). The selection is best early in the week.

• Many boat, bike and walking tour companies offer discounts (about 10 per cent or so) if you book online.

• The Go Chicago Card (*smartdestinations.com/chicago*) provides several configurations of discounts for museums, tours and other attractions.

09 **SummerDance**

It's an open-air global dance party. Every weekend during summer, a multi-ethnic mash-up of locals gathers to boogie together in the Spirit of Music Garden in downtown's Grant Park. Bands play rumba, samba and other world music, preceded by hour-long dance lessons in the matching style. Ballroom-quality moves not required. *cityofchicago.org; 601 S Michigan Ave; 6-9.30pm Fri & Sat, 4-7pm Sun late Jun–mid-Sep; free.*

10 **The Whistler**

Hometown indie bands, punk, soul, country and jazz combos rock the wee, artsy Whistler most nights. The bar, located in the super-hip Logan Square neighbourhood, never has a cover charge. Instead, everyone purchases the fabulous cocktails to keep the music going. Whistler is also a record label, venue and gallery: the window showcases local artists' work. *whistlerchicago.com; 2421 N Milwaukee Ave; 6pm-2am Mon-Thu, from 5pm Fri-Sun; free.*

11 **John Hancock Center**

Chicago is well known as being a dandy place to get high. You know: in its abundant skyscrapers. The loftiest have viewing decks where you can pay about $20 to look out, such as the Hancock Center with its observatory on the 94th floor. But go two storeys *higher* to the Signature Lounge, and the view is completely free if you buy a drink. *signatureroom.com; 875 N Michigan Ave; 9am-11pm; drinks from $6.*

12 **Millennium Park events**

Downtown's public-art-studded showpiece is a trove of freebies in summer, with gratis garden tours, no-cost yoga classes and complimentary kids' activities. But nothing beats the free nightly concerts at Pritzker Pavilion, especially the weekend classical gigs. Patrons bring wine and picnics as the sun dips, the skyscraper lights flicker on and glorious music fills the twilight. *cityofchicago.org (search for 'Millennium Park'); 201 E Randolph St; 6am-11pm; free.*

TOP CHEFS ON THE CHEAP

You don't have to break the bank to eat a meal by Chicago's top chefs. Many have opened lower-priced eateries next to their signature restaurants. Take Stephanie Izard: opposite top-end Girl and the Goat, she has Little Goat (*littlegoatchicago.com; 820 W Randolph St; 7am-10pm Sun-Thu, 7am-midnight Fri & Sat; mains $10-19*), a comfort-food diner. Same goes for Rick Bayless. Next door to his swanky Topolobampo Mexican restaurant, he wafts high-quality but much cheaper tortas, churros and other street food at Xoco (*rickbayless.com/restaurants/xoco; 449 N Clark St; 8am-9pm Tue-Thu, 8am-10pm Fri & Sat; mains $10-14*).

 ARTS & CULTURE | MUSIC & FILM |  SPORTS & LEISURE | FOOD & DRINK | FESTIVALS & EVENTS

DETROIT

Motor City. Motown. Hockey Town, USA. When it comes to cars, music and sports, Detroit can compete with any other city. It also tops the list for urban blight. Detroit has its problems, but this renaissance city has new-found optimism – and unbeatable bargains – if you're in the know.

01 Architectural tours

Get a glimpse of Detroit's best architecture on free guided tours offered by Pure Detroit (*puredetroit.com*). Circle around the cylindrical **Renaissance Center** (*gmrencen.com; 330 E Jefferson Ave, tours noon & 2pm Mon-Fri*), the city's glossy centrepiece. Or admire the mosaics, murals and stained glass that adorn the **Guardian Building** (*guardianbuilding.com; 500 Griswold St*) and **Fisher Building** (*3011 W Grand Blvd; tours 11am, 1pm & 3pm Sat*).

02 Heidelberg Project

There are strange goings-on here: stuffed animals sharing tea in ruined houses; household appliances in vacant lots; giant clocks that tell no time. Street artist Tyree Guyton created the Heidelberg Project to beautify and bring attention to his rundown street; some 30 years later, the multi-block outdoor installation still brightens the surroundings and bewilders passers-by. *heidelberg.org; 3600 Heidelberg St; 24hr; free.*

03 Detroit Jazz Festival

Over the Labor Day weekend, Detroiters turn down the volume of their rock and roll music and turn up the jazz, as Motown hosts the world's premier free jazz festival. For four days, the festival takes over several city blocks in downtown Detroit, including Hart Plaza and Campus Martius. There is music on five stages, along with late-night jam sessions at area clubs and many other associated events. And it's all free. *detroitjazzfest.com; see website for venues and times.*

02

© dannyjameslane | 500px

DETROIT

MUSICIANS' PICKS

"My favourite spot is Cliff Bells (*cliffbells.com; 2030 Park Ave; 8pm Tue-Thu & 6pm Sun*)," says the Savage Rascals' Jim Habarth. "It has a great atmosphere and top jazz acts like Dr Lonnie Smith." Singer-songwriter Paulina Jayne plugs the Shelter (*saintandrewsdetroit.com; 431 East Congress St; shows $13-17*): "It's such an intimate experience. You're right there with the singer."

04 Belle Isle

An urban oasis designed by Frederick Law Olmsted in the 1880s, the 982-acre Belle Isle sits in the Detroit River between the USA and Canada, and is covered with wetlands, paths and manicured spaces. There are also beaux-arts buildings, picnic areas, playgrounds, botanical gardens, bike trails, museums, a beach, a zoo, an aquarium and a giant slide. *belleisleconservancy.org; cars $10 to cross the MacArthur Bridge, cyclists and pedestrians free.*

05 Slow Roll

The Slow Roll offers a novel perspective on the city: the view from the seat of a bicycle. Each week, hundreds – if not thousands – of cyclists meet at a designated starting point for a slow, safe, community ride around Detroit. There's a new route every week, guaranteeing you'll see something unexpected. *slowroll.bike; 6pm Mon; registration $10 for the year, but nobody is turned away for inability to pay.*

06 Markets

There's always something doing at **Eastern Market** (*easternmarket.com; 2934 Russell St; free*), Detroit's flourishing farmers' market. Saturday is the liveliest day (*6am-4pm year-round*), but there's also a smaller Tuesday market and a Sunday artist market (*10am-3pm, Jun-Oct*). Look for gourmet goodies, fresh produce, live music and yoga classes, as well as tours and other events. Nearby, the **Detroit Market Garden** (*greeningofdetroit.com; Orleans St; free*) is one of the city's famous urban farms.

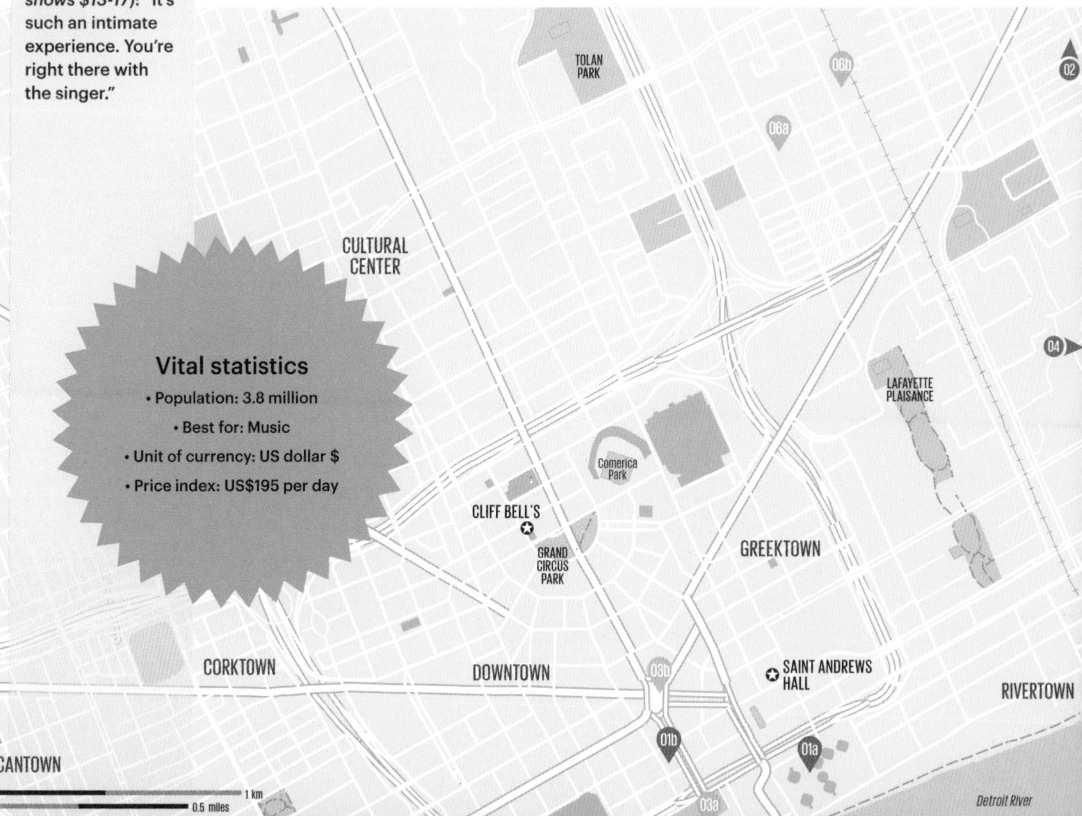

Vital statistics

- Population: 3.8 million
- Best for: Music
- Unit of currency: US dollar $
- Price index: US$195 per day

TOP

© Stephen Frink | Getty Images

In search of budget thrills and spills in the land of the free and home of the brave.

LIFE AQUATIC

Armed with fins and a snorkel set, explore Florida Keys National Marine Sanctuary, which protects the planet's third-largest reef and contains the submerged statue Christ of the Abyss. *floridakeys.noaa.gov; Key Largo, FL; free.*

GLACIER-SPOTTING

In summer, the roadside Child's Glacier near Cordova, Alaska, sees a collapse of ice every 15 minutes. For a glacier you can walk up to, visit Matanuska, a 27-mile/43-km tongue of ice poking out from the Chugach Mountains. *Free.*

BODY-SURFING

No board? No money? No worries! Point Panic beach in Hawai'i, in the midst of a surfing mecca, has a wave so tailor-made for body-surfing that boarders stay away, leaving it to the penny-pinching purists. *Hawai'i, HI; free.*

DEEPWATER SOLOING

DWS is rock climbing without the encumbrance (and expense) of safety gear – it's just you, the rock and the water below. Lake Powell's extensive shoreline is the perfect venue. *lakepowell.com; Glen Canyon National Recreation Area, UT; free.*

STORM-CHASING

The self-proclaimed 'storm-watching Capital of the World', Bandon-by-the-Sea's beaches become wind- and wave-whipped once winter riles the Pacific into a rage. Watch the action from behind the sea stacks and spires on Bullards Beach, OR. *Free.*

NORDIC SKIING

Forget expensive lift passes, extortionate on-mountain

accommodation rates and crowded runs, try your arm (and legs) at Nordic skiing somewhere like Higgins Lake, Michigan, where you can ski a groomed 12-mile/19-km network of trails for just $8 per day.

SAN FRAN PARKOUR

It's hard to keep flowers in your hair during a monkey vault, but whether you're a trained traceur or a free-running virgin, the San Fran parkour scene is both developed and welcoming. Complimentary intro sessions offered. *facebook.com/SFParkour; free.*

CANYONEERING

A non-technical introduction to an addictive art, the spectacular Peekaboo–Spooky Gulch Loop and Escalante-Grand Staircase National Monument in Utah can be spliced into easy 3-mile/5-km (three-hour) return scrambles, with plenty of slots and arches to explore. *utah.com/hiking; free.*

TRAIL-RUNNING

In autumn, go trail-running around Lake Placid, NY, and explore the tracks that wend through 6 million acres (24,200 sq km) of fantastic forest in the Adirondack Mountains to experience an explosion of leaf-turning colour. *lakeplacid.com; Lake Placid, NY; free.*

BOULDERING

Another essentially equipment-free pursuit, bouldering is all about solving small climbing problems on, yep, boulders... Bishop, in California's lower Sierra Nevada Mountain Range, is one of the world's best bouldering destinations. *bishopvisitor.info; Bishop, CA; free.*

FREE WHEELIN' ALL-AMERICAN ADVENTURES

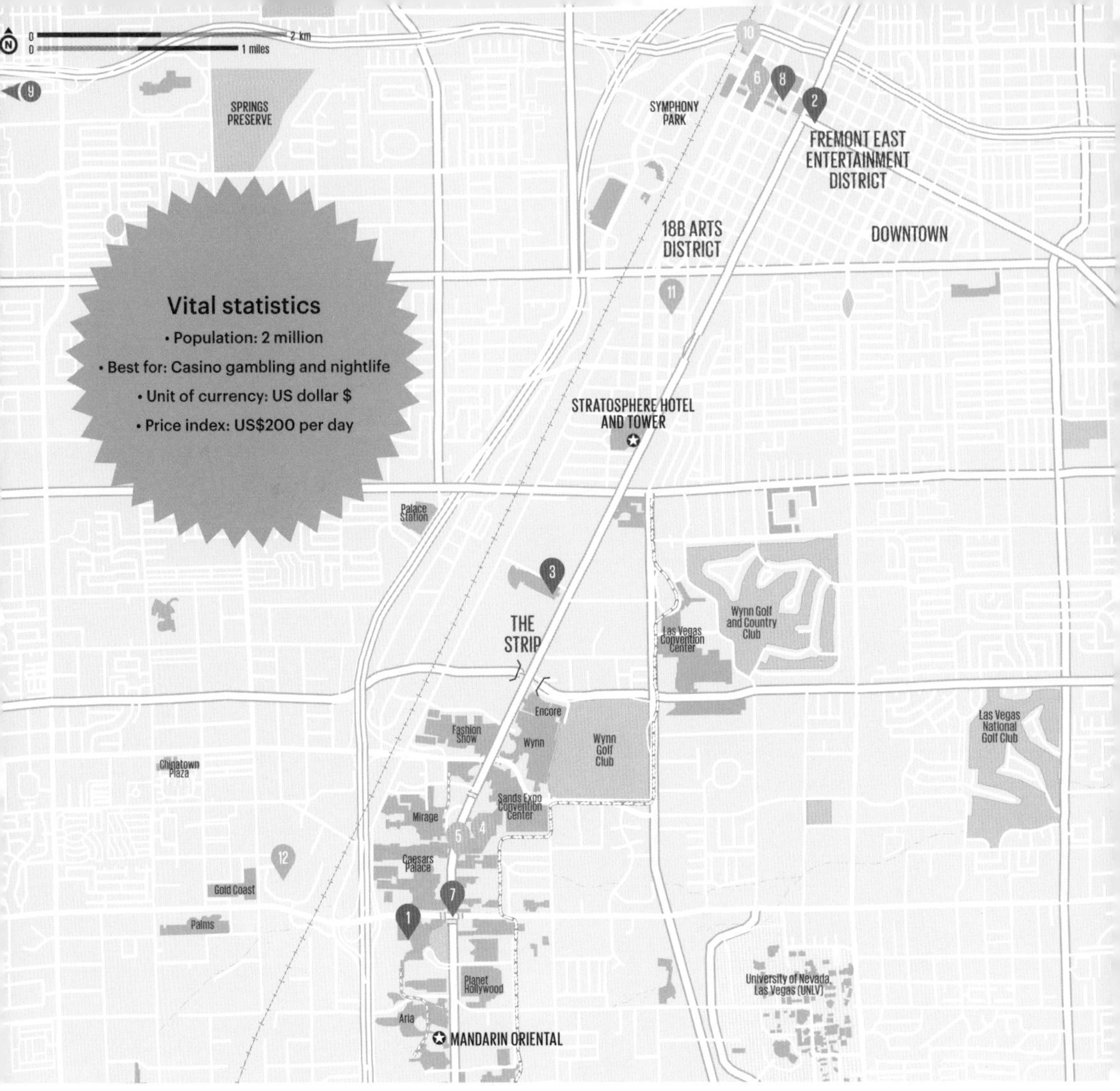

LAS VEGAS

Nobody needs an excuse to visit 'Sin City'. Neon-lit casinos, glamorous nightclubs, all-night wedding chapels and the ding-ding-ding of slot machines all make up this American siren's call. You could easily drop over a thousand dollars a day, but you really don't have to – freebies and deals abound.

ARTS & CULTURE MUSIC & FILM SPORTS & LEISURE FOOD & DRINK FESTIVALS & EVENTS

01 Bellagio Conservatory and Botanical Gardens

Often, Vegas feels way too artificial, with no real greenery or sunlight visible inside its smoke-filled casinos. One refreshingly different oasis on the Strip is this opulent casino's indoor conservatory. Here, show-stopping floral displays jauntily change themes with the seasons and holidays. Some botanical creations are so elaborate that they have to be lowered into position by crane through the glass ceiling. *3600 Las Vegas Blvd S; 24hr; free.*

02 Burlesque Hall of Fame

For cheaper entertainment than most casinos offer, head to the alternative, arty Fremont East entertainment district, a short walk east of downtown's 'Glitter Gulch' casino row. Pop in the Emergency Arts collective to peruse the deliciously retro photos and sequinned, barely-there costumes worn by Vegas' exotic dancers in decades past. *burlesquehall.com; 520 Fremont St; 11am-7pm Tue-Sat, noon-5pm Sun; free, small donation suggested.*

03 Circus acts at Circus Circus

You're not hallucinating: that really is a tightrope-walker balancing in mid-air above the blackjack tables and roulette wheels. Welcome to Circus Circus casino, where loads of free entertainment will distract you from your betting losses (or from winning in the first place). There's no charge to be an onlooker watching the human contortionists, jugglers and clowns. *circuscircus.com; 2880 Las Vegas Blvd S; 11am-11pm Sun-Thu, 11am-midnight Fri, 11am-1am Sat; free.*

04 Big Elvis

At the Piano Bar inside Harrah's fun Mardi Gras-themed casino on the Strip, Pete Vallee has given more than 7000 performances as 'Big Elvis'. Although there's a two-drink minimum for lounge seating, it won't cost you a thing to stand inside the casino and listen. Bonus: Big Elvis takes audience requests. *bigelvislasvegas.com; 3475 Las Vegas Blvd S; show times may vary, usually 2pm, 3.30pm & 5pm Mon, Wed & Fri; free.*

05 Carnaval Court

Smack bang in the middle of the Strip, this outdoor nightclub welcomes everybody with no entry fee, except late at night on weekends. Watch flair bartenders expertly juggle flaming bottles of liquor as they mix elaborate cocktails

VEGAS' BEST FREE VIEWS

You could fork out for the High Roller (*3545 S Las Vegas Blvd*), the world's tallest observation wheel, but why pay? Instead, ride the glass elevator at the Delano hotel (*3940 S Las Vegas Blvd*) up to the 64th-floor Skyfall Lounge, or check out the Strip views from the Mandarin Oriental hotel's (*3752 S Las Vegas Blvd*) 23rd-floor 'sky lobby'. You can't get any higher than the Stratosphere Tower (*stratospherehotel.com; 2000 S Las Vegas Blvd*). To avoid paying the exorbitant observation deck fee, go for cocktails in the revolving Level 107 lounge (the elevator ride is complimentary for bar patrons).

while high-energy cover bands rock out on stage. There's an anything-goes crowd of all-ages party-people here, from cheapskate students to Baby Boomers. *3475 Las Vegas Blvd S; 11am-3am; usually no cover charge.*

06 Fremont Street Experience

It's trippy and unbelievably hokey, yet you can't ignore the Viva Vision light show playing overhead on a 1500ft/450m-long canopy that blasts you with 550,000 watts of sound and around 12.5 million LED lights. Free live bands play along the pedestrian mall for gamblers stumbling out of the casinos. *vegasexperience.com; Fremont St, btwn Main St & Las Vegas Blvd; 24hr, shows hourly from dusk until midnight or 1am; free.*

07 Las Vegas Strip

Copying world landmarks, the Strip's free attractions include watching the **Mirage**'s (*mirage.com; 3400 S Las Vegas Blvd*) exploding volcano and the **Bellagio**'s (*bellagio.com; 3600 S Las Vegas Blvd*) musical dancing fountains and singing gondoliers rowing the artificial canals. Head south for a photo with an Elvis impersonator (tip expected) in front of the 'Welcome to Fabulous Las Vegas' sign. *Las Vegas Blvd S, btwn Tropicana Ave & Sahara Ave; 24hr; free.*

08 Neon Museum's Urban Gallery

This outdoor collection of restored neon signs will take you back to Vegas' 'Fabulous Fifties' and the Rat Pack era. More signs spiral around the central elevator inside the Neonopolis mall next door, outside which is a giant Aladdin's lamp. Beware: touring the museum's 'boneyard' of neon signs is not cheap, however. *neonmuseum.org; Fremont St & N 3rd St; 24hr; free.*

FREE CASINO DRINKS

While you're gambling in a Las Vegas casino, drinks are on the house. Even if you're only playing penny slot machines, you've still earned the right to free booze. Place your order with a roving cocktail waitress on the casino floor – don't forget to tip at least $1 when they deliver your drink. For big gamblers (aka high rollers, or 'whales'), RFB (room, food and board) is complimentary. When checking into a casino hotel, low rollers can ask for promotional coupons (sometimes called a casino 'fun book'), which is good for 2-for-1 drinks, discounted show tickets and much more.

Red Rock Canyon National Conservation Area

You could drive for many hours and pay $30 to visit the Grand Canyon National Park, or you could save yourself some money by taking a scenic drive through Red Rock Canyon, which is just outside Las Vegas' city limits. Its iconic desert scenery will make your eyes and brain pop. *3205 Hwy 159; visitor centre 8am-4.30pm, scenic drive open from 6am, closing time varies seasonally from 5pm to 8pm; entry per car $7.*

Garden Court Buffet

Everything is cheaper in ol' downtown than it is on the Strip. That rule applies not just for booze, but also for all-you-can-eat buffets, such as this popular spread of eclectic cuisines at Main Street Station casino. The Friday-night seafood dinner costs extra, yet for an endless supply of cracked crab legs and freshly shucked oysters, it's still a great deal. *200 N Main St; 7am-9pm Mon-Thu, 7am-10pm Fri-Sun; $8-15.*

First Friday Las Vegas

Local artists, musicians, street performers, hipsters and hangers-on gather in their masses for this free monthly extravaganza. Walk through buzzing art galleries, grab a cheap fusion bite from a food truck and listen to live indie bands. It all happens in downtown's 18b Arts District and the Fremont East district, and there are several after-parties too. *Casino Center Blvd, btwn Colorado & California Sts; 5-11pm first Fri of month; free.*

World Series of Poker

Major players who have perfected their poker faces compete in the popular no-limit Texas Hold 'Em poker tournament, aka the 'Main Event'. This series of poker tournaments happens every year at the Rio casino, which is just west of the Strip. It's free if all you want to do is spectate, but if you want to buy in, it will set you back $565 or more. *3700 W Flamingo Rd; late May–mid-July & mid-November; free to watch.*

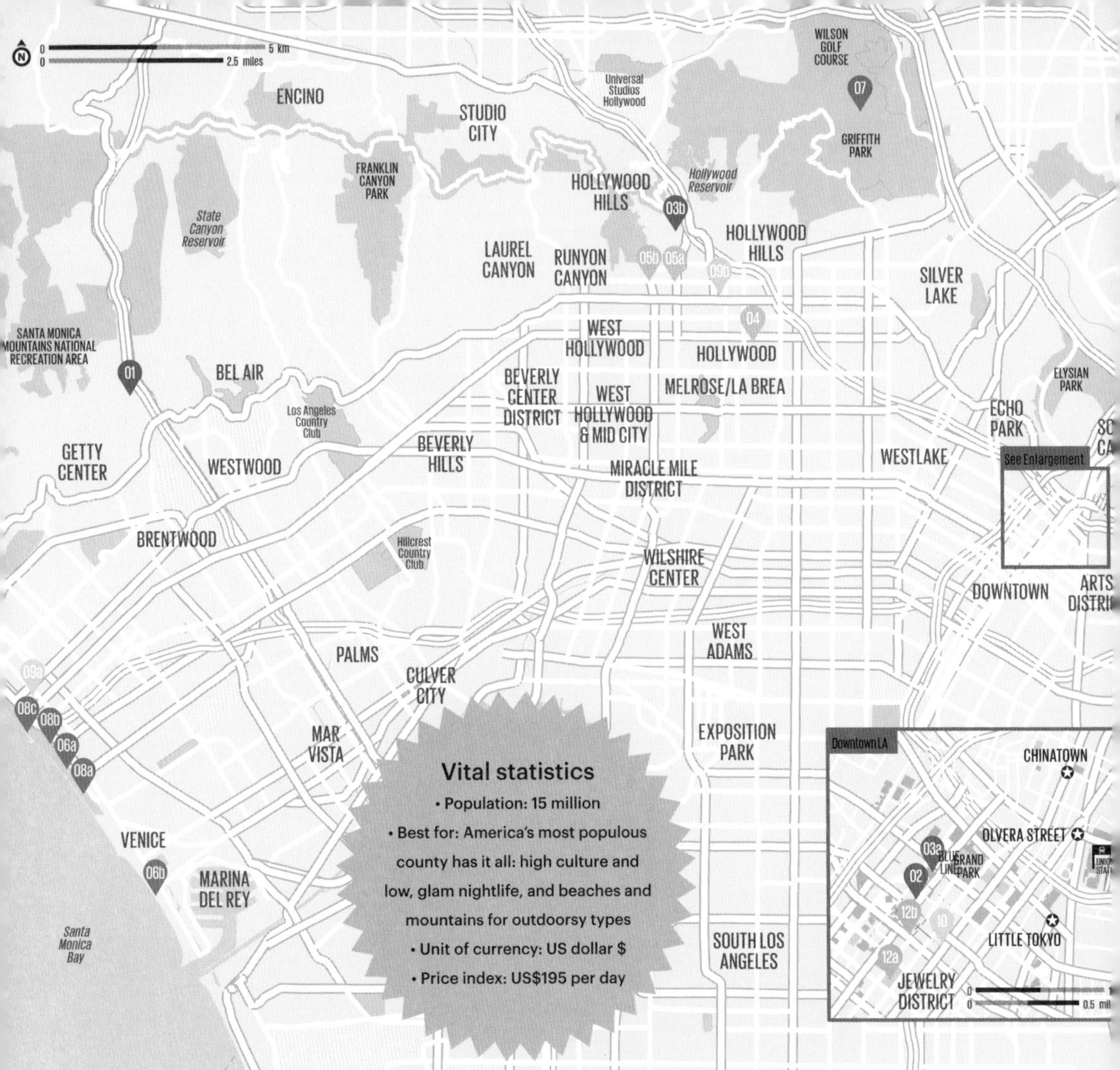

Vital statistics

- Population: 15 million
- Best for: America's most populous county has it all: high culture and low, glam nightlife, and beaches and mountains for outdoorsy types
- Unit of currency: US dollar $
- Price index: US$195 per day

LOS ANGELES

LA is a beacon for dreamers, rockers and risk-takers – and those who love them. Venture beyond starry-eyed Hollywood glamour to world-class cultural institutions, beaches, hikes and a mini-UN of ethnicities. Even if LA is one of America's more expensive cities, many of the best activities don't cost a cent.

ARTS & CULTURE | MUSIC & FILM | SPORTS & LEISURE | FOOD & DRINK | FESTIVALS & EVENTS

01 Getty Center

In its billion-dollar, in-the-clouds perch, one of America's favourite museums presents quadruple delights: a stellar art collection (from Renaissance greats through to David Hockney); gleaming-white cutting-edge architecture; the visual splendour of seasonally changing gardens; and kingly views across LA Basin from Downtown to the Pacific. *getty.edu; 1200 Getty Center Dr, Westside; 10am-5.30pm Tue-Fri & Sun, 10am-9pm Sat; admission free, but parking $15 ($10 after 4pm).*

02 The Broad Museum

The newest jewel in LA's cultural crown, the Broad Museum opened in September 2015 to house the 2000-piece-and-growing contemporary art collection of billionaire philanthropists Eli and Edythe Broad (rhymes with 'road'). A who's who of the post-war to 21st-century art world is stunningly displayed behind the perforated exterior walls collectively nicknamed 'the veil'. *thebroad.org; 221 S Grand Ave; 11am-5pm Tue & Wed, 11am-8pm Thu & Fri, 10am-8pm Sat, 10am-6pm Sun; free.*

03 LA Philharmonic buildings

Architect Frank Gehry pulled out all the stops on **Walt Disney Concert Hall** (3a), a gravity-defying sculpture of heaving and billowing stainless steel. If you can't fork out for an LA Phil' concert, explore the building on a free 45-minute, self-guided audio tour. At the Phil's summer home, the awe-inspiring, nearly 18,000-seat **Hollywood Bowl** (3b; *hollywoodbowl.com; 2301 Highland Ave*), the cheapest seats cost just $1! *laphil.org; 111 S Grand Ave; see website for details.*

04 Saturday night at the movies

Savvy Angelenos go for only-in-LA movie venues, including the **Last Remaining Seats Film Series** (*laconservancy.org*), which screens classics in theatres from cinema's golden age. Across town, **Cinespia** (*cinespia.org*) has a 'to-die-for' location at **Hollywood Forever Cemetery** (*6000 Santa Monica Blvd*), eternal resting place of film legends. It's a hipster heaven of picnics, cocktails and DJs, and there are screenings on a mausoleum wall. *Times & prices vary, see websites for details.*

05 Step out on Hollywood Boulevard

Marilyn Monroe, Michael Jackson, Aretha Franklin and Big Bird are among the 2400 stars sought out, worshipped and stepped on along the **Hollywood Walk of Fame** (3a; *walkoffame.com; Hollywood Blvd; free*). Its epicentre is

05

LOS ANGELES

TCL Chinese Theatre (5b; *tclchinese theatres.com; 6925 Hollywood Blvd; free*), where hand- and footprints of the biggest stars are enshrined in concrete. If you take a picture with a costumed character, tip a coupla bucks, or face wrath...

06 Golden beaches

LA is an epic beach destination with miles of golden sand, swaying palms, towering bluffs, volleyball, bike and skate trails, and waves surmounted by surfer dudes. Start at close-in **Santa Monica State Beach** (6a; *smgov.net/portals/beach; 24hr; free*) with its century-old pleasure pier. Just south, **Venice Beach** (6b; *venicebeach.com; 24hr; free*) offers boardwalk, bodybuilders, skaters and hippies old and new peddling goods bizarre, bland and beautiful; the Sunday drum circle is an institution.

07 Griffith Park

If you don't associate LA with hiking, think again. Griffith Park is just the biggest of dozens of options. One of the USA's largest urban green spaces (five times the size of New York's Central Park), it boasts 53 miles (85km) of hiking trails, Batman's caves and the Hollywood sign – plus an amphitheatre, zoo, observatory, museums, golf and playgrounds for non-hikers. *laparks.org/dos/parks/griffithpk; 4730 Crystal Springs Dr; 5am-10.30pm, trails sunrise-sunset; free.*

08 Work out, baby!

Rent a bike at **Perry's** (*perryscafe.com, multiple locations; per hr/day $10/30*) to cruise the 22-mile/35-km **South Bay Bicycle Trail** (8a; *traillink.com*). Further south, the original **Muscle Beach Venice** (8b; *musclebeach.net; 1800 Ocean Front Walk; 24hr; free*) is where the SoCal (Southern California) exercise

ONE-DAY FREE PASS

For a tiny sample of LA's vibrant ethnic neighbourhoods, follow the Metro Gold Line Downtown. Pedestrianised Olvera St (*olvera-street.com; 24hr; free*), LA's original settlement, feels like a festive (if kitschy) Mexican *mercado*; browse historic adobes, slurp Mexican-style hot chocolate or pick up Day of the Dead trinkets. Just north, beyond a modern dragon gate, Chinatown (*chinatownla.com; 24hr; free*) beckons with dim sum, shops overflowing with herbal remedies, faux silk slippers and lucky bamboo. Then take the Gold Line to Little Tokyo (*littletokyola.org; 24hr; free*), which buzzes with Buddhist temples, modern-art galleries, traditional gardens, pop-culture shops and authentic sushi.

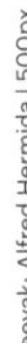

THRIFTY COMMUTING

LA may have practically invented car culture, but modern Angelenos, fed up with the nation's worst traffic, are increasingly demanding transit and pedestrian- and bike-friendly neighbourhoods. The Metro (*metro.net*) rail network now connects Downtown with Santa Monica, Hollywood, Koreatown, Olvera Street, Chinatown and Little Tokyo for a bargain fare of $1.75 (day/week pass $7/25). And Angelenos adore app-based ride services such as Uber (*uber.com/cities/los-angeles*) and Lyft (*lyft.com*), which charge a fraction of taxi fares. An airport train is in the works; for now, $8 Flyaway buses (*lawa.org*) connect LAX with Hollywood, Santa Monica and Downtown.

craze began in the 1930s and updated equipment draws today's generation. The competition is just as intense at **Santa Monica International Chess Park** (8c; *Ocean Front Walk; daylight hrs; free*).

09 Farmers' markets

LA has just about the best farmers' markets in the country. This is not surprising, given that California grows much of America's agricultural bounty. **Santa Monica's markets** (9a; *smgov.net/portals/farmersmarket; Third Street Promenade & Arizona Ave, Santa Monica; 8.30am-1.30pm Wed, 8.30am-1pm Sat*) on Wednesdays and Saturdays set the standard (check out the professional chefs), while **Hollywood's** (9b; *hollywoodfarmersmarket.org; cnr Ivar & Selma Aves, Hollywood; 8am-1pm Sun*) *serves great food, crafts and community. Admission free.*

10 Grand Central Market

Much of LA's best food doesn't come with a hefty price tag. Exhibit A: Grand Central Market, where sawdust-sprinkled aisles and old-timey neon signs in a 1905 beaux-arts building lead foodie aficionados to, among other stalls, a gourmet deli (Wexler's), Thai street food (Sticky Rice), decadent breakfasts (Eggslut), chichi cheeses (DTLA Cheese) and coffee and patisseries (Valerie), alongside historic produce stalls. *grandcentralmarket.com; 317 S Broadway; 8am-6pm Sun-Wed, 8am-9pm Thu-Sat; admission free.*

11 Artwalk Gallery Tours

A mad swirl of art lovers invades the city centre for monthly Downtown art walks, which are self-guided, liberally lubricated excursions that link more than 40 galleries and museums. You'll find most of them between 3rd and 9th and Broadway and Main. Even if the scene sometimes surpasses the art, it's usually a fun time. If not, you can always try one of the other walks next time... *downtownartwalk.org; noon-9pm 2nd Thu of month; free.*

12 Summer Concerts For All

Summertime means free outdoor concerts in LA. The biggest crowds turn out for the **Twilight Dance Series** (*santamonicapier.org/twilightconcerts; free*), which turns the Santa Monica Pier and adjacent beaches into a dance party. Downtown, **Pershing Square** (12a; *laparks.org/pershingsquare; 525 S Olive St; free*) hosts live acts on Saturday and Thursday nights, while **Grand Performances** (12b; *grandperformances.org; free*) brings international music, dance and theatre acts to California Plaza on Friday and Saturday nights.

LOS ANGELES

ARTS & CULTURE · MUSIC & FILM · SPORTS & LEISURE · FOOD & DRINK · FESTIVALS & EVENTS

MIAMI

MIAMI

More than just a beach town (although, wow, it is a great beach town), Miami is the crossroads of Latin America, North America and the Caribbean. Consistently wonderful weather, a cosmopolitan arts scene and a lust for life makes the Magic City a world-class destination that can be very affordable.

05

01 Wynwood Walls

With its edgy warehouses and studio spaces, the neighbourhood of Wynwood has, since 2009, assumed the role of Miami's bohemian heartbeat. Art walks, gallery nights and ever-expanding food and nightlife options revolve around the wonderful Wynwood Walls, a collection of mind-boggling murals that never ceases to drop a jaw. *thewynwoodwalls.com; btwn NW 25th & 26th Sts and NW 2nd Ave; 11am-11.30pm Mon-Thu, 11am-midnight Fri & Sat, 11am-8pm Sun; free.*

02 WALLCAST at the New World Symphony

The New World Center is the Frank Gehry-designed performing arts pride of Miami Beach. If you'd like to see a concert but skip a ticket (and take advantage of South Florida's great weather), the WALLCAST series brings the symphony's shows to the public; performances are projected on to the Symphony building's walls while families lounge in a nearby park. *nws.edu/wallcasts.aspx; Miami Beach, 500 17th St; check website for details; free.*

03 A1A/MacArthur Causeway

This one is free, but you need a car to do it, because it's a drive. And not just any drive, but the iconic Miami scenic route: a jaunt over teal and deep blue, between the condo canyons and high-rises of Miami

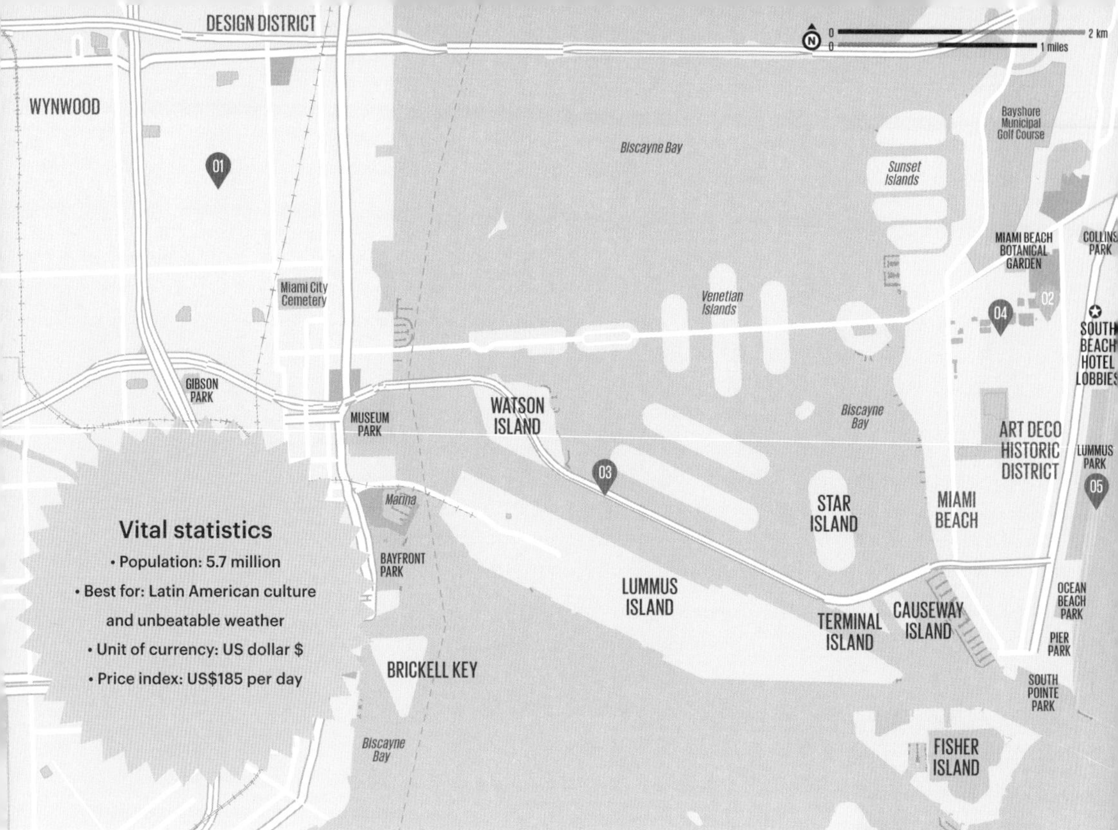

and Miami Beach. Hit this route during a deep-pink Florida sunset, when the palms sway in the breeze, and keep those windows rolled down. *24hr; free.*

04 Lincoln Road Mall

South Florida likes to strut, and she shows it off like nowhere else on the Lincoln Road Mall. A pedestrian thoroughfare located at the nexus of the area's hippest hotels and nightlife, Lincoln Rd is a people-watching paradise with a constant procession of the beautiful, the brash, those who wish to be seen and those who really make the scene. *Miami Beach, btwn 16th & 17th Sts; 24hr; free*

05 Miami Beach

Miami Beach is both a city on an island located offshore Miami proper, and the name for said city's municipal sand. South Beach, which lasts from 1st to roughly 23rd St, is the most popular area for tourists; below 11th St is a younger, party-oriented scene that lures the rich and famous, while the beach becomes more family friendly the higher up the street numbers you go. *miamibeachfl.gov; 5am-midnight; free.*

06 Viernes Culturales

On the last Friday of every month, Miami celebrates her Latin heritage and vibrant arts scene at *Viernes Culturales*, or cultural Fridays. This enormous street party takes over the heart of Little Havana, and features a free walking tour, arts markets, gallery shows, lots of refreshing tropical drinks (for adults and kids) and music, dancing and food from across Latin America. *viernesculturales.org; SW 15th Ave & 8th St; 7-11pm; free.*

SOBE HOTELS

The hotels of South Beach unashamedly flaunt wealth, opulence and sexiness. Even if this isn't your speed, the indulgence of their design and landscaping – huge pools flanked by open-air lounges and vaulted, columned ceilings – is a jaw-dropper. Explore via their lobbies and outdoor lounge areas; order a drink from a hotel bar if you're staying awhile.

ARTS & CULTURE

MUSIC & FILM

SPORTS & LEISURE
FOOD & DRINK

FESTIVALS & EVENTS

NEW ORLEANS

There is nowhere quite like New Orleans: historical architecture, candy-coloured homes, the greatest indigenous cuisine in the USA, unstoppable live music, a deep well of Afro-Caribbean culture, and bars that just don't quit. It's all about hedonism and beauty here, and both of these qualities abound around every street corner.

01

02

03

01 Jackson Square

Jackson Square sits at the heart of the French Quarter but away from major roads; instead, it fronts the Mississippi River, the original 'road' into New Orleans. The well-manicured green space is backed by St Louis Cathedral, one of the oldest French cathedrals in North America, and filled with buskers, tarot card-readers, travelling street musicians and sketch artists. *jackson-square.com; btwn St Peter, St Ann & Decatur Sts; 24hr; free.*

06

02 Lafayette Cemetery No. 1

Cloaked under an umbrella of ancient trees and one of the most evocative of New Orleans' many 'cities of the dead', Lafayette No. 1 contains a glut of gently mouldering tombs and mausoleums, the slightly maudlin atmosphere caused by their leisurely decay offset by the rapid green fecundity of the surrounding Garden District neighbourhood. *Btwn Prytania St, Coliseum St & Washington Ave; 7am-3.30pm Mon-Fri, 8am-4pm Sat & Sun; free.*

03 Frenchmen Street

It's safe to say that 'music' is a term people identify with New Orleans, and the most accessible strip of live music in the city is Frenchmen. It's not where the locals hang out according to tour guides, but there's a fantastic concentration of venues, bands and the people who love them, and you can hear plenty on the street without ever paying a cover. *Music from 6pm-2am; free.*

NEW ORLEANS

04 City Park

The biggest park in New Orleans, and one of the largest urban green spaces in the country, City Park's myriad elements would take a book to catalogue. There are live oaks draped with Spanish moss, classical Greek pavilions, the New Orleans Museum of Art and its attached sculpture garden, and a jungle landscape not far removed from that of the South Louisiana wilderness. *neworleanscitypark.com; 1 Palm Dr; sunrise-sunset; free.*

05 Mardi Gras

No one event encapsulates New Orleans like Mardi Gras. All of the city's demographic threads start to unravel: Uptown, the crowds cheer for beads tossed from floats staffed by semi-secretive parading 'krewes'. In black neighbourhoods, Second Lines and the Mardi Gras Indians take over the streets. And downriver, artists and musicians dress in madcap homemade costumes. *mardigrasneworleans.com; Feb, check website for routes and schedules; free.*

06 Second Lines Festival & Event

New Orleans' Afro-Caribbean culture manifests at Second Lines – neighbourhood parades held every Sunday (not in summer) and to commemorate major events. Each Second Line is put on by Social Aid & Pleasure Clubs (black community organisations), and feature brass bands (the 'First Line') and dancing. Check the website of radio station WWOZ *(wwoz.org/new-orleans-community/inthestreet)* for listings and parade route sheets. *Free.*

STREETCAR DESIRE

An indelible piece of the New Orleans' landscape, the St Charles Avenue Streetcar (*norta.com; 24hr; one-way ticket $1.25, all-day pass $3*) trundles up and down the street it was named after, one of the most beautiful roads in North America. Rolling past enormous trees and mansions, the streetcar stops every 20 minutes or so throughout the Garden District and Uptown; a ride on the rail is a wonderful way of seeing the city at slow pace.

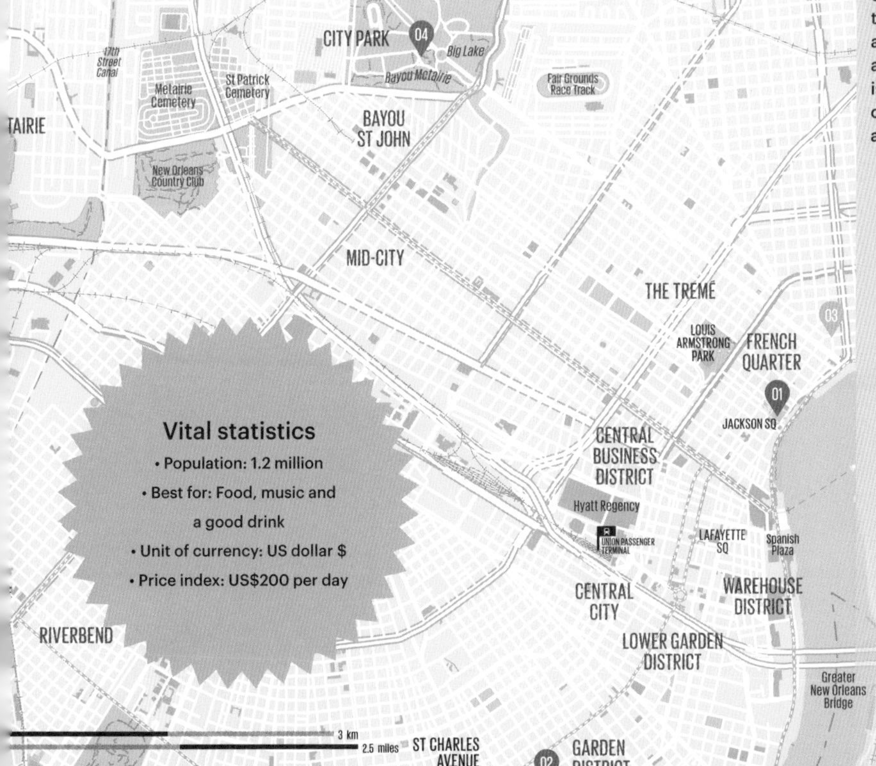

Vital statistics

- Population: 1.2 million
- Best for: Food, music and a good drink
- Unit of currency: US dollar $
- Price index: US$200 per day

NORTH AMERICA'S BEST FREE MOVIE NIGHTS

MOVIES WITH A VIEW - BROOKLYN, NY

With a Manhattan skyline backdrop, Brooklyn Bridge Park presents a mash-up of classic and cult films on a yearly theme. Hipster meets Boho meets Woody Allen...only in New York. *brooklynbridge-park.org; 334 Furman St, Brooklyn; Thurs at sunset, July-August.*

SCREEN ON THE GREEN - WASHINGTON, DC

Surrounded by the Smithsonian and a view of the National Monument, this free summer movie festival is a new way to experience the National Mall. *hbo.com/screenonthegreen/. On the National Mall btwn 4th & 7th Sts; Mon at dusk, July-August.*

NEW ORLEANS FILM SOCIETY: MOONLIGHT MOVIES - NEW ORLEANS, LA

An exquisite curation of mostly free, outdoor movies at unique venues across the city (Old U.S. Mint, Sculpture Garden) ramps up the cultural quotient. *neworleansfilm society.org; spring and fall schedules.*

LITTLE ITALY OPEN AIR FILM FESTIVAL - BALTIMORE, MD

Infused with the inimitable Italian community spirit, free movies are projected on an unfinished billboard on the side of a restaurant... from the window of a family home. *littleitalymd.com/t/Open_Air_Film_Fest; Crnr of High & Stiles Sts; Fridays, 9pm, July- August.*

FREE FRIDAY FILMS AT INNIS TOWN HALL - TORONTO, ON

Well connected with Toronto's many film festivals, U of Toronto's Cinema Studies Students' Union delivers advance screenings, art films, and director visits. *cinssu.ca/fff-schedule/. Innis Town Hall, 2 Sussex Ave; 7pm Fri, Sept-Apr.*

EN PLEIN AIR - MONTRÉAL, QC

Feeling curious? Catch some of the world's best documentaries for free at screenings curated by the Montréal International Documentary Festival at parks and other locations. *ridm.qc.ca/en/ridm-en-plein-air; screenings throughout the week, Jul-Sept.*

CAPRI DRIVE-IN THEATER - COLDWATER, MI

A slice of Americana between Detroit and Chicago, operating since the 1960s, the twin-screen Capri has retained a cool vintage vibe. From the long car line-ups, to the sound system (your radio) it's worth the $8 (adult). *119 West Chicago Rd; Weekends, opens 7.30pm.*

MIAMI BEACH SOUNDSCAPE CINEMA SERIES - MIAMI, FL

Palm trees and bougainvillea provide the setting for movies on a 7000 foot projection wall at this urban park, steps from Lincoln Road. *mbculture.com; Soundscape ExoStage, 17 Street and Washington Avenue; Oct-May, Wed 8pm.*

OLD PASADENA FILM FESTIVAL - PASADENA, CA

Home to Hollywood's earliest movie stars, Pasadena offers a free month-long festival featuring an eclectic selection of movies at several venues. Locals grab snacks from the flocking food trucks. *oldpasadena.org; Jul-Aug, starting 7-8.30pm.*

FILM ON THE ROCKS - MORRISON, CO

Your only chance to see movies in a geologically created, red sandstone natural amphitheatre. Just outside Denver, the cost is $12 but the experience is priceless. *redrocksonline.com; Jun-Sept, doors open 6:30pm.*

Illustration | Thomas Burden

ARTS & CULTURE | MUSIC & FILM | SPORTS & LEISURE | FOOD & DRINK | FESTIVALS & EVENTS

NEW YORK CITY

NEW YORK CITY

One of the world's most captivating cities, NYC is famed for its many world-class museums and theatres, fascinatingly diverse neighbourhoods and unrivalled dining scene. Though prices are high, there are plenty of ways to save money, from catching free outdoor concerts or art exhibitions to chowing down cheaply at markets.

01 American Folk Art Museum

For a glimpse into an alternative art world – where self-taught and outsider artists steal the show – don't miss this small museum on Manhattan's Upper West Side. You'll find wood carvings, paintings, textiles, hand-tinted photographs and many curiosities, including works by Henry Darger (known for his girl-filled 'battlescapes'). There's free music on Friday evenings. *folkartmuseum.org; 2 Lincoln Sq; 11.30am-7pm Tue-Thu & Sat, noon-7.30pm Fri, noon-6pm Sun; free.*

02 Chelsea Galleries

The epicentre of New York's art world lies in West Chelsea, a formerly industrial neighbourhood containing hundreds of galleries. It's gratis to browse works by famous artists and up-and-comers, and if you visit the district on Thursday nights you can usually enjoy free wine at art openings. Start your tour at top-class galleries such as **David Zwirner** (2a; *davidzwirner.com*), **Gagosian** (2b; *gagosian.com*) and

04

06

10

Vital statistics

- Population: 8.5 million
- Best for: The dizzying array of cultural attractions
- Unit of currency: US dollar $
- Price index: US$300 per day

Barbara Gladstone (2c; *gladstonegallery.com*). *chelseagallerymap.com; from 10th to 11th Aves, btwn 18th & 25th Sts; free.*

03 Met Museum

A Promised Land for art-lovers, the Metropolitan Museum boggles the imagination with its 17 acres of gallery space containing about two million treasures that range from beautifully wrought works from Ancient Egypt to exquisite paintings by European masters. You could spend days there and still go back for more. Admission isn't free, but you could pay less than the suggested amount. *metmuseum.org; 1000 Fifth Ave; 10am-5.30pm Sun-Thu, 10am-9pm Fri + Sat; $25 suggested donation.*

04 National Museum of the American Indian

Despite its setting inside a grand beaux-arts building in Lower Manhattan, this Smithsonian affiliate often gets overlooked among the big-hitting museums of NYC. But don't you miss out: the collections here include stunning decorative arts, textiles and ceremonial objects that document America's diverse native cultures. Check the calendar for dance and music performances, craft demonstrations, films and workshops. *nmai.si.edu; 1 Bowling Green; 10am-5pm Fri-Wed, 10am-8pm Thu; free.*

05 Celebrate Brooklyn!

Not to be outshone by its better-known sibling across the East River, Brooklyn hosts its own outdoor summer shows in leafy Prospect Park. This free series features eclectic bands, from New Orleans-style jazz, African funk and Brazilian dance to bluegrass and indie rock. There's also decent food and drink on hand, including Brooklyn-made craft brews. *bricartsmedia.org/performing-arts/celebrate-brooklyn; Prospect Park, entrance at 9th St & Prospect Park W; free.*

06 SummerStage

One of the best ways to spend a summer evening in NYC is to go to

THE LOCALS' VIEW

"I spend a lot of time in the park, where there's always something going on – free films, yoga, concerts... For shopping, look for sample sales, where you can find some great deals. I tend to use Refinery 29 (*refinery29.com*) and Flavorpill (*flavorpill.com*)." – Florence Foley, fashion designer

"Shop for clothing and household items at Housing Works (*housing works.org*) thrift shops, which have great stuff at citywide locations. The summer concerts are well worth going to. For those that aren't free, I like to take a picnic and sit on the lawn outside." – Heungman R Kwan, photographer (*heungman-photography.com*)

a concert in Central Park. From June through to August, you can catch more than 20 free shows in an incredible line-up of dance and music. Django Django, Femi Kuti, the Metropolitan Opera and the Martha Graham Dance Company have all taken the stage previously. *cityparksfoundation.org/summerstage; Central Park, entrance near Fifth Ave & 72nd St; free, but donations appreciated.*

07 **Sunny's**

Down near the waterfront in Brooklyn's Red Hook district, you'll find an old-school bar that serves up strong drinks to a mostly local crowd. Come Saturday nights, however, folks come from all over to hear some of the best bluegrass in the city. It happens in the small back room, so arrive early to get a spot. There's no charge, though it's polite to drop some dollars in the hat for the musicians. *sunnysredhook.com; 253 Conover St; 2pm-4am Sat; free.*

08 **Brooklyn Bridge Park**

It's difficult not to fall for Brooklyn after a wander through this picturesque 85-acre/34-hectare green space hugging the East River. In addition to admiring the jaw-dropping views of Lower Manhattan, there's plenty to get involved in here, from roller skating on Pier 2 and playing sand volleyball off Pier 6 to riding the historic Jane's Carousel near the foot of the Brooklyn Bridge. *brooklynbridgepark.org; 6am-1am; free.*

09 **Central Park**

New York's quintessential green space offers free fun of all varieties, from waterside strolls along the Lake to Frisbee-throwing and picnicking on Sheep Meadow. Come on weekdays for the bucolic experience (head to the North Woods to escape the crowds); while weekends are a fun-fest of busking musicians, disco-grooving roller skaters, and families lining up for carousel rides and animal encounters in the **Tisch Children's Zoo**. *centralparknyc.org; 6am-1am; free.*

10 **High Line**

A stroll along Manhattan's longest green space provides some of the best vantage points of the city. This once-industrial rail line has been converted into a greenway, complete with wildflowers, art installations and cut-outs where you can gaze at the action 30 feet (9m) below. The park runs for 1.5 miles (2.4km) from Gansevoort St in the Meatpacking District to W 34th St. *thehighline.org; 7am-7pm Dec-Mar, 7am-10pm Apr-May & Oct-Nov, 7am-11pm Jun-Sep; free.*

11 **Staten Island Ferry**

Skip the long lines for the (not-free) boat ride out to the Statue of Liberty, and instead board the classic bright-orange Staten Island Ferry. The 25-minute journey across the harbour won't cost a penny, and you'll have fabulous open-air views of the torch-holding dame (not to mention

NEW YORK CITY

soaring skyscrapers) along the way. Bonus: you can purchase beer on board. *siferry.com; east end of Battery Park; 24hr; free.*

12 Joe's Pizza

Joe's is the Meryl Streep of pizza parlours, collecting dozens of awards and accolades over the past three decades while safely cementing its reputation as one of the top pizza destinations in New York City. Slices are served up indiscriminately to students, tourists and celebrities alike (everyone from Kirsten Dunst to Bill Murray has stopped by for a bite). *joespizzanyc.com; 7 Carmine St; 10am-4am; pizza slices from $2.75.*

13 Roosevelt Avenue food trucks

When it comes to sidewalk grazing, it's hard to beat Roosevelt Ave and its

KAYAKING IN THE CITY

It's easy to forget that NYC is surrounded by water. One of the best ways to reconnect with the aquatic landscape is to head out on a free kayak ride from one of the boathouses around town. All you have to do is show up and register for a free 20-minute paddle on the water, against a backdrop of million-dollar views. Here's where to find a kayak: the Downtown Boathouse (*Hudson River Park nr N Moore St; 9am-4.30pm Sat + Sun mid-May–early Oct*); Governors Island (*10.30am-4pm Sat Jun-Aug*) and Brooklyn Bridge Park, near Pier 2 (*10am-3pm Sat, 5.30-6.45pm Jun-Aug*).

army of late-night Latino food trucks, carts and stalls. Just one stroll from 90th St to 103rd St will have you sipping on *champurrados* (a warm, thick, corn-based chocolate drink), nibbling on a *cemita* (a Mexican sandwich) and making room for some Ecuadorian fish stew. It's a cheap and quintessentially Queens experience. *Times vary.*

14 Smorgasburg

One of the greatest foodie events in New York City happens every weekend in Brooklyn. It's called Smorgasburg and features a staggering line-up of food vendors serving up dishes from every corner of the planet. You'll find Indian-style masala sandwiches, donuts, ramen burgers, Salvadoran *pupusas* (stuffed tortilla), tart cherry popsicles, and much more. Check the website for locations. *smorgasburg.com; 11am-6pm Sat + Sun; admission free.*

15 Brooklyn Flea

When the weekend arrives, head to Brooklyn to experience one of the best markets in the whole city. More than 100 vendors ply their wares here, with plenty of treasures on offer from the past and the present. You'll find everything from records to 1930s posters, vintage clothing, jewellery, homewares, artwork, antique collectables and craft items. More than two-dozen food vendors are also on hand, meaning you won't go hungry while you browse. Check the website for locations, which change seasonally. *brooklynflea.com; admission free.*

17

16 Independence Day

Nearly every city in America celebrates Independence Day with fireworks, but it's pretty hard to top New York's brilliant pyrotechnics display against the backdrop of soaring skyscrapers. The big event usually happens over the East River, allowing Brooklynites, Queens' residents and Manhattan's East Siders grand views. Plan ahead; it gets crowded, so arrive well ahead of sunset for a prime spot. *social.macys.com/fireworks; 4 Jul; free.*

17 Mermaid Parade

Celebrating sand, sea and the commencement of summer is this wonderfully quirky afternoon parade. It's a flash of glitter (and plenty of flesh), as elaborately costumed folks display their fish finery on Coney Island. It takes place annually in June on the closest Saturday to the beginning of summer. It's even more fun to take part, of course – although this is not free ($25 per participant). *coneyisland.com/programs/mermaid-parade; Jun free.*

18 Village Halloween Parade

It's great fun to come along to watch this outrageous parade, but it's even more fun to take part in it. Grab a costume, plaster your face with make-up and join in the action. The parade runs from Spring St to 16th St. All are welcome, as long as you're in costume. Just show up on Sixth Ave near Canal St between 7pm and 9pm on Halloween. *halloween-nyc.com; 31 Oct; free.*

Plan your schedule right and you can visit three of the best museums in the country without busting out your wallet. The Museum of Modern Art (MoMA; *moma.org; 11 W 53rd St*) gives free admission on Fridays from 4pm to 8pm. Go after 6pm to avoid the crowds. At the Guggenheim (*guggenheim.org; 1071 Fifth Ave at 89th St*), Saturday is the night to save with pay-what-you-wish admission from 5.45pm to 7.45pm. Meanwhile, the brand-new Whitney Museum (*whitney.org; 99 Gansevoort St*) near the High Line also has a discount night. Friday is pay what you wish from 7pm to 10pm.

ARTS & CULTURE · MUSIC & FILM · SPORTS & LEISURE · FOOD & DRINK · FESTIVALS & EVENTS

PORTLAND, OR

PORTLAND, OR

Portland is known for its craft beer and quirky vibe, and it's now also earning respect for its dining scene. Eating isn't as cheap as it once was, but meals in high-end restaurants are still a bargain compared with those in similar cities. For budget meals, food carts are everywhere.

02

03

04

© Danielle D. Hughson; Anthony Pidgeon | Getty Images; © Irvin Hayes Jr. | 500px

01 OMSI Science Pub

This series presents lectures about cutting-edge ideas in science, technology, history and geology, everything from the origin of quince to the future of the polar seas, presented with a pop spin to make them as entertaining as they are informative. Ever made a beer geyser using sound waves? Pondered the life cycle of a thermophile? Here's your chance. *omsi.edu; suggested donation $5.*

02 Powell's City of Books

Powell's is a Portland institution – almost a museum. Most evenings, the flagship store – which occupies a whole block – brings visiting authors to read from and sign new books. Get lost in the many colour-coded rooms and search for bargain-priced used copies of titles you want. *powells.com; 1005 W Burnside St; 9am-11pm; readings free.*

03 Forest Park

This 5000-acre urban wilderness area contains more than 80 miles

NORTH PARK BLOCKS
CYCLE PORTLAND BIKE TOURS & RENTALS
Burnside Bridge
EASTBANK ESPLANADE
Pioneer Courthouse Sq
Pioneer Pl
DOWNTOWN
Morrison Bridge
LOWNSDALE SQ
CHAPMAN SQ
Willamette River
Hawthorne Bridge
SOUTH PARK BLOCKS
TOM MCCALL WATERFRONT PARK
Portland State University
PETTYGROVE PARK
RIVER PLACE
500 m
0.25 miles

Vital statistics

- Population: 2 million
- Best for: Cyclists and food-cart fanatics
- Unit of currency: US dollar $
- Price index: US$200 per day

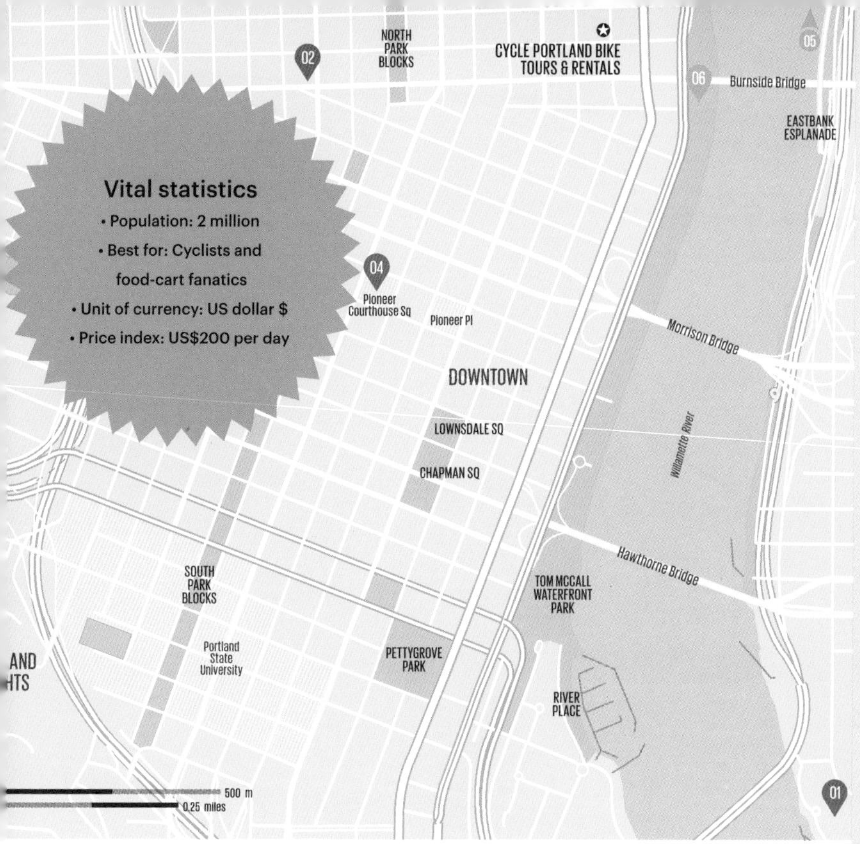

(130km) of hiking paths, including the popular 30-mile/48-km Wildwood Trail, which snakes through the park and intersects several other, shorter trails. Parking is free at most trailheads; Lower MacLeay Park is a handy starting point. *forestparkconservancy.org; NW 29th Ave & Upshur St; 5am-10pm daily; free.*

04 Pioneer Courthouse Square

The heart of downtown (often called Portland's 'living room'), Pioneer Square offers top-notch people-watching opportunities and convenient stairs on which to sit while you devour whatever you've picked up from a nearby food cart. On Mondays from 10am to 2pm there's a farmers' market. Other events and festivals fill the square throughout the year. *thesquarepdx.org; SW Broadway & Morrison St; 24 hours; free.*

05 Last Thursday Art Walk

This loose-knit, oblong carnival brings monthly mayhem (in a good way; just don't try to park close) to hip-and-arty NE Alberta St. Sure, you can shop here – your souvenirs will be one-of-a-kind – but it's equally fun just to browse, check out a gallery and stop for ice cream. *lastthurs pdx.org; NE 15th-30th Ave along Alberta St; 6-9.30pm last Thu of month; free.*

06 Saturday Market

Technically a crafts market, this weekend event (it opens Sundays too) shines as a street theatre venue. Stroll through at leisure to avoid missing anything. Pause for buskers, scope the waterfront and enjoy observing your fellow humans. *portlandsaturdaymarket.com; 2 SW Naito Pkwy; 10am-5pm Sat, 10am-4.30pm Sun Mar-Dec; free.*

TWO-WHEEL TOURING

The best way to get around Portland – both for purposes of sightseeing and for the environment – is by bicycle. The city's car traffic has grown increasingly frustrating; public transport is well run and affordable, but bicycling is more fun and offers even greater flexibility. And there are bike lanes and specially marked cycle streets all over town. If you're not bringing your own, rent a set of wheels through Cycle Portland Bike Tours (*portlandbicycle tours.com, rentals from $5*), then grab a bike-route map and hit the road.

SAN DIEGO

San Diego calls itself 'America's Finest City', and that's hard to dispute. The nation's most perfect weather, sunny coastlines, distant mountains, hilly parks and a buzzing downtown provide the backdrop for tons of free fun for all interests: surfers, sailors, beaches, brew pubs, historic haunts and a world-famous zoo.

ARTS & CULTURE MUSIC & FILM SPORTS & LEISURE FOOD & DRINK FESTIVALS & EVENTS

01 Balboa Park

Balboa Park occupies prime real estate smack in the centre of the city and is packed with museums and gardens that will keep you entertained for days. Some venues are free, such as **Timken Museum of Art** (1a; *timkenmuseum.org; 1500 El Prado; 10am-4.30pm Tue-Sat, noon-4.30pm Sun; free*), while others are big-city-pricey, so it's worth stopping by the **Visitors Center** (1b; *1549 El Prado; 9.30am-4.30pm*) to plan your time (and budget) effectively. *balboapark.org*

02 Hotel Del Coronado

It costs nothing to wander the all-timber, whitewashed main building of this much-beloved hotel (built 1888) with its conical towers, cupolas, turrets, balconies and acres of polished wood that conjure visions of panama hats and linen suits. The 1959 Marilyn Monroe film *Some Like It Hot* was filmed here, and a century-plus of photos of famous guests line the walls. *hoteldel.com; 1500 Orange Ave, Coronado; 24hr; admission free.*

03 Old Town State Historic Park

In 1821, when California was under Mexican control, this area became the territory's first civilian settlement. Now the plaza is surrounded by trees and period buildings housing museums, shops and restaurants. You can take a free guided tour from the Visitor Center at 11am and 2pm daily. *www.parks.ca.gov; 4002 Wallace St; visitor center & museums Mon-Thu 10am-4pm, 10am-5pm Fri-Sun May-Sep; admission free to park, most museums & historic buildings.*

04 Movie night

The always-buzzing pool at the mid-century modern **Pearl Hotel** (4a; *thepearlsd.com; 1410 Rosecrans St; Wed*) offers free 'dive-in' movies on a big screen most Wednesdays. Just buy a drink if you want to jump in! Other nights, it's worth paying a little to catch an art-house flick at the 1928 art-deco landmark **La Paloma Theatre** (4b; *lapalomatheatre.com; 471 S Coast Hwy 101, Encinitas; $10 cash only*), in northern San Diego County.

05 Spreckels Organ Pavilion

The sugar-beet-rich Spreckels family donated the Spreckels Organ Pavilion in Balboa Park with the stipulation that San Diego must always have an official organist. The pipe organ here is said to be the world's second-largest outdoor pipe organ, and is situated in a curved colonnade. *Free concerts take place at 2pm Sundays year-round. spreckelsorgan.org; House of Hospitality, 1549 El Prado #10; 2pm Sun; free.*

02

SAN DIEGO ZOO

The justifiably famous San Diego Zoo is well worth the splurge. More than 3000 animals represent over 800 species, and this zoo has long set the standard for beautifully landscaped locations that replicate natural habitats. The koalas are so popular that they're an unofficial city mascot, and elephants, tigers, gorillas and Komodo dragons all get their moment in the sun (well, except for nocturnal species, visible indoors). ***sandiegozoo.org; 2920 Zoo Dr; 1-day pass adult/child from $48/38; 9am-9pm mid Jun–early Sep, 9am-5pm or 6pm early Sep–mid Jun. See San Diego Savings (p217) for discount passes.***

06 Beach life

Choosing San Diego's best beaches is like comparing jewels at Tiffany & Co. **Coronado Municipal Beach** has appeared on just about every Top 10 list, but away from this deservedly famous star, there's a beach for pretty much any scene: bodysurfing (**Pacific Beach**), surf breaks (**Sunset Cliffs** in Ocean Beach), family-friendly (**Shell Beach** in La Jolla), teen scene (**Mission Beach**) and even clothing-optional (**Black's Beach** in La Jolla). *24hr; free.*

07 Harbor Drive

A manicured waterfront promenade, the **Embarcadero** (7a) is perfect for strolling or jogging (or watching US Navy personnel doing likewise). Visit the **USS Midway Museum** (7b; *midway.org; 910 N Harbor Dr; 10am-5pm; adult/child $20/10*), a former aircraft carrier that's now one of the USA's top museums, then dine at chichi shopping centre **The Headquarters at Seaport** (7c; *theheadquarters.com; 789 W Harbor Dr; 10am-9pm Mon-Sat, 10am-8pm Sun; admission free*).

08 Brew pubs

America's Finest City is home to some of America's finest brew pubs, including the 40-or-so members of **San Diego Brewers Guild** (*sandiegobrewersguild.org*). There's no such thing as a free beer, but the drinks cost a lot less than they would at local cocktail bars and nightclubs. **Try Stone Brewing Company** (*stonelibertystation.com; 2816 Historic Decatur Rd; 11.30am-10pm Mon-Sat, 11am-9pm Sun; mains $14-29*), which is set in a former naval training centre.

09 Clayton's Coffee Shop

Some diners are imitation-old-

SAN DIEGO SAVINGS

Go ahead; forget the rental car. Most of San Diego is reachable via the Metropolitan Transit System (*sdmts.com*). Bus/tram rides cost $2.25/2.50, or day passes are a steal (*1-/2-/3-/4-day passes $5/9/12/15, plus a one-time $2 purchase of a reusable Compass Card*). For discounted admission to attractions, buy the Passport to Balboa Park (*good for one-time entry to 14 museums within one week; adult/child $53/29*), a Stay For The Day pass (*five museums; $43*) or the Combo Pass (*Passport plus zoo-admission; adult/child $89/52*). All can be purchased at the Transit Store (*sdmts.com; 102 Broadway*).

fashioned, but the 1940s-era Clayton's Coffee Shop is the real deal, with red leatherette swivel stools and booths with mini-jukeboxes. It does reasonably priced all-American breakfasts and some Mexican specialities such as *machaca* (spiced meat) with eggs and cheese, and it's not above panini and croque-monsieur sandwiches. For dessert: mile-high pie from the counter. *979 Orange Ave, Coronado; 6am-9pm Sun-Thu, 6am-10pm Fri + Sat; mains $8-12.*

10 Mission Hills eateries

A little out of the way, the Mission Hills neighbourhood doesn't look like much, but it's worth the trip for some of the city's favourite cheap ethnic holes-in-the-wall. Multi-award-winning **Saffron** (10a; *saffronsandiego.com; 3731-B India St; 10.30am-9pm Mon-Sat, 11am-8pm Sun; mains $8-11*) creates Thai grilled chicken, noodles and satay. Steps away, **El Indio** (10b; *el-indio.com; 3695 India St; 8am-9pm; dishes $3-9*) has been doing counter-service taquitos, tamales and breakfast burritos since 1940.

11 Comic-Con International

Every year in July, Comic-Con International turns normally, well, normal San Diego into a mega-centre of geek chic. Visitors from the world over shell out to gawk at America's largest event for collectors of comic and pop culture, from superheroes to anime, as well as the Hollywood types who attend. Tickets cost $50, but you can see plenty of wacky costumes around town for free. *comic-con.org; late Jul; free.*

12 Fleet Week

San Diego is headquarters of the US Navy's Pacific fleet, and during Fleet Week, actually more like 'Fleet Month', the military shows off with free events including a sea and air parade, classic car exhibitions, special tours of ships, the Miramar Air Show (the world's largest) and the Cabrillo Festival, which ceremonially welcomes the Spanish explorer who 'discovered' California. Look for sailors in dress whites. *fleetweeksandiego.org; mid-Sep–early Oct; 24hr; free.*

SAN DIEGO

ARTS & CULTURE | MUSIC & FILM | SPORTS & LEISURE | FOOD & DRINK | FESTIVALS & EVENTS

SAN FRANCISCO

From beatnik poetry and flower-powered hippies to Silicon Valley start-ups, San Francisco has long stood at the edge of American culture. For travellers, hilltop bay views and cable cars capture the city's romantic side. You can definitely leave your heart here, but there's no need to leave your wallet too.

01 Balmy Alley

Colourful murals have been an artistic fixture of the Mission District since the 1980s. Today, Balmy Alley has the biggest concentration of politically conscious murals in the city. Stop by the **Precita Eyes Muralists Center** (*precitaeyes.org/tours.html*) nearby to pick up a self-guided walking tour map of neighbourhood murals, whose themes range from everyday Bay area life to world peace. *balmyalley.com; Balmy St, btwn 24th & 25th Sts; 24hr; free.*

02 Cable Car Museum

Cable cars trundling up unbelievably steep hills is an enduring image of the City by the Bay. While cable-car boarding tickets aren't cheap ($7 per ride), this little museum of cable car history, which houses some antique cars, won't cost you a penny. You can even see the steel cable-car line whirring as it runs underneath the street. *cablecarmuseum.org; 1201 Mason St; 10am-5pm Oct-Mar, 10am-6pm Apr-Sep; free.*

02

04

11

Vital statistics
• Population: 6 million
• Best for: A tie for tech innovation and bohemian creativity
• Unit of currency: US dollar $
• Price index: US$205 per day
0 2 km
0 1 miles
Horseshoe Bay
ALCATRAZ
San Francisco Bay
Golden Gate Bridge
Aquatic Park
POWELL-HYDE (FRIEDEL KLUSSMANN) CABLE CAR TURNAROUND
POWELL-MASON CABLE CAR TURNAROUND
FISHERMAN'S WHARF
GHIRARDELLI SQUARE
TELEGRAPH HILL
THE MARINA
George R Moscone Recreation Center
PRESIDIO NATIONAL PARK
MAIN POST
RUSSIAN HILL
NORTH BEACH
PRESIDIO
COW HOLLOW
NOB HILL
CHINATOWN
FERRY BUILDING MARKETPLACE
GOLDEN GATE FORTUNE COOKIE FACTORY
EMBARCADERO
FINANCIAL DISTRICT (FIDI)
ALTA PLAZA PARK
LAFAYETTE PARK
CALIFORNIA ST CABLE CAR TURNAROUND
PACIFIC HEIGHTS
MONTGOMERY ST
UNION SQUARE
JAPANTOWN
THE TENDERLOIN
POWELL ST
YERBA BUENA GARDENS
FILLMORE
JEFFERSON SQUARE
THE RICHMOND
WESTERN ADDITION
University of San Francisco
CIVIC CENTER
Civic Center Plaza
CIVIC CENTER
SOUTH OF MARKET (SOMA)
NOPA
VAN NESS
UPPER HAIGHT
LOWER HAIGHT
HAYES VALLEY
MISSION BAY
GOLDEN GATE PARK
BUENA VISTA PARK
CHURCH ST
POTRERO FLATS
COLE VALLEY
CORONA HEIGHTS PARK
16TH ST MISSION
CASTRO ST
University of California San Francisco
DOLORES PARK
THE MISSION
POTRERO HILL
THE CASTRO
THE SUNSET
24T ST MISSION
TWIN PEAKS
NOE VALLEY
BERNAL HEIGHTS PARK
GLEN CANYON PARK
BERNAL HEIGHTS
GLEN PARK
MT DAVIDSON
STERN GROVE
12
17
16
06
08
05
14
04
11
03
02
09
15
01
10

03 **City Lights Books**
San Francisco's landmark independent bookstore was co-founded by poet Lawrence Ferlinghetti in 1953. Its tradition of political radicalism began when City Lights published Beat-poet Allen Ginsberg's *Howl*, which was put on trial for obscenity (Ferlinghetti won). The bookstore has a busy calendar of author readings that are free to attend, or just show up to browse the bookshelves. *citylights.com; 261 Columbus Ave; 10am-midnight; admission free.*

04 **Coit Tower**
Since 1933, this dazzling-white art-deco tower has topped Telegraph Hill in the North Beach neighbourhood. It's free to visit the tower's lower level, which displays political murals painted by Works Progress Administration (WPA) artists during the Depression. Find panoramic views by shelling out a little dough for an elevator ride to the top. *1 Telegraph Hill Blvd; 10am-5pm Nov-Apr, 10am-6pm May-Oct; admission free, elevator $8.*

05 **Musée Mécanique**
At the foot of Taylor St, this family-owned jewel box spills over with antique arcade games, retro pinball machines, hand-cranked music boxes and other child-like entertainment to delight all ages. Playing the games isn't free, but it is very, very cheap; some games cost just a penny (don't worry about bringing coins – there are change machines). *museemecaniquesf.com; Shed A, Pier 45, the Embarcadero; usually 10am-8pm; admission free.*

06 **Presidio Officers' Club**
In the green belt of the Presidio parklands, this restored military officers' club boasts adobe walls dating from

ONE-DAY FREE PASS

Start your morning with a cappuccino and an Italian pastry in North Beach. Climb the Filbert Street Steps to Coit Tower. Afterwards, wander into City Lights Books and then over to Chinatown for a bowl of noodles. Walk to waterfront Fisherman's Wharf, where sea lions bark at Pier 39 (p222) and historical ships moor at Hyde St Pier. Ride a cable car uphill to the tiny Cable Car Museum (p218). Downhill on Market St, take a BART train to the Mission District for an enormous San Francisco-style burrito.

the late 18th-century Spanish Colonial period. Museum exhibits, which cover the city's cultural heritage and the Bay's natural history, are free to browse. Check the online calendar and pre-register for free tickets to concerts, readings and archaeology tours. *presidioofficersclub.com; 50 Moraga Ave; 10am-6pm Tue-Sun, special event schedules vary; free.*

07 San Francisco City Guides

Free guided walking tours of the city are led by enthusiastic volunteers who treasure historical knowledge ranging from colourful gossip to little-known trivia. Take your pick of themed neighbourhood tours, perhaps 'Gold Rush City' or 'Art-deco Marina'. For San Francisco newcomers, the Chinatown walking tour is a classic (meet at Portsmouth Square Park). No reservations required. *sfcityguides.org; various meet-up locations; tour schedules vary; free, but donations are welcome.*

08 San Francisco Maritime National Historical Park

Near Fisherman's Wharf, you can whistle a sea shanty while viewing the free exhibits inside this national park visitor centre and maritime museum. The latter inhabits a 1930s Streamline Moderne building resembling an ocean liner. On Hyde St Pier, inspect floating ships from centuries past. *nps.gov/safr; 499 Jefferson St & 900 Beach St; 9.30am-5pm; visitor centre, museum & pier free, ship $10.*

09 Amoeba Music

Situated in the historically hippie, radical Haight neighbourhood, this is the city's definitive independent music shop. In-store performances by bands from as far away as Europe (or just LA) are free – no tickets required. Listen while you browse the endless racks of hip-hop, electronica, world beats and other ear-tickling albums – staff picks may blow your mind with experimental sounds. *amoeba.com; 1855 Haight St; live show schedules vary; free.*

10 Stern Grove Festival

Now in its 80th season, this free outdoor festival stages both fine performing arts groups, like the city's symphony and ballet, and more modern sounds such as mambo bands and folk music. Concerts are held on Sunday afternoons in summer. Show up early to get a good view of the stage, or any seat at all. *sterngrove.org; off Sloat Blvd at 19th Ave; mid-Jun–mid-Aug; free.*

11 Exploratorium

San Francisco's most beloved museum is an interactive new world of science and the senses. The admission fee for the Exploratorium's brand-new bayside campus is a little steep, but anyone can visit the outdoor galleries for free. Open-air exhibits range from a giant wind harp to a camera obscura hidden inside a painted rickshaw. *exploratorium.edu; Pier 15, the Embarcadero; 10am-5pm Tue-Sun, also 6-10pm Thu; outdoor exhibits free, museum admission adult/child $29/19.*

12 Golden Gate Bridge

Painted 'International Orange', this iconic landmark bridge soars over the Golden Gate Strait at the wind-whipped entrance to San Francisco Bay. Standing underneath one of the span's skyscraping art-deco towers, you can peer out at the tawny Marin Headlands or maybe spot a school of migratory whales as they breach offshore during the winter. *goldengatebridge.org; Hwy 101; vehicle* *traffic 24hr, pedestrian sidewalk 5am-6.30pm, 5am-9pm mid-March–early Nov; pedestrians free, vehicle toll from $7.25.*

13 Golden Gate Park

Ending at Ocean Beach, this 1000-acre/4 sq km urban park is a forested haven of botanical gardens and dirt paths worth ambling around. Don't miss gawking at the Dutch-style windmills and the bison paddock. Free events include everything from outdoor yoga classes to Italian opera concerts. *goldengatepark.com; btwn Fulton St & Lincoln Way, Stanyan St & Great Hwy; 24hr, individual attraction hours vary; admission free, surcharges apply for some attractions.*

14 Sea Lions at Pier 39

After the 6.9-magnitude Loma Prieta earthquake hit in 1989, California sea lions began hauling out on Pier 39 at Fisherman's Wharf. They've noisily stayed there ever since – up to 1700 of these marine mammals can be spotted lounging on the dock at one time. Go ahead, take a selfie with the city's unofficial mascots. *Pier 39, the Embarcadero; 10am-9pm, 10am-11pm late May-late Sep; free.*

15 El Farolito

Taco shops abound in the Mission District, a neighbourhood with Latin American roots. For cheapskates and gannets, the most famous hunger fix is an enormous San Francisco-style burrito, stuffed with extra rice, beans and veggies. Just try getting your mouth around the entire thing on your first bite. El Farolito adds fat slices of avocado too – mmmm-hmmm. *2779 Mission St; 10am-2.30pm Sun-Thu, 10am-3.30am Fri + Sat; meals under $10.*

16 Off the Grid

Calling itself a 'roaming mobile food extravaganza', this round-up of food trucks takes place every day of the week at different locations around the city and beyond. Favourite spots include 'Picnic at the Presidio' on Sunday afternoons

GRAZING AROUND THE CITY

San Francisco is a foodie town. Epicurean multi-course tasting menus of molecular gastronomy easily run into the hundreds of dollars, but you can also sample some of the city's most famous flavours for free. Chinatown's Golden Gate Fortune Cookie Factory (*56 Ross Alley; 8am-6pm*) gives out free samples, as does the sprawling Ghirardelli Square chocolate factory (*ghirardelli.com; 900 North Point St; 9am-11pm Sun-Thu, 9am-midnight Sat + Sun*). For more gourmet tastes, scope out the free samples offered by artisanal vendors at the Ferry Building Marketplace and the thrice-weekly farmers' market outside.

SAN FRANCISCO

and 'Twilight at the Presidio' on Thursday nights, which feature live music and fire pits. *offthegrid.com; Main Parade Ground, the Presidio; 5-9pm Thu & 11am-4pm Sun; admission free, food from $2.*

17 Fleet Week

Getting to board and to walk around US Navy ships or watch the parade of boats on San Francisco Bay is great, but it's really just a warm-up to the main event. A spectacular air show brings in the Blue Angels for gasp-worthy aerial tricks and feats of derring-do. It's best to watch the thrilling action from a picnic blanket spread out on the lawn at Marina Green. *fleetweeksf.org; various locations; early Oct; free.*

18 Hardly Strictly Bluegrass Festival

For more than a decade, this ginormous outdoor music festival has taken over Golden Gate Park during the first long weekend in October. True to its name, it's not just bluegrass, folk and country musicians who play on seven different stages, but also rockers, punks, indie bands and world beat masters. More than 100 different musical acts perform here each year. Come and listen! *hardlystrictlybluegrass.com; Golden Gate Park; early Oct; free.*

18

The USA's largest celebration of LGBT pride takes place in San Francisco, a city well known for its progressive activism for gay civil rights. Entry to a long weekend of wildly creative, fun events held in late June is free, although a small donation is requested at the gates. The biggest party is the Sunday parade, when more than 200 groups march down Market St while over a million spectators dressed in anything from rainbow-coloured ballerina tutus to all-black leather gear cheer. Held separately, the Dyke March and Trans March are also massively popular events. *sfpride.org*

TOP 10 FREE-RANGE ADVENTURES IN AMERICA'S NATIONAL PARKS

The national parks are America's wild playground. Some charge a nominal entry fee, but once you're in, they're full of fantastic free escapades.

Illustration | Hayley Warnham

VERTICAL HIKING

The 1.8 mile-/3.2km-long Precipice Trail dramatically ascends the east face of Champlain Mountain, along super-narrow ledges with vertical climbs up via ferrata-style rungs. *nps.gov/acad; Mount Desert Island, Acadia NP; opening hours vary; $15 individual 7-day pass.*

WILD HOT-TUBBING

Park on the 45th parallel and follow the steam to Boiling River, a bathing spot where hot springs enter Gardner River to create perfect soaking conditions. *www.nps.gov/yell; Mammoth Hot Springs, Yellowstone NP, ID, MT + WY; 24hr; $15 individual 7-day pass.*

FLOWER POWER

More than 1500 wildflowers explode into colour beneath the Appalachians during spring. Go backcountry hiking and wild camping ($14 to $23 per night) amid the blooming ephemerals. Watch out for black bears. *nps.gov/grsm; Great Smoky Mountains NP, NC + TN; 24hr; free.*

SNORKEL AROUND A FORT

Seventy miles (110km) from Key West, perched on a coral atoll, Fort Jefferson is the scene of much marine activity. Snorkel around the moat and sea wall, amid fish, coral and wrecks. *nps.gov/drto; Dry Tortugas NP, FL; 24hr; $5 7-day pass.*

WATERFALL-WALKING

The best short hike in an epic Sierra Nevada nirvana, this 6.5 mile/10.4km-long trail passes through the thundering mist created by two magnificent cascades: Vernal Falls and Nevada Falls. *nps.gov/yose; Mist Trail, Yosemite NP, CA; 24hr; $15 individual 7-day pass.*

GO BEAR

Few encounters are as exciting as running into a big brown bear. Fortunately, at Brooks Camp, the bears have tastier fish to fry than you. July-September is the best time to see them. *nps.gov/katm; 24hr; Brooks Camp, Katmai NP, AL; free.*

MOON-WALKING

Two hours' drive from the neon glow of Vegas, the night sky is so clear you can regularly see five planets. Rangers offer free lunar-lit night hikes in summer when there's a full moon. *nps.gov/grba; Great Basin NP, NV; 24hr; free.*

VOLCANO VOYEURISM

Surf's up in Hawai'i, and so is the lava... Kīlauea volcano remains active, and the spitting vent in Halema'uma'u crater can be viewed from the overlook at Jaggar Museum. *nps.gov/havo; Hawai'i Volcanoes NP, HI; 24hr; $8 individual 7-day pass.*

HUNT BISON

Follow in the footsteps of the Conservationist President in the park named in his honour, by exploring the badland prairies and fixing a mighty bison in your camera's crosshairs. *nps.gov/thro; Theodore Roosevelt NP, ND; 24hr; $10 individual 7-day pass.*

TRAVEL THROUGH SPACE AND TIME

A dark-sky park, Chaco has terrestrial wonders to complement its heavenly delights, with 1000-year-old Puebloan ruins, built to align with the stars during the equinox. Rangers offer free tours. *nps.gov/chcu; Chaco Culture National Historical Park, NM; 7am-sunset; $6 individual 7-day pass.*

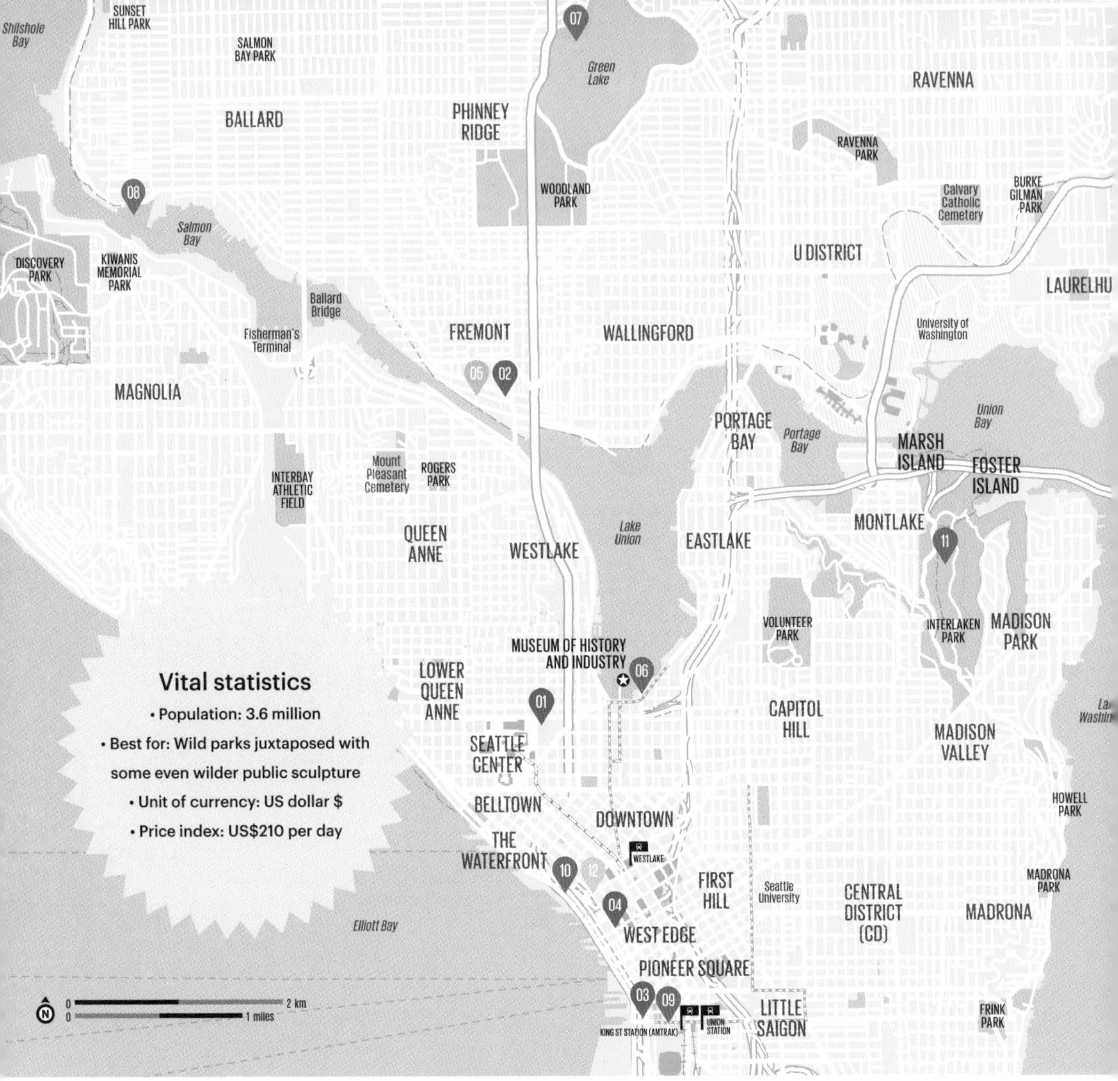

Vital statistics

- Population: 3.6 million
- Best for: Wild parks juxtaposed with some even wilder public sculpture
- Unit of currency: US dollar $
- Price index: US$210 per day

SEATTLE

Seattle is home to internet millionaires, hi-tech gadgetry and the world's richest man, but that doesn't necessarily mean it's expensive. You can give your credit card a rest while admiring cool public art, wandering through luxuriant urban parks, or finding plenty of gastronomic bargains in the USA's oldest farmers' market.

ARTS & CULTURE | MUSIC & FILM | SPORTS & LEISURE | FOOD & DRINK | FESTIVALS & EVENTS

01 Bill & Melinda Gates Foundation Visitor Center

This sustainable building cost about $500 million to construct in 2011 and is owned by the world's richest man, but, fear not, entry is free. Well set up for visitors, it focuses on Gates' philanthropic activities, displaying exhibits that are inspiring and interactive. Visitors are invited to add their own ideas to the foundation's intellectual bank. *gatesfoundation.org/visitor-center; 440 5th Ave N; 10am-5pm Tue-Sat, to 6pm summer months; free.*

02 Fremont Public Sculpture

The Seattle neighbourhood of Fremont lives up to its 'De Liberta Quirkas' ('freedom to be peculiar') motto with a bewildering array of public sculptures. Strange apparitions include a troll crushing a Volkswagen Beetle, a Cold War rocket attached to a fashion boutique, a cluster of commuters waiting for a train that never comes, and a statue of Vladimir Lenin rescued from a Czechoslovakian junkyard in the 1990s. *Fremont neighbourhood; 24hr; free.*

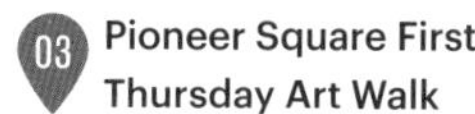

03 Pioneer Square First Thursday Art Walk

The craze for city art walks was apparently born in Seattle's red-bricked Pioneer Square in the 1980s. Still going strong, this self-guided walk links together some of the neighbourhood's 50-plus galleries, allowing punters to appreciate creative public sculpture, sip decent coffee, browse through temporary stalls in Occidental Park, and meet local artists to see what inspires them. *pioneersquare.org/experiences/first-thursday-art-walk; Pioneer Sq; 6-8pm 1st Thu of month; free.*

04 Seattle Art Museum (SAM)

Seattle's art culture is thriving thanks to the avant-garde presence of SAM, entrance to which is free on the first Thursday of every month. The museum's permanent collection emphasises Native American art along with dazzling modern creations, while surreal sculpture is amply represented in the nearby **Olympic Sculpture Park** (*2901 Western Ave; dawn-dusk; free*). *seattleartmuseum.org; 1300 1st Ave; 10am-5pm Wed & Fri-Sun, 10am-9pm Thu; free 1st Thu of month.*

05 Fremont Almost-free Outdoor Cinema

Summer isn't summer until you've taken in a movie at Fremont's 'almost free' al-fresco cinema bivouacked in a diminutive parking lot and guarded over by murals

THE CITY BY BIKE

Seattle enhanced its already bicycle-friendly reputation in 2014 by introducing the Pronto bike-sharing scheme (*prontocycleshare.com*). In common with similar bike-sharing schemes around the world, the idea is simple. For a small fee (*$8 for 24 hours; $16 for three days*), you can borrow a bicycle from one of 50 docking stations scattered around central Seattle. Return it to any station within 30 minutes and you'll incur no extra cost. Take it for longer, and there's a small charge (*$2 for up to one hour*). For visitors not averse to some pedalling, it's a no-brainer – stay fit, reduce congestion and save money.

of Bogart and Bergman. On a good night, half of the neighbourhood turns out, some dragging armchairs, others dressed in movie-themed garb (zombies are especially popular). Mobile food carts lay on cheap, delicious, aromatic snacks. *fremontoutdoormovies.com; 3501 Phinney Ave N; Jul & Aug; $5.*

06 Center for Wooden Boats

Seattle is surrounded by water, so it is practically obligatory to hop on a boat at some point to view the city from afar, framed by gliding sea birds and rippling waves. For 25 years, this maritime museum has been offering free one-hour boat rides on an assortment of watercraft. To board, arrive any Sunday after 10am and sign up; first-come-first-served. *cwb.org; 1010 Valley St; 10am-7pm; free.*

07 Green Lake Park

This always-busy park that encircles a small natural lake in one of North Seattle's most affluent neighbourhoods is where you can view the city with its guard down, a place where the locals congregate to run, bike, date and debate. Dodge roller-skaters and dot-com entrepreneurs getting bullied by their personal trainers as you stroll along the pleasant paved paths. *7201 E Greenlake Dr N; 24hr; free.*

08 Hiram M Chittenden Locks

Commonly known as the Ballard Locks, this ingenious system allows an assortment of boats to negotiate a 22ft height difference between Lake Union and Puget Sound. Flanked by manicured botanical gardens, it's a glorious place to linger and watch passing birds, boats, motor yachts, kayaks and the odd sea lion. There's even a viewable underwater fish ladder built to accommodate spawning salmon. *myballard.com/ballard-locks-seattle; 3015 NW 54th St; 24hr; free.*

09 Klondike Gold Rush National Historic Park

Seattle was the main embarkation point for history's most legendary gold rush, providing gear and logistics for prospectors heading north to Canada's

FREE FIRST THURSDAYS

If you have plenty of wiggle-room when planning a trip to Seattle, try to be in town on the first Thursday of the month when many of the city's museums waive their entrance fees. Up to a dozen museums participate in this generous scheme. Schedule a visit to a couple of the big-hitters, such as the Seattle Art Museum (p227) – *normally $19.50* – or the Museum of History and Industry (*mohai.org; 860 Terry Ave N; 10am-5pm Fri-Wed, 10am-8pm Thu, normally $17*) and you'll save a packet.

Klondike region. This free museum run by the US National Parks Service recreates the atmosphere of frenetic energy of 1897-98 by tracking the stories of five gold-rush pioneers on their journeys from rags to occasional riches. *nps.gov/klgo; 117 S Main St; 9am-5pm daily; free.*

10 Seattle Free Walking Tours

Seattle offers an impressive cache of walking tours, from coffee crawls to beer-supping, but few are as good as these gratis excursions set up by a couple of Seattle-based world-travellers in 2012. Drawing inspiration from similar jaunts offered in European cities, these short culture-heavy ambles around downtown are rich in anecdotes and historical details. Book places online. *seattlefreewalkingtours.org; Pike Place Market; tours 9.30am, 11am, 2pm; free.*

11 Washington Park Arboretum

Fittingly, the Pacific Northwest's 'evergreen city' is home to a huge alfresco plant 'museum' of some 5500 species contained within one of Seattle's most salubrious parks. There might be wilder green spaces in Seattle, but few are as multifarious as this one which, come the spring, displays a giddy array of pink- and orange-flowered azaleas and rhododendrons. Free guided walks are offered at weekends. *depts.washington.edu/uwbg/gardens/wpa.shtml; 2300 Arboretum Dr E; dawn-dusk; free.*

12 Pike Place Market

Seattle's biggest tourist site is also, ironically, its ultimate 'local' experience, an unofficial confederation of small-scale farmers, family bakers, halibut-tossing fisherfolk, artisan cheesemakers and fresh-from-the-fields fruit stalls that sprawls like a colourful slice of street theatre overlooking Seattle's waterfront. Work up an appetite, dive into the melee and go off in search of Seattle's cheapest soul food. *pikeplacemarket.org; 1st Ave and Pike St; 9am-6pm Mon-Sat, 9am-5pm Sun; admission free.*

ARTS & CULTURE · MUSIC & FILM · SPORTS & LEISURE · FOOD & DRINK · FESTIVALS & EVENTS

TORONTO

A relatively young city on the world stage, Toronto is becoming increasingly sophisticated, with newer and glitzier landmarks. Luckily, she prides herself on inclusiveness and there's always one way or another to take part in festivals, events and attractions at less-than-full-ticket-price, if not completely free.

01 Bata Shoe Museum

This mammoth and airy shoe box draws on the world's largest shoe collection, featuring 1000 at a time. Covering 4500 years of global shoe history, it offers imaginative exhibits. If you go along on a pay-what-you-can Thursday evening it's sooo much cheaper than shoe shopping. *batashoemuseum.ca; 327 Bloor St W; 5-8pm Thu; suggested donation C$5.*

02 Evergreen Brickworks

Dating from 1889, the Don Valley Brick Factory has been re-imagined as a community gathering place after years of disuse. Learn its history, hike a nature trail through ravine forest and meadows in the former quarry and poke around the city's largest farmers' market (weekends). *evergreenbrickworks.com; 550 Bayview Ave; 9am-5pm Mon-Fri, 8am-5pm Sat, 10am-5pm Sun; free.*

03 Skating at Nathan Phillips Square

Under decorated arches surrounded by skyscrapers in front of downtown

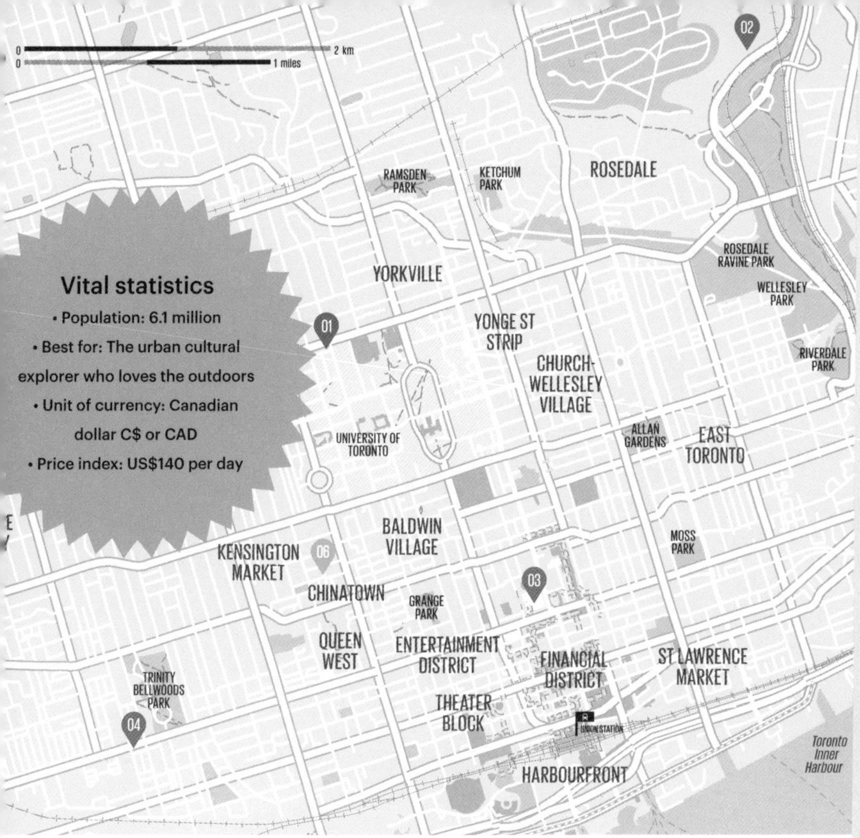

0 2 km
0 1 miles

RAMSDEN PARK
KETCHUM PARK
ROSEDALE
ROSEDALE RAVINE PARK
WELLESLEY PARK
YORKVILLE
YONGE ST STRIP
CHURCH-WELLESLEY VILLAGE
RIVERDALE PARK
UNIVERSITY OF TORONTO
ALLAN GARDENS
EAST TORONTO
BALDWIN VILLAGE
KENSINGTON MARKET
MOSS PARK
CHINATOWN
GRANGE PARK
QUEEN WEST
ENTERTAINMENT DISTRICT
FINANCIAL DISTRICT
ST LAWRENCE MARKET
TRINITY BELLWOODS PARK
THEATER BLOCK
UNION STATION
Toronto Inner Harbour
HARBOURFRONT
EAST VIEW PARK
Lake Ontario

Vital statistics

- Population: 6.1 million
- Best for: The urban cultural explorer who loves the outdoors
- Unit of currency: Canadian dollar C$ or CAD
- Price index: US$140 per day

City Hall, the rink provides a low-cost, all-Toronto outdoor experience. Cheap chip wagons and hot chocolate are steps away. *nathanphillipssquareskaterentals.com; 100 Queen St W; late Nov–mid-March, 10am-10pm; C$10 for two hours.*

04 West Queen West

Queen Street, west from Bathurst St to Dufferin St, is one of Toronto's hippest strips. Explore independent shops, cafes, galleries and eateries that showcase the city's multicultural and entrepreneurial spirit. Then sit and people-watch in **Trinity Bellwoods Park**. *Queen Street West btwn Bathurst + Dufferin Sts; 24hr; free.*

05 Contact Photography Festival

The world's largest international photography festival runs throughout May. Some 1500 artists are curated from an open call, ramping up the creativity. At dozens of different venues, including shops and even billboards, simply check out the programme, pick a neighbourhood and plan your own photographic tour. *scotiabankcontactphoto.com; most exhibits free*

06 Kensington Market

A long-time cultural conglomeration arising from waves of immigration, the market features Portuguese, West Indian and Central American elements (to name a few). Particularly sensory in summer, it's set in a neighbourhood of Victorian row houses, featuring ethnic food stalls, bakeries and vintage shops that spill on to the street (check out pedestrian Sundays). *kensington-market.ca; btwn Spadina Ave & Bathurst, College & Dundas Sts; times vary, daily; admission free.*

THE LOCAL'S VIEW

"I walk everywhere – it's the best way to experience this city – and if you need to transit more than three times in a day, get a day pass (C$*11.50*). Toronto's food is phenomenal but can be pricey: I visit food trucks and many ethnic eateries (several Indian roti places along Queen West) and eat out more during Summerlicious (*toronto.ca/summerlicious*) and Winterlicious (*toronto.ca/winterlicious*) festivals, which offer reduced prix-fixe at popular restaurants. *NOW* magazine (*nowtoronto.com*), available every Thursday, lists free one-off events and countless festivals, street and food fairs, so you can make low-cost plans on the spot." – Gino Pugliano, Toronto-dweller

FREE SPECTATOR SPORTS IN THE USA

Sports are a big deal in the US, and prime tickets can cost a bomb – but you can be part of the action and atmosphere for nowt at these athletic alternatives.

US POND HOCKEY CHAMPS – MINNEAPOLIS, MN

Simple: if you can stand the cold, you can stand and watch. Minnesota hosts this championship every January, which see amateur teams do battle on frozen Lake Nokomis. With no seats (or fees), there's nothing between you and the puck-tussling action. *uspondhockey.com.*

BOSTON MARATHON – BOSTON, MA

The world's oldest annual marathon has been held every Patriots' Day (third Monday in April) since 1897. Standing by the roadside, you're not simply watching 30,000 runners, you're celebrating the history, tradition and – after the bombings of 2013 – a sense of solidarity engendered by all those pounding feet. *baa.org.*

VENICE BEACH STREET-BALL – LA, CA

As well as ogling at the outdoor gym, Venice Beach is the place to see raw, back-to-roots basketball. Street-ball is fluid, free-form basketball, with no ref, fewer rules and lots of showing off. Watch a spontaneous game or come on summer Sundays for the Venice Basketball League.

LITTLE LEAGUE BASEBALL WORLD SERIES – WILLIAMSPORT, PA

Tickets for the Baseball World Series can nudge $1000. Tickets for the Little League version don't cost a dime. This competition has run every August since 1947, and sees players aged 11 to 13 dashing around the Williamsport diamond in front of thousands. *llbws.org.*

IDITAROD – ANCHORAGE, AK

They call this 1000 mile/1600km-long dog-sled dash across Alaska to Nome 'The Last Great Race on Earth®'. Fortunately, watching the ceremonial start on the first Saturday in March – from Anchorage's Fourth Ave to Campbell Creek – is less challenging. *iditarod.com.*

EAST COAST SURFING CHAMPIONSHIPS – VIRGINIA BEACH, VA

Admire pros and amateurs alike every August at the USA's oldest surfing competition. Since it began in 1963, the event has evolved; it's now a free sports festival, with top skateboarders, skimboarders, stand-up paddleboarders and beach volleyballers on show too. *surfecsc.com.*

PHILADELPHIA INTERNATIONAL CYCLING CHAMPIONSHIP – PHILADELPHIA, PA

This cycle race is the most prestigious outside Europe. Good spectator spots around the city include Manayunk, to watch riders climb the 'Manayunk Wall', and Midvale Ave, with its party and Sprint Zone views. *procyclingtour.com.*

SPRING FOOTBALL – COUNTRYWIDE

American Football games aren't cheap. Even College League game costs a pretty penny – unless you catch a practice game in March/April. At these, fans can assess the best new players, grab autographs and get pumped for the upcoming season, for free. *fbschedules.com.*

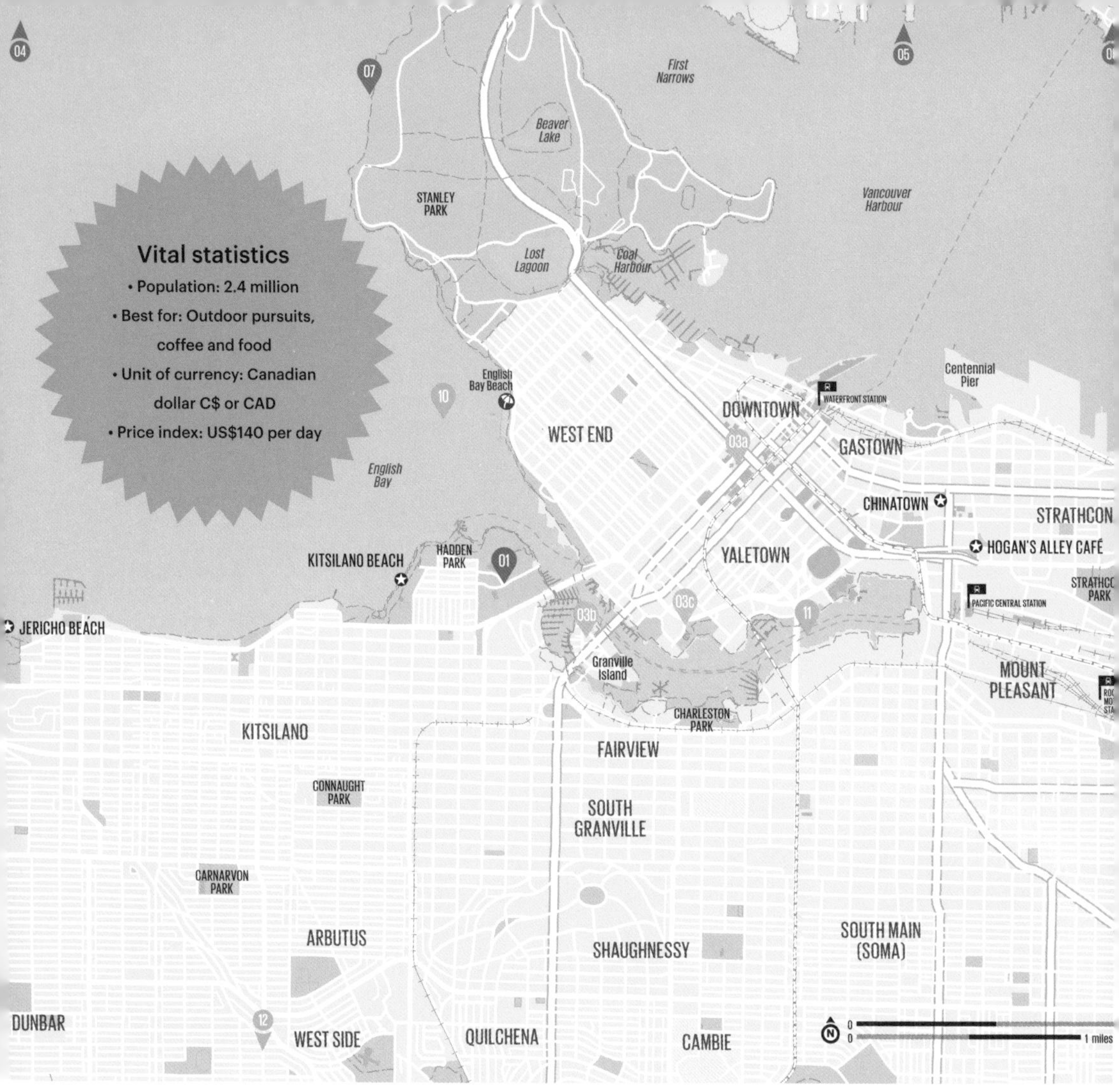

VANCOUVER

Vancouver is like a child's drawing – it has everything in it: the ocean, snow-capped mountains, beaches, skyscrapers, forests and people of all colours enjoying it. And then there's the food! While property prices have soared, the cost of travel (for those in the know) has not. Your playground awaits...

01 Gordon MacMillan Southam Observatory

Visit the GMS Observatory for a look into the heavens – the view of space through the 0.5m Cassegrain telescope beneath the 10m-high dome will astound you. The observatory was designed to be part of a community outreach programme, so it doesn't incur the entrance fees of the adjacent HR MacMillan Space Centre. *spacecentre.ca/gms; 1100 Chestnut St; 8pm-midnight Sat Jul-Aug; admission by voluntary donation.*

02 Fresh Air Cinema

Bring a pillow, bring a lawn chair, bring your friends – get comfortable and enjoy a great film, projected on to a giant inflatable movie screen under the stars. These free pop-up cinemas pop up throughout the year, though more take place in the summer when the weather is more conducive to outdoor airings. Follow @OutdoormoviesBC on Twitter for dates and locations. *freshaircinema.ca; free.*

03 Vancouver International Jazz Festival

This lively music festival has been going for over 30 years, and while many of its events are ticketed, there are hundreds of free concerts throughout the city during its two-week run, so the impecunious can join in too. Free venues include the **Vancouver Art Gallery** (3a; *vanartgallery.bc.ca; 750 Hornby St*), **Granville Island** (3b; *granvilleisland.com; 1661 Duranleau St*) and **David Lam Park** (3c; *1300 Pacific Blvd*) in Yale Town. *coastaljazz.ca; Jun; free.*

04 Bowen Island Ferry

The Howe Sound network of fjords is one of the most remarkable sights on the west coast of Canada, and it is best viewed from the water. Instead of hiring a costly powerboat in Horseshoe Bay, just hop aboard the ferry there to Bowen Island – the view from the deck is just as good. Before your return voyage, go for a wander or spend that saved cash on a meal. *bcferries.com; Horseshoe Bay; return fare C$12.*

05 Grouse Grind

Why pay C$40 for a gondola ride up Grouse Mountain when you could take on such a rewarding urban workout? 'Mother Nature's Stairmaster' will lead you up 853m over roughly 3km and wind you through dense coastal forest. The view from the 'Peak of Vancouver' will be well worth the effort. Pay C$10 for the gondola down or descend the nearby BCMC trail for free. *grousemountain.com; 6400 Nancy Green Way; free.*

ONE-DAY FREE PASS

Breakfast at Hogan's Alley Café (*hogansalleycafe.com; 789 Gore St; 6.30am-5pm Mon-Fri, 8am-4pm Sat, 8am-2pm Sun; mains C$8-10*) before exploring atmospheric Chinatown on foot. Next, stroll along False Creek, or nab one of the mini ferries (*$5.50*), to Granville Island Public Market (*granvilleisland.com/public market; Johnston St; 9am-7pm*). Continue west on foot and bus to the University of British Columbia, savouring Kitsilano Beach and Jericho Beach en route. At UBC, dine cheaply at the AMS Student Nest (*ams.ubc.ca/nest; 6133 University Blvd; 7am-11.30pm*) and visit the incredible Museum of Anthropology (*moa.ubc.ca; 6393 NW Marine Dr; 10am-5pm Wed-Mon, 10am-9pm Tue; C$16.75, C$9 Tue evenings*).

06 Lynn Canyon Park

Although the vertiginous drop to the rushing waters of Lynn Creek from the swaying suspension bridge may be less than that dividing the Capilano Suspension Bridge from the ground beneath, this particular park's wobbly offering is totally free. Included in the non-existent price tag are numerous trails beneath evergreen stands. The bravest of the visitors here are those who take a dip in the creek's frigid waters. *lynncanyon.ca; 7am-9pm summer, reduced hours off-season; free.*

07 Stanley Park Seawall

Whether you choose to walk, run, skate or cycle it, the Seawall that runs around the city's iconic Stanley Park is perhaps Vancouver's quintessential experience. The paved 8.8km-long path snakes beneath towering trees and along the seashore, offering staggering views of English Bay, the mountains and the gleaming skyline. If you are longing for more once you've completed the trail, continue around False Creek and west along the beaches to the University of British Columbia. *Downtown & West End; free.*

08 Dine Out Vancouver

This 17-day celebration of culinary delights features many of the city's finest restaurants offering three-course tasting menus for the sum of C$18, C$28 and C$38. Although certainly not free, these offerings represent great value for money and give you a chance to try out some top-notch food that may otherwise be beyond your means. There are also other epicurean events that take place in the city, such as street-food markets and local craft beer-tasting sessions. *dineoutvancouver.com; Jan.*

THRIFTY COMMUTING

Transit day passes (C$9.75) are a great way to cover a lot of ground at minimal cost. These passes include the SeaBus, which enables users to get to and from the North Shore's many attractions, such as Grouse Grind (p235) and Lynn Canyon Park. The best option, however, is the mighty bicycle. If you have the option to bring (or borrow) one, do so – the city has a great network of cycle lanes, and for longer journeys buses have bike racks mounted on them (the SeaBus also allows bikes).

05

12

09 Shipyards Night Market

Filling the historic Wallace Shipyard on Vancouver's North Shore, this weekly night market is a great place to pick up fresh produce from farmers, devour a meal from one of the dozen or so food trucks, and enjoy live entertainment. It's perfectly placed next to the SeaBus terminal, which means you can also take a budget-friendly scenic cruise to and from downtown. *northshoregreenmarket.com; Shipyard Plaza; 5-10pm Fri May-Sep; admission free.*

10 Celebration of Light

The entire shoreline and the waters of English Bay are bathed in light during this annual fireworks competition, which is one of the finest in the world. Three countries take turns to best choreograph their displays to music, which is played on loudspeakers and over local radio. The prime viewing spot is on English Bay Beach and in Vanier Park, which are the closest viewpoints to the floating barge that launches the pyrotechnic displays. *hondacelebrationoflight.com; English Bay; Jul; free.*

11 Dragon Boat Festival

Hundreds of dragon boat teams, many from around the world, congregate near Science World in False Creek every year during the third week of June for a weekend of choreographed and colourful water-bashing. Besides the excitement of the dragon boat racing itself, the festival highlights include plenty of food stalls, children's activities, art installations and shopping, as well as free music concerts and theatrical events. *dragonboatbc.ca; False Creek; free.*

12 Ships to Shore Festival

On Canada Day (1 July) and during the days that precede it, the port of Steveston in Richmond plays host to a fleet of historic and working ships. There are loads of fabulous free activities, including on-board tours of the vessels. The event coincides with the annual **Steveston Salmon Festival** (*stevestonsalmonfest.ca*), which takes place a short walk away in Steveston Park. *richmond.ca/shipstoshore; Britannia Shipyard, 5180 Westwater Dr, Steveston; free.*

ARTS & CULTURE | MUSIC & FILM | SPORTS & LEISURE | FOOD & DRINK | FESTIVALS & EVENTS

WASHINGTON, DC

When it comes to freebies, Washington DC tops the world. The cost of museums? Gratis. Concerts? Nada. Jaunts through the White House and Congress? Zilch. Even drinking establishments throw in no-pay, or discounted, beverages. The sum of the capital? You can spend weeks having fun, almost without spending a dime.

01 Bureau of Engraving and Printing

Just in case (with all these freebies) you've forgotten what money actually looks like, head here to see US dollars being printed. Free 40-minute tours, which run every 15 minutes or so, feature an introductory film after which you can view the production floor and watch million$ roll off the presses. You can even spend some bucks yourself on the currency products on sale. *moneyfactory.gov/washingtondctours.html; 14th & C Sts, SW; 8.30am-3pm; free.*

02 Library of Congress

Strangely, the site with the most boring name is one of the most exciting city highlights. Not only does it hold one of the world's largest collections of books, but beyond the covers, the stunning Thomas Jefferson building is replete with mosaics, paintings and fascinating history. Regular free daily tours give a rundown of the many chapters of this palace of pages. *loc.gov; 101 Independence Ave SE; free; 8.30am-5pm Mon-Sat; free.*

Vital statistics

- Population: 4.8 million
- Best for: Cultural stars and happening bars
- Unit of currency: US dollar $
- Price index: US$195 per day

03 **National Archives**
This is the place where locals' hearts go aflutter. The reason? It houses the country's Constitution, the Bill of Rights and the Declaration of Independence. Although John Hancock's *John Hancock* (American slang for 'signature') is highly important, also interesting here are the public vaults, a fascinating, interactive collection of original records from Abraham Lincoln's telegrams to recordings from the Oval Office. *archives.gov; 700 Pennsylvania Ave NW; 10am-5.30pm; free.*

04 **National Theater**
Children, too, can get their free fun on Saturday mornings at a series of programmes that inspire creativity and imagination through play, laughter, puppets, interactive performances, dance and music – and consist of everything from reptile presentations to flamenco dance steps. See the website for the schedules and bear in mind that tickets are distributed on a first-come-first-served basis 30 minutes before the curtain rises. *thenationaldc.org/saturday-morning-at-the-national; 1321 Pennsylvania Ave NW; 9.30am Sat; free.*

05 **Pentagon tour**
Not surprisingly, there are numerous rules surrounding any visits to the Pentagon (visits must be reserved from 14 to 90 days in advance, for example), but it's well worth making the effort for a glimpse inside the US Department of Defense's headquarters. Tours cram a lot into the hour: an informative run-down on the military, visits to memorials and plenty of unusual facts and figures. *pentagontours.osd.mil/tour-selection.jsp; The Pentagon; 1hr-tours Mon-Fri 9am-3pm; free.*

THE LOCALS' VIEW

"Head to 7th St in Shaw, DC's new trendy neighbourhood, the perfect destination for both day-drinking and nightlife. Think killer cocktails and local beer for less than $10, great bar snacks for about $5 and plenty of delicious food to prevent hangovers." – Erin Petrey, Shaw resident

"Don't miss Captain White's Seafood City (*1100 Maine Ave SW*), an outdoor fish market where you can eat a paper bag-full of steamed crabs (while standing on a barge!) for about $7. It's a true favourite of DC locals." – Molly Cox, local cheap-eat connoisseur

06 Jazz at the National Gallery's Sculpture Garden

On balmy summertime Friday evenings at the National Gallery of Art Sculpture Garden you can swing in to catch free performances of salsa, xylophone and Afrofunk. DC is a bastion of jazz – greats such as Duke Ellington and Shirley Horn cut their teeth here – and these al-fresco soirées make it available to the masses. *Constitution Ave NW, btwn 3rd & 9th Sts; 5-8.30pm Fri May-Sep; free.*

07 John F Kennedy Center for the Performing Arts' Millennium Stage

Every evening, whether or not you're attending a ticketed performance, you can grab a live act at the Millennium Stage at DC's performing arts memorial, the Kennedy Center. The acts vary from the sublime (Washington National Opera youngsters) to the ridiculous (skateboarders improvising to music). The class act goes to the setting – on the banks of the Potomac River. *kennedy-center.org/programs/millennium; 2700 F St NW; 6pm; free.*

08 DC cultural tours

You can pound the pavements on your own using the free maps, apps and audio of **Cultural Tourism DC** (*culturaltourismdc.org*). For a more local flavour, head off on a day or night tour with a guide from **DC by Foot** (*freetoursbyfoot.com/washington-dc-tours*). Guide quality can vary so take pot luck; themes range from secrets and scandals to a more straightforward National Mall stroll. *Venues & times vary; tip appreciated.*

09 Dumbarton Oaks Park

This compact but beautiful park designed by landscape architect Beatrix Farrand on the northern edge of Georgetown is one of DC's local secrets. Enter off the hidden Lovers' Lane (off R St) and wander through lush foliage, over quaint bridges and past grazing deer. This spot is among the coolest of places in these humid climes. *nps.gov/olst/planyourvisit/dumbarton.htm; R St NW; sunrise-sunset; free.*

10 Explore on a Capital Bikeshare cycle

Share bikes are a great, cheap and often speedy way to make your way between site highlights. You must change bike every 30 minutes or you will be charged $2 per half hour thereafter (they are commuter bikes, after all), but there are plenty of stations. The downsides? No helmets are provided and stations can be full or empty, especially at the end of the day. *capitalbikeshare.com; $8 per 24hr.*

11 Meander the National Mall's monuments

Whatever you think of **The Mall** (11a) – a 3-mile/5km-long rectangle of patchy grass – it is 'America's front yard'. Anchored by the US Capitol at one end and the **Lincoln Memorial** (11b) at the other, The Mall is dotted with other memorials, including ones for Vietnam veterans and Martin Luther King, Jr. Be sure to ascend the **Washington Monument** (11c; also free) for a bird's-eye view. *900 Ohio Dr SW; 24hr; free.*

12 Smithsonian National Zoological Park Conservation Biology Dept

More than two million people per year visit this zoo to see its various critters and to watch demonstrations and feeding sessions. Pandas are the star attractions, but over 400 species of animals (2000 animals in total) occupy enclosures that are built to replicate their natural habitat. Even if you aren't particularly into zoos, the grounds are pleasant and worth a little wander. *nationalzoo.si.edu; 3001 Connecticut Ave NW; 6am-8pm summer, 6am-6pm winter; free.*

13 Ben's Chili Bowl

Ben's Chili Bowl is the quintessential cheap and cheerful hangout, considered a 'landmark', not only for its location on U St (where riots took place in the 1960s), but also for its inexpensive chilli dogs and milkshakes, and the fact that President Barack Obama once munched on a half-smoke (a hotdog with chilli and onion) here. *benschilibowl.com/menu; 1213 U St NW; 6am-2am Mon-Thu, 6am-4am Fri, 7am-4am Sat, 11am-midnight Sun; chilli dog $4.40.*

14 Food trucks

A bevy of food trucks park around DC's 'hoods. Some snacks are sublime, others just 'meh', but it depends on your taste (and to a certain extent your budget), of course. Big-name chefs have rolled up, too, so you may hit the culinary jackpot. A few bucks will get you anything from Ibérico pork sandwiches to crab salads. And a (cheap) street party. *foodtruckfiesta.com; various locations & times; small filled bun $4.*

15 Happy hours

Love 'em or hate 'em, happy hours – a DC institution – are guaranteed to pull in the punters, from students to staffers heading home from 'the Hill'. Between approximately 4pm and 7pm many establishments, from highly glossed restaurants to grungy bars, offer some type of two-for-one or reduced-priced special, so you can tank up cheaply. *dchappyhours.com or bardc.com/happyhour; various locations & times; beer $3-5.*

16 DC Jazz Festival

Celebrating DC's historic contribution to jazz (many world-famous performers first hit the stage here), the

14

A FREE EDUCATION

Washington, DC surely boasts the world's highest number of free-entry museums in any city thanks to the Smithsonian Institution – a collection of 19 museums and galleries, plus a zoo and research centres. And all of this is thanks to an eccentric Brit, Mr James Smithson who, despite never having stepped foot in the USA, left his fortune to the country for the 'profusion of knowledge'. Visitors to the museums located along the Mall, among other locations, can learn about virtually everything, from dinosaurs to space shuttles, gold nuggets to the star-spangled banner, the Constitution to botanic plants. The most extraordinary part? Entry to the museums costs nada.

WASHINGTON, DC

DC Jazz Festival promotes established and emerging jazz artists alike. Numerous styles – from blues to swing, bebop to soul – are played at museums, restaurants and clubs throughout the capital, often for as little as a few dollars per head. And generally, they hit the right note. *dcjazzfest.org; locations & times vary, summer; tickets from $5.*

17 National Cherry Blossom Parade

It's a short and sweet season and it's no Japan, but the tidal basin definitely shimmers pink when the cherry trees bloom around March or April. It costs nothing to wander around appreciating it all, but there's also a parade in the blossom's honour, featuring floats, giant inflatables, marching bands, music and entertainment, which you can stand and watch for free. *nationalcherryblossomfestival.org; parade Constitution Ave NW, btwn 9th & 15th Sts, 10am-noon; free.*

18 Watch the Washington Nationals

The only 'free pass' at a Nationals (baseball) game is on the field; to attend you'll need to dig out your wallet. But hey, it's about time you paid for something. And it's a case of 'you can't leave DC without...' Students get the best deals but some ticket combinations include entrance and a portion of the game's ubiquitous munchies: hot dogs and fries. *Nationals Park; summer; tickets from $7.*

17

THE SEATS OF POWER

The closest you've probably been to the country's seats of power is your TV screen but, incredibly, you can experience the three branches of government – Executive (The White House); Legislative (US Capitol) and Judicial (The Supreme Court) – in one day. Visiting the hallowed halls is surprisingly easy, though The White House (*whitehouse.gov; 1600 Pennsylvania Ave NW*) requires advance planning. You can roll up to the US Capitol (*visitthecapitol.gov; East Capitol St NE & First St SE*) for a same-day ticket, though it's best to book online beforehand. The Supreme Court of The United States (*supremecourt.gov; 1 First St NE*) offers a three-minute glimpse of court in session or you can sit for an entire hearing.

OCEANIA

ARTS & CULTURE | MUSIC & FILM | SPORTS & LEISURE | FOOD & DRINK | FESTIVALS & EVENTS

BRISBANE

Brisbane may be Australia's third city (by size anyway) but a host of new bars, independent stores and cultural events see Brissy rivalling its southern competitors. Due to its tropical climate and outdoor lifestyle, Brisbane is a magnet for the fit and beautiful and doesn't have to cost you big bucks.

01 Museum of Brisbane

Brisbane was 'blessed' with a construction boom during one of Australia's less aesthetically pleasing eras, leaving it with little in the way of heritage buildings. Thankfully, the 1920s City Hall remains intact and you can learn about Brisbane's history and people on a free guided tour at the museum (register early). There are also art exhibitions to take in if time allows. *museumofbrisbane.com.au; Level 3, City Hall; 10am-5pm; free.*

02 Brisbane Botanic Gardens Mount Coot-Tha

One of many excellent Australian botanic gardens to explore, the gardens here are arranged by theme and geography, and there are self-guided walks – including one on plants used by Queensland's indigenous people. Behind the gardens is Mt Cooth-Tha, which has numerous forested walking tracks. Hike the 2km-long trail to the summit for views over Brisbane. *brisbane.qld.gov.au; Mt Coot-Tha Rd, Toowong; 8am-5.30pm; free.*

03 Street Beach

Just near Brisbane River you'll find an artificial beach that descends to a shallow lagoon suitable for paddling. This is a popular spot in which to chill, particularly with families. On warm weekends, if you don't want to jostle for space on the sand there is plenty of lawn space nearby on which to picnic and people-watch all afternoon. *visitbrisbane.com.au/south-bank; Stanley St, South Bank parklands; daylight hrs; free.*

02

NORTH STRADBROKE ISLAND

An easy 30-minute ferry chug from the Brisbane suburb of Cleveland, this unpretentious holiday isle is like Noosa and Byron Bay rolled into one. There's a string of glorious powdery white beaches, great surf and some quality places to stay and eat. It's also a hotspot for spying dolphins, turtles, manta rays and, between June and November, hundreds of hump-back whales. It's a cheap and must-do day trip from Brisbane but you need to plan around the bus timetable on 'Straddie'. *strad brokeisland.com*

04 Eat Street market

This hawker-style food market takes place on a disused container wharf by the Brisbane River. You can grab a cheap bite to eat, listen to live music, or mingle with locals drinking cocktails and cold lagers. Foodies are spoilt for choice with a global offering from Mexico to the Middle East and plenty of Southeast Asian options. *eatstreetmarkets.com; Macarthur Ave, Hamilton; 4-10pm Fri + Sat, 10am-3pm Sun over winter; admission over-12s A$2.*

05 Brisbane Festival free events

For most of September when the weather is at its best, Brisbane hosts a major international arts festival featuring music, dance, opera and circus acts. Events change yearly so check the website. The lawn by the **Queensland Performing Arts Centre** (*cnr Melbourne & Grey Sts*) often hosts free live music, while buskers and dancers are found around South Bank. *brisbanefestival.com.au; various locations; Sep; free.*

06 Knockoff comedy and LiveSpark music

Thanks to a sponsorship deal, the Powerhouse shows Brisbane's comedic talent to a generally appreciative crowd every Friday from 6pm. On Sunday afternoons there's live music on offer for no cost in the Turbine Hall. If the stand-up comedy or alternative rock are not your thing, then make a quiet exit and explore the cavernous Powerhouse with its bars, restaurants and mini-exhibitions. *brisbanepowerhouse.org; Brisbane Powerhouse Arts, 119 Lamington St; free.*

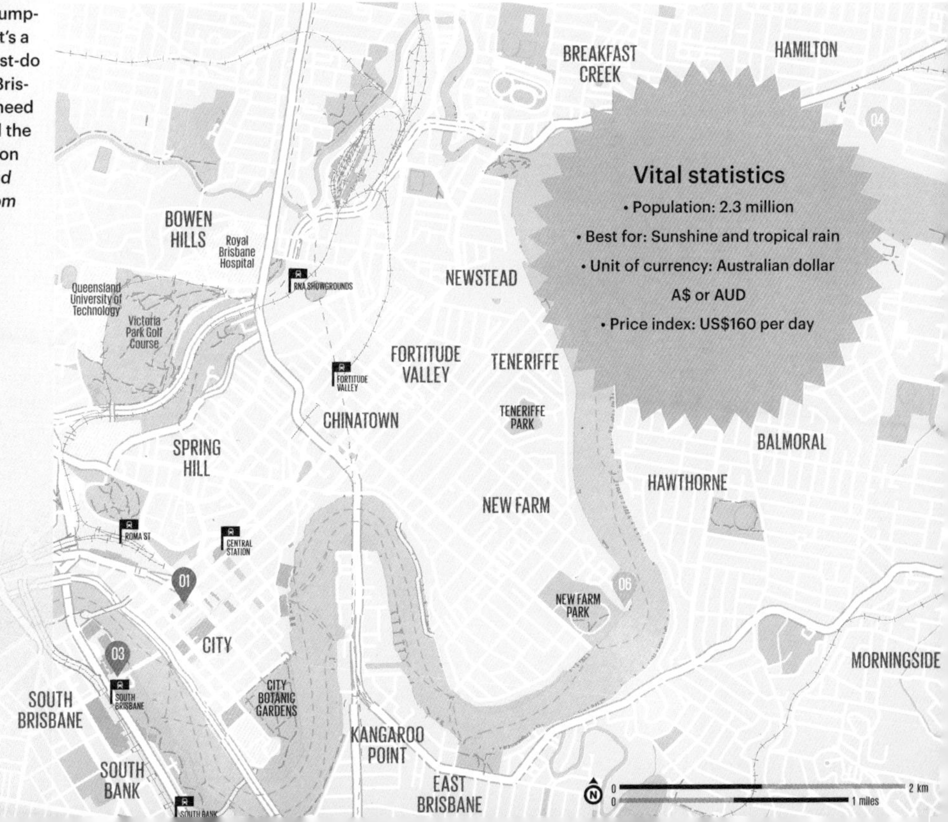

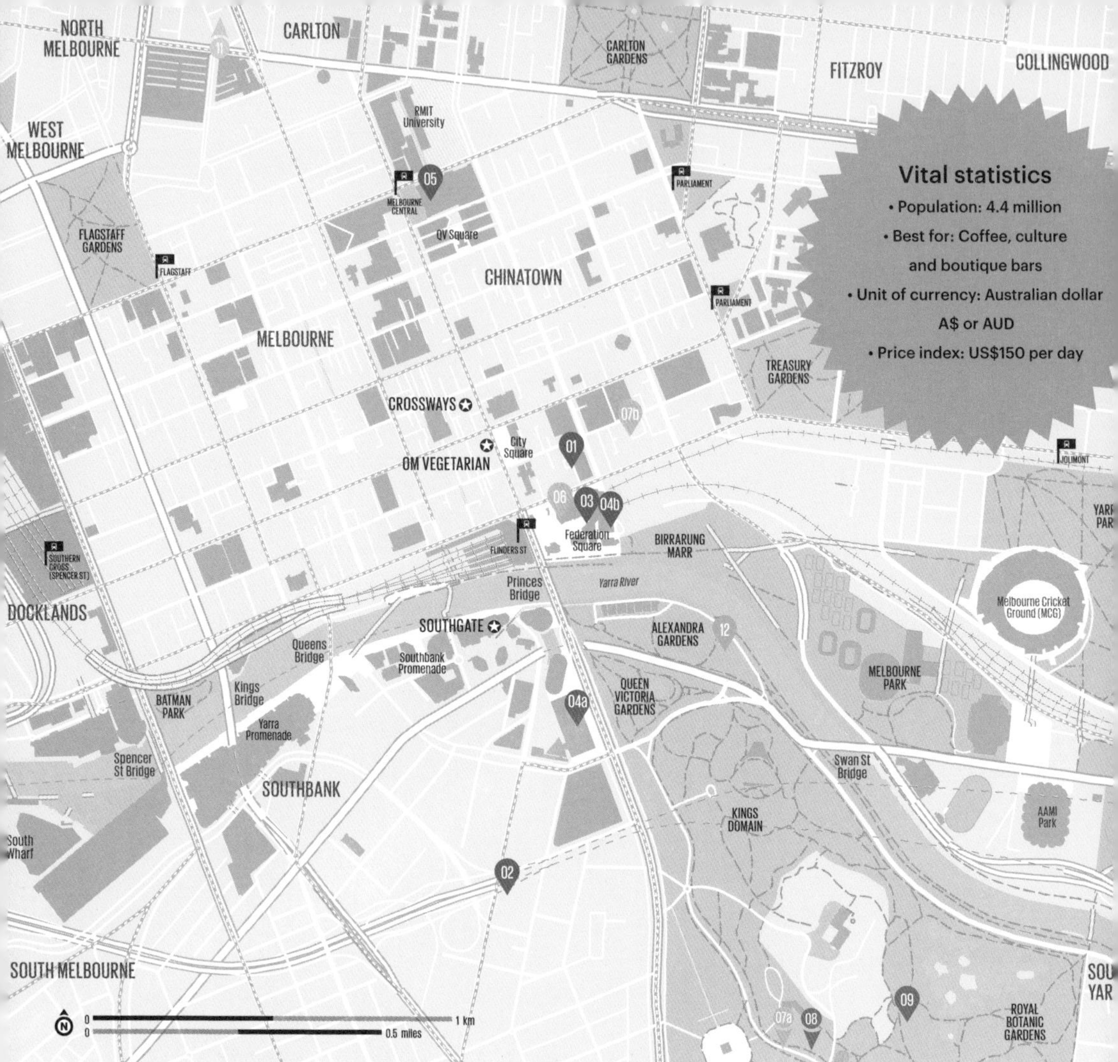

MELBOURNE

Australia's culture capital is one of the world's most liveable cities. Lacking Sydney's superficial sex appeal, Melbourne instead seduces inquisitive visitors with a more nuanced dance, revealing its manifold charms layer by layer over time. Whether you also spend loadsa money depends on what you know and where you go...

ARTS & CULTURE | MUSIC & FILM | SPORTS & LEISURE | FOOD & DRINK | FESTIVALS & EVENTS

01 Arty alleyways

Melbourne is grid-based, but it's anything but square. The city's labyrinthine laneways are lined with coffee houses, bars and the colourful work of guerrilla graffiti artists. You can pay to do a tour, but it's easy to freestyle it, starting from Hosier Lane and weaving north(ish). Besides local talent, many international artists have contributed, including Banksy, Blek le Rat and Shepard Fairey. *24hr; free.*

02 Australian Centre for Contemporary Art (ACCA)

In a rusty angular building that evokes the site's industrial past and resembles a work of modern art in itself, this contemporary gallery exhibits challenging work by Australian and international artists. Out the front, you can't miss *Vault*, a controversial sculpture by Ron Robertson-Swann, dubbed the 'Yellow Peril' and 'Steelhenge' by critics. *accaonline.org.au; 111 Sturt St; 10am-5pm Tue-Fri, 10am-8pm Wed; noon-5pm Sat-Sun; free.*

03 Koorie Heritage Trust

Melbourne is scarcely 175, but little remains of those who occupied this land for 30,000-plus years before John Batman arrived. This centre addresses that, sharing the traditions, displaying artefacts, staging exhibitions and explaining the oral history of the south-eastern Aboriginal peoples. You can buy bush food, craftwork and books on Indigenous affairs, and join tours (charge) to Flagstaff Gardens and the Yarra. *koorieheritagetrust.com; Yarra Bldg, Federation Square; 10am-5pm; free.*

04 National Gallery of Victoria (NGV)

The always-free NGV (4a) has a permanent collection of classical and contemporary work by the likes of Constable and Rodin. The St Kilda Rd site is stunning, with a moat out front and stained-glass atrium inside. Nearby, the **Ian Potter Centre** (4b; *Federation Square; 10am-5pm; free*) houses the Australian collection, including a gallery dedicated to mind-blowing Aboriginal art. *ngv.vic.gov.au; 180 St Kilda Rd; 10am-5pm; free.*

05 State Library of Victoria

From the funky pavement sculpture to the epic domed reading room, this is a house of stories about Victoria's past, present and future, with books (two million), exhibitions (including Ned Kelly's armour) and talks/debates – some held in the **Wheeler Centre** (*wheelercentre.com; 176 Little Lonsdale St*) and many free. There's a cafe/bar and free wi-fi. *slv.vic.gov.au; 328 Swanston St; 10am-9pm Mon-Thu, 10am-6pm Fri-Sun; free.*

THRIFTY COMMUTING

Exploring Melbourne for next-to-nowt is simple – thanks to an easy-to-navigate street grid and several initiatives. Since 2015, the CBD has been a 'free zone', so you can ride trams (*ptv.vic.gov.au; free*) for nothing. Alternatively, board the City Circle Free Tourist Tram (*yarratrams.com.au; free*), which trundles around town from Flinders St through Docklands and out to Nicholson St, with running commentary. Melbourne Bike Share (*melbournebike share.com.au*) provides blue bikes (and free helmets) for nothing for the first half-hour, and cheaply thereafter, and you can enjoy a free two/four-hour walking tour led by volunteers for the City of Melbourne (*thats melbourne.com.au/greeter; free*).

06 Australian Centre for the Moving Image (ACMI)

An Aussie-accented celebration of movies, television and dynamic digital culture, ACMI is a cave of wonders for film fans. The star is the interactive Screen Worlds exhibit, which explores the evolution of moving art from zoetrope to modern game labs. Upstairs in the **Australian Mediatheque** you can watch programmes from the National Film and Sound Archive. *acmi.net.au; Federation Sq; free entry 10am-5pm, free tours 11am & 2.30pm.*

07 Free gigs

Live comedy and music is in Melbourne's blood, and there's plenty of both at venues throughout the city and in the suburbs – often with no entry charge. **St Kilda's Espy** (7a; *espy.com.au; 11 The Esplanade)* is an iconic live-band boozer, where front-bar gigs are typically free. In town, **Cherry Bar** (7b; *cherrybar.com.au; AC/DC Lane)* puts on the type of acts that suit its rock and roll address. Listings appear in free street-press publications such as *Beat*.

08 Beach-bumming

St Kilda is great for bars and boho chic, but on beach-weather days take the train (A$4) out of town on the Sandringham line from Flinders St Station and alight at **Brighton Beach** (where iconic beach huts frame views of the city) or go all the way to **Sandringham** (30 minutes) for Melbourne's best suburban beach. There's no surf within the bay, but the swimming, snorkelling and sunbathing are sensational. Free barbecues can be found along the foreshore.

09 Royal Botanic Gardens

These 38-hectare gardens dominate a corner of the city south of the river, providing breathing space and acting as

12

11

THE LOCAL'S VIEW

"In Melbourne, food is expensive – as are drinks – but Crossways (*crosswaysfood forlife.com.au; 123 Swanston St; 11.30am-8pm Mon-Sat; all-you-can-eat A$7.50*) and Om (*omvegetarian.com; 113 Swanston St; 11am-9pm; all-you-can-eat A$6.50*), serve mountains of healthy vegetarian tucker. Check out *thehappiest hour.com* for more bargains. I'm a footloose freelancer, and while cafes provide wi-fi, there's a limit to how many world-class coffees you can consume, so free access at the State Library (p249), Federation Square (*fedsquare.com; cnr Swanston & Flinders Sts; free*) and Southgate (*southgatemel bourne.com.au; 3 Southgate Ave; 10am-late; free*) is handy." – Simon Madden, journalist

a free natural gym for those who flock here before and after work to run 3.84km around the loop of 'The Tan'. The park features a lake, myriad picnicking spots and a purpose-built **Children's Garden**, complete with water fountain and a creek to splash around in. *rbg.vic.gov.au; Birdwood Ave; 7.30am-sunset; free.*

10 Yarra Bend Park

Easily accessible from central Melbourne, this riparian retreat is the city's largest remaining chunk of wild bushland. Walking and cycling trails wend alongside the water and thread through the trees, and there's 16km of river frontage to explore. Paths lead from Studley Park (where you can hire boats) to the cascade at Dights Falls and the colony of grey-headed flying foxes opposite Bellbird picnic area. Free barbecues available. *parkweb.vic.gov.au; Kew; free.*

11 Coffee cupping

Coffee is a religion here, where well-inked and bushy-bearded baristas brew bean juice from increasingly complicated/pretentious menus at hipster cafes everywhere. Become an expert by doing a cupping session – the coffee equivalent of wine tasting, where you'll learn the differences between single-source beans from around the world. Free sessions are offered by various cafes, including an eight-taste experience at **Seven Seeds** (*sevenseeds.com.au; 114 Berkeley St, Carlton; 9am Fri + Sat*).

12 Moomba

The biggest free festival in the city, Moomba attracts more than a million people to the banks of the Yarra for a feast of fireworks, live music, waterskiing and aquatic shenanigans, including the **Bird Man Rally**, where people attempt to 'fly' over the river in homemade contraptions. Apparently, the name – proposed by the President of the Australian Aborigines League in the 1950s – means 'up your bum' in the local indigenous language. *facebook.com/moombafestival; Mar; free.*

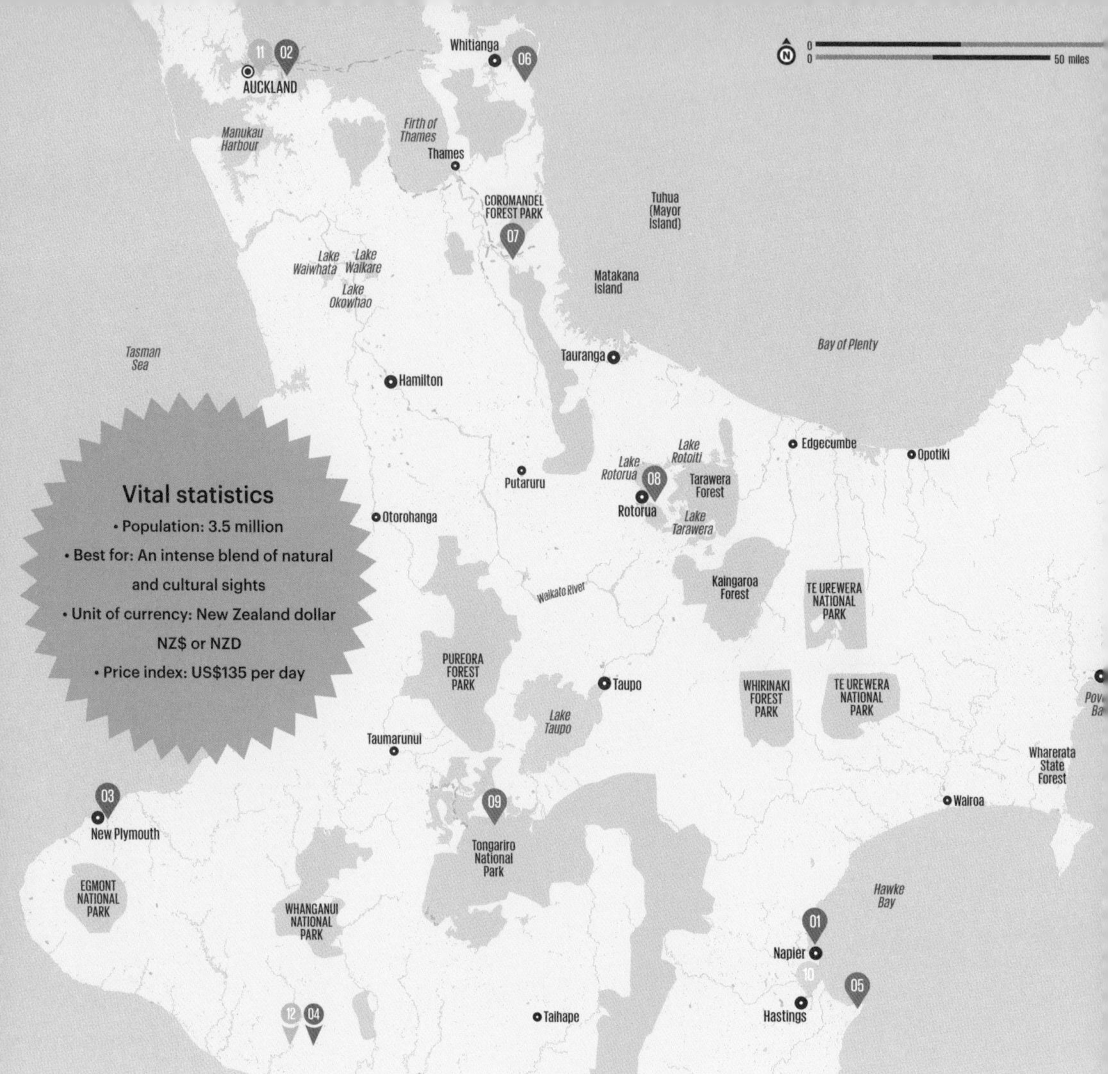

NORTH ISLAND, NZ

Rumour has it that New Zealand travel is pricey, but while food, accommodation and transport can stretch the budget, masses of free and cheap experiences more than make up for it. Whether you're a culture-vulture, wildlife-watcher or outdoor explorer, shake some pennies from your pocket and get going.

ARTS & CULTURE MUSIC & FILM SPORTS & LEISURE FOOD & DRINK FESTIVALS & EVENTS

01 Art-deco Napier

Essentially an outdoor museum of art-deco architecture, Napier city was rebuilt after a catastrophic 1931 earthquake. Its uniformly fine streets are full of colourful eye candy, and make a wonderful venue for a walk or bicycle ride. Guided tours are available, but to see it on the cheap just follow your nose around Tennyson and Emerson Sts, ideally with the illuminating self-guided art-deco walk map (NZ$7.50) in hand. *artdeconapier.com; 24hr; free.*

02 Auckland Art Gallery

'Free guided tour' – music to the ears of art fans everywhere. Auckland's public art gallery, housed in a beautiful 1887 building with a *très moderne* facelift, offers two daily at 11.30am and 1.30pm. International stars include Picasso, Cézanne and Gauguin, but it's local luminaries of all eras and media that make this gallery *the* place for a New Zealand Art 101. *aucklandartgallery.com; cnr Kitchener & Wellesley Sts; 10am-5pm; free.*

03 Len Lye Centre

Opened in 2015, the Len Lye Centre is the dazzling new wing of the Govett-Brewster, a dearly beloved provincial art gallery. Arguably New Zealand's most quirky, colourful and optimistic artist, who has a motto of 'individual happiness now', Lye will work magic on your soul as his vibe fizzes, crackles and pops throughout the sky-high gallery space. *lenlyefoundation.com; 42 Queen St, New Plymouth; 10am-6pm Fri-Mon & Wed, 10am-9pm Thu; free.*

04 Museum of New Zealand Te Papa Tongarewa

Free national museums may be ten-a-penny, but few are such fun. Te Papa's colourful displays include heaps of hands-on stuff and digital bling, plus the hilarious Golden Days movie hall that may *mooooove* you to tears (you'll get that joke when you go, trust us). One visit won't be enough so that makes it double value, right? *tepapa.govt.nz; 55 Cable St, Wellington; 10am-6pm Fri-Wed, 10am-9pm Thu; free.*

05 Cape Kidnappers Gannet Colony

One of New Zealand's best bird circuses, such rowdy gaggles of gannets usually nest on remote islands but here about 20,000 settle happily on an accessible cliff top. The best time to see them is November to late February, when the fun tractor tour cranks up, but you can reach them under your own steam on a fascinating five-hour return walk from Clifton. *doc.govt.nz; Clifton Rd; free.*

01

05

07

04

NORTH ISLAND, NZ

CHEAP CAMPS & CABINS

Dirty campers have caused a clamp-down on freedom camping around the North Island, but those with a toilet on board their campervan will still find plenty of designated spots where they can park up for free. Meanwhile, those in loo-less campervans and tents can avail themselves of about 100 Department of Conservation campsites, ranging in cost from free to NZ$15 per adult per night. Even the next step-up – the classic Kiwi holiday park – offers great value for money, with some very cute cabins making an affordable and atmospheric alternative to hostel and budget motel rooms. *doc.govt.nz; hapnz.co.nz.*

06 Hot Water Beach

Enjoy the therapeutic benefits of New Zealand's thermal waters without having to shell out for a fancy spa resort. At this beautiful Coromandel beach you can dig your own personal hot pool in the sand (spade hire is available from the cafe) two hours either side of low tide, then relax while enjoying the salty, sociable atmosphere. *thecoromandel.com/new-zealand/hot-water-beach; Hot Water Beach Rd (off SH25), Coromandel; free.*

07 Karangahake Gorge

If you like a little spookiness along with your scenery, Karangahake Gorge will certainly float your boat. The Hauraki Rail Trail's most picturesque leg features ghostly gold-mining relics and a cobwebby museum, the wacko Windows Walkway and a freaky tunnel. Even with the cost of bicycle hire and the cost of a cup of tea at Waikino Station Cafe taken into account, this is marvellous entertainment for peanuts. *karangahakegorge.co.nz/mainpage.html; SH2 btwn Waihi & Paeroa; free.*

08 Kuirau Park, Rotorua

Although major thermal parks such as Whakarewarewa and Te Puia are well worth the entry fee for the spirited Māori culture surrounding spurting geysers and colourful silica terraces, they're not the only way to see Rotorua's steamy side. Kuirau Park Precinct, 10 minutes' walk from central Rotorua, has a crater lake, bubbling mud pools and plenty of steam wafting about. *rotoruanz.com/kuirauparkprecinct; Ranolf & Pukuatua Sts; free.*

09 Tongariro Alpine Crossing

One of the finest day walks in the world needn't cost you any more than trailhead transport, some shoe rubber

02

09

PUB GIGS

Nary a corner of the North Island is a stranger to the pub band, and outsiders who seek out or accidentally stumble across gig nights will find themselves richly rewarded, particularly as many are free. Yes, whether it's a black-singlet-wearing shearer twanging out country classics, or hormonal twentysomethings murdering mainstream rock ballads, entertainment in some form is guaranteed. Competent cover bands are a speciality, especially outside the cities, so expect to hear Kiwi anthems such as Dragon's 'April Sun in Cuba' (*whoa ho ho!*) and the Exponents '(*I don't know... o-o-o!*) Why Does Love Do This To Me?'.

and sweat. The walk traverses the volcanic heart of Tongariro National Park; a peculiar moonscape of steaming vents and springs, surreal lakes, craters and ridges offering magnificent views. The more sure-footed types can embark on a side trip up conical Mount Ngauruhoe, which doubled as Mount Doom in *The Lord of the Rings. doc.govt.nz; Tongariro NP; free.*

10 Hawke's Bay Farmers' Market

Picture yourself on a warm, sunny weekend morning, lazing barefoot on the grass, while serenaded by local musicians and surrounded by stalls overflowing with delicious local picnic supplies, such as world-beating fruit, bread, cheese and wine, direct from the producer. This very fine farmers' market is an indulgent and highly satisfying way to while away a Sunday morning on a shoestring. *hawkesbayfarmersmarket.co.nz; A&P Showgrounds, Kenilworth Rd; 8.30am-12.30pm Sun; admission free.*

11 Pasifika Festival

The world's biggest Polynesian party is held in Auckland over a weekend in late summer. Celebrating the colourful Pacific Islands' culture that makes up so many strands of New Zealand's collective identity, it's a fulfilling (and filling) fiesta of food, art, craft and more live music than you can shake a *rakau* (stick) at. Love those island vibes! *aucklandnz.com/pasifika; Western Springs, Auckland; early-mid Mar; free.*

12 Wellington Summer City

So absolutely positively ecstatic are Wellingtonians at the arrival of the balmy season that they erupt into a riotous carousal of concerts, dances and assorted cultural happenings, most of which occur outdoors, thereby adding an extra, weather-related frisson of excitement. In all, the windy city's three-month long festival strings together nearly 100 events, most of which are as free as the, um, breeze. *wellington.govt.nz; Jan-Mar; free.*

AUSTRALIA & NEW ZEALAND'S BEST FREE WALKS

Dawdlers Down Under often have to pay to plod around many popular parks and paths, but here's a selection of freestyle footpaths...

BONDI TO COOGEE BEACH

A classic cliff-top canter around five of Sydney's best beaches, this urban adventure starts amid the backpackers and breakers on Bondi and traces the curvaceous coastline south, taking in Tamarama, Bronte, Clovelly and finally Coogee Beach. Allow ample time for swimming breaks and beachside beers. *bonditocoogeewalk.com.au; Sydney, NSW, Australia; 5.5km; free.*

ORMISTON GORGE AND POUND

There's more to explore in the Red Centre than the Rock. An offshoot of the epic Larapinta Trail, this dramatic day-long desert adventure takes you through a gorge and the West MacDonnell ranges to a croc-free swimming hole. *nt.gov.au/westmacs/docs/Ormiston_Gorge.pdf; West MacDonnell NP, NT, Australia; 7.5km; free.*

REES-DART TRACK

This challenging four to five-day adventure near Queenstown follows the spectacular Rees and Dart Rivers. Considerate backcountry camping is permitted and free unless you're using hut campgrounds. *doc.govt.nz/parks-and-recreation/places-to-go; Mt Aspiring NP, South Island, New Zealand; 86km; free.*

MT FEATHERTOP AND THE RAZORBACK

One of the Victorian Alps' top trails, this two-day mission takes trekkers along a fantastic ridgeline to the second-highest – but prettiest – peak in the state. A demanding exercise for experienced walkers, it's also cross-country skiable in winter. *parkweb.vic.gov.au; Vic, Australia; 36km; free.*

CAPE-TO-CAPE

Running between Cape Naturaliste and Cape Leeuwin, this lighthouse-to-lighthouse seven-day epic is one colossal coastal walk, promising everything from whale sightings to wine tasting. Wild camping is possible. *capetocapetrack.com.au; W Australia; 135km; free.*

TONGARIRO ALPINE CROSSING

This fabulous one-day trail tiptoes past active volcanoes and luminous lakes. The weather can be as confronting as the terrain, so be prepared (for almost anything). You'll need to arrange a car drop. *tongarirocrossing.org.nz; Tongariro NP, North Island, New Zealand; 19.5km; free.*

BARTLE FRERE TRAIL

From Josephine Falls, 75km south of Cairns, return-hike to Queensland's highest point. Tropical trails climb dramatically through lush rainforest until you pop out of the canopy and cop a view across the Tablelands to the Great Barrier Reef, vaguely visible through the iridescence of the Coral Sea. *nprsr.qld.gov.au/parks/bartle-frere; Tropical North Queensland, Australia; 16km; free.*

MT WELLINGTON AND THE ORGAN PIPES

The best spot to absorb Hobart's end-of-the-world ambience is atop Mt Wellington, the apex of this rock-strewn scramble, which starts with a cheap-as-chips bus ride into the suburbs. A stern climb earns stunning views over the Organ Pipes (a rock-climbing mecca) to the harbour, where icebreakers prepare for Antarctica. *parks.tas.gov.au; Hobart, Tas, Australia; 13km; free.*

Illustration | Owen Gatley

ARTS & CULTURE | MUSIC & FILM | SPORTS & LEISURE | FOOD & DRINK | FESTIVALS & EVENTS

SOUTH ISLAND, NZ

The biggest bargain here is the conservation estate, which covers vast parts of the South Island, offering endless free adventures in amazing places. In between is a raft of other experiences that won't cost the earth, from food-foraging and festivals to wildlife-spotting, gallery-hopping and admiring colonial architecture.

01 Canterbury Museum

In the category of free cultural attractions, Canterbury Museum is up there with the best. The wow factor comes via characterful local content, such as Fred and Myrtle's Paua Shell House, Māori artefacts, a replicated street from Christchurch's colonial era, and frequently changing exhibits of admirable diversity. Try to time your visit for free guided tours on Tuesdays and Thursdays at 3.30pm. *canterburymuseum.com; Rolleston Ave; 9am-5pm; free.*

02 Eastern Southland Gallery

Fondly known as the 'Goreggenheim', this outstanding art gallery occupies the old public library in the unassuming rural town of Gore. Highlights include works by Ralph Hotere, a Māori artist famed for his poetic 'black' series, while the John Money Collection combines indigenous folk art from West Africa and Australia with works by New Zealander Rita Angus. *esgallery.co.nz; 14 Hokonui Dr, Gore; 10am-4.30pm Mon-Fri, 1-4pm Sat + Sun, free.*

Vital statistics

- Population: 1 million
- Best for: Life-changing outdoors experiences
- Unit of currency: New Zealand dollar NZ$ or NZD
- Price index: US$135 per day

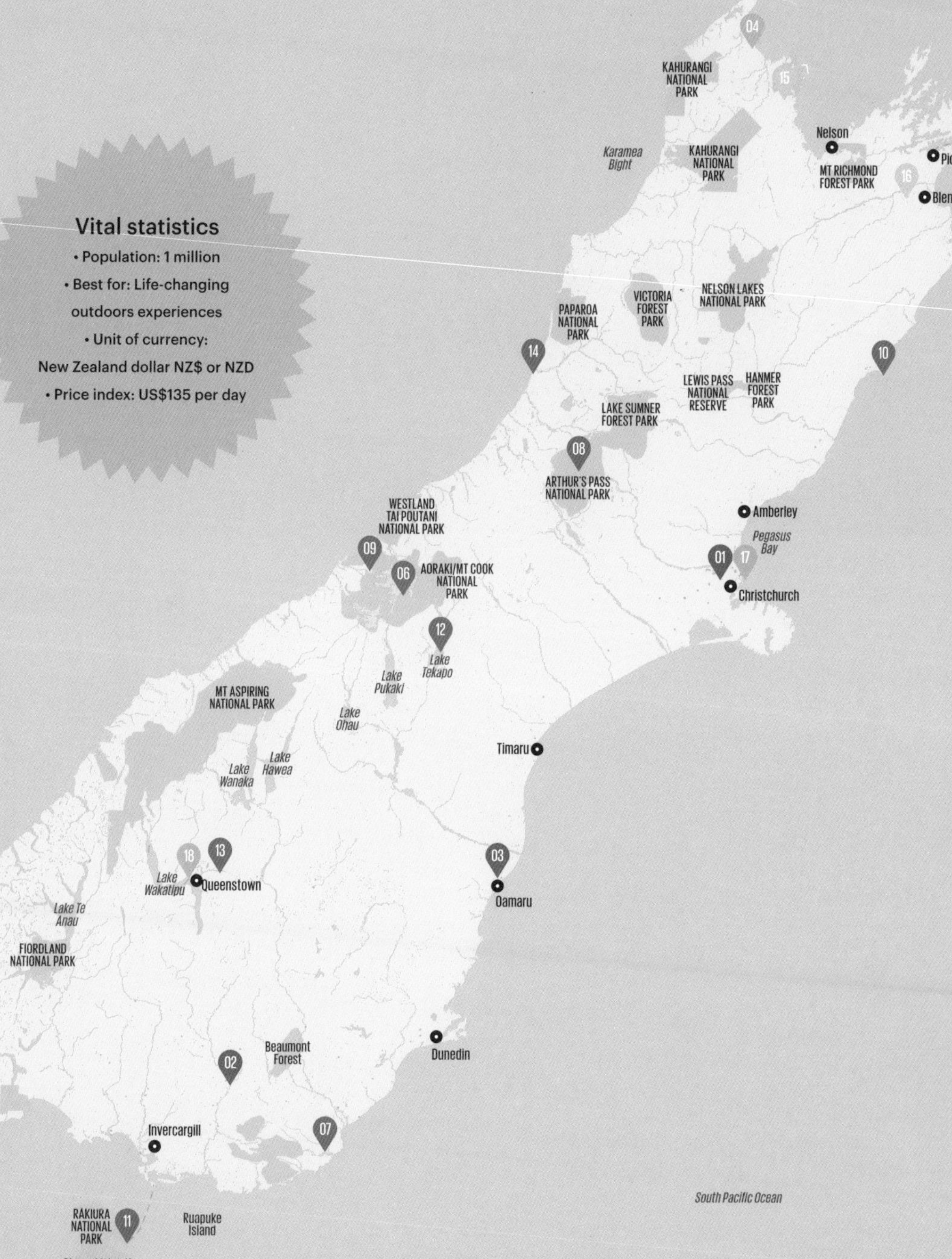

03 Victorian Precinct

With its colonial architecture befitting one of those costly outdoor heritage museums, Oamaru's Victorian Precinct packs plenty of punch for the price of perhaps a pie and a slightly foxed paperback. Stroll through its cobbled lanes lined with Dickensian stone buildings, dodging penny-farthings and visiting period-vibe shops, including a bakery, bookshop, antique store, artist studios and galleries. Costumed locals add atmosphere and moustaches. *victorianoamaru.co.nz; 2 Harbour St; free.*

04 Five-dollar gigs at the Mussel Inn

Although you could easily blow your budget on this brew-pub's tasty beers alone, a rollicking night out at the Inn needn't cost your shirt. Genuinely rustic – complete with creaky timbers and a rambling beer garden – it also hosts regular NZ$5 gigs featuring musicians from all over the show. For a little libation to get the toe tapping, we suggest the manuka-infused Captain Cooker. *musselinn.co.nz; 1259 State Highway, Onekaka; 11am-late (closed mid-Jul–mid-Sep); NZ$5.*

05 *The Lord of the Rings* and *Hobbit* film sets

There's no need to go on a costly guided movie-location tour, as a personalised one requires little more than your own transport, reliable intel and a vivid imagination. South Island landscapes stole many a Middle-earth scene, with the Queenstown region showing some star quality as Lothlórien, the Ford of Bruinen and Gladden Fields, among others. Look for Ian Brodie's *The Lord of the Rings Location Guidebook*, or search for Middle-earth on *newzealand.com*. *Free.*

06 Aoraki/Mt Cook National Park Visitor Centre

Spectacularly located in the shadow of its tallest mountain, New Zealand's grand-prize national park visitor centre does Aoraki justice with impressive exhibits alongside racks of maps and feathery fridge magnets. Intriguing natural history

DAY WALKS

Justifiably popular for their jaw-dropping scenery, New Zealand's multi-day Great Walks aren't the only way to go bush. Just as well, as hut passes and transport can certainly add up. Then there's the burden of a heavy backpack. Happily, sections of Great Walks and hundreds of other amazing trails can be experienced on day walks, ranging from a 10-minute nature trail to an all-day epic. What's more, many feature excellent interpretation panels that bring the landscapes to life, adding even more value to New Zealand's free outdoor adventures. *doc.govt.nz; free.*

vies for attention with spine-tingling stories of human endeavour amid the Alps. People would pay good money for this, so make sure you feed the donation box... *doc.govt.nz/parks-and-recreation; 1 Larch Grove, Canterbury; 8.30am-4.30pm May-Sep, 8.30am-5pm Oct-Apr; free.*

07 Catlins Wildlife Tour

On the Southern Scenic Route, the Catlins is a beguiling blend of rolling farmland, wetlands, forest and rugged coastline punctuated by caves, cliffs, blowholes and various other oddball phenomena. Inhabiting this wild place are scores of special animals such as penguins at **Nugget Point**, spoonbills at **Pounawea**, and sea lions at **Surat Bay**. All you need to see them is walking shoes, patience and a modicum of good luck. *catlins.org.nz; free.*

08 Climb Avalanche Peak

It ain't Everest, but this summit can be bagged in a day by moderately fit hikers unfettered by oxygen tanks. Saddle up with appropriate gear and supplies, check on conditions at the national park visitor centre, and may the glory be yours. It's a 1100m grind to the 1833m-high peak where the views rival those of the mighty Himalayas (well, nearly, and this one is free). *doc.govt.nz; Arthur's Pass NP, Canterbury; free.*

09 Glacier Lookouts

The West Coast's twin glaciers – **Franz Josef** and **Fox** – are magnets for ice-hikers and scenic flight-takers happy to part with big bucks to get right up close. Budget travellers, however, can admire their awe-inspiring forms from excellent vantage points within the glacier valleys, along walkways featuring sublime forest, waterfalls and epic rock gardens, and where interesting information panels will serve as your guide. *doc.govt.nz; Westland Tai Poutini NP; free.*

10 Kaikoura Seal Colony

Can't afford whale-watching? No worries. Head to Point Kean to see blubbery seals for free. It's not exactly all-singing, all-dancing entertainment, but watching these whiskery critters sleep, sniff the breeze and loll around the rocky reef is strangely mesmerising. Seal TV can be combined with the **Kaikoura Peninsula Walkway**, a three-to-four-hour loop featuring whirling seabirds and stupendous ocean and mountain views. Priceless. *doc.govt.nz; Fyffe Quay, Kaikoura; free.*

11 Kiwi-spotting on Stewart Island

There are an estimated 20,000 kiwi (*tokoeka*) roaming wild on Stewart Island, a few of which will probably appear on a pricey night tour. Bag a bargain by befriending a local and asking them on the quiet about a particular Oban sports field, upon which the inimitable bird may forage around dawn and dusk. While you're at it, ask about the penguin parade near the wharf. *Oban, Stewart Island; free.*

09

11

16

12 Stargaze in the Mackenzie Country

More fun than meditation and cheaper than drugs, stargazing is a mind-expanding trip into mysterious worlds. One of five International Dark Sky Reserves, the Aoraki Mackenzie region offers nightly astronomical tours at Lake Tekapo's **Mt John Observatory** (*earthandskynz.com; adult/child NZ$145/80*), but you could rug up on a blanket, for free. Use an app to identify constellations such as Matariki and the Southern Cross. *mtcooknz.com; free.*

13 Watch bungy jumpers

The numerous reasons not to partake of a bungy jump include many compelling ones, such as the prospect of leaping head first from a great height while attached to a rubber band... Then there's the cost. Fortunately, it is possible

13

SWIMMING SPOTS

"While some might argue that plunging into a frigid lake or river isn't the most enjoyable free activity on the planet, such memories tend to linger a lot longer than those of the 10-buck museum. The South Island offers plenty of swimming opportunities, readily identified by suspiciously popular car parks, rope swings hanging from trees, moored rafts and lifeguards. The ultimate giveaway is a bunch of locals taking the plunge. Only swim where you know it's safe as New Zealand's beaches, lakes and rivers can be wild and dangerous."
– Sarah Bennett, author, *Lonely Planet New Zealand*

SOUTH ISLAND, NZ

to hijack the heart-stopping thrills by watching others jump, with the best place for spectators being the world's original jump site at creaky Kawarau Bridge. *AJ Hackett Bungy, SH6 btw Queenstown & Cromwell; free.*

14 West Coast Wilderness Trail

This is just one of 23 New Zealand Cycle Trails constructed in recent years, each representing a mammoth investment of time and money. And you, dear traveller, can reap the benefits. The trail is a 120km-long humdinger between Greymouth and Ross, revealing spectacular landscapes along historic pathways at the foot of the Southern Alps. Bike-hire depots make these adventures affordable, although they can be walked. *westcoastwildernesstrail.co.nz; nzcycletrail.com; admission free.*

15 Cockling at Marahau

On the fringe of Abel Tasman National Park, Marahau beach hides beds of delicious cockles (aka clams) that can be gathered when the tide is low. It's by no means easy work, and each cockle yields merely a nibble, but simmered open with garlic and white wine and served on pasta, they make a first-class meal at a rock-bottom price. Catch limits are posted by the beach. *Marahau Beach Rd; free.*

16 Marlborough wine tasting

Spread across several golden valleys, New Zealand's vinous colossus offers refreshingly snoot-free touring around 35 small-scale cellar doors. Many of these can be reached by hire bike, or even on foot around vine-lined Renwick, and although some venues on the Marlborough Wine Trail charge a small tasting fee, it's still a cheap and cheerful education and is normally refundable against a purchase. Some spectacular wines can be sniffed out at bargain prices – just follow your nose! *wine-marlborough.co.nz; free-NZ$5.*

17 Christchurch World Buskers Festival

Shake out your pockets and head to the garden city's colourful annual outdoor extravaganza, held over 10 days around mid-January. Acrobats, jugglers, stand-up comedians and burlesque performers join a crazy Christchurch line-up of more than 40 acts that assemble from around the world. Hagley Park serves as the performance hub, with many other hotspots drawing crowds throughout the city. Check the website for details. *worldbuskersfestival.com; venues & dates vary, Jan; free.*

18 Queenstown Winter Festival

New Zealand's fanciest Alpine resort can get pretty blingy during the ski season, but budget travellers are able to bluff their way in during the 10-day Winter Festival. There are loads of free events amid all the frivolity, beginning with a firework-laden, lake-front party, followed by a street parade, craft markets and musical events. It's also free to enter the 'suitcase race' down the slopes of Coronet Peak. *winterfestival.co.nz; late Jun-early Jul; free.*

SAVVY SHOPPING

New Zealand's produce scene is highly seasonal, the year punctuated by frequent gluts that see the likes of avocados, asparagus and berries plunge to rock-bottom prices at peak output – an absolute boon for self-catering travellers. Farmers' markets, held in most towns on Saturdays or Sundays, are a great place to bag a bargain as well as delicious local products including meat, cheese and preserves. Free-range eggs, lemons and salad veg are regularly offered at roadside stalls, with the accompanying honesty box a fundamental pillar of Kiwi culture. ***farmersmarkets.org.nz; free.***

ARTS & CULTURE · MUSIC & FILM · SPORTS & LEISURE · FOOD & DRINK · FESTIVALS & EVENTS

SYDNEY

Australia's de facto capital – in the eyes of its residents anyway – Sydney is an instantly identifiable city, with iconic buildings and a stunning setting on one of the world's greatest harbours. It's big, bold and beautiful, but can also be a bit brash and rather a budget-buster, unless...

01 Art Gallery NSW

Behind a neoclassical facade lies a fantastic gallery, exhibiting works by international artists as well as locals, including Sidney Nolan, Grace Cossington Smith, John Olsen and Arthur Boyd. The **Yiribana Gallery** features a display of Aboriginal and Torres Strait Islander art, and there's also an impressive Asian collection. Complimentary tours are available, and free talks and films take place here on Wednesday nights. *artgallery.nsw.gov.au; Art Gallery Rd, The Domain 2000; 10am-5pm Thu-Tue, 10am-10pm Wed; free.*

02 Conservatorium of Music

Above the Royal Botanic Gardens, behind 200-year-old battlements, musical magic happens. Wander around the halls of this international musical school for free, or book a tour (they cost) to hear about the building's past life. Most excitingly, you can wrap your ears around some world-class classical music at one of many free monthly recitals and

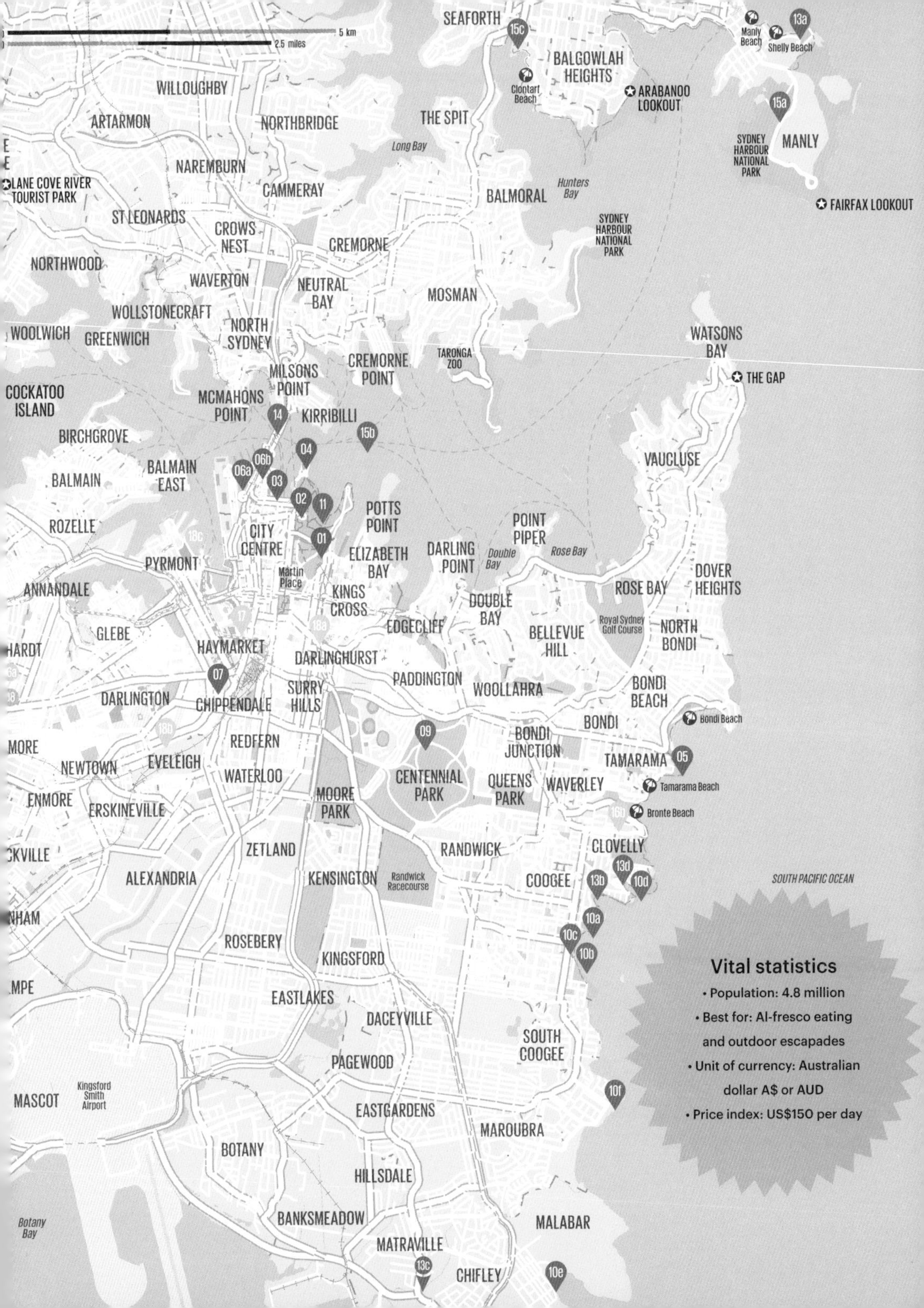
5 km
2.5 miles
SEAFORTH
15c
Manly Beach
Shelly Beach
13a
BALGOWLAH HEIGHTS
Clontarf Beach
ARABANOO LOOKOUT
WILLOUGHBY
ARTARMON
NORTHBRIDGE
THE SPIT
15a
Long Bay
SYDNEY HARBOUR NATIONAL PARK
MANLY
NAREMBURN
LANE COVE RIVER TOURIST PARK
CAMMERAY
Hunters Bay
BALMORAL
FAIRFAX LOOKOUT
ST LEONARDS
CROWS NEST
CREMORNE
SYDNEY HARBOUR NATIONAL PARK
NORTHWOOD
WAVERTON
NEUTRAL BAY
MOSMAN
WOLLSTONECRAFT
WOOLWICH
GREENWICH
NORTH SYDNEY
WATSONS BAY
TARONGA ZOO
CREMORNE POINT
MILSONS POINT
THE GAP
COCKATOO ISLAND
MCMAHONS POINT
14
KIRRIBILLI
15b
BIRCHGROVE
04
06b
06a
03
BALMAIN EAST
BALMAIN
VAUCLUSE
02
11
POTTS POINT
POINT PIPER
ROZELLE
18c
CITY CENTRE
01
ELIZABETH BAY
DARLING POINT
Double Bay
Rose Bay
DOVER HEIGHTS
PYRMONT
Martin Place
ANNANDALE
KINGS CROSS
DOUBLE BAY
ROSE BAY
17
18a
EDGECLIFF
Royal Sydney Golf Course
NORTH BONDI
GLEBE
BELLEVUE HILL
HARDT
HAYMARKET
DARLINGHURST
07
PADDINGTON
WOOLLAHRA
BONDI BEACH
DARLINGTON
CHIPPENDALE
SURRY HILLS
BONDI
Bondi Beach
18b
09
BONDI JUNCTION
REDFERN
TAMARAMA
05
MORE
NEWTOWN
EVELEIGH
WATERLOO
CENTENNIAL PARK
QUEENS PARK
WAVERLEY
Tamarama Beach
ENMORE
ERSKINEVILLE
MOORE PARK
16b
Bronte Beach
ZETLAND
RANDWICK
CLOVELLY
CKVILLE
ALEXANDRIA
KENSINGTON
Randwick Racecourse
COOGEE
13b
13d
10d
SOUTH PACIFIC OCEAN
NHAM
10a
10c
ROSEBERY
10b
KINGSFORD
MPE
EASTLAKES
DACEYVILLE
SOUTH COOGEE
PAGEWOOD
MASCOT
Kingsford Smith Airport
10f
EASTGARDENS
MAROUBRA
BOTANY
HILLSDALE
BANKSMEADOW
MALABAR
Botany Bay
MATRAVILLE
13c
CHIFLEY
10e
Vital statistics
• Population: 4.8 million
• Best for: Al-fresco eating and outdoor escapades
• Unit of currency: Australian dollar A$ or AUD
• Price index: US$150 per day

concerts. See the website for details. *music.sydney.edu.au; University of Sydney, Crnr Bridge & Macquarie Sts; 8am-6pm Mon-Sat; free.*

03 Museum of Contemporary Art

Sitting on the iconic waterfront overlooking Circular Quay, this enormous art-deco building is something of a cathedral of creativity in all its kaleidoscopically colourful forms. Entry to the main galleries is free (featured exhibitions may be ticketed, see website for details), and you can also join complimentary tours, including some conducted by teenagers, to gain a youthful insight into modern art. *mca.com.au; 140 George St, The Rocks; 10am-5pm Fri-Wed, 10am-9pm Thu; free.*

04 Opera House

Opera House architect Jørn Utzon never beheld his fantastically funky design fully finished – the Dane stormed out after a row – but you can see his creation for free. If your budget doesn't stretch to experiencing a performance, explore the base of the sails or nip inside for a nibble in one of the restaurants – **Opera Kitchen** (*operabar.com.au; 8am-midnight Mon-Thu, 8am-1am Fri-Sun*) is the least expensive. *sydneyoperahouse.com; admission free.*

05 Sculpture by the Sea

As if the beach-combing clifftop trek from Bondi to Coogee Beach (p256) doesn't already deliver enough eye candy, in the early summer months the free Sculpture by the Sea project lines the preliminary route with a selection of al-fresco arty installations. A Tactile Tour programme, led by guides from the Art Gallery NSW, provides free touching-tours of the sculptures for the visually

WHALE WATCHING

Few cities offer complimentary whale-watching opportunities, but Sydney sits on a major migration route and here the thrill of seeing one of nature's biggest beasts cavorting in the wild is free. From mid-May to August, 20,000 humpback and right whales swim past, performing breaches, pectoral slaps and lobtails, and often calling in for harbour views. Top spots for whale-spotting include Cape Solander (at the mouth of Botany Bay); Arabanoo Lookout (overlooking Manly); Fairfax Lookout (North Head), where calves are often born; the Gap (Watsons Bay, South Head), from where killer whales are sometimes seen too; and Barrenjoey Head (Palm Beach).

impaired. *sculpturebythesea.com; Bondi to Tamarama coastal walk; Oct-Nov; free.*

06 The Rocks

Sydney's oldest quarter is crowned by **Observatory Hill** (6a; *24hr; free*). The First Fleet fell ashore here in 1788, spelling disaster for the indigenous population. Once a den of iniquity, now food markets, Aboriginal art galleries and cafes line the cobbled catacomb. The historic sandstone buildings were nearly lost to developers, but building unions refused to demolish them – the **Rocks Discovery Museum** (6b; *2-8 Kendall Lane; 10am-5pm; free*) explains all. *therocks.com.*

07 White Rabbit Gallery

Housed in what once served as a Rolls-Royce service depot, this eccentric gallery showcases Chinese contemporary art that's been created this millennium. It sounds as if it's esoteric, but free tours will help to explain more. The White Rabbit Collection contains 1400 works by more than 500 artists, which are rotated regularly. There's also a teahouse, serving Taiwanese teas and Chinese *cha* in chilled-out surrounds. Brews include blossom-in-the-pot chrysanthemum, lychee and green tea. *whiterabbitcollection.org; 30 Balfour St, Chippendale; 10am-5pm Wed-Sun; free.*

08 Movies by the Boulevard

Blessed with balmy evenings, Sydney offers numerous al-fresco cinema experiences. Big screens appear everywhere during summer, including one that emerges from the harbour outside the Opera House, in front of the bridge, where tickets cost more than A$30. **Olympic Park** in the west, however, screens new, cult and classic flicks for free throughout the summer; you can bring a picnic, and it's easy to reach via public transport. *sydneyolympicpark.com.au; Olympic Park; free.*

09 Centennial Park

Reminiscent of London's great green gardens, this 125-year-old city park is home to lakes, an intricate labyrinth, more than 15,000 trees, free barbecues and playgrounds, and a colony of flying foxes, which you can meet at a monthly **Bat Chat**, one of many free events. It's a peach of a picnic spot, and for a few dollars you can hire bikes or go horse riding. *centennialparklands.com.au; opening times vary; free.*

10 Ocean pools

Sydney boasts about 40 ocean pools, perfect for those who like to swim laps and anyone with a shark phobia. Some, including Bondi's Icebergs, cost money to access, but most are free. Check out **Giles Baths** (10a; a natural rockpool or 'bogey hole'), **McIvers Baths** (10b; women only) and **Ross Jones Memorial Pool**, (10c) all in Coogee, plus **Clovelly Ocean Pool** (10d), Long Bay's **Malabar Ocean Pool** (10e) and Maroubra's spectacular **Mahon Pool** (10f). *See randwick.nsw.gov.au for details; free.*

11 Royal Botanic Gardens

Sydney is commonly criticised for its big-city manners and expensive prices, but this free-access 730-hectare park between the CBD and the harbour is an oasis of tranquillity. Take a free tour daily at 10.30am, or just explore the environs. The 200-year-old collection of plants is stunning, and displays include 'Cadi Jam Ora – First Encounters', which honours the Cadigal, Sydney's original inhabitants, and their relationship with the land. *rbgsyd.nsw.gov.au; 24hr; free.*

12 **Royal National Park**

The planet's second-oldest national park offers bush-covered and ocean-stroked wilderness. Over 100km of walking trails wend through the park, across cliffs and through rainforest-fringed gullies to deserted beaches. Wild camping at Uloola Falls and North Era sites costs A$12 (possibly Sydney's cheapest accommodation). Cars are charged A$12 per day, but visit via public transport (train to Waterfall, or ferry from Cronulla) for free admission. *nationalparks.nsw.gov.au/Royal-National-Park; Audley Rd, Audley; 7am-8.30pm.*

13 **Snorkelling**

Scuba diving isn't cheap, and Sydney Aquarium is pricey too, but fish-spotting is free from loads of the city's beaches if you're packing a snorkel and a mask. Manly's **Shelly Beach** (13a) is a great spot, as is **Gordon's Bay** (13b) between Coogee and Clovelly. You can swim with wonderful weedy sea dragons off **Bare Island** (13c) in Botany Bay, and at **Clovelly** (13d) snorkellers regularly meet a resident blue groper nicknamed Bluey. *24hr; free.*

14 **Sydney Harbour Bridge**

The giant 'coat hanger' no longer dominates the ever-changing and growing Sydney skyline, but it does define it; with the Opera House, this structure is one of the twin icons of the Harbour City. An official climb over the top of the bridge is expensive – a budget alternative is to wander along the pedestrian pathway at the bridge's eastern edge – from where the views are still stunning. *24hr; free.*

15 **Sydney Harbour National Park**

This 4-sq km NP protects sections of Sydney's foreshore and several islands within the harbour. Most attractions are free, including the **Quarantine Station** (15a; *quarantinestation.com.au; 1 North Head Scenic Dr; museum 10am-4pm Sun-Thu, 10am-8pm Fri + Sat*) and **Fort Denison** (15b; *fortdenison.com.au*) on Pinchgut Island, although you need to buy ferry tickets and there's a charge

THRIFTY COMMUTING

Travelling around Sydney needn't cost a fortune. On public transport, buy an Opal Card (*opal.com.au*), and after eight paid train/bus/tram/ferry journeys between Monday and Sunday, you travel free for the rest of the week. When driving, be aware that fuel is cheaper earlier in the week, with prices rising around the weekend (especially during public holidays); Check *motormouth.com.au* for the best up-to-date petrol prices. Sydney and its suburbs are ideal for exploring on foot, and free/cheap walking-tour apps are available for lots of places, including Observatory Hill and the Rocks (p267) and Centennial Park (p267). Free maps for Sydney's cracking coastal walks can be downloaded at *walkingcoastalsydney.com.au*.

SYDNEY

for tours. There's hiking in the park, including the **Spit to Manly** walk (15c; *walkingcoastalsydney.com.au; free). nationalparks.nsw.gov.au; 24hr; free for pedestrians.*

16 Barbecue bargain

Eating out costs a fortune in Sydney, but eating outside will only set you back the price of a few 'snags' (sausages). In numerous public places throughout the city and suburbs, from **Western Sydney Parklands** (16a; *westernsydneyparklands.com.au; Richmond Rd; Dean Park, 8am-5pm May-Jul, 8am-7pm Aug-Apr; free*) to **Bronte Park** (16b; *Bronte Rd; free*), you will find free (occasionally coin-operated) barbecues, where a variety of families, backpackers and travellers bond over a shared, if very well used, hotplate.

17 Chinatown night markets

Chinatown is full of fragrances and frenetic activity. Sydney has a long-established Chinese population, but this area is now a pan-Asian melting pot, where you can chow on a whole host of delicious cuisines, including Cantonese, Thai, Malaysian, Japanese and Vietnamese. Sydneysiders have embraced *yum cha* (eating dim sum and drinking tea) especially at weekend lunchtimes, but Friday evening is when the sensational street-eats market takes place. *Dixon St; Fri 4-11pm; admission free.*

18 Farmers' markets

Sydney's street markets offer a source of good, fresh and usually locally grown/made produce. Time your run right, and you can often pick up tasty bargains at places such as **Sydney Sustainable Markets** (18a; *sydneysustainablemarkets.org; Taylor Sq, Darlinghurst; 8am-1pm Sat; admission free*), **Carriageworks Farmers Market** (18b; *carriageworks.com.au; 245 Wilson St, Eveleigh; 8am–1pm Sat; admission free*), and **Growers' Market Pyrmont** (18c; *growersmarketpyrmont.com.au; Pyrmont Bay Park, Sydney Harbour; 7-11am 1st Sat of the month except Jan*).

"Sydney isn't cheap, but there are ways to keep things affordable. We're members at the local independent cinema, which means tickets are super-cheap. Australian wine is fantastic, but the country makes too much of it; to avoid flooding the market, loads of top-quality vino is sold in Sydney bottleshops as 'cleanskins', with no branding and at a fraction of the price. Because of Sydney's climate, camping is brilliant and cheap – Lane Cove River Tourist Park (*Plassey Rd, Macquarie Park*) and The Basin Campground in Ku-Ring-Gai Chase National Park both offer sites close to the city. Check *nationalparks.nsw.gov.au* for details." – Oran Redmond, Sydneysider

SOUTH AMERICA

ARTS & CULTURE | MUSIC & FILM | SPORTS & LEISURE | FOOD & DRINK | FESTIVALS & EVENTS

BOGOTÁ

Bogotá is Colombia's beating heart, an engaging and vibrant capital cradled by chilly Andean peaks and steeped in sophisticated urban cool. During the day, history and culture call, from the atmospheric colonial quarter of La Candelaria to nearly 80 museums dotted about the city; at night, brace yourself: Bogotá boogies!

01 Bogotá Graffiti Tour

This fascinating 2½-hour cultural walking tour focuses on Bogotá's impressive urban art scene. The tour itself is free but a COP$20,000 to COP$30,000 gratuity is recommended for the guide. It's a great (and cheap!) way to dive deeper into a colourful and creative underworld you might otherwise stroll right past on your way to more well-known attractions. *bogotagraffiti.com; Parque de los Periodistas; 10am & 2pm; free.*

02 Museo Botero

Banco de la República's massive museum complex dedicates several halls to all things chubby: hands, oranges, women, mustachioed men, children, birds, Fuerzas Armadas Revolucionarias de Colombia (FARC) leaders – all, of course, the robust paintings and sculptures of Colombia's famed artist, Fernando Botero (who donated these works). *banrepcultural.org/museo-botero; Calle 11 No 4-41; 9am-7pm Mon & Wed-Sat, 10am-5pm Sun; free.*

03 Cine Tonalá

One of Bogotá's few independent cinemas champions Latin/Colombian films and international cult classics, but this Mexico City import refuses to be categorised. The multifaceted cultural centre in a renovated 1930s La Merced mansion is a shelter for artistic refugees, who retreat here for its hip bar, fine cheap Mexican food and rousing club nights. *cinetonala.co; Carrera 6A No 35-27; noon-3am Tue-Sun; films COP$7000-9000.*

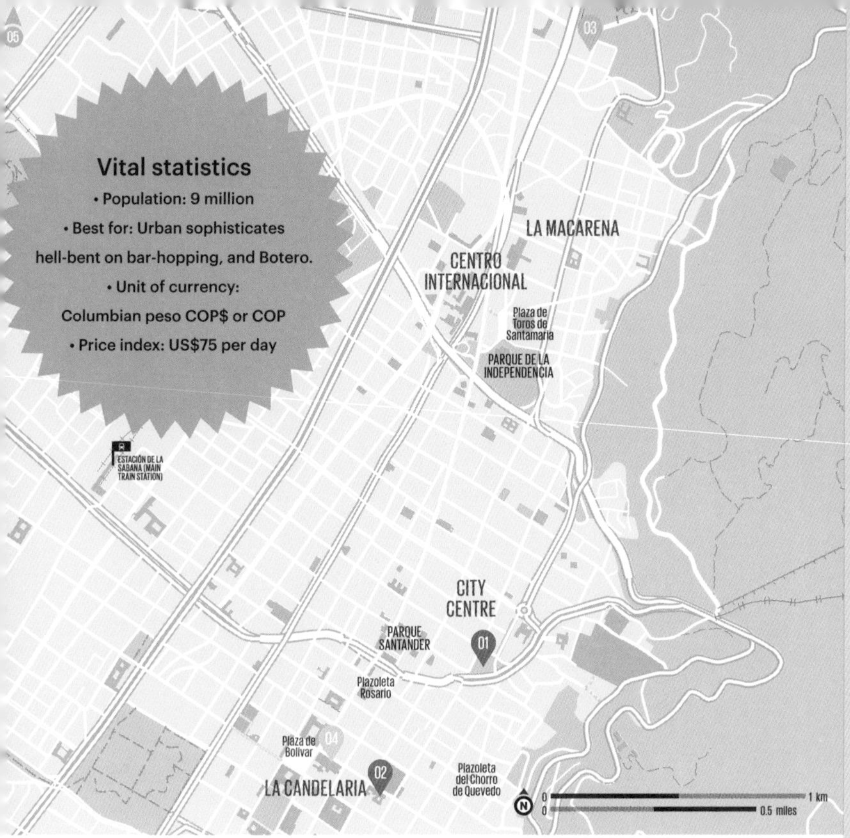

Vital statistics

- Population: 9 million
- Best for: Urban sophisticates hell-bent on bar-hopping, and Botero.
- Unit of currency: Columbian peso COP$ or COP
- Price index: US$75 per day

LA MACARENA
CENTRO INTERNACIONAL
Plaza de Toros de Santamaría
PARQUE DE LA INDEPENDENCIA
ESTACIÓN DE LA SABANA (MAIN TRAIN STATION)
CITY CENTRE
PARQUE SANTANDER
Plazoleta Rosario
Plaza de Bolívar
LA CANDELARIA
Plazoleta del Chorro de Quevedo
0 1 km
0 0.5 miles

04 La Puerta Falsa

Bogotá's most famous snack shop, where a rainbow display of candies beckons you into a tiny interior, remains the place to eat and drink a piece of history in the colonial quarter. The moist tamales and luscious *chocolate completo* (hot chocolate served with cheese, buttered bread and a biscuit) are local favourites – and priced to please. *Calle 11 No 6-50; 7am-9pm Mon-Sat, 8am-7pm Sun; candies COP$1500-2000, snacks COP$3500-6300.*

05 Noche de Galerías

Get drunk on culture? *And free wine?* Where do I sign up, you say? No signature necessary! Once a quarter, several of Bogotá's coolest galleries open their doors for Noche de Galerías (Gallery Nights). Think of it as a wine-driven gallery crawl, with free drinks, guided tours and a generally festive atmosphere all fuelled by some of the city's most creative and interesting people. *nochedegalerias.co; see website for details; free.*

06 Free music for all

Bogotá is one of the best cities in the world for free concerts, including the three days of (mostly South American) rock/metal/pop/funk/reggae bands that feature at **Rock al Parque** (*rockalparque.gov.co; Parque Simón Bolívar; check website for details; free*). Other notable events include **Salsa al Parque** (*salsaalparque.gov.co; see website for details; free*), **Hip-Hop al Parque** (*hiphopalparque.gov.co; Oct/Nov, see website for details; free*) and the 10-day **Festival de Verano** (*idrd.gov.co/sitio/idrd; see website for details; free*).

TIP BOX

- Biking is perhaps the best way to get around the city. Bogotá is home to one of the world's most extensive bike-route networks, with over 350km of separated, clearly marked bike paths called *CicloRuta;* and the city goes nuts for the citywide *Ciclovía,* when 121km of city roads are closed to traffic from 7am to 2pm on Sundays and holidays.

- Save your museum visiting for Sundays, when at least 35 of the city's myriad museums offer free admission.

ARTS & CULTURE · MUSIC & FILM · SPORTS & LEISURE · FOOD & DRINK · FESTIVALS & EVENTS

BUENOS AIRES

Buenos Aires is a city that pumps with passion. From football to politics, emotions often run high and find expression in a vibrant arts scene. And it's not just the many free concerts and exhibitions; take a stroll around the neighbourhood and you'll find street art, buskers and armchair philosophers.

01 Caminito

Wander down this street of brightly coloured houses that are typical of the places once inhabited by many Italian immigrant shipyard workers. It's a good place in which to see street performers dancing tango and La Boca's famous Maradona mural. There's a wonderful view from the roof terrace of the **Quinquela Martin Museum** *(Ave Don Pedro de Mendoza 1835; 10am-6pm Tue-Fri, 11am-6pm Sat & Sun; suggested donation AR$10). 24hr; free.*

01

02 Carlos Gardel Museum

Even if you don't know much about Carlos Gardel, spend any time in Buenos Aires and you'll soon recognise his face – it's everywhere. The celebrated tango crooner's former home is now a museum worth a look, and don't miss the murals of Gardel painted in the nearby Calle Zelaya and Calle Agüero. *museocasacarlosgardel.buenosaires.gob.ar/; Jean Jaurés 735; 11am-6pm Mon & Wed-Fri, 10am-7pm Sat & Sun; AR$5, free on Wed.*

02

05

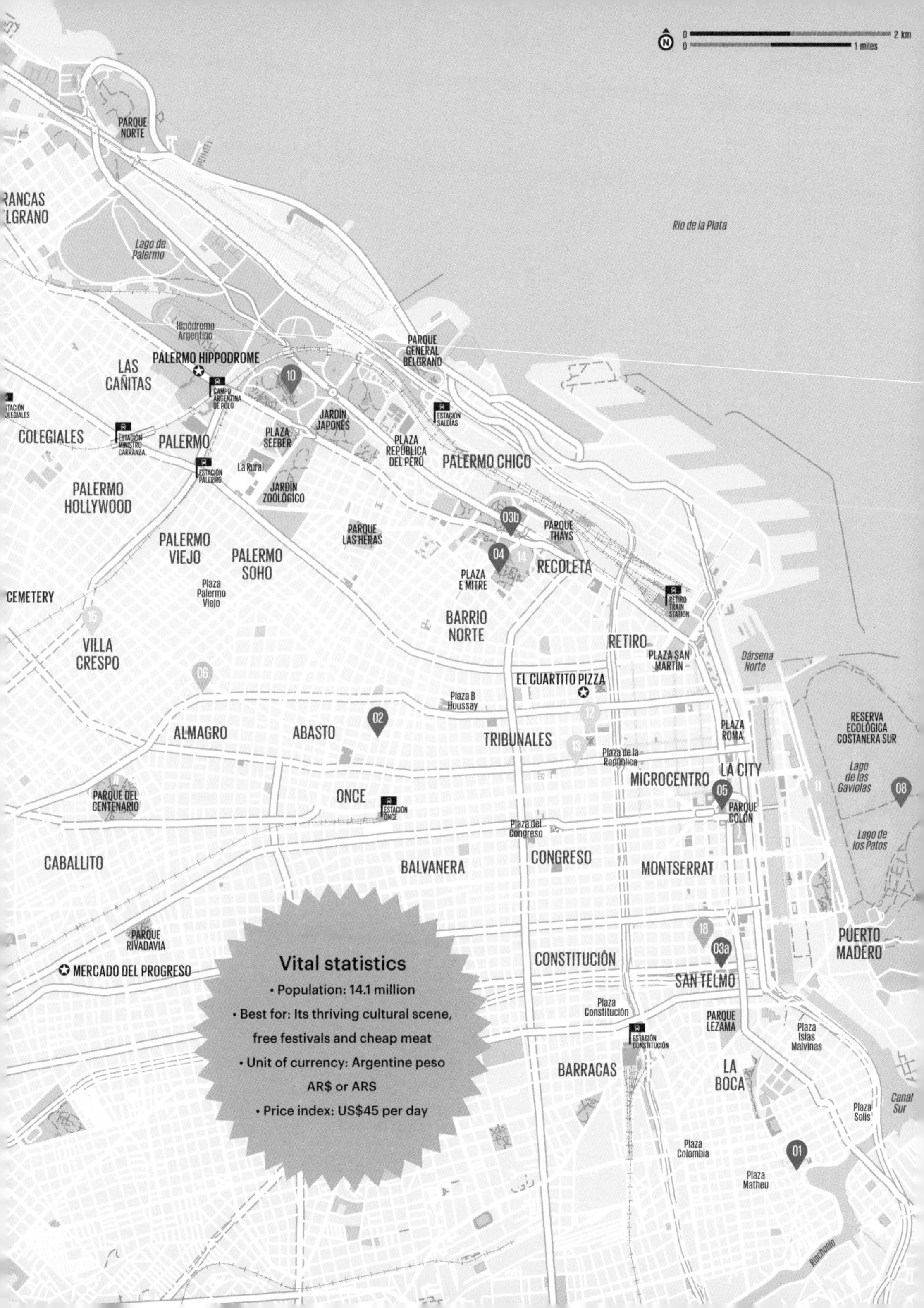

0
2 km
0
1 miles
PARQUE NORTE
RANCAS
LGRANO
Río de la Plata
Lago de Palermo
Hipódromo Argentino
PARQUE GENERAL BELGRANO
PALERMO HIPPODROME
LAS CAÑITAS
CAMPO ARGENTINA DE POLO
10
ESTACIÓN SALDÍAS
JARDÍN JAPONÉS
PLAZA SEEBER
ESTACIÓN MINISTRO CARRANZA
COLEGIALES
PALERMO
PLAZA REPÚBLICA DEL PERÚ
PALERMO CHICO
ESTACIÓN PALERMO
La Rural
JARDÍN ZOOLÓGICO
PALERMO HOLLYWOOD
03b
PARQUE THAYS
PARQUE LAS HERAS
PALERMO VIEJO
PALERMO SOHO
04
14
RECOLETA
PLAZA E MITRE
CEMETERY
Plaza Palermo Viejo
RETIRO TRAIN STATION
15
VILLA CRESPO
BARRIO NORTE
RETIRO
PLAZA SAN MARTÍN
Dársena Norte
06
EL CUARTITO PIZZA
Plaza B Houssay
12
02
ALMAGRO
ABASTO
TRIBUNALES
PLAZA ROMA
RESERVA ECOLÓGICA COSTANERA SUR
13
Plaza de la República
LA CITY
Lago de las Gaviolas
MICROCENTRO
05
11
08
PARQUE DEL CENTENARIO
ONCE
ESTACIÓN ONCE
PARQUE COLÓN
Plaza del Congreso
Lago de los Patos
CABALLITO
BALVANERA
CONGRESO
MONTSERRAT
18
PUERTO MADERO
PARQUE RIVADAVIA
03a
CONSTITUCIÓN
MERCADO DEL PROGRESO
SAN TELMO
Plaza Constitución
PARQUE LEZAMA
Plaza Islas Malvinas
ESTACIÓN CONSTITUCIÓN
BARRACAS
LA BOCA
Canal Sur
Plaza Solís
Plaza Colombia
01
Plaza Matheu
Riachuelo
Vital statistics
• Population: 14.1 million
• Best for: Its thriving cultural scene, free festivals and cheap meat
• Unit of currency: Argentine peso AR$ or ARS
• Price index: US$45 per day

03 Free art for all

Get a free midweek dose of culture by visiting the **Museum of Modern Art** (3a; MAMBA; *buenosaires.gob.ar/museoartemoderno; Ave San Juan 350; 11am-7pm Tue-Fri, 11am-8pm Sat & Sun; free on Tue)*, housed in a former cigarette factory that has been transformed into a spacious gallery. Or check out the fine art museum, the **Museo Nacional de Bellas Artes** (3b; MNBA; *mnba.gob.ar; Ave del Libertador 1473; 12.30-8.30pm Tue-Fri, 9.30am-8.30pm Sat & Sun; free)*.

04 Recoleta Cemetery

The mausoleums at Recoleta are world famous, but while that of Eva Perón draws the crowds, the cemetery's most elaborate tombs are elsewhere. Look for the grand mausoleum of newspaper magnate José C Paz (the William Randolph Hearst of his day) and the 'tomb' of Dorrego Ortíz Basualdo, which has its own chapel. In the city of the dead, the only living residents are cats. *Junín 1760; 8am-5.45pm; free.*

05 Casa Rosada

Take a free guided tour of the President's executive building and see the balcony from which Juan and Evita Perón would address enraptured crowds. Every Thursday at 3.30pm, the Mothers of the Plaza de Mayo, whose children were 'disappeared' during the military dictatorship of 1976–83, circle the monument in front of the Casa Rosada in a moving act of remembrance. *casarosada.gob.ar/la-casa-rosada/visitas-guiadas; Balcarce 50; 10am-6pm Sat & Sun; free.*

06 Club Cultural Matienzo

Matienzo is just one of the city's fantastic cultural centres, laid-back neighbourhood places that serve cheap drinks and food (usually empanadas) and host concerts, workshops and exhibitions, among other things. Have a look at the website to see what's scheduled; Matienzo regularly hosts great up-and-coming local bands that you can often listen to for free, as well as music festivals

ONE-DAY FREE PASS

Begin with a typical Buenos Aires breakfast of *medialunas* (croissants), but instead of going to a cafe, pick them up from a bakery and eat them in a park (look out for dog-walkers and their multiple charges). Spend the morning checking out San Telmo's market (p279), antiques shops and street art, making your way along Calle Defensa to Plaza de Mayo. Jump on the *subte* (underground) to Retiro and walk through mansion-lined streets to Recoleta Cemetery. Refuel with empanadas – eaten at the counter – in El Cuartito *(Talcahuano 937; 12.30pm-1am)*.

and literary evenings. *ccmatienzo.com.ar; Pringles 1249; times and prices vary.*

07 La Glorieta

Don't waste your money on an expensive, tacky tourist show; the best place to see real tango is at a *milonga* (dance hall). Many have a small cover charge but one of the most atmospheric, La Glorieta, is free. It's hard to imagine a more romantic setting than the park bandstand where, every weekend, dancers of all ages and levels come to tango together. *Barrancas de Belgrano; 7-10pm Fri-Sun; free.*

08 Costanera Sur Ecological Reserve

One of the best things about this place is that coming here feels almost like you've left the city. Sandwiched between the waters of the Río de la Plata estuary and the high-rise prime real estate of Puerto Madero, the reserve is a 360-hectare wild, open space full of fragrant flora and interesting fauna that's great for walking, jogging, cycling or a spot of birdwatching. *Costanera Sur; 8am-6pm Tue-Sun; free.*

09 Buenos Aires Local Tours

There is plenty to see for yourself as you stroll around Buenos Aires, but the history of the city really comes alive when you learn the stories behind the buildings and monuments on a guided walking tour. Described as 'pay what you want' tours, the idea is that you tip your guide with an amount you think is appropriate. Or not. *buenosaireslocaltours.com; see website for location; daily at 10am; free.*

10 Rollerskating in the Bosques de Palermo

With an artificial lake surrounded by a smooth, tarmacked path, Parque Tres de Febrero (as the Bosques is officially known) is the perfect place in which to roll, not to mention people-watch – the park-goers here are usually a colourful crowd. If you don't have your own skates then you can hire them at the park; there are bikes available for rent too. *Cnr Ave Sarmiento & Ave Libertador; 24hr; admission free.*

11 Costanera Sur sandwiches

When *porteños* (port-dwellers) return home from their travels, one of the first places they'll come is the Costanera Sur for *choripán* (chorizo sandwich) or *bondiola* (braised pork shoulder). This is street food Buenos Aires-style: a long line of roadside *parrillas* selling meaty sandwiches for bargain prices. The smell of barbecuing meat – perhaps the essence of the city – is difficult to resist. *Ave Int Hernán M. Giralt; 24hr; choripán AR$25-30.*

07

08

11

12 *Mate*-drinking at Plaza Lavalle

This pleasant way to combine two very Argentine activities – *mate*-drinking and dog-walking – costs only as much as a bag of *yerba* (loose-leaf tea). Bring your vacuum flask of hot (but not boiled!) water, *yerba*, *mate* (drinking gourd) and *bombilla* (metal straw) to Plaza Lavalle and watch the professional dog-walkers arrive with their multi-leaded packs, while you sip your morning brew. *Cnr Libertad & Tucuman; mornings; free.*

13 Pizzería Güerrin

Forget what you think you know about pizza; Güerrin doesn't mess around with delicate thin crusts. A slice or two of this doughy, greasy, satisfying carb-fest can be eaten standing up at the counter for a snip of the price of sitting at a table. Increase the stodge factor by topping it with a slice of *fainá*, a chickpea-based

09

BUENOS AIRES BY BIKE

The best way to explore Buenos Aires is by bike: it's almost completely flat and has a network of bike lanes that makes cycling easy. To pick up one of the 3000 free EcoBici bikes and take advantage of the government's bike scheme, take a photocopy of your passport and immigration stamp to one of the 32 yellow bike stations and sign up. The bike is now yours for an hour. Drop it off at any of the stations around the city; these are marked on a map that you can pick up when you register. *buenosaires.gob.ar/ecobici; 24hr; free.*

flatbread. *pizzeriaguerrin.com; Ave Corrientes 1368; 11am-2am; pizza from AR$25 per slice.*

14 Plaza Francia Feria Artesanal

The weekend artisan market in Plaza Francia is not only a place to come for handicrafts. Also keep an eye out for sellers of homemade *pan relleno* (bread stuffed with cheese and tomato), which is one of the cheapest and most filling meals you'll find in town. The vendors are usually to be seen wandering among the stalls carrying a basket of their tasty wares. *Recoleta; 11am-8pm Sat & Sun; pan relleno AR$20-25.*

15 Sabores Entrerrianos

It might look a bit rough around the edges but this *parrilla* in Villa Crespo serves the best-value steaks in town – significantly cheaper than those of its flasher neighbours – and its servings are so generous that even the waiter suggests ordering half portions. The owners clearly believe in substance over style; the meat here is good-quality and always perfectly cooked. *Serrano 954; 12-3pm & 8pm-midnight; meals around AR$70.*

16 Buenos Aires festivals

There are so many festivals taking place in Buenos Aires – celebrating jazz, cycling, rock music, film and even mathematics – that it seems as if no sooner has one finished than the next one begins. They feature first-rate performances and workshops, for free. Check the website (*festivales.buenosaires.gob.ar*) for details about individual festivals. Two of the best are the **Buenos Aires International Festival** (FIBA) *(September-October; free)* and **Tango BA** *(August & April; free).*

17 Feria de Mataderos

To get a piece of rural *gaucho* (Argentine cowboy) action in the city, head to the neighbourhood of Mataderos for the Sunday fair. Displays of horsemanship, folk music, dancing and plenty of leather goods are some of the highlights. It's also the place to try *locro*, a traditional hearty soup. *feriademataderos.com.ar; cnr Ave Lisandro de la Torre & Ave de los Corrales; 11am Sun, 6pm Sat during summer; free.*

18 San Telmo Sunday Market

It doesn't matter if you're not keen on shopping, the Sunday street fair in San Telmo has plenty more going on to keep you entertained, from buskers to tango dancers. Stretching a whole 10 blocks from Plaza Dorrego to Plaza de Mayo, the stalls here sell a sometimes-bizarre collection of antiques and handicrafts, as well as the usual souvenirs. *Calle Defensa; 10am-6pm Sun; admission free.*

THE LOCAL'S VIEW

"I live next to one of the oldest markets, Mercado del Progreso *(mercadodelprogreso.com; Ave Rivadavia 5430; 7.30am-2pm & 5-8.30pm Mon-Sat; free)*. The vendors there sell top-quality meat that's no more expensive than at a regular butcher. If I'm having an *asado* I'll shop there, and buy wine from the Chinese-owned neighbourhood supermarket. Two of my favourite places to go are Chacarita cemetery *(Ave Guzmán 680; 7.30am-5pm; free)*, where the tango singer Carlos Gardel is buried; and the horse-racing venue Palermo Hippodrome *(palermo.com.ar; Ave del Libertador 4101; free entrance, minimum bet AR$5)*."
– Patricio Santos, Spanish teacher at Che Vos Spanish

WINE TASTING ON A SHOESTRING IN SOUTH AMERICA

South American wine regions are romantic destinations, but you don't have to kiss goodbye to all your pesos to sample the fruit of the harvest.

CAFAYATE WINE REGION – ARGENTINA

Fewer tourists make it to Cafayate, Argentina's 'other' wine country, famous for the aromatic white varietal Torrontés, but it's an easy side trip from Salta, a city many travellers pass through on their way to or from Bolivia. *welcomeargentina.com/cafayate.*

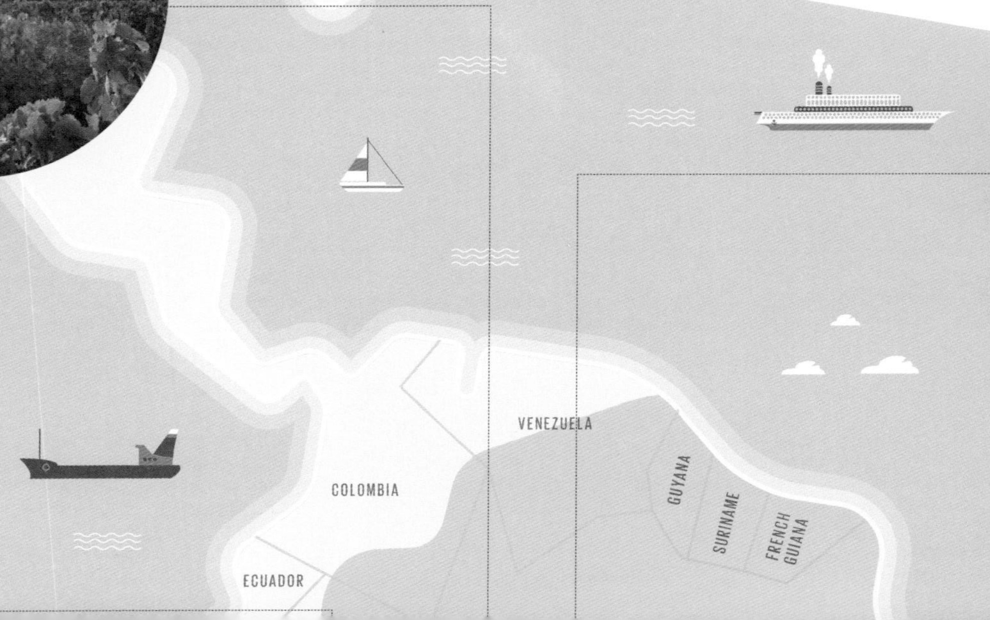

VENEZUELA
COLOMBIA
ECUADOR
GUYANA
SURINAME
FRENCH GUIANA

FINCA NARBONA – URUGUAY

The wineries around Carmelo are the places to sample little-known Tannat. You don't need to be an overnight guest at Narbona Wine Lodge to see the impressive winery: just come for lunch with wine pairings. *narbona.com.uy; Ruta 21, km 267, Carmelo, Uruguay.*

VIÑA CONCHA Y TORO – CHILE

The largest wine producer in Latin America may not be especially quaint, but you can at least get to it on the metro from downtown Santiago. *conchaytoro.com; Virginia Subercaseaux 210, Pirque, Chile; 10am-5pm; tastings CH$12,000.*

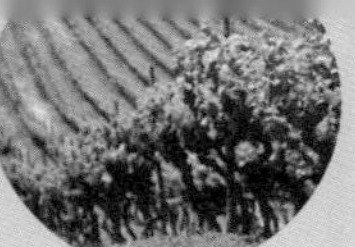

CASABLANCA VALLEY – CHILE

You came to Valparaíso for picturesque architecture and Pablo Neruda, now take a day tour with Wine Tours Valparaíso – the perfect way to see the nearby Casablanca Valley. *winetoursvalparaiso.cl; Cerro Alegre, Valparaíso, Chile.*

MONTGRAS WINERY – SANTA CRUZ, CHILE

Make a day of it at this beautiful winery located in Chilean wine region Colchagua Valley: in addition to tasting Carménère, you can go hiking or mountain biking. *montgras.cl; Camino Isla de Yáquil s/n, Palmilla; 10am-4.30pm; tasting with food pairing CH$15,000.*

SALENTEIN WINERY – VALLE DE UCO, ARGENTINA

In Argentina's buzzed-about Uco Valley, you'll get more bang for your peso if you time your winery visit with one of the many cultural events on schedule at Salentein's amphitheatre. *bodega-salentein.com; RP 89, Los Árboles, Tunuyán, Argentina; 9am-5pm Mon-Sat; tastings AR$150.*

MENDOZA ON TWO WHEELS – ARGENTINA

Rent a bicycle and explore los caminos del vino (roads of wine) close to the city of Mendoza. Mr. Hugo Bikes offers bicycles, lockers and maps, and organises tours. *mrhugobikes.com; Urquiza 2288, Maipú, Mendoza; reservations online.*

CASA VALDUGA – BRAZIL

One of the big players in Vale Dos Vinhedos – ground zero for Brazil's up-and-coming wine scene – the popular Casa Valduga offers a basic tasting of three wines for free. *casavalduga.com.br; Via Trento 2355, Vale Dos Vinhedos, Brazil; 9.30am-6.15pm; free.*

ARTS & CULTURE | MUSIC & FILM | SPORTS & LEISURE | FOOD & DRINK | FESTIVALS & EVENTS

LIMA

LIMA

Lima is no mere stopover. Its leafy suburbs overlooking the ocean have made countless travellers gush, 'I'd love to live here.' Many have stayed, bringing an international attitude to Peru's fusion culture, and you can sense this thrill of thenew as keenly as the scent of the ocean.

01 Museo de Arte de Lima (MALI)

Lima's principal fine art museum is housed in a lovely beaux-arts building – some of the columns are from the workshops of Gustave Eiffel himself. Subjects range from pre-Columbian to contemporary art and give good insight into Chavín and other pre-Incan cultures. On Sundays the normal S12 admission fee drops to S1 and includes a guided tour and kids' activities. *mali.pe; Paseo Colón 25; 10am-5pm, closed Wed; S1 on Sun.*

02 Museo de la Inquisición

The Spanish Inquisition once plied its trade in this diminutive museum. You can tour the basement, where morbidly hilarious wax figures are stretched on racks and flogged – to the delight of visiting eight-year-olds. The old 1st-floor library retains a baroque wooden ceiling that is scarily beautiful. Entry is by half-hour guided tours in Spanish and English, after which you can wander about. www. *congreso.gob.pe/museo.htm; Jirón Junín 548; 9am-5pm; free.*

03 Free walking tour

Lima is full of curious places that most people overlook. This walking tour is led by an enthusiastic guide who will tell you about such compelling events as the pirate attacks on old Lima, and bring to life the humble post office, which once was Lima's first train station. The tour is free with little hard sell but most people leave a tip. *fwtperu.com/fwt-lima.html; tours start at the north entrance to Parque Kennedy; 11am Mon-Sat; free.*

03

© Danny García | 500px

MENÚ DEL DÍA

The best way to try Lima's cuisine is also the cheapest. Forget dinner, fill up on a huge set-lunch *menú del día* on nearly any street. Just look for a whiteboard list at the restaurant entrance. Even in ritzy Miraflores you're likely to only pay S7 to S14. Places can be no-fuss family-run joints or white-tablecloth establishments with nicer desserts. Either way, you'll rub shoulders with office workers and families as you try a three-course meal that usually includes a hearty soup, rice, salad and a drink, often tea. Some serve up ceviche, so you'll get your daily fix of marinated raw seafood.

04 Parque del Amor

A stroll along the clifftop green spaces of Milaflores is relaxing and full of surprises. The best of these is this park perched over the Pacific Ocean, with its Gaudí-esque curved benches and arches decorated in mosaics spelling out messages of love in Spanish. It's an expanse that feels like a gallery with no walls. Lovers come here to whisper sweet nothings and watch the paragliders launch across Lima's beaches. *Malecón Cisneros; 24hr; free.*

05 Puente de los Suspiros and the Barranco district

Take the hand of your lover and cross this bridge while holding your breath. If you can make it across in one lungful of air, you'll apparently have a love life as beautiful as the surrounding Barranco district. Walk up the winding paths by the church then out to the ocean viewpoint: your date will surely be bewitched. *Paseo Chabuca Granda, a block west of the plaza, Barranco; 24hr; free.*

06 Choco Museo Miraflores

It's actually more of a shop, but the free tours at this 'museum' serve up the history of chocolate and you can cop a feel of the ingredients. The taste-testing is what everybody really comes for, with free samples of raw cacao, sublime chocolate bars, chocolate tea and fair-trade hot cocoa. The venue also hosts affordable workshops – see the website for details. *chocomuseo.com; Calle Berlin 375; 11am-8.30pm Sun-Thu, 11am-9.30pm Fri + Sat; admission free.*

02
LIMA
LIMA CENTRO
01
BREÑA
SANTA BEATRIZ
EL AGUSTINO
LA VICTORIA
JESÚS MARÍA
SAN LUIS
PARQUE ZONAL TÚPAC AMARU
LINCE
RÍO SURCO
Hipódromo de Monterrico
LA MOLINA
SAN ISIDRO
Lima Golf Club
SAN BORJA
SURQUILLO
MONTERRICO
06
03
04
MIRAFLORES
Universidad Ricardo Palma
Pacific Ocean
SANTIAGO DE SURCO
VILLA MARÍA DEL TRIUNFO
BARRANCO
05
5 km
2.5 miles

Vital statistics

- Population: 10.8 million
- Best for: History, outdoors
- Unit of currency: Nuevo sol S or PEN
- Price index: US$80 per day

ARTS & CULTURE · MUSIC & FILM · SPORTS & LEISURE · FOOD & DRINK · FESTIVALS & EVENTS

RIO DE JANEIRO

It's hard not to fall for Rio de Janeiro, with its gorgeous beaches, rainforest-covered mountains and samba-fuelled nightlife. While it's easy to blow the budget here (beachfront hotels, high-end restaurants, expensive tours), the Rio experience doesn't have to be costly; some of the best activities in the city are free.

01 Centro Cultural Banco do Brasil (CCBB)

Housed in a beautifully restored 1906 building, the Centro Cultural Banco do Brasil hosts some of Rio's best exhibitions – all of which are free. You're set for a good time roaming the galleries, which often have multimedia exhibits, or attending evening concerts and film screenings. If you come on weekdays there's rarely a crowd. *culturabancodobrasil.com.br; Primeiro de Março 66, Centro; 9am-9pm Wed-Mon; free.*

02 Escadaria Selarón

One of Rio's best-loved attractions is the magnificent tiled staircase connecting Lapa with Santa Teresa. Created by the Chilean-born artist Jorge Selarón, these wildly decorated stairs (215 in all), have become a symbol of Lapa's creative and bohemian spirit. They were Selarón's gift to the Brazilian people and contain tiles from all over the globe. A sign in English and Portuguese explains his vision. *Off Joaquim Silva, Lapa; 24hr; free.*

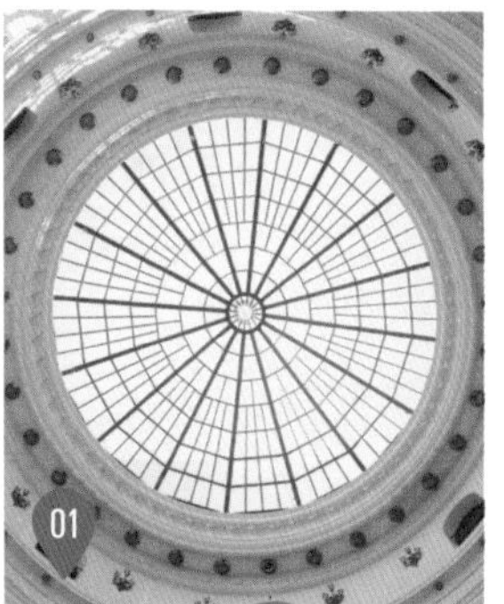

01

14

02

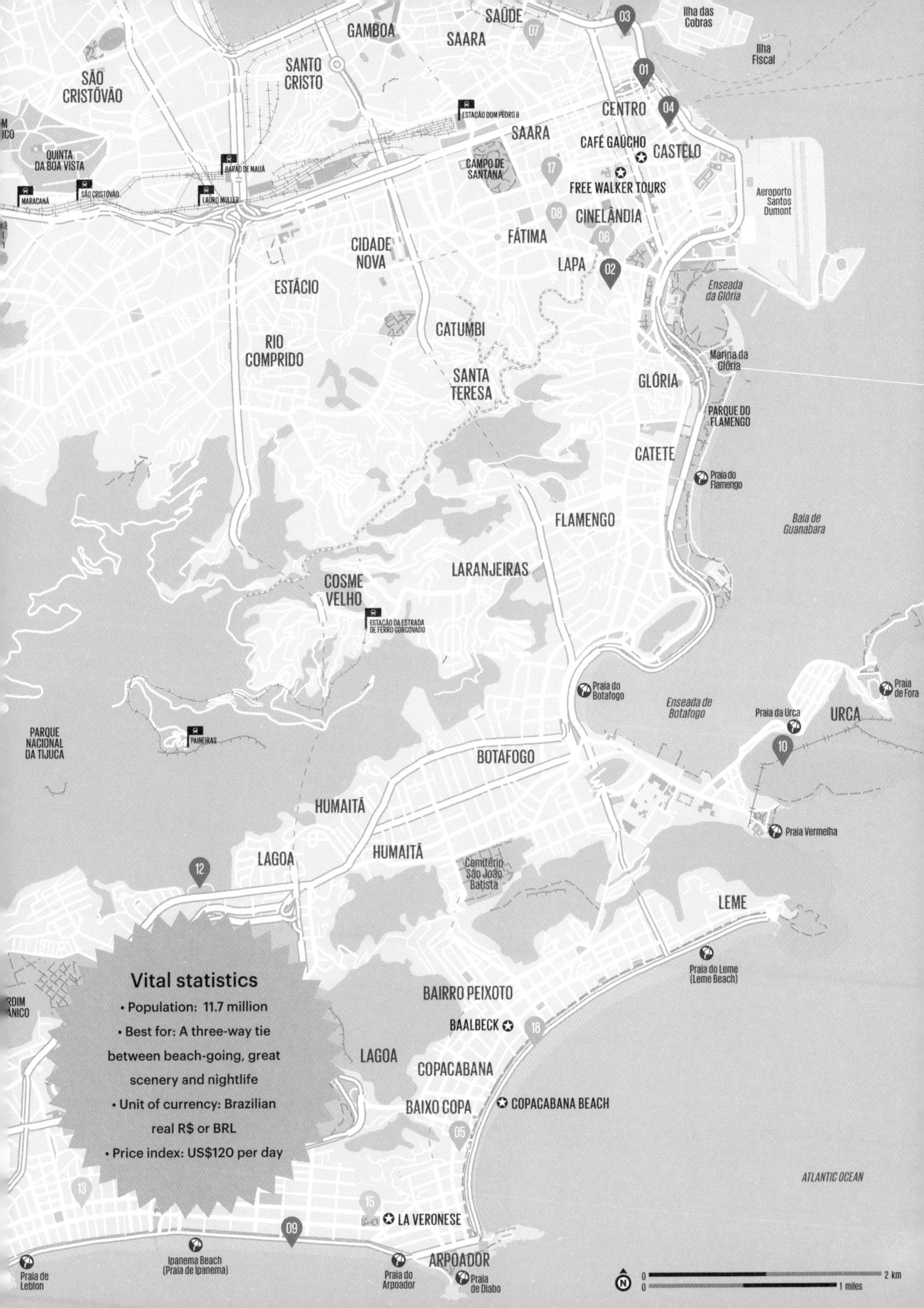

SAÚDE
GAMBOA
SAARA
Ilha das Cobras
Ilha Fiscal
SÃO CRISTÓVÃO
SANTO CRISTO
CENTRO
ESTAÇÃO DOM PEDRO II
SAARA
CAFÉ GAÚCHO
CASTELO
QUINTA DA BOA VISTA
BARÃO DE MAUÁ
CAMPO DE SANTANA
FREE WALKER TOURS
MARACANÃ
SÃO CRISTÓVÃO
LAURO MULLER
Aeroporto Santos Dumont
CINELÂNDIA
FÁTIMA
CIDADE NOVA
LAPA
ESTÁCIO
Enseada da Glória
CATUMBI
RIO COMPRIDO
Marina da Glória
SANTA TERESA
GLÓRIA
PARQUE DO FLAMENGO
CATETE
Praia do Flamengo
FLAMENGO
Baía de Guanabara
LARANJEIRAS
COSME VELHO
ESTAÇÃO DA ESTRADA DE FERRO CORCOVADO
Praia do Botafogo
Enseada de Botafogo
Praia de Fora
Praia da Urca
URCA
PARQUE NACIONAL DA TIJUCA
PAINEIRAS
BOTAFOGO
HUMAITÁ
Praia Vermelha
LAGOA
HUMAITÁ
Cemitério São João Batista
LEME
Vital statistics
• Population: 11.7 million
• Best for: A three-way tie between beach-going, great scenery and nightlife
• Unit of currency: Brazilian real R$ or BRL
• Price index: US$120 per day
Praia do Leme (Leme Beach)
BAIRRO PEIXOTO
BAALBECK
LAGOA
COPACABANA
BAIXO COPA
COPACABANA BEACH
ATLANTIC OCEAN
LA VERONESE
Ipanema Beach (Praia de Ipanema)
ARPOADOR
Praia de Leblon
Praia do Arpoador
Praia de Diabo
0 2 km
0 1 miles

03 Mosteiro de São Bento

In the northern reaches of downtown you'll find one of the finest colonial churches in Brazil. Built between 1617 and 1641 on the hilltop perch of Morro de São Bento, the monastery has a magnificent baroque interior, with beautiful sculptures and striking side chapels adding to the majesty. For the full experience, come for mass (weekdays 7.30am) when the monks sing Gregorian chants. *Rua Dom Gerardo 68, Centro; 7am-5.30pm; free.*

04 Paço Imperial

This former palace (1743) once housed the royal family of Portugal, who set up shop here after fleeing Napoleon and sailing to their New World colony in the early 1800s. The building has been turned into galleries hosting free exhibitions. Vestiges of the past remain, including the huge adjoining plaza where Princesa Isabel announced the liberation of slaves in 1888. *Praça XV (Quinze) de Novembro 48; noon-6pm Tue-Sun; free.*

05 Bip Bip

For years, Bip Bip has been one of the top spots in which to catch a *roda de samba* (informal samba played around a table). Although the place is just a storefront and some tables, it becomes the backdrop to serious jam sessions as the evening progresses, with music and revellers spilling into the street. There's no cover charge, but do tip the musicians. *Almirante Gonçalves 50, Copacabana; from 8pm Sun-Fri; free.*

06 Lapa

The epicentre of Rio's live music scene is the neighbourhood of Lapa, a former red-light district lined with open-air bars and old-fashioned samba clubs. On weekends, a wildly festive

09

12

WALKING TOURS

For an in-depth look at Rio's history, join one of the outfits offering free walking tours downtown. The aptly named Free Walker Tours (*freewalkertours.com*) takes visitors to Travessa do Comércio, Praça XV, Cinelândia, the Arcos da Lapa and Escadaria Selarón (p284), among other places, on insightful three-hour strolls. Although it's free, the guide asks for tips at the end. Most people give about R$25. The same outfit also leads good-value pub crawls in Ipanema and Lapa (*each R$55, including drinks and admission to several clubs*) as well as a free Copacabana walking tour.

air prevails, and the plaza by the Lapa Arches becomes an open-air dance party. Vendors sell cocktails from makeshift drink carts and there's live music. Later, stroll down **Ave Mem de Sá**, Lapa's liveliest strip. *Largo da Lapa; Sat + Sun, free.*

07 Pedra do Sal

The Monday- and Friday-night street parties are extremely popular with lovers of samba. The lively *samba da mesa* features a pool of changing players who deliver well-known songs to joyful crowds surrounding the tiny plaza. The atmospheric but run-down venue is rich in history – samba in fact was born in the Bahian community that once flourished here. *Largo João da Baiana, Gamboa; 8pm-midnight Mon & Fri; free.*

08 Vaca Atolada

For an authentic samba experience, head to this simple, brightly lit, tile-covered eating and drinking den. You'll find a *samba de roda* and a local crowd who gather around, join in the songs and dance (when space allows). This is old-school Lapa, friendly, ungentrified and lively. Arrive early to score a table, and be prepared to move; these rhythms were made for dancing! *Rua Gomes Freire 533, Centro; 8pm-2am Tue-Sat; free.*

09 Ipanema Beach

One of the best places to spend a sun-drenched day is out on Ipanema Beach. You can frolic in the waves, go surfing, take long walks or simply sit back and engage in the discreet art of people-watching. You also needn't leave the sands when hunger strikes. *Barracas* (beach stalls) sell everything from sandwiches to caipirinhas, and wandering vendors bring by cold drinks and snacks. *Off Av Vieira Souto, Ipanema; 24hr; free.*

10 Morro da Urca

Rio's lush hillsides have fabulous views, but getting to them generally means ponying up for a pricey funicular ride. If you're willing to hoof it, however, you can hike your way up to some jaw-dropping lookouts. One of the best is the Morro da Urca. It's a steep climb through forest along a well-marked trail, and you might spy monkeys en route. *Access off Claudio Coutinho trail in Urca; 24hr; free.*

11 Beachside paths

Take a seaside stroll along Copacabana or Ipanema Beach and it is easy to see why Rio is called the *cidade maravilhosa* (marvellous city). To take it all in, head out on foot or bike along the pavement that skirts the beach. Sunday is one of the best times to do this; the beach road closes to traffic, and cyclists, joggers, walkers and in-line skaters rule the street. *Copacabana & Ipanema beaches; 24hr; free.*

12 Parque Lage

You can still find pockets of Atlantic rainforest in Rio de Janeiro if you know where to look. A fine setting for a taste of the tropics is Parque Lage. This lush park has lovely forested walking trails, a koi pond, caves and a mini castle where kids enjoy clambering about. And you can sometimes spot marmosets and parrots in the trees. *eavparquelage.rj.gov.br; Rua Jardim Botânico 414; 9am-7pm; free.*

13 Bibi Sucos

The lively juice bar is a Rio institution, and most of them serve delicious concoctions from morning till late. Bibi Sucos, one of the best snack spots in Rio, serves dozens of flavours, including juices made from Amazonian fruits and berries. A favourite is açaí juice, a vitamin-packed berry that's blended up so thick you'll need a spoon to eat it. *bibisucos.com.br; Ave Ataúlfo de Paiva, Leblon; 8am-1am; açaí R$6-15.*

14 Coconut water

Drink of the gods, *água de coco* (coconut water) is wildly popular in Rio de Janeiro. It's the perfect refreshment for the tropical heat and is served from the husk – plus it's a bargain at R$5. Best of all, you don't even have to leave the sand to find it; beachside kiosks all along Ipanema and Copacabana serve it. As a bonus, coconut water is loaded with potassium and rich in electrolytes – all of which is excellent for hangovers...

15 Hippie fair

On Sundays, this is the best place to be in Ipanema. Although there's plenty of souvenir-shopping to be had, we suggest you come for the food. At the corners of the plaza you'll find delicious Bahian street snacks, such as *acarajé* (a black-eyed-pea fritter topped with shrimp and spices), which costs a mere R$12. And at that generous price, you can definitely afford dessert. *Praça General Osório, Ipanema; 9am-6pm Sun; admission free.*

16 Carnaval

Although hotels are expensive during Carnaval, there are many ways to join in the fun without spending a lot of cash. In the weeks leading up to the big event, *Blocos* and *Bandas*, aka roving street parties, happen all across town (see p290). There are also free concerts, and parties at the samba schools that host the big parade. *rio-carnival.net; locations and times vary, two weeks leading up to Ash Wednesday; free.*

17 Feira Rio Antigo

If you're around on the first Saturday of the month, don't miss this fair – there's live music, food and drink vendors and countless stalls selling crafts, clothing and antiques. It all goes down on one of Lapa's oldest streets, Rua do Lavradio, which is lined with picturesque buildings.

06

RIO DE JANEIRO

ONE-DAY FREE PASS

First thing, stroll or jog along Copacabana Beach, then stop to refuel on *água de coco* at a beachside kiosk. Afterwards, head to downtown and grab a sandwich at Café Gaúcho *(Rua São Jose 86; 7am-7pm Mon-Fri, 7am-1pm Sat)* before continuing on to the exhibitions in Paço Imperial (p286) and at Centro Cultural Banco do Brasil (p284). In the afternoon, come back to Ipanema and watch the sunset from Arpoador. That evening, grab your dancing shoes and head up to Lapa (p286). Buy a drink from a sidewalk vendor, then stroll along Ave Mem de Sá.

You'll be assured a great time, though it's best to go early to beat the crowds. *Rua do Lavradio, Lapa; 10am-6pm 1st Sat of month; admission free.*

18 **Réveillon**

Give frosty Times Square or rainy London a miss and head to the tropics to ring in the New Year. Rio de Janeiro throws a truly incredible bash, with some two-million people taking to **Copacabana Beach** to watch fireworks light up the night sky. Revellers traditionally wear all-white for the big night, and some even take a plunge in the ocean, an activity that is said to bring good luck for the year ahead). *rioguiaoficial.com.br; Copacabana Beach; free.*

16

"I save money by eating a *prato feito* (fixed-price meal) at lunch. One of my favourite places is the Middle-Eastern-style eatery Baalbeck *(Ave Nossa Sra de Copacabana, 664, 9am-8pm Mon-Sat)*, where you can eat well for R$15. Snack bars are also good, including La Veronese *(Rua Visc de Pirajá, 29)*, which serves mini pizzas for R$15, and Café Gaúcho, which sells R$10 steak sandwiches. At night, I go where there are street parties – Empório, Pedra do Sal, Baixo Gávea, Pavão Azul – and you can buy beer from street vendors." – Cristiano Nogueira, author of *Rio For Partiers*

HOW TO PARTY AT CARNIVAL IN RIO

You don't need to splash cash to celebrate Carnival. Some of the best events – especially Rio's festive street parties – are free.

SALGUEIRO SAMBA SCHOOL

One of the most exciting places to be in the build-up to Carnaval is at a samba school rehearsal, and Salgueiro is a favourite. Don your red and white (Salgueira's colours) and plan a late night of dancing! *salgueiro.com.br; Rua Silva Teles 104, Andaraí; 10pm-4am Sat; admission R$20-40.*

MANGUEIRA SAMBA SCHOOL

Every Saturday night from September to Carnaval, this traditional samba school throws a great party. Expect heavy percussion, ever-flowing caipirinhas and a festive crowd. *www.mangueira.com.br; Rua Visconde de Niterói, Mangueira; 10pm-4am Sat; admission R$20-40.*

BANDA DE IPANEMA

One of the best roving celebrations in Ipanema happens twice during Carnaval. You can don a costume (or not), and join the massive crowds as they dance through the neighbourhood. *Praça General Osório, Ipanema; 4pm Sat of Carnaval & Sat prior; free.*

MONOBLOCO

The festivities in Rio don't end abruptly on Ash Wednesday. You can join half a million revellers at this huge party downtown that bids adieu to Carnaval. *Ave Rio Branco near Presidente Vargas, Centro; 9am 1st Sun after Carnaval; free.*

BANDA CARMELITAS

There's nothing quite like shimmying your way through the cobblestone streets of Santa Teresa – preferably dressed as a nun (the costume of choice). *Cnr Rua Dias de Barros & Ladeira de Santa Teresa, Santa Teresa; 1pm Carnaval Fri & 10am Carnaval Tue; free.*

CORDÃO DO BOLA PRETA

Arrive early to join the oldest and biggest street party in Rio, with some two million joining the celebration. Costumes are encouraged – especially something creative with black-and-white spots. *cordaodabolapreta.com; Primeiro de Março near Rua Rosário, Centro; 8am Carnaval Sat; free.*

PARADE OF CHAMPIONS

If you don't want to pay up for the big parades during Carnaval, come the Saturday just after the big week, when the top six samba schools march through the Sambódromo. It's a dazzling performance, well worth catching. *Sambódromo; 9pm-4am Sat after Carnaval; tickets from R$145.*

SAMBA LAND

This huge square near the Sambódromo transforms into party central during Carnaval (and the weekend before), with a wide range of live music throughout the night, plus ample food and drink vendors. *Praça Onze, Centro; 7pm-6am Fri-Tue of Carnaval; admission around R$40.*

RIO FOLIA

During Carnaval, head to the plaza in front of the Lapa Arches for some of the city's best free shows. There's great dancing and people-watching at these open-air concerts. *Praça Cardeal Câmara, Lapa; 8pm-late Fri-Tue of Carnaval; free.*

Photography | Daniel Di Paolo, Styling | Hayley Warnham

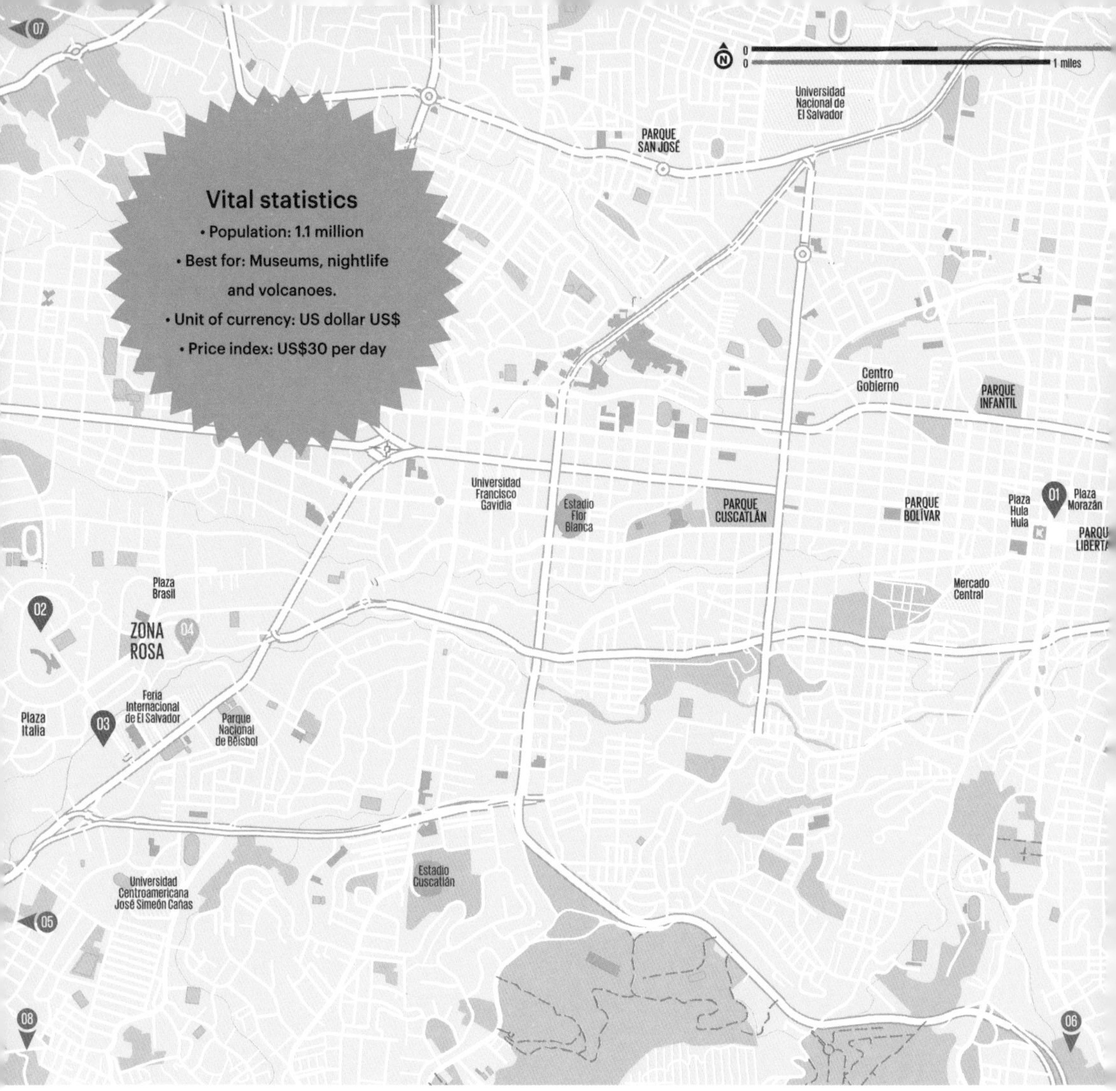

SAN SALVADOR

El Salvador is a postage stamp-size country that delivers. Black-sand beaches and rolling surf, volcanic lakes and the Ruta de las Flores, artisan villages and a compact capital, there's not much worth doing here that costs more than a few bucks. San Salvador is the quintessential Central America on a shoestring experience.

ARTS & CULTURE | MUSIC & FILM | SPORTS & LEISURE | FOOD & DRINK | FESTIVALS & EVENTS

01 Catedral Metropolitana

Archbishop Oscar Romero, an outspoken critic of government 'death squads' during the 1980s, was murdered while giving mass at the Catedral Metropolitana. His body still rests here beneath impressive stained-glass windows and among icons dating back to the 16th century. The downtown building is well maintained. Religious monuments may not be your thing, but this one tells a crucial story. *Calle Ruben Dario; 8am-noon & 2-4pm; free.*

02 Museo de Arte

The artwork on display at this small national gallery in Colonia San Benito is always impressive. The evolution of local art as a form of political expression is cleverly documented, while the contemporary exhibitions are vibrant and playful. You can easily while away half a day here, especially in summer when it provides a cooling refuge from the heat. *marte.org.sv; Ave de la Revolución, Colonia San Benito; 10am-6pm Tue-Sun; adults/students US$1.50/0.50.*

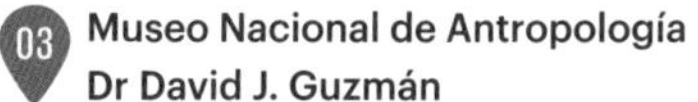

03 Museo Nacional de Antropología Dr David J. Guzmán

David J Guzmán was a 19th-century natural scientist who espoused liberal European values and knew how to curate a museum. His namesake houses artefacts spanning epochs and explains the historical context of the region in an accessible manner. The Pipils and Mayans are featured and their influence still lingers in modern Meso-America. The venue also hosts free concerts and movie nights. *cultura.gob.sv; Ave de la Revolución; 10am-5pm Tue-Sat, 10am-6pm Sun; US$3.*

04 Zona Rosa

The flashiest suburb in the capital is also the best place in which to dance with friendly locals. Salsa, merengue, cumbia and hip-hop are on rotation in the clubs, while ska, reggae and heavy metal (and the occasional traditional xuc band) can also be heard blasting out of the speakers in the coolest capital in Central America. If you arrive at most establishments before 10pm you'll avoid a cover charge. *Locations and times vary.*

05 Paseo El Carmen

In Santa Tecla, 10km southwest of the CBD, Paseo el Carmen is worthy of an afternoon or evening stroll to see Salvadorans fighting back against the city's dangerous reputation. The attractive restored street is car-free, with cafes, bars and shops opening on to the pavement,

07

08

11

01

THE LOCAL'S VIEW

"If you want to see incredible Mayan ruins, save yourself the trouble of travelling all the way to Guatemala. The pyramids of Tazumal (*Chalchuapa; Tue-Sun; US$5*) are only an hour away. A section built by the Olmecas, *Finca San Antonio*, predates the Mayans and has recently been opened to the public. Chalchuapa itself is a great place to catch local reggae bands for free at Trench Town Rock (*Carretera Panamericana desvio a Chalchuapa, 7pm-late, Wed-Sat*). You might even find somebody to teach you a little Nahuatl, the root language of Mayan civilisation. You probably know one word already... tequila!" – Jorge, Chalchuapa local

and the weekend night market feels more cosmopolitan than those of other Central American capital cities. It doesn't cost much for a coffee either. *Free.*

06 Puerta del Diablo

The Devil's Door is a rocky ridge 13km south of San Salvador, which was a sacrificial site for the ancient Mayans and a place of execution during the Civil War. Today, it is a fabulous place for an easy, if slightly precarious, climb to the summit, where you can peer between two enormous boulders and enjoy unhindered panoramic views to the Pacific Ocean and the village of Panchimalco below. *Free.*

07 Volcan El Boquerón

Grab an oxygen boost 19km north-west of the city by hiking to the top section of two massive craters in Boquerón National Park. It takes a mere 30 minutes by bus to get to Boquerón village from Parque Cuscatlán in the capital – take bus 101A or B to Santa Tecla, then bus 103 from 6a Ave Sur. Buy wild berries and flowers along the 1km walk to the summit. *Free.*

08 Playa El Tunco

Beach-bumming is cheap and cheerful pursuit and Playa El Tunco, just 35km south-west of the capital, is perfecto for mastering its elusive charms. But this black-sand beauty, famed for neat, hollow waves on a long stretch of Pacific Ocean, is not exactly quiet on weekends. The pumping surf is matched by jumping nightlife when the throngs shuffle about its sandy paths to hang very loose, man. *24hr; free.*

ON THE HOUSE ART

Street art abounds in El Salvador, and any stroll around the capital will take you past impressive murals. Some pay testament to the recent past, while others are simply upbeat creative expressions attempting to capture the zeitgeist. Stick to the areas around Colonia Escalon and Zona Rosa, or why not venture the 84km north to La Palma, a cool mountain village with probably more murals per capita than anywhere else on earth. Painter Fernando Llort, pioneer of naïve art, lived here in the 1970s and his influence remains in the nation's art today.

06

09 Street food: *Pupusas* and *chilate*

Every second roadside stand in the city is a humble *pupuseria*, serving El Salvador's staple food for about 50 cents a pop. These hand-size flour pouches are lightly fried and filled with beans, cheese and meat. Smother on the *cortida*, a pickled cabbage relish. *Chilate* is a mild corn drink served in a bowl made from a calabash gourd. The Salvadoran version adds ginger and peppercorn. Healthy and delicious! *Pupusa c US$0.50, chilate c US$0.75.*

10 Fiestas Agostinas

This week-long party, which is held in honour of El Salvador del Mundo (the saviour of the world), starts very early and doesn't let up until you literally can't stand up any longer. Marching bands kick things off at 4am, before the dancing, food and merriment take over. A parade snakes around San Salvador on 3-4 August. Oh, and lots of people will be wearing masks, so be careful who you kiss. *1-6 Aug; free.*

11 Mercado Central

Stalls spilling on to the streets sell fruit and vegetables and daily essentials at this covered market – an excellent place in which to pick up handicrafts brought in from the villages, especially the famous hammocks that still swing many a Salvadoran to sleep on summer evenings. Keep your wits about you to avoid being pickpocketed, and avoid driving there. *6 Calle Oriente, 7.30am-6pm Mon-Sat, 7.30am-2pm Sun; admission free.*

12 Holy Week

El Salvador is an exuberantly Catholic country and Semana Santa is celebrated with panache. The capital has the most ostentatious public ceremonies, especially the Procession of the Flagellation around Catedral Metropolitana, but you will also find smaller gatherings where locals are happy to spend a few days with family and – if you loiter with intent in this overwhelmingly friendly part of the world – no doubt strangers like you too. *Free.*

ARTS & CULTURE | MUSIC & FILM | SPORTS & LEISURE | FOOD & DRINK | FESTIVALS & EVENTS

SÃO PAULO

Enormous, intimidating and home to whatever pleasures you might covet, São Paulo is a 24/7 workhorse of culture and cuisine. Plus you don't need big bucks to get a taste of the avalanche of first-rate museums, cultural centres, experimental theatres and rabid nightlife, or South America's most enticing epicurean delights.

01 Museu Afro Brasil

The important, fascinating Parque do Ibirapuera museum hosts a permanent collection chronicling 500 years of African immigration (and a nod to the 10 million African lives lost in the construction of Brazil) as well as a rotating array of contemporary Afro-centric exhibitions. *museuafrobrasil.org.br; Ave Pedro Álvares Cabral s/n, Parque Ibirapuera, Gate 10; 10am-5pm Tue-Sun, 10am-9pm last Thu of month; adult/student R$6/3, free Sat.*

02 Sala São Paulo

The city's world-renowned concert hall is located in the gorgeously restored Júlio Prestes train station, a neoclassical downtown icon that is home to the São Paulo State Symphonic Orchestra (OSESP). On Sundays, concerts in the acoustically marvellous space are free. Nab your tickets (up to five per person) at the box office on the Monday prior to the performance. *salasaopaulo.art.br; Praça Júlio Prestes, 16; times vary; free Sun.*

03 Parque do Ibirapuera

This 2 sq km-park is the biggest green space in central São Paulo and is a thriving centre of cultural life. Designed by renowned landscape architect Roberto Burle Marx, the space features a series of landmark buildings by Oscar Niemeyer and several museums and performance arenas. Whether on foot, rollerskates, bike or skateboard, Paulistanos' devotion to their beloved park cannot be understated. *parqueibirapuera.org/ibirapuera-park; Ave Pedro Álvares Cabral; 5am-midnight; free.*

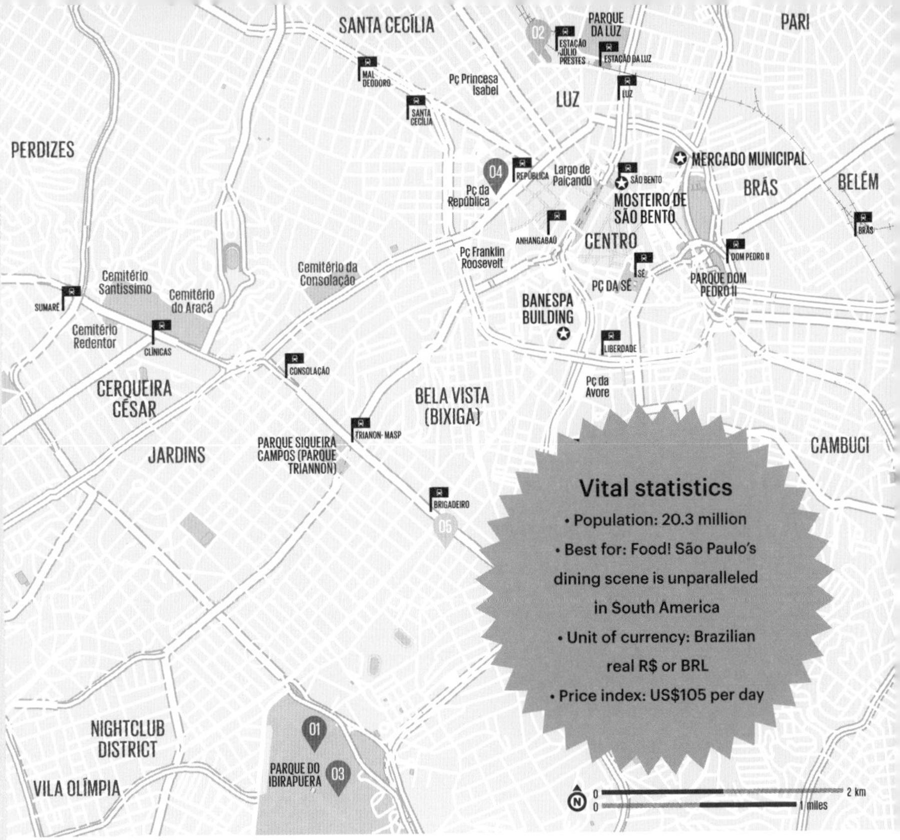

ONE-DAY FREE PASS

From Luz metro station it's a short walk to one of South America's best urban markets, Mercado Municipal (*oportaldomercadao.com.br; Rua da Cantareira 306; 6am-6pm Mon-Sat, 6am-4pm Sun; admission free*). Pick up a cheap lunch there, then take the metro to São Bento to see the city's oldest church, Mosteiro de Sao Bento (*mosteiro.org.br; Largo de São Bento s/n; 6am-6pm Mon-Wed & Fri, 6am-8am Thu, 6am-noon & 4-6pm Sat & Sun; free*), a neo-Gothic stained-glass wonder. Finish by ascending the Banespa Building (*Edifício Altino Arantes; Rua João Brícola 24; 10am-3pm Mon-Fri; free*) for a panoramic view of this megalopolis.

Vital statistics

- Population: 20.3 million
- Best for: Food! São Paulo's dining scene is unparalleled in South America
- Unit of currency: Brazilian real R$ or BRL
- Price index: US$105 per day

04 São Paulo 'Old Downtown' Free Walking Tour

This tri-weekly 'Old Downtown' walk condenses more than 450 years of Sampa history into a fascinating couple of hours. It is without doubt the best way to get to know the atmospheric old centre of São Paulo, a pedestrianised maze offering a cornucopia of architectural styles that are easily missed without the guidance of these local experts. *spfreewalkingtour.com; Praça da República; 11.30am Mon, Wed & Sat; free, but tips appreciated.*

05 Kan

São Paulo is world-famous for its top-notch Japanese cuisine, but the most authentic hotspots are often prohibitively pricey. But fret not – at normally expensive Kan restaurant you can snag an eight-piece *Jiro Dreams of Sushi*-level set lunch from sushi superman Keisuke Egashira (he barely speaks Portuguese!) for a mere R$50! Now that's a bargain. *restaurantekan.com.br; Rua Manoel da Nóbrega 76, Jardins; 11.30am-2pm & 6-10pm Tue-Sat, 6-10pm Sun; omakase R$230-280.*

06 Virada Cultural

This non-stop city-wide festival of cultural and musical events, usually held in May, is concentrated in and around some of Centro's most-known public squares, such as **Estação Júlio Prestes**, **Praça da Republica**, **Largo do Arouche** and **Ave São João**. The extensive programme includes circus and theatre performances, dance, music of all kinds, children's events and more, all for free. *viradacultural.prefeitura.sp.gov.br; check website for venues, dates & times; free.*

PRICE INDEX

This chart compares the price of an average day in each destination featured in the book.*

**including one night in midrange accommodation, three reasonable-priced meals, entry to one cultural attraction, one day's travel and one pint of beer or glass of wine.*

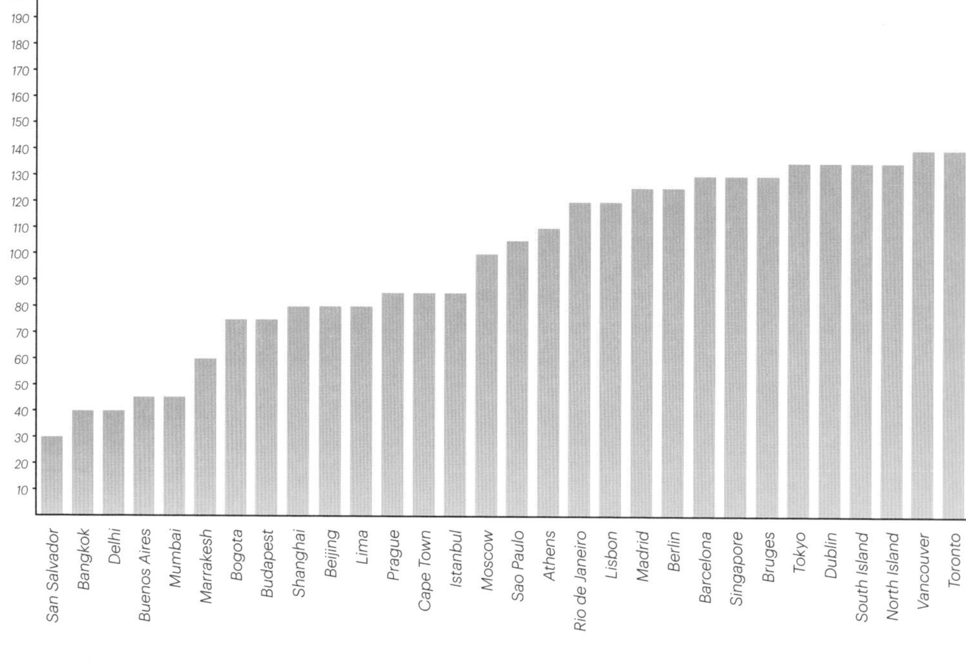

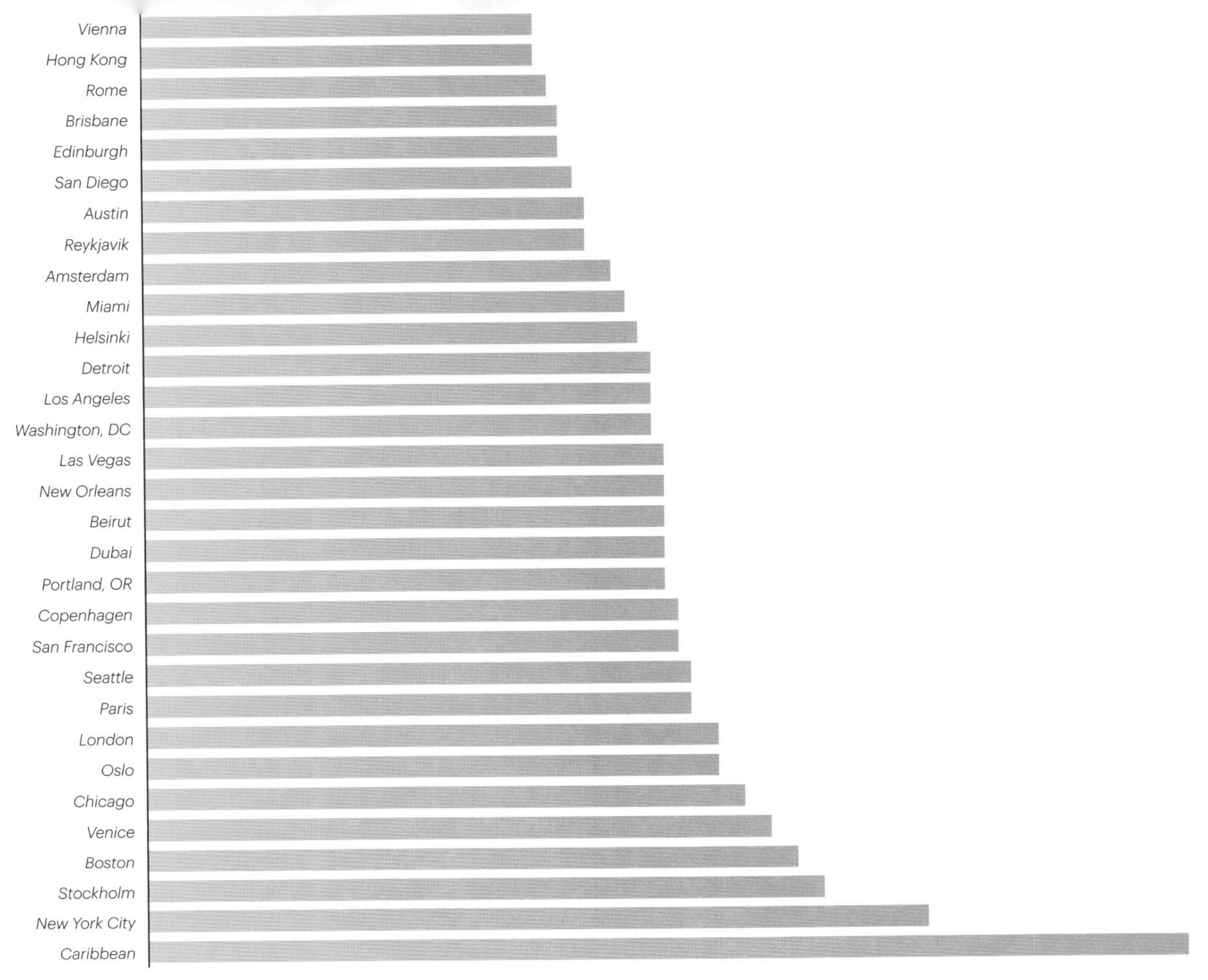
Vienna
Hong Kong
Rome
Brisbane
Edinburgh
San Diego
Austin
Reykjavik
Amsterdam
Miami
Helsinki
Detroit
Los Angeles
Washington, DC
Las Vegas
New Orleans
Beirut
Dubai
Portland, OR
Copenhagen
San Francisco
Seattle
Paris
London
Oslo
Chicago
Venice
Boston
Stockholm
New York City
Caribbean

PRICE INDEX

AUTHORS

A writer and San Lorenzo fan, **Isabel Albiston** spent four years drinking mate and Malbec in the Buenos Aires neighbourhood of Boedo.

Kate Armstrong's favourite travel moments include a tasty meal, stimulating sights and local company, many of which come (nearly) free.

Prague-based writer **Mark Baker** is the author of several Lonely Planet titles, including LP's *Prague* pocket guide and *The Best of Prague and the Czech Republic*.

Travel writer, author, editor and cheapskate **Sarah Baxter** loves nothing better than bagging bargains around the globe.

A true Californian (by choice if not by birth), **Andrew Bender** covers San Diego for Lonely Planet guidebooks.

Joe Bindloss is Lonely Planet's destination editor for the Indian Subcontinent and the author of more than 50 books for Lonely Planet.

Sarah Bennett's author credits include Lonely Planet *New Zealand, Hiking New Zealand* and *The Best of Wellington*. www.bennettandslater.co.nz

A Californian, but not by birth, **Sara Benson** calls Oakland home. She escapes to Las Vegas more than she'll willingly admit.

Piera Chen is a travel writer, film reviewer and poet who is happy to call Hong Kong home most days.

Janine Eberle is a Francophile who spends as much time as possible in Paris, spending her entire budget on cheese and wine.

Based in Buenos Aires, **Bridget Gleeson** has travelled widely in South America, tasting a variety of wines along the way.

Tom Hall has been writing for Lonely Planet for most of his adult life and when not doing so composes love letters to Hagia Sophia in Istanbul.

Anthony Ham fell irretrievably in love with Madrid on his first visit and later lived there for a decade. He speaks fluent Spanish and returns regularly to a city he considers his spiritual home.

From Lido beaches to backstreet bacari, **Paula Hardy** has contributed to Lonely Planet's Italian guides for over 15 years. Find her tweets @paula6hardy.

Daniel McCrohan is the creator of iPhone app Beijing on a Budget, author of 28 guidebooks, and a budget-travel expert who has been living in China for more than a decade.

Virginia Jealous is presently on the trail of poet Laurence Hope – aka Violet Nicolson – who died in India in 1904.

Adam Karlin has written multiple guidebooks for New Orleans and Miami, and loves spending time – and sometimes, money – in both cities.

After two decades of scraping, scrimping, haggling and hitching around the planet, **Patrick Kinsella** has experienced more by trying things than buying things.

Mariella Krause has been writing for Lonely Planet since 2006, and enjoying cheap margaritas in Austin since long before that.

Since 2002, **Alex Leviton** has contributed to roughly half a gabillion Lonely Planet titles, most recently about Italy, food, and happiness.

Karyn Noble is a senior editor in Lonely Planet's London office, and a freelance writer specialising in luxury and gourmet travel. But some of her most memorable experiences didn't cost a thing. She tweets @MsKarynNoble.

Virginia Maxwell is a long-time and regular visitor to the Middle East, covering destinations including Turkey, Iran and Lebanon for Lonely Planet.

Rebecca Milner is a Tokyo resident and co-author of Lonely Planet guides to Japan and Korea.

Kate Morgan is a freelance travel writer and editor, and has worked on several guidebooks and trade titles for Lonely Planet.

Becky Ohlsen is a freelance writer in Portland, Oregon, and is always happy to stumble across a good deal.

Stephanie Ong is an Australian editor/writer based in Milan. When not immersed in writing and travel, she's eating well and complaining about tax – like every good Italian.

Matt Phillips loves free things (who doesn't?), particularly those involving the great outdoors. Writes about Africa, Europe, Asia and his native Vancouver.

Brendan Sainsbury is a Britrish writer based near Vancouver, Canada. He has been exploring and writing about Seattle for over a decade.

Brandon Presser is an award-winning travel writer and television personality who has visited over 100 countries and penned over 40 books for Lonely Planet.

Kevin Raub is a São Paulo-based travel journalist and a co-author of four Lonely Planet Brazil travel guides.

Travel writer **Sarah Reid** loves discovering a new side to Singapore during every visit – especially when it's free.

Andrea Schulte-Peevers lives in Berlin and has been the author of all nine editions of Lonely Planet's guide to the city.

Lee Slater's author credits include Lonely Planet *New Zealand*, *Hiking New Zealand* and *The Best of Wellington*. www.bennettandslater.co.nz

Tom Spurling is a writer and teacher based in Hong Kong. He has contributed to 11 Lonely Planet guidebooks, including *Central America on a Shoestring*.

Phillip Tang likes to show off the best-value thrills for many Lonely Planet publications, including *Peru* and *Discover Peru*. More at philliptang.co.uk

Mara Vorhees is a travel writer, city dweller and mother of twins. Follow her adventures at www.havetwinswilltravel.com.

Regis St. Louis is a full-time travel writer and the author of Lonely Planet guides to New York City and Rio de Janeiro.

A contributor to numerous LP books on culture and travel, **Caroline Veldhuis** continues her lifelong mission to sample vegetarian food in situ around the world.

Tasmin Waby is a broke London-based writer and editor who travels at every opportunity (usually with her kids – but not always).

British writer **Nicola Williams** lives on the southern side of Lake Geneva. She writes Lonely Planet's Switzerland guide and tweets at @tripalong.

Based in Chicago for over 25 years, **Karla Zimmerman** knows where the bargains hide (especially when it comes to beer and donuts).

INDEX

The Best Things in Life are Free
August 2016
Published by Lonely Planet Publications Pty Ltd
ABN 36 005 607 983
www.lonelyplanet.com
1 2 3 4 5 6 7 8 9 10

Printed in China
ISBN 978 1 76034 062 9

Written by **Isabel Albiston, Kate Armstrong, Mark Baker, Sarah Baxter, Andrew Bender, Sarah Bennett, Sara Benson, Joe Bindloss, Piera Chen, Janine Eberle, Bridget Gleeson, Anthony Ham, Paula Hardy, Virginia Jealous, Adam Karlin, Patrick Kinsella, Mariella Krause, Alex Leviton, Virginia Maxwell, Daniel McCrohan, Rebecca Milner, Kate Morgan, Karyn Noble, Becky Ohlsen, Stephanie Ong, Matt Phillips, Brandon Presser, Kevin Raub, Sarah Reid, Brendan Sainsbury, Andrea Schulte-Peevers, Lee Slater, Tom Spurling, Regis St. Louis, Phillip Tang, Caroline Veldhuis, Mara Vorhees, Tasmin Waby, Nicola Williams and Karla Zimmerman.**
Foreword writen by **Tom Hall.**

Managing Director, Publishing **Piers Pickard**
Associate Publisher **Robin Barton**
Commissioning Editor **Jessica Cole**
Art Director **Daniel Di Paolo**
Layout Designer **Hayley Warnham**
Thanks to **Lucy Doncaster, Gabrielle Green, Nick Mee**
Print Production **Nigel Longuet, Larissa Frost**

Lonely Planet Offices

Australia
The Malt Store, Level 3, 551 Swanston Street,
Carlton 3053, Victoria
Phone 03 8379 8000 Fax 03 8379 8111
Email talk2us@lonelyplanet.com.au

USA
150 Linden St, Oakland, CA 94607
Phone 510 250 6400 Toll free 800 275 8555
Fax 510 893 8572
Email info@lonelyplanet.com

Europe
240 Blackfriars Road, London, SE1 8NW
Phone 020 3771 5100 Fax 020 3771 5101
Email go@lonelyplanet.co.uk

Paper in this book is certified against the Forest Stewardship Council™ standards. FSC™ promotes environmentally responsible, socially beneficial and economically viable management of the world's forests.